D1255379

LANGUAGE AND LANGUAGE LEARNING

The Edinburgh Course in
Applied Linguistics

Volume 3

LANGUAGE AND LANGUAGE LEARNING

General Editors: RONALD MACKIN *and* PETER STREVENS

The Edinburgh Course in Applied
Linguistics

Edited by J. P. B. ALLEN *and* S. PIT CORDER

VOLUME THREE

Techniques in
Applied Linguistics

LONDON

OXFORD UNIVERSITY PRESS

1974

Oxford University Press, Ely House, London W.1

GLASGOW NEW YORK TORONTO MELBOURNE WELLINGTON
CAPE TOWN IBADAN NAIROBI DAR ES SALAAM LUSAKA ADDIS ABABA
DELHI BOMBAY CALCUTTA MADRAS KARACHI LAHORE DACCA
KUALA LUMPUR SINGAPORE HONG KONG TOKYO

Library Edition ISBN 0 19 437124 7

Paperbound Edition ISBN 0 19 437059 3

© Oxford University Press 1974

Typeset by The Lancashire Typesetting Co. Ltd.
Bolton, Lancashire, England
Printed in Great Britain by
Robert MacLehose & Co. Ltd
The University Press, Glasgow

To Julian Dakin
1939–71

*In memory of a valued colleague and friend whose thinking
has had an important influence on
the preparation of this volume*

Contents

Editors' Preface

This third volume of the Edinburgh Course in Applied Linguistics presents a variety of techniques which exemplify the practical application of the principles discussed in Volume 2. The material takes its present form as a result of its use in postgraduate teaching over a number of years. Most of the chapters incorporate modifications and contributions made by various people during that period. In particular every part of the book shows the influence of our students, who have been a constant source of valuable material and ideas. This book, then, although it has received its final shaping at the hands of the authors whose names appear at the head of each chapter, is in a very real sense the work of the Department as a whole.

The ten chapters of this book are based on material originally designed for use in 'practical classes', which must form a central part of any teaching of applied linguistics. The purpose of such classes is to get students to think about ways in which the knowledge derived from the linguistic sciences about the nature of language and how it is learned can be put to use in the planning and execution of teaching programmes and in finding solutions to problems which have arisen during the course of the student's own professional career. The arrangement of the book reflects this original purpose. The chapters necessarily differ in details of presentation because of the wide variety of topics covered, but all the chapters are alike in that they provide an introductory discussion, and most provide a number of exercises. In some of the exercises the problems posed are of a general nature and no specific answer is provided; in these cases it is up to each reader to find a solution based on his own particular experience. Sometimes an answer is given at the end of the chapter or at the back of the book, and at other times the questions are followed by a detailed discussion in the main body of the text. In all cases we suggest that the reader should attempt to work out his own solution before going on to check the answer given, since it is only in this way that he will derive maximum benefit from the book. Where the book is used as a class text, in colleges of education for example, it is hoped that the instructor will devise supplementary exercises on the basis of those provided.

The first four chapters—those dealing with course design, practical phonetics and phonology, pedagogic grammar and language laboratory materials—may be regarded as basic in that no discussion of language teaching could take place without some reference to these topics. The remaining chapters are more specialized, either in the sense that they are particularly relevant to certain types of language teaching, or because the topics themselves constitute a comparatively new development in applied linguistic studies. For example, although teachers have long been aware of the importance of learners' errors, the possible contribution of error analysis to our understanding of the learning process has only recently begun to be explored in detail. Another specialized topic to attract a great deal of attention in recent years is advanced reading and writing, an area which contains problems quite different from those associated with the elementary stages of language learning.

Since the book covers a wide range of topics, it is inevitable that at first sight some chapters will appear more difficult than others. The chapter on contrastive analysis, for example, is more theoretically oriented than the rest of the book, since this topic involves a number of issues which cannot be adequately discussed without developing a fairly complex theoretical apparatus. In other chapters, dealing with the presentation of material in the classroom, the argument is developed in terms which may be more immediately familiar to the language teacher. The reader should not be lulled into a false sense of security by the straightforward style of the 'practical' chapters, nor should he be deterred by the use of symbols and technical terminology in the more theoretical discussions. *Techniques in Applied Linguistics* is a practical book, and the general approach is eclectic. It is not our aim to promulgate an 'Edinburgh School' of applied linguistics; rather, we hope to encourage teachers to think for themselves, to investigate a variety of techniques, and thus to make their own contribution to the development of applied linguistics.

The writing of this book has been a collaborative undertaking and we have, consequently, not acknowledged the very extensive criticism and advice which the authors have given to one another. We wish, however, to acknowledge the generous help given by colleagues who were not directly involved in writing the book. We are in particular grateful to David Abercrombie, Keith Brown, Sandy Hutcheson, John Lyons and Jim Miller, who suggested a number of improvements which have been incorporated into the book; they are not, of course, in any way responsible for the imperfections that remain. Our thanks are also due to

Ethel Bacon, who has borne the brunt of typing the manuscript, and to Mary Bratt who has helped with the bibliography and other editorial duties.

Department of Linguistics, Edinburgh   J. P. B. Allen
July 1973   S. Pit Corder

1 The Background to Course Design

ANTHONY HOWATT

1 Approaching the problem

Creating materials to teach a foreign language is a complicated, demanding and many-sided task. The purpose of this chapter is to describe some of the points which a course-writer has to bear in mind as he sets about his work.

The first point is that writing a language teaching course is a *pedagogic* problem. Although it is obviously sensible to seek help and advice from specialists in linguistics, psychology and so on, the choices and decisions that we make are our own responsibility as teachers, and the wisdom or otherwise of these decisions can be seen only in the results we obtain from our pupils. Our task is to produce good teaching materials which will fit the situation they are intended for, allow the pupil to learn quickly and well, and make the teacher's job as interesting and profitable as possible. As a first step towards this goal, we should ask ourselves who the learner is, and why he is learning a foreign language; then we can decide what he should be taught in order to achieve this aim.

In the first place, the learner is a member of a community which has certain views about the purpose of teaching languages, and the role that language teaching fulfils in the general system of education. These views are a reflection of the attitudes the community adopts towards the languages being taught. There are various labels to describe these attitudes, and we shall mention three of them. Firstly, the language may be regarded as a *foreign* language. This label implies that there is a fairly clear distinction in people's minds between a home community and a foreign community, each speaking a different language. Secondly, there is the situation where two languages are used for different purposes in the same community. Some people in such communities will be bilingual from childhood, but others will have to learn the other language at school, as a *second* language. The third situation is where people with different native languages communicate by using a third language, often referred to as a *lingua franca*. For example, French is still a foreign language to most British children, but it is a second language to the Flemish-speaking community in Belgium and needed as a lingua franca by many learners in continental Europe.

The implication of these attitudes and views can be far-reaching. A British child learning French may never have to use his foreign language, except perhaps during short holiday trips to France. So when we ask why we teach French in this country the answer must stress the general educational value of French, quite apart from its usefulness as a practical skill. On the other hand, if a language is a second language in the pupil's own community, it has a clear practical use in everyday life, and the pupil will be aware of this. Similarly, if the learner knows that he is learning an international lingua franca, he will see its practical relevance for his future life, and more general questions concerning the educational and literary value of the language will seem less important. It is right that the economic and social needs of the community should exert the most powerful influence on shaping the content and methodology of language teaching courses, and in this connection, it is interesting to see how French-teaching materials in Britain are gradually being transformed as the European continent comes to exert a greater influence on our economic welfare.

As well as being a member of a community, the pupil is a member of a particular learning group in his school or college of higher education. We must, therefore, discover how old he is, how much he has already learnt, how good he is at learning languages, and how interested he is likely to be in learning the language, before we can start constructing materials for him to use. For example, very young children seem to prefer lessons with plenty of activity and concrete goals which do not take too long to reach. Adults, on the other hand, can tolerate longer periods of instruction and a more formal approach, but they too need evidence that they are making progress. They may possibly lack some of the young child's flexibility in adapting to new speech habits, but they are better able to take advantage of the short cuts offered by rules and generalizations about the language they are learning. In between, the adolescent learner has some of the mature adult's power of abstract reasoning, but still needs plenty of variety in the teaching materials to attract and hold his somewhat unpredictable attention. He also demands a serious approach that genuinely involves his interests and preoccupations.

Figure 1 sums up some of the points which have been made so far. We shall return to the question of learning objectives. First, in order to fit the teacher into the picture, the diagram has to be extended a little.

Every teacher wants materials which will allow him to work easily and effectively according to principles which he thinks are right. These principles may derive in part from his practical experience and in part

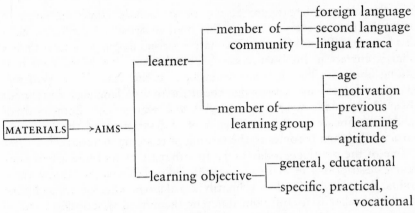

Figure 1

from a more formal study of psychology. Taken together, the results of study and experience constitute a body of method which can be put into effect by developing teaching techniques to suit the special circumstances of a particular teaching situation. In other words, it is not always possible to apply a principle in its pure form. For instance, the principle of encouraging spontaneous conversation would have to be heavily adapted to suit a class of 40 or 50 pupils in a classroom built to hold half that number. The teacher will have to find a technique which is workable even if it is not ideal.

Principles of method are obviously not principles in any absolute sense. They are rather guesses and hypotheses about the best way of tackling a practical problem. For example, a principle that stresses oral work is a hypothesis that this will lead to better and more efficient learning in the long run. Principles are useful so long as they remain open to discussion and change in the light of further experience or new ideas put forward by the theorists. In this respect, teachers and psychologists have complementary roles—the teacher has to show that his practical ideas are widely applicable and the psychologist has to prove that his suggestions will work in a real-life situation.

We can now extend figure 1, omitting some of the earlier details:

TEACHING TECHNIQUES⟶MATERIALS⟵AIMS
↑
Practical Restrictions
↑
THEORY OF LEARNING⟶PRINCIPLES OF METHOD

Figure 2

In order to complete figure 2, we must include some reference to language. Just as every teacher is his own informal psychologist, he is also his own informal linguist. The native second language teacher knows what is correct in his own language, but he may not be very good at talking about it. The non-native teacher, on the other hand, probably has quite an extensive knowledge about the foreign language, but cannot always tell exactly what is acceptable and what is not. Both kinds of teacher obviously need to make use of a description of the language, particularly when it comes to the writing of teaching materials.

One of the problems today is the fact that there are quite a few competing descriptions of language written from different theoretical viewpoints. But since our task is primarily a pedagogic one, we are at liberty to choose what is useful from different theoretical descriptions and to disregard what is irrelevant or impractical for our purposes. Some language learning difficulties are well described in traditional grammars, others become clearer if they are looked at from a structural or a transformational point of view. A study of recent developments in descriptive linguistics is useful because it gives us a choice of ways in which the pupil's difficulties can be approached, and perhaps explained.

Language descriptions provide us with information, but this information has to be presented to the pupils in some form or other. Arguments about 'grammar' often run aground because of a failure to notice the distinction between the knowledge that the teacher or course-writer possesses about the foreign language and the way in which this knowledge is passed on to the learners. The teacher will probably acquire his information about the language within the framework of some terminology or other, but this does not necessarily mean that he will use a linguistic terminology in order to pass this knowledge on to his pupils. He may use only a selection of example sentences or texts. Broadly speaking, the grammatical system of a language can be taught in three different ways—by giving rules, by giving examples, or by a combination of these methods. If the teacher gives rules, he will have to use a terminology which the pupils already know. At the present time this will almost certainly derive from traditional grammar. If the pupils do not know a terminology, they will have to be taught one, provided that the teacher thinks it worth the time and effort. If no formal rules are given, all the teaching will have to depend on specially written examples. It is arguable whether either technique is reliable by itself, but it is important to notice that the argument is pedagogic and not linguistic. It is up to the teacher to discover which approach is more likely to be helpful to different groups of pupils.

Figure 2 can be completed as follows:

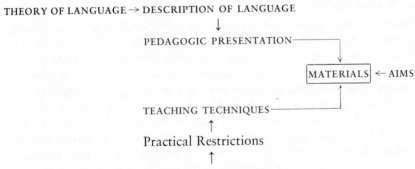

THEORY OF LANGUAGE → DESCRIPTION OF LANGUAGE
↓
PEDAGOGIC PRESENTATION
MATERIALS ← AIMS
TEACHING TECHNIQUES
↑
Practical Restrictions
↑
THEORY OF LEARNING → PRINCIPLES OF METHOD

Figure 3

The content of teaching materials derives from a description of the language being taught, assuming of course that a description is not restricted to information about grammar but includes information about all aspects of language use. But before the descriptive information can be used by the pupils, the course-writer must work out suitable techniques for presenting it to them.

2 Choosing what to teach

Having outlined a general framework for our task, we can return to the question of choosing what to teach. In order to do so, we must examine the purpose of the teaching course in more detail.

It seems useful to distinguish between different types of course. The categories suggested below are not meant to indicate hard and fast distinctions, but merely serve as a framework for discussion:

Special courses
   Problem-based
   Activity-based
   Role-based

General courses

Special courses have fairly specific objectives and are rather simpler to discuss. General courses tend to be diffuse in their aims and take their overall shape more from tradition, contemporary fashion and the vague but powerful influences exerted by the social attitudes and economic needs of the community.

2.1 Special courses

Problem-based courses are intended to help pupils who have specific language difficulties, for instance in pronunciation, spelling or grammar. The choice of what to teach depends on noting the kinds of mistakes that the learners make. From his experience, the course-writer can draw up a list of difficulties and problems and then try to work out the best way of helping the pupils. The form this help takes will depend on our explanation of how the difficulties arose in the first place, and we shall come back to this point later. It is important here to stress that the causes of error are many—faulty initial teaching, misconceptions, mother-tongue interference, over-generalizations and so on. It is not a simple matter to explain mistakes, but it is necessary to make an attempt as it is the only way of working out remedial exercises.

Activity-based courses aim to train the pupil to use the foreign language better. They may concentrate on conversation, on reading or on writing, or they may try to develop two or more of these skills at the same time.

For example, a course may set out to improve the pupils' ability to read a foreign language. There is a linguistic side to the question: what is written language like, how is it similar to spoken language, how is it different, what features of language do we use when we read, and so on? And there is a psychological side: how do people read, what skills are involved, why are some people good at reading when others are not, etc? All these questions require thought, but the most important point is that people read for a reason. They may want to be entertained, or they may want to find something out. But, unless they are interested in the topic, they will not read well. The first consideration of a course-writer making reading materials for foreign learners must be the choice of a wide range of suitable topics which will interest the learner, provoke him into reading and encourage him to continue. If we are successful in this choice, we are half-way home.

However, it is not enough just to provoke interest. We also need to provide the pupil with some advice on how to read to get the most out of it in the most efficient and enjoyable way. Furthermore, it is necessary to grade the materials so that they gradually become more demanding.

The S.R.A. Reading Laboratory is a good example of reading materials meant for native-speakers, but the principles apply to foreign learners as well. The first principle is to provide a wide choice of subject matter to suit different age-groups. The second is to encourage the learners to use a reading technique which starts from the general sense and only goes into the details later on. The third principle is to grade the texts by gradually making them longer and by using more complicated grammar and less common vocabulary as the series progresses.

The third type of course is *role-based*. Role-based courses depend on the reason why the pupil needs the foreign language. He may want to learn it for his job, or because he wants to visit the country where it is spoken, or because he wants to help his children who are learning it at school, and so on. Being a businessman, a tourist or a parent are different roles that people play in life, and the kind of language we need to play one role is different from the language needed for another. The language for role-based courses is tailored, as far as possible, to the requirements of the particular group of pupils who will use it.

If a man wants to learn a foreign language for his job, the writer must first discover what activities the job entails and what part is played in these activities by language of different kinds. He must decide how much emphasis is to be placed on talking and how much on reading or writing. He must find out what topics come up often enough to be worth discussing in class and he must also bear in mind the kind of people the pupil will eventually have to deal with. For example, a doctor may have to deal with fellow-doctors, or he may have to cope with the problems of the patients themselves or their relatives. We could summarize these points under five headings:

(i) The *role* itself: doctor, businessman, teacher, parent, tourist, etc.

(ii) The *language activities* that the role involves: talking, reading, corresponding, writing reports, etc.

(iii) The *topics* that arise: health, symptoms, insurance arrangements, money, etc.

(iv) The *intentions* behind the use of language: polite social chit-chat, persuading, arguing, giving opinions, describing, explaining, etc.

(v) The need for different *styles* of language when addressing different kinds of people: talking to fellow specialists, public officials, friends, customers, etc.

To sum up so far, we have dealt with teaching problems that can be described in some detail because the objectives are reasonably clear: helping the pupils with their language difficulties and problems, improving their ability to use the foreign language, or teaching the special language of a particular role in life. It is now necessary to turn to the more common general courses and see what can be done if the pupils have no very clear objective, except that they want to learn a foreign language.

2.2 General courses

It is often extremely difficult to decide what to teach in a general course unless the problem is simplified by having an examination to work towards. In a situation which is as vague as this, it is natural that the course-writer should come to depend almost entirely on a linguistic description to guide his choice of teaching points. He makes what seems to him to be a reasonable choice, organizes it and then exemplifies each of his points in some suitable text or dialogue, practises them and constructs some activity in which they can be used.

The real difficulty lies not so much in choosing what to teach as in arranging and grading the materials. Since a general course has no particular practical objectives, it must set out to teach more or less everything—all the sounds, spelling rules and grammar. The learners follow the course for a certain length of time and so get to know the main outlines of the linguistic structure of the language without having to specialize in the kind of language needed for any particular purpose in life. The principal objective of Book 1 in such a course must be the ability to go on to Book 2, and the objective of Book 2 is to advance to Book 3 and so on. Of course a great deal is learnt this way, and a pupil who follows the course through to the end should acquire a foundation knowledge of the language which will permit him to take up a more specialized course later on, if he wishes.

However, there is one area of language where there is a need for choice and selection—the vocabulary. It is not an accident that most suggestions for controlling the content of language courses have concentrated on the problem of deciding which words to teach, given the vast number of possible choices. Three such suggestions involve the concepts of frequency, coverage and availability. We shall examine each of these in turn, beginning with frequency, which is probably the best known.

Frequency studies developed in the early years of this century as a means of determining which words were the most useful for a learner of a foreign language, and tended to be a weapon in the hands of those who sought to free language teaching from a predominantly literary orientation. It was valuable from this point of view to be able to point to objective evidence that *cup* and *saucer* were more useful words to learn than *skylark* and *daffodil*. In order to make a frequency list, the investigators chose a large number of texts of various kinds, sometimes running into millions of words. They then counted the number of times a particular word occurred in these texts and computed the relative frequency of each word. The general assumption was that, if the original texts were varied and general enough, the frequency of the words in the texts would reflect their frequency in 'the language as a whole'. And frequent words were held to be useful words for foreign learners to know.

In many ways these investigations provided useful information. However, they had their limitations. The most important fact to emerge was that a very small number of words accounted for a very high proportion of the total text. About 1,000 words occurred so frequently that they accounted for nearly 95% of the total number of words counted by the investigators. Perhaps there were 15,000 other words in the texts, but none of them turned up often enough for anybody to get much useful information. If, for example, *language* turns up 75 times in a million words, this tells us next to nothing about the potential 'usefulness' of the word. We have to ask a different kind of question. We have to ask whether the word *language* is going to be useful to the kind of pupil we are teaching.

A practical procedure is to compare a number of frequency studies, find out which words appear in all of them and in this way make a check-list of words that definitely ought to be included in the course. In their *Key Words and the Teaching of Literacy*, McNally and Murray (1968) followed this procedure to provide a basis for reading materials for native-speakers of English. There is no comparable list, so far as I know, which takes into account the learning problems of the foreign student of English.

There are other problems which arise in connection with the use of frequency counts. We have said that the compilers list 'words' but we have not discussed what a 'word' is. In most, but not all, frequency lists, the concept of a 'word' appears to be equated with the spelling of a word. For example, *her* may be regarded as a single word, whether it is an adjective (*I like her dress*) or a pronoun (*I like her*). There are other unfortunate effects of treating words only as they appear on the printed page without considering what they mean or how they fit into the grammar of the language. Let us take as an example the word *right*, which has a very high frequency of occurrence. This is not surprising when we consider that *right* can be a noun, a verb, an adjective or an adverb. Secondly, the word can have more than one meaning in each of its parts of speech. As an adjective, for example, it can mean 'correct', 'not left' or in geometry 'not acute or obtuse'. Thirdly, no account is taken of the way we use the word when we speak. We can say 'Right' with a falling intonation at the beginning of a classroom lesson to mean 'Let's begin, shall we?' and at the end to mean 'That's enough for today'. Fourthly, the meaning of a word is related to the other words that it is used with. We must know that you can 'put something right', 'put somebody right', 'get something right' and so on. Finally, there is no information about differences in style. There are times when *right* (meaning 'correct') would be used and other times when *acceptable* would be better.

It is clear, I think, that one of the reasons why many words come so high in frequency counts is because they are so ambiguous. If this is true it makes them particularly difficult to learn, and each item on a word frequency list should be treated as the tip of a learning iceberg. We should not only worry about including high frequency words in our course, we should also make sure that we have worked out all the different meanings of the word which make it so frequent in the first place.

Coverage and availability are the other two concepts that have been put forward as a basis for controlling the vocabulary content of language courses and thus lightening the pupil's learning burden. Coverage refers to the fact that one word can do the work of many words. We have met a similar idea in connection with frequency, and the same problems arise. If a word really can 'stand in' for many other words, it increases the pupil's problems in another direction by requiring him to learn many different meanings of the same item. If the student learns *get*, he does not need to learn *become* and *receive* because *get* covers the meanings of the other two. But of course what he does have to learn is two different meanings of *get*. What we gain on the roundabouts (i.e. fewer different items to remember), we lose on the swings (i.e. more possible meanings expressed by the same item).

The idea of coverage can be useful if it is used sensibly. For instance as W. F. Mackey (1965) points out, the student can avoid having to remember the three words *calf*, *puppy*, *kitten* by learning the single word *young* and applying it to *cow*, *dog* and *cat*. However, before long this system will break down because the language that it produces will conflict with what people actually say. Ogden and Richards in their *Basic English* system, which relied heavily on the notion of coverage, were forced to use clumsy circumlocutions like 'have a desire for' to avoid the ordinary word 'want'.

'Availability' is the English translation of the French term *disponibilité* which refers to a technique worked out by Gougenheim, Rivenc and others to supplement the frequency studies of French made for *Le français fondamental*. Briefly, the idea of availability is to discover which words come up most readily in particular contexts. These are the most 'available' words. The technique was to ask people to write down the words that occurred to them when they thought of a particular context, e.g., 'the street'. By comparing the resulting lists, it was possible to discover which words came at the top of most lists and which were mentioned by only a few people. It is clearly not possible for most people to do full-scale availability studies, and in any case such studies tend to deal only with isolated nouns. But the idea can be usefully applied in an informal manner to the construction of check-lists of vocabulary items connected with certain topics.

The techniques of frequency, coverage and availability are all essentially counting techniques. They have their uses, but they tend to distract attention from other ways of looking at the problem of vocabulary selection that cannot be expressed in statistical terms. The most important of these is the idea of *appropriate* language. For example, the language of winter sports is not going to appear high on any numerically determined list of 'useful words in English'. But to a Norwegian or a Swiss learner, it is especially important to their interests and to the situations where they are likely to use their English, e.g. talking to foreign visitors at ski resorts and so on.

If a pupil is to learn what kind of language is appropriate to particular circumstances, he must be able to recognize what is distinctive about different styles and varieties of language use. But the features which are distinctive do not necessarily show up in a statistical study of frequency: we are not concerned with how often a particular grammatical pattern or a particular word is used, but how typical it is of the kind of language we are interested in.

To sum up this section, we want to choose language that is useful to the learner. This means choosing common, everyday language which is continually being used by native speakers and writers. Frequency counts and studies of availability can help, but they have to be used with care. Secondly, we want to select language which can be used in a wide range of contexts and which is not limited to very specialized situations. The idea of coverage can be of some help here, though we have seen that a word which covers a wide range of meanings (like *get* or *put*) has its own learning difficulties. Thirdly, we need to teach language that is appropriate to the interests of the pupil and the situations in which he might possibly use his linguistic knowledge. There is little to guide us here except our own intuitions about what is distinctive about different language varieties and usages. These three criteria of usefulness may well conflict with one another. For example, the interests of the pupils may involve topics and situations which are not particularly common. In this case some compromise must be sought which will take their special interests into account without imposing too drastic a limitation on their general knowledge of the language. This is particularly important with school pupils who are learning a foreign language for use in adult life. If they study the language for a few years at school and learn only about jolly outings to the seaside, the practical application of their work in later life will obviously be rather limited.

In addition to teaching useful language, we should also try to choose language that is easy to learn and to teach. This brings us to the problem of organizing and grading materials.

3 Organizing the course

The purpose of organizing and grading a course is to make the content easy and quick to learn. We must, therefore, try to

decide *in which order* new teaching points should come,

decide *how much* to expect from the pupil in a given time, and

arrange for enough *revision* without causing boredom.

3.1 The question of order

In principle, we want to teach easy points first and leave the more difficult features of the language until later on. What makes a new point easy or difficult to learn? There is a methodological side to this question, which we will look at first, before moving on to more linguistic matters. In the very early stages of a foreign language course, meaning can only be learnt through translation or demonstration techniques. Afterwards meaning can be learnt through the context of language which is already known. If translation is rejected, then the teacher has certain other resources—pictures, objects, actions, mime and so on. Early in the course the language must be selected so that these resources can be used to their full advantage. It is for this reason that many courses begin with the language of demonstration, teaching patterns such as *This is a book, That's John*, etc. These patterns are not particularly easy, indeed their pronunciation is quite difficult for most foreign learners. But they are needed by the method, so they are taught first. Similarly, the audio-visual technique of matching recorded dialogues with film-strip pictures forces the writer to introduce simple conversation pieces at the beginning of his course, whether these are easy to learn from other points of view or not. To a large extent, therefore, the sequential grading of material is determined in the early stages of a course by the teaching method that has been chosen to implement it.

As a course progresses, pictures and demonstrations play a smaller role, and the problems that arise are increasingly linguistic in origin. For instance, there are the difficulties that are caused by the pupil transferring the patterns of his own language into the new language. Sometimes this transfer will work because the languages share a concept and express it in more or less the same way. For example, the tenses in English and German have a very great deal in common. Similarly, the foreign language may contain words which are evidently cognate to words in the pupil's own language. Again, German and English share many cognate items: *Mutter, Vater, Haus, Garten*, etc. Of course, at some point the pupil will have to learn the ways that apparently similar items differ in the two languages, but there is no doubt that it is the existence of cognate words which makes it easier for an English-speaking pupil to learn German than Russian or Arabic. On the other hand, the transfer of native language patterns to the new language can often land the pupil in trouble. Mother-tongue interference, as this source of difficulty is often called, is most noticeable in pronunciation and results in the markedly different accents with which foreigners with different native languages speak English. However, interference is most troublesome at a conceptual level. For example, both English and German have a perfect tense, formed in more or less the same way in the two languages and with enough in common semantically for a learner to suppose that they are equivalent in all respects. This results in the German learner of English making errors such as *I have seen him yesterday* and *I am here since Christmas*.

Grading can help to lessen the effects of interference, though it cannot preclude it altogether. Care must be taken to distinguish between different usages of the same grammatical pattern or lexical item, and to introduce them into the materials at intervals rather than all at once. In addition, great attention must be paid to providing an unambiguous context for the different meanings, particularly when these may be unclear to a learner or unexpected. For example, it is easier to see why the perfect tense is used in English if it is presented with adverbials like *often, just, many times* and so on, than to see why it is used in a question like *Who's broken the window?* when there is no overt time phrase present.

The idea of mother-tongue interference should not be pursued too far. It is not true that every difference between two languages is going to cause a learning problem. Differences can exist which cause relatively little trouble for a foreigner because the point itself is easy to learn. For example, the past tense in Russian is formed very differently from English because it changes with the gender and number of the subject. Since it is easy in Russian to tell what gender and number a noun is, the past tense is easy too. In fact it is easier to learn than the present tense where there are two conjugations, each with six endings and exceptions as well. It makes sense, therefore, to teach the past tense before the present tense in a Russian course for English speakers.

The main questions we are faced with are as follows: Is a particular point difficult to learn? If it seems to be, is there any apparent reason for this? If so, can anything be done about it in terms of grading, or not? We have already mentioned the misleading similarity of the foreign language to the mother-tongue as a possible source of difficulty. However, there are a number of other problems which cause at least as much trouble, but have nothing to do with interference. We will now go on to discuss these.

Diffuse concepts

Many pupils find it difficult to learn how to use *a* and *the* properly in English. The reason is that we find it difficult to explain the difference between the two articles except by presenting lists of examples which illustrate various usages. We would probably find it difficult to sum up the difference between *a* and *the* in a rule that the pupil can easily apply. Other examples in English are the use of the perfect and the continuous forms of the verb, the distinctions between these and the imperfect and non-continuous forms and so on. Can grading make the task lighter for the pupil? Up to a point it can, by distinguishing between different meanings, and by making sure that they are introduced in clearly defined contexts. But in the end success in learning is a matter of sufficient experience—gradually the pupil will come to 'feel' the difference in meaning between different forms of the verb. We cannot do much to help because in many cases we ourselves cannot clearly describe the differences in meaning that we intuitively recognize.

Problems of class assignment

In learning a language we have to group items into classes, and then subdivide these classes into subclasses. For example, French nouns are either masculine or feminine, they may or may not begin with a vowel, and so on. The learner's problem is to assign a new noun to the proper subclass, to say whether it is masculine or feminine, for instance. In French this is extremely difficult because there is little that a teacher can say which will help. By and large the pupil has to learn the gender of each new word separately. In English a similar problem arises between verbs which take the infinitive (*I want to go home*) and those which take a gerund (*I enjoy skating*). There is also a subclass which may take either infinitive or gerund with different meanings (*I stopped smoking/I stopped to smoke*). If a new verb comes up, e.g., *forget*, which subclass does it belong to? There is nothing about the form of the verb, or its meaning which can help the learner much. The class-assignment of each verb has to be learnt separately.

Can grading help? Probably not, except by controlling the number of class-assignment problems that have to be handled by the pupil at any one time.

Exceptions

It is obviously sensible to grade a course so that the pupils learn the 'major' rules before they learn the 'minor' ones. Some rules will only produce one example, for instance the rule for forming the past tense of *go*, i.e., *went*. Exceptions also have to be learnt as single items for the most part, and they therefore cause a considerable learning problem. Grading can assist by limiting the number of exceptions introduced at any one time and postponing the unimportant ones until late in the course.

Apparent anomalies

By anomalies I mean the unexpected features of a language. For example, the fact that the third person of the present tense in English is inflected (*he comes*) unlike the other present tense forms is an anomaly to a learner. This is obviously not an 'exception' in the usual sense, but nevertheless it is unexpected and has to be remembered as an odd, isolated form. Grading cannot protect the pupil from such problems, of course, but care has to be taken to remind the pupil of the rule fairly often and to provide plenty of revision.

Complexities

By 'complexity' I mean either (i) that the pupil has to apply a number of rules simultaneously in order to produce a correct sentence or (ii) that he has to make the right choice from a number of related possibilities. For example, in order to produce the correct form of the verb in a question like *Where does your father work?* the learner must use the (meaningless) question-marker 'do' before the subject, attach the 's' inflection to make the form *does*, and remember not to attach an 's' to the lexical part of the verb (*work*). Until he can do all this fluently, he will make a variety of errors such as *Where your father work(s)*, *Where do your father work(s)*, *Where does your father works*, etc. An example of the second kind of complexity is the choice that a learner has to make between inflectional endings in, say, the imperfect tense in French, bearing in mind that the inflexions of the future and the conditional tenses will almost certainly interfere with the right selection.

Problems such as this raise an interesting grading question. It is common practice to introduce more than one form of a grammatical structure into a course at the same time. It seems a reasonable alternative to suggest that we might introduce selected examples of the structure as set phrases over a number of lessons. The pupils would then learn, for instance, *I don't know* as a set phrase quite early in the course without having to learn how to produce *Do you know?*, *He doesn't know*, and so on. They could then learn to ask *Do you want?* or *Do you like?*, again as set phrases. Gradually a number of such set phrases which have an obvious use in the classroom situation could be introduced and learnt, so that when the students arrive at the lesson where the rules governing the use of *do* as an auxiliary are the main learning point, they will already be familiar with a number of instances and examples. This notion is sometimes frowned on as 'unsystematic'. However, since the traditional procedure has not shown itself to be particularly successful, there is a good argument for trying a new approach.

'Meaningless' choices

We have already noticed that the 'do' in a question like *Do you live in Bristol?* is meaningless except as a formal marker of interrogatives. There are many other examples of grammatical choices which carry no semantic implication, e.g., the prepositions in such phrases as *to be fond of*, *to be interested in*, *on purpose*, *by mistake*, etc. Each of these prepositions has to be learnt separately and, as we have already seen a number of times, whenever the pupil has to learn individual items for which there is no meaningful general rule, he takes a long time to master each item and frequently makes mistakes.

Grading cannot help in a problem of this kind, if by grading we mean simply the ordering of items that are introduced into the course. However, we said earlier that grading also has to do with deciding how much can be expected from a learner in a particular time and how much revision he will need.

In general it is clear that the ordering of items in a language course is not always particularly important. Choosing one sequence of items rather than another cannot help much in making diffuse and difficult concepts any clearer, nor can it help the pupil to classify new items if each one has to be classified separately. It can lighten the learner's burden to a certain extent by delaying the introduction of exceptions, and also by breaking up complicated paradigms into more manageable and more easily learnt sections. But, again, it cannot ease the memory problems of 'meaningless' choices such as exist in prepositional phrases.

3.2 How much to teach?

At first sight the question of how much to teach in a course appears relatively simple to answer: as much as the average member of the class can master in the time available. However, this raises the problem of what is meant by 'master'. Secondly, it begs the question of how this mastery is to be achieved.

As soon as we begin to analyse what we mean by 'knowing a foreign language', we are faced with a host of difficult decisions. Does 'mastery' mean the ability to talk, read and write like a native speaker in any situation? Or does it mean something less than this and, if so, what is the criterion of success? Clearly, in order to answer these questions we must return to the learner's purposes in acquiring the language. For instance, it may be sufficient for a pupil to acquire the ability to understand the language over quite a wide range of topics, without being able to produce very much. On the other hand, an ability to speak the language may be more important than an extensive reading knowledge. We cannot decide how much to include in the materials for a course unless we know how much the pupil is expected to recognize in reading and listening.

We must also consider the question of performance standards. If the pupil is expected to be completely accurate, he will obviously learn less in a given time than he would if he were working to a less demanding (and perhaps more useful) criterion, e.g., fluent intelligibility.

We have seen that many features of the grammar and pronunciation of a foreign language carry little, if any, semantic information. Verb endings, case inflexions, gender distinctions, prepositions and many spelling rules can all be inaccurately deployed without affecting intelligibility. Of course, such errors are irritating and must be dealt with if the learner's ultimate aim requires accurate performance, for example if he wishes to teach the foreign language. It is, in the end, a matter of priorities: do we want an emphasis on fluency in the early stages which will probably result in inaccuracies but which will provide the pupil with a useful command of the language relatively quickly, or do we want slower progress with stress laid on accurate performance of new points as they turn up in the course? It is tempting to go for the latter aim, particularly if one believes that inaccuracies tolerated early in the learning will be more difficult to deal with later on. However, it is noticeable that, even if the teaching is very precise and careful, the pupils find it extremely difficult to achieve a high standard of accuracy in the details of the language, particularly if they have little semantic content. *I go yesterday* is comprehensible enough, after all.

It is very important not to attach irrelevant value-judgements to the two different approaches by thinking of one of them as 'disciplined' and the other as 'slapdash', for example. This misrepresents the whole issue, which is basically one of timing. If our aim is fluency we can let the pupil get on as fast as possible in the beginning stages, aiming only at a reasonably confident comprehension and production of the foreign language in spite of inaccuracies in semantically unimportant rules such as gender, declension, conjugation, etc. Then at a later stage we can take up the details and train a more correct performance. If we do this, there will be certain consequences. Firstly, some pupils will leave the course before the question of detailed accuracy has been seriously raised. Their performance will be faulty, but at least it should be useful. Secondly, the pupils may resist the teacher's attempts to enforce accuracy because it temporarily slows up their fluency of expression. Finally, there may be a problem of 'unlearning' points which have been allowed to pass without much comment in the past. If one believes very strongly that language learning is essentially a matter of habit formation, then this argument is likely to carry a great deal of weight. It should be remembered, however, that inaccuracies persist even with the most stringent teaching methods. This suggests that there is a 'natural' timetable for learning a foreign language just as there undoubtedly is for learning one's native language. The utterances of small children are full of inaccuracies if measured against the standard of developed speech and for the most part they go unchecked because they are not thought of as inaccuracies but as 'underdeveloped speech'. However, if a six-year-old still talks like a three-year-old, then

B

his behaviour does not match the expectations of society, and he will be given special attention of some sort.

If we adopt the more usual aim of accurate performance, one advantage is immediately obvious: the pupils can be examined and tested to see whether they have acquired this accuracy or not. Accuracy is simple to examine, mainly because it tests grammatical rules which can easily be judged right or wrong, and so tests can be marked without too much argument. Fluency is almost impossible to mark fairly, which is a pity because it is a more important skill in most real-life situations. The second consequence of an accuracy-dominated approach is that some pupils leave the course before they have learnt enough of the foreign language to be of much practical use. There is only a limited amount of time at the teacher's disposal in any teaching situation. If he spends that time insisting on accuracy in all the details, he will obviously not have time to train a fluent, more wide-ranging command of the language. Finally, there is always the thought that insistence on detailed accuracy is premature in the early stages, rather like forcing a plant in a hot-house.

Faced with a choice between accuracy and fluency, most teachers will naturally tend towards a compromise position: as much accuracy and as much fluency as possible in the time available. However, teaching systems being what they are with their inevitable demand for testable behaviour from the pupils, the accuracy criterion is almost bound to find favour with the majority of teachers. In fact the problem goes deeper than this. Fluency in the early stages of learning is very difficult to recognize. After all, if a student has not learnt very much, he cannot easily demonstrate how good he is at expressing his ideas. Accuracy, however, is very easy to recognize, with the result that an inaccurate learner is a much louder comment on the teacher's skill than an inarticulate pupil. As a teacher one dislikes inaccuracy because it is an affront to one's abilities and, ultimately, to one's authority. It is not irrelevant that accuracy tends to be the shibboleth of authoritarians.

To sum up, the amount of material contained in a language teaching course reflects not only how much the pupils can be expected to learn in a given time, but also the kind of learning that the teacher expects them to achieve.

3.3 Revision

The lack of opportunity for constant revision is the most glaring defect in foreign language teaching courses. Certainly, most courses include 'revision lessons' at certain points but this does not really provide an answer. Before going on to discuss this point it is necessary to establish what should be understood by 'revision' in a language teaching course.

Revision should be both cumulative and recurrent. When a learning point has been introduced into the materials, it should be used again and again in the succeeding units. Of course, some points are more important than others and it would be physically impossible to bring back every single item in every unit, so choices have to be made. However, if the notion of cumulative recurrence were to be applied to teaching materials in even the most limited way, the effect would be startling. The greatest problem in foreign language teaching is to provide enough interesting repetition. It is only by constantly using the language which has already been taught in new and different contexts (stories, dialogues, reading and listening texts, etc.) that the pupils can be continually reminded of what they met in previous lessons, and boredom is avoided by the fact that each story, song and dialogue is based on a different topic. Provided the previously introduced language recurs in a very wide variety of materials, the pupils will not get bored.

In contrast to the idea of cumulative recurrence, the common technique at the present time is to try and teach a new point 'thoroughly' at the time it is introduced into the syllabus. It is presented, practised, drilled and tested, and then in the next lesson it is forgotten.[1]

There is an obvious practical objection to the notion of cumulative recurrence. It would require a very large body of teaching material—readers, listening texts, comics, magazines and so on—if the twin aims of constant revision and varied activity were to be realized. But even a limited realization of this concept could lead to valuable improvements in the construction of language teaching materials.

4 'Linear' and 'spiral' syllabuses

Our use of language, for either production or reception, is marked by two important characteristics. First, we continually use the same resources of language in different combinations to express different meanings. We know from a study of grammar that the same limited number of rules are employed over and over again to produce different sentences. And we also know from word frequency studies that a fairly small number of lexical items tend to occur and recur. But unlike grammatical rules the number of lexical items is unlimited, and the second aspect of our experience of language reflects this fact. We meet new words every day, whose meaning we guess from their contexts (or, sometimes, ask somebody about or look up in a dictionary). Some time later we hear the word again and then

[1] The concept of frequency was discussed earlier. Its most revealing (and most logical) application would be to count how often particular items appear in language teaching courses and compare that figure with the established frequency lists. After all, a measure of frequency should tell us how often items should appear in our materials.

again, and perhaps learn more of its meaning each time we hear it.

The implication of these ideas for language learning is that we cannot reasonably expect full control of a new bit of language at a first encounter. In the case of our own language, we learn new bits of language gradually by experiencing them intermittently in different contexts. Of course, we have to notice that they recur—and in language instruction it is part of the teacher's job to draw the pupil's attention to those features of language that it is important for him to notice. In addition, we need to have repeated experience of the same features of language, always in context and preferably in different contexts. The concept behind all this is that of a 'cyclical', or 'spiral' experience of new language; i.e., we continually experience a new word or phrase and endeavour to assimilate it by trying it out on people and listening to the way other people use it.

If we compare the above remarks with the way in which language teaching courses are often organized, we see that the latter adopt a very different point of view. The tendency is to isolate learning points; to present these points one after the other in some order and to practise each of them in rather a lot of detail before moving on to the next. In addition, there is a feature of teaching courses which is not often noticed, but which seems astonishing once we have had our attention drawn to it— they contain hardly any language. A native speaker of English, for example, could easily read the whole of a year's course for foreigners in an hour or two. The result is that the teacher must squeeze every drop of instruction out of every page, and the pupil must make an enormous effort to assimilate each new learning point the first time it appears because when he turns the page he will go on to something else. Whereas the natural process of learning a language is 'spiral', i.e., the same things keep turning up in different combinations with different meanings, the language teaching process is usually 'linear', i.e., new points are strung along in a line and each one is, so to speak, sucked dry before moving to the next.

These remarks should not be interpreted as a plea for revolution, but rather for evolution. The economic arguments against duplicating and distributing a wide variety of teaching materials are not so strong as they were before the introduction of photographic processes, and the language laboratory provides unlimited access to examples of recorded speech. Before long, the videotape will provide a visual element to support and elucidate the spoken texts. What is necessary is a sophisticated linguistic control of the content of the materials so that the pupil is not simply 'immersed' in a bewildering mass of uncoordinated bits and pieces of language. No matter how interesting each separate bit might be, it is better that the student should be given the opportunity to experience the same features turning up in many different combinations, so that he may gradually 'grow into' the language as his experience of it increases.

5 Practical work and further reading

This chapter is not intended to tell you how to write a language course, but only to raise certain background issues which might be interesting to discuss. The exercise which follows asks you, therefore, to do some research on existing courses rather than to construct one of your own. Have a look at a selection of courses and try to analyse them with the following questions in mind:

1 What sort of learner is the course intended for? How does it reflect his supposed purpose in learning the language? Do the materials (choice of texts, etc.) show a concern with general educational values or with more specific and practical objectives?

2 What account is taken of the prospective learner's mother-tongue?

3 How does the course reflect the prospective pupil's age, previous learning experience, aptitude and motivation?

4 Is the language it contains likely to be useful to the learner? (In this connection consider not only the choice of vocabulary and grammatical patterns, but also the actual example sentences. Some courses have rather strange examples which nobody would normally use, e.g., *The sun is shining in the sky, Are you my mother?, Am I English?*, etc. If such sentences exist in the materials, what purpose are they intended to serve?)

5 Does the author merely exemplify the grammar or does he explain it as well?

6 What principles can you discern in the grading and organization of the course? If it is a beginner's course, to what extent does the grading in the early stages depend on the choice of teaching method and techniques?

7 Does the author introduce whole paradigms at once, or does the pupil learn various examples as set-phrases beforehand? (If the course is intended to teach English as a foreign language to beginners, see how the author handles questions with 'do'.)

8 Is the pupil asked to use the language in some activity, or only practise it in formal exercises and drills, i.e., to what extent does fluency seem to be an aim of the course as well as accuracy?

9 How is revision provided for? Take a grammar pattern and one or two reasonably important vocabulary words from the early part of the course. How often do they turn up later on in the tests, exercises, etc.?

10 How long is the course supposed to last? How much experience of language should the pupil have had in that time? (You will have to ignore the teacher's contribution.)

If possible, try to look at the following courses for comparative purposes:

Alexander, L. G. *First Things First*. London: Longmans, 1967. An example of a modern approach using pictures and dialogues in the early stages.

Buckby, M. and others. *En Avant, Stage 4A*. The Schools Council French Course. Leeds: E. J. Arnold and Son, 1970. Look at this course particularly with respect to question 9 above. This is the only course I know which systematically applies the idea of recurrence to language teaching materials. Notice how the authors treat the teaching of *pouvoir, savoir* and *vouloir* in particular.

Derrick, June and others. *SCOPE: An Introductory English Course for Immigrant Children*. Books for Schools, Ltd., 1969, for the Schools Council. Look at this course particularly with respect to questions 1, 3, 4, 6, 7 and 8 above. Unlike the first two courses in this list, *SCOPE* has a specific type of learner in mind with a clearly definable need for English.

Hornby, A. S. and Mackin, R. *The Oxford Progressive English Alternative Course*. London: Oxford University Press, 1966. A very good example of a standard, structurally graded course for use throughout the world.

Also try to look at:

McNally, J. and Murray, W. *Key Words to Literacy and the Teaching of Reading*. London: Schoolmaster Publishing Co., 1968. A discussion on transforming frequency studies into a pedagogically useful word-list. Take a selection of items on the final list and consider each of them as the 'tip of a learning iceberg' for a foreign learner of English. What learning problems are involved in each of the words you have chosen?

S.R.A. Reading Laboratory. Various levels. Chicago: Science Research Associates, 1958 (Revised 1960). An example of carefully graded materials with a specialized objective.

The following works are also relevant to the problem of preparing teaching materials:

Dakin, J., Tiffin, B. and Widdowson, H. G. *Language in Education*. London: Oxford University Press, 1968. See section 3 by H. G. Widdowson.

Fries, C. C. and Traver, A. A. *English Word Lists and Their Adaptability for Instruction*. Ann Arbor: University of Michigan Press, 1955.

Mackey, W. F. *Language Teaching Analysis*. London: Longmans, 1965. A thorough and valuable encyclopedia of the subject with a very extensive bibliography.

Ogden, C. K. *Basic English* Series. London: Kegan Paul, 1930–. A series of books written by Ogden and I. A. Richards was published at various dates in the 1930s in Kegan Paul's Psyche Miniatures General Series.

Thorndike, E. L. and Lorge, I. *The Teacher's Book of 30,000 Words*. New York: University of Columbia Press, 1944.

West, Michael. *A General Service List of English Words*. London: Longmans, 1955.

There are many books about teaching languages to particular types of learner but the following are interesting if read in conjunction with *SCOPE* (see above):

Derrick, June. *Teaching English to Immigrants*. London: Longmans, 1968.

Stern, H. H. *Foreign Languages in Primary Education*. London: Oxford University Press, 1967.

Stern, H. H. *Languages and the Young School Child*. London: Oxford University Press, 1968.

2 GILLIAN BROWN
Practical Phonetics and Phonology

1 General phonetics

1.1 Introduction

General phonetic theory is concerned to describe the production and reception of speech sounds. Description of the productive processes would ideally include an account both of the neurological and the physiological operations by which speech is produced. The neurological control of speech is an area which is only just beginning to be systematically explored (see Laver 1970). Much more is known about the physiological control of speech, though no-one would claim that anything like an adequate description of the physiological processes involved yet exists. Description of the reception of speech should include an account of the acoustics of the waveform which mediates between speaker and listener—this is one of the most intensively explored areas of phonetic theory. On the other hand the investigation of the processes of perception of speech by a listener is a comparatively recent field of research.

Traditionally, general phonetic theory has been chiefly concerned with the description of the movements of the articulators during the production of speech sounds. At the beginning of this century a strong impetus was given to the study of phonetics in Britain by the work of Daniel Jones. His main concern, in his published works at least, was with the description of speech sounds used in English and the ways in which they differed from speech sounds used in other well-known languages, especially French (See, for example, Jones 1956a, 1956b). The result of his influence was not only the rapid expansion of the subject but also that phonetic interest tended to concentrate on isolatable speech sounds, each of which was described as if a static posture of the articulators existed during its articulation. This approach to phonetic description is exemplified in many well-known accounts of the phonetics of English (Jones 1956a, 1956b, Ward 1948, to mention only a few).

I am deeply grateful to David Abercrombie who has made detailed comments on this paper and to Keith Brown and Tim Johns who have made very helpful suggestions. Expressions of opinion together with any remaining errors are, of course, my own.

The development of interest in phonetics, especially in the context of pronunciation teaching, coincided with the development of the theory of the phoneme. The segments isolated from the stream of speech by the phoneticians tended to be phoneme-sized segments. A great deal of very valuable work was done in terms of this approach and no-one would wish to question its value—or indeed to deny that in all future attempts at phonetic description we shall be standing on the shoulders of the giants of the past. Despite this positive contribution to human knowledge, it is clear that in some fields some damage has been done by the insistently segmental approach to phonetic description. One field which has suffered considerably from undue reliance on the concept of isolatable segments strung together in the stream of speech is certainly that of pronunciation teaching. There appears to be a widespread view that by identifying the contrastive speech sounds (those which can distinguish between the meanings of words, the phonemes of a given language) and by stating some of the more obvious variations in their phonetic realization in different contexts (stating the allophonic distribution) one has said all that can usefully be said about the phonetics of a given language. I believe this to be a fundamentally mistaken view and one which has led to disillusion and despair among many pronunciation teachers. In the following sections I shall first outline a classificatory phonetic taxonomy, and then a plain man's phoneme theory, in order to be able to discuss some of the approaches which I believe can help the pronunciation teacher in his uphill struggle.

1.2 Articulatory phonetic taxonomy

The conscientious reader should read this section with a mirror in his hand and pause frequently to peer into his mouth.

The vocal tract from the larynx to the lips may be regarded as a curved tube with flexible sides. When an airstream is passed into this tube the articulators (the flexible sides of the tube) may modify it in various ways and thus determine the acoustic quality of the resulting soundwave. The most usual input to the tube is pulmonic air coming out of the lungs. The first possibility of modification arises in the larynx itself.

(a) The state of the glottis

The *vocal cords* (which look rather like thick muscular lips lying horizontally across the larynx) bound the space known as the *glottis*. They can be in a state of vibration, called *voicing*; or lying apart, not impeding the airstream in any way, in a state of *voicelessness*; or completely closed in a *glottal stop*.

Say *zzzzzzz* like a bee buzzing. While you are doing this put your cupped hand round your throat, covering the larynx. You should feel a distinct vibration. Now block your ears completely while still buzzing—you should feel as if you had a pneumatic drill inside your head. *zzzzzz* is a *voiced* sound.

Say *sssss* like a snake hissing. Do the same exercises again. This time there should be no vibration at the larynx and no buzzing in the head. *sssss* is a *voiceless* sound.

Many people find it very difficult to bring the state of the glottis under conscious control. Try alternating *sszzsszzss*. Now try alternating *ffvvffvvff* with no break in between them. If this isn't difficult try saying *mmmm* and then make that voiceless. You should find that voiceless *mmmm* is just breathing out with your mouth closed. (This sound occurs in Icelandic, Welsh and Burmese.) Now try alternating voiced and voiceless *llll*. (Voiceless *llll* occurs in Welsh, for instance, at the beginning of the place name Llandudno.)

Most sounds in all languages are voiced sounds.

When you have mastered voicing control (and it often takes a lot of practice) try making a *glottal stop*. This is the sound you make when you cough—you jerk from one glottal stop to the next. It turns up as a speech sound in many languages—it is often remarked on in urban British accents when it occurs instead of *t* in a word like 'butter'.

(b) *The root of the tongue*

The root of the tongue lies just above the glottis in that part of the vocal tract which is round the bend—you can't see it in a mirror. Because the root of the tongue is not directly visible, and because it is difficult to teach oneself to feel what's going on down there, we know remarkably little about its action and the effects of its action. It can certainly bulge out to constrict the passage of air and it is very active, especially in front vowels, as X-rays show us. It seems likely that its characteristic posture influences the sort of voice quality an individual has—whether harsh or hollow, etc.

(c) *The velum*

The *velum* is the soft area of muscle attached behind your hard palate. (The hard palate is the bony arch spanning that part of the roof of the mouth which is surrounded on three sides by teeth.) If you look in the mirror and yawn you will see the velum moving. One of its important functions is to control *nasality*. If the velum is raised, as it is most of the time in typical British speech, the airstream doesn't seep up into the nasal cavities and produce nasal resonance. If, however, the velum is lowered, part of the airstream is diverted into the nasal cavities and nasal resonance results. If there is a complete stop in the mouth the whole of the airstream behind the stop is diverted into the nasal cavities. Most languages have one or two *nasal consonants*, for example *m* and *n* in English. If you can say *bmmbmmbmmbmm* with no vowel creeping in (keep your lips closed) you may be able to feel your velum flapping up and down, alternately allowing the airstream into the nasal cavities and keeping it out. (This action is especially noticeable if you have a cold.) Both consonants (other than stops) and vowels are said to be *nasalized* when the airstream is bifurcated so that part of it passes out through the lips while simultaneously there is nasal resonance. Nasalized vowels occur in many languages, for example French, as in 'banc'.

(d) *The tongue*

The tongue is a very large and flexible organ—it is very much bulkier than the part we can see at the tip would suggest. It can rear up vertically at the front or at the back of the mouth. It can spread out horizontally or curve itself round to form a groove extending right along its length. For convenience of reference it is usually divided into four parts—the *tip*, the very front vertical edge, the *blade* which is the area lying imme-diately behind the tip (the part which shows when someone sticks his tongue out in a rude gesture), the *front* which is identified as the part which lies immediately beneath the hard palate when at rest, and the *back* which lies beneath the velum. (We have already mentioned the *root* of the tongue.) The characteristic posture of the tongue varies a great deal from one language to another—whether it is normally held convex or concave to the roof of the mouth for example, whether the tip or blade of the tongue characteristically articulates against the back of the upper teeth as in French (*dental* articulation) or against the alveolar ridge (which lies just behind the teeth) as in English (*alveolar* articulation), whether the back of the tongue frequently sweeps back to articulate with the tiny piece of flesh dangling down from the back of the velum (*uvular* articulation—as in French), or whether the main activity of the tongue is concentrated in the front of the mouth, as in English.

Any movement of one part of the tongue necessarily constrains the possibilities of movement in other parts of the tongue, since the tongue is a single organ. Little is known of the nature and extent of these constraints.

(e) *The lips*

The lips are readily observable and modify the airstream in a way that can be fairly adequately described. They are very flexible, can open and shut in a vertical dimension (as in *baa, baa*), can form a narrow round opening as in *oooh!*, or a wider opening when they curl outwards exposing some of the soft inner lip as in *shhh!* (Look at this in your mirror.) Protrusion of the lips obviously has an effect on the whole vocal tract, not only lengthening the tract but also constricting the inner dimensions, since the cheeks are necessarily pulled forward with the lips. Sounds articulated with both lips are called *labial* (sometimes *bilabial*), e.g. *p, m, w* in English. When the lips are pursed round a narrow opening, they are said to be *rounded*, as in English 'woo', where the whole word is rounded. Sweet (1906, p. 18) called the second sort of rounding 'protrusion or pouting'. *Protrusion* is characteristic of several English consonants, for example the sound at the beginning of 'shake'. Whereas most languages have some rounded sounds, the type and degree of protrusion varies a good deal from one language to another, and varies to some extent among speakers of any one language. Many French speakers typically protrude the lower lip all the time they are talking.

The lower lip can function independently of the upper lip. It is attached to the lower jaw, which can move backwards, forwards, and sideways in relation to the upper jaw, as well as vertically. In many languages *labio-dental* articulation occurs when the lower lip articulates with the upper teeth (as in English *f* and *v*). The point at which it articulates with the upper teeth varies from one language to another. Whereas in English *f* is typically articulated with the inner, soft side of the lower lip against the front edge of the upper teeth, in some German accents and in many Slavic languages *f* is typically articulated with the top outside rim of the bottom lip against the inner edge of the upper teeth, so that the bottom edge of the upper teeth is visible during the articulation.

The above sections are concerned with the *active articulators*—the tongue and the lips. Consonants are usually classified however in terms of articulation with the *passive* or *fixed articulators*. Some common classes are *dental* (the back of the upper teeth), *alveolar* (the teeth ridge), *palatal* (the hard palate) and *velar* (the soft palate).

So far we have discussed the articulators which can modify the airstream as it passes through the vocal tract. There are many different ways in which the airstream can be modified—we shall only have space to mention some of the more common ones.

(f) *Stop*

The most dramatic way of modifying the airstream is to obstruct it completely at some point along the vocal tract by putting one articulator against another in such a way that no air can escape from the mouth. This is called a *stop*. Examples of *oral stops* are *p, k, d*. If you make the closure for any one of these you will find that you can build up pressure behind it, and make yourself red in the face with the effort, but no air will escape from any part of the articulatory tract while you maintain the stop. (We need to distinguish a closing phase, a holding phase, and a release phase for all stops used in speech. The holding phase is the one which obstructs the airstream.) Examples of *nasal stops* are *m* and *n*. (During nasal stops no air escapes from the mouth but the airstream is diverted into the nasal cavity.)

(g) *Fricative*

Whereas during the holding phase of a stop the passage of air in the mouth is completely obstructed, during a *fricative* the passage of air is only partially obstructed—but sufficiently to be heard as a slight 'roughness' in the quality of sound. Examples of fricatives are *s* and *z*. Notice that you cannot build up much pressure behind these strictures of *close approximation*.

Stops and fricatives are sometimes grouped together as a class of *obstruents*.

(h) *Aspiration and affrication*

Aspirated consonants are stops (and, rarely, fricatives) which are released with a moment of voicelessness before the onset of voicing for the following vowel. The voicelessness normally has the quality of the following vowel. English *p, t, k* are normally aspirated when initial in stressed syllables, whereas French *p, t, k* are not aspirated. Try to prolong the aspiration in 'peat' 'part' 'port' and notice the difference in quality. *Affricated* consonants are stops which are released with a more or less strongly fricative noise. The sounds at the beginning and end of 'church' and 'judge' are called affricated stops (or affricates).

(i) *Trill, tap and flap*

These are three rather unusual ways of modifying the airstream. They are all characterized by a very delicate adjustment of air pressure in relation to the muscular tension of the relevant articulator. The *trill* (sometimes called a *roll*) occurs when an extremely rapid series of stops occurs in such rapid succession that their articulation lasts no longer than any other single segment. An alveolar trill occurs in some Scots speech in words like 'burr', and is characteristic of stage Scots speech. The *tap* has been described as 'one tap trill' by Abercrombie (1967, p. 49). An alveolar tap occurs between vowels in words like 'very' and 'orange' in the speech of some English speakers, and commonly occurs instead of *t* in the speech of many American speakers in words like 'butter', 'writer'. It sounds like a very rapid *d*. The flat tongue tip rises and taps once, rapidly, against the alveolar ridge. For a *flap*, on the other hand, the tip and blade of the tongue are curled back in a rapid movement, and the underside of the tip strikes the back of the alveolar ridge as the tongue flaps back down. Flaps are found in some Indian and Scandinavian languages. (The terms *tap* and *flap* are not kept distinct by all authors.)

(j) *Central and lateral*

The airstream usually passes through a *central* passage in the vocal tract. In *s*, for example, the sides of the tongue are raised to make a complete closure with the gums right round to the front incisors. X-rays show that the sides of the tongue, in English at any rate, are raised much higher than the centre of the tongue, not only along the gums but also right back round the bend under the uvula. The air escapes through a very narrow opening just behind the front teeth—a *central* opening. If you try to breathe in through the mouth while saying *s* you should feel the cold air rushing in down the centre of your tongue.

Most languages have an alveolar *lateral* consonant—*l*. (Some have more than one lateral as, for example, Italian, which has a palatal lateral—spelt *gl*—in words like 'figlia'.) The tip of the tongue is raised as in a *d*, but the side of the tongue is lowered on one or both sides to allow the air to escape laterally. If you breathe in through your mouth while saying a voiceless *l* you should feel the cold air rushing in down the side(s) of your tongue.

(k) *Vocoid*

All modifications which obstruct the airstream less than those we have considered so far are grouped together under the general heading *vocoid* which involves a stricture of *open approximation*. This term includes those sounds which have traditionally been called 'vowels', as well as sounds which have received a number of rather unsatisfactory labels like 'semi-vowel' and 'semi-consonant'—the sort of sounds at the beginning of the English words 'yet', 'wet', 'rat' and 'hat'.

(i) *Vowels*. Vowels have traditionally been classified by the part of the tongue highest in the mouth, how far the highest part is from the roof of the mouth, and the posture of the lips—whether they are rounded or unrounded. It is taken for granted that a vowel is voiced and that the tongue is convex to the roof of the mouth, with the tongue tip down, and that there is no nasal resonance, unless otherwise stated. If the front of the tongue is highest in the mouth (as in 'peat') the vowel is said to be *front*. If the back of the tongue is highest, the vowel is said to be a *back* vowel (e.g. in 'boot'). If you slowly alternate the vowels in these two words you can feel the hump rolling like a wave along your tongue. If the hump consists of the part where front and back meet, the vowel is said to be *central* (e.g. the two vowels in 'above'). So much for the front-back dimension. In the vertical dimension, if the hump of the tongue is close to the roof of the mouth—as in the vowels in 'beat' and 'boot'—the vowel is said to be a *close* vowel. If the jaw is dropped and the highest part of the tongue is lying pretty close to the bottom of the mouth—as in 'pat'—the vowel is an *open* vowel. If a vowel is just a little more open than close it is called *half-close*—as in the beginning of the vowel in 'day'—and if it is a little more open but still not fully open it is called *half-open*—as in 'egg'.

Vowels, like consonants, can be rounded. In many languages back vowels are rounded, as in 'boot' and 'naught' in English, and front vowels are not. In some languages with large vowel systems there are rounded front vowels as well as back (e.g. French), and unrounded back vowels (e.g. Korean or Gaelic). In other languages with large vowel systems *diphthongs* (vowels of constantly changing quality occurring as the nucleus of one syllable, e.g. the vowels in 'eye', 'how') are found, as well as the more usual *monophthongs* (vowels of unvarying quality). *Retroflex*, *nasalized* and *long* vowels are also found.

(ii) *'Semi-vowels'*. It has often been pointed out that if you prolong the pronunciation of *y* or *w* (the sounds initial in 'yet' and 'wet'), the result is exactly like the vowels *i* and *u* found in 'beat' and 'boot'. The main distinguishing characteristic cannot be stated in terms of difference of articulation since the posture of the articulators can be identical in each case. The distinguishing characteristic is rather the way these sounds function in different languages as *syllable onset* or *syllable nucleus*. When one of these sounds occurs as onset to a syllable it functions like a consonant and is transcribed as *w* or *y*; when it occurs as nucleus of a syllable it functions like a vowel and is transcribed with a vowel symbol. (Pike 1943 characterized these as nonsyllabic vocoid and syllabic vocoid respectively.) A similar relation exists between the sound at the beginning of 'red' and the sound in the middle of 'bird' in the speech of some 'r pronouncing' English and American speakers. If *r* is prolonged it may sound like a central vowel.

r is one of the sounds of English which is realized in a wide variety of ways. For many speakers it is characterized by a drawing back and raising of the tip and blade of the tongue with a simultaneous drawing back of the back of the tongue. This sort of articulation is called *retroflex*. Retroflexion of the tongue characterizes the pronunciation of quite a number of vowels in many English accents—those which are followed in the orthography by an *r* as in 'poor', 'heard', 'hard'. Retroflexion is one of the best known characteristics of many Indian languages. Here the drawing back of the tip and blade may be much more marked than it is in English, and the tip may actually be curled back so that the underside of the tongue tip is presented to the roof of the mouth.

Finally under the general heading of 'vocoid' we shall briefly discuss the vexed question of *h*. The pronunciation of *h* varies a good deal between languages. In English *h* is usually a voiceless onset to the following vowel —so if you prolong *h* at the beginning of 'heat', 'hat' and 'hoot' for example, you will find that the quality of the *h* varies considerably—what remains constant is the voiceless onset. In some languages, for example many Bantu languages, *h* is pronounced with a far more fricative effect. It is often difficult to determine whether the friction is due to 'glottal friction', as is sometimes claimed, or to more general cavity friction in the whole oral chamber.

(l) *Coarticulation*

We have already mentioned the distortion of description which can arise from considering the stream of speech as a sequence of isolated segments. As soon as you begin to consider how a word is pronounced, you will notice the mutual interaction of the 'segments' it contains; indeed you may find it hard to decide in any non-arbitrary way where one segment ends and the next begins. Consider the gesture made just by the tip and blade of the tongue in pronouncing the English word 'stroke'. (Ignore the complex lip gesture and the movement of the back of the tongue and the onset of vocal cord activity for the moment, though you might like to consider them by yourself later.) Throughout the gesture the sides of the tongue make contact with the upper gums—they may slide back a bit during *r* but otherwise we will ignore them. The blade of the tongue is in close approximation to the centre of the alveolar ridge during *s*, then it slides back through a point of closure that is difficult to isolate if you say the word at anything like normal speed, and *r* is released as the tip of the tongue slides back off the alveolar ridge. It is extremely difficult to think of this cluster as a well demarcated sequence of segments —much easier to think of it as one complex gesture.

There are many relationships of *coarticulation* which are sometimes described under the rubric 'secondary articulation'. These include the palatalizing of consonants before front (palatal) vowels (compare palatalized *s*, *t*, *n* in 'seat', 'teat', 'neat' with the same set non-palatalized in 'sat', 'tat', 'gnat'—the palatalization is particularly noticeable in the pitch of the hiss in *s*.) Another type of coarticulation is the rounding of consonants before round vowels. (Look in the mirror at *p*, *m*, in 'poor', 'moot' and compare them with *p* and *m* in 'peat', 'meat'.) Another type is the tendency to nasalize vowels adjacent to nasal consonants (try saying 'moon' in English—is the vowel identical to that in 'boot'?). There are many other examples that we could list. In general it is not too much to claim that every segment will interact to some degree with any adjacent segment, whether consonant or vowel. You may rely on finding coarticulation in all speech, but notice that coarticulation habits will vary widely with different languages. How much a *k* is fronted before a front vowel cannot be predicted by a universal law, nor whether it is the vowel before or after a nasal consonant which will tend to be nasalized. (Compare English *k* in 'key' with an East African rendering which may sound like 'chee'—or consider the difficulty of a West African speaker accustomed to strongly nasalize vowels *before* nasals, in pronouncing English 'him'.)

(m) *Airstream mechanisms*

In all languages most speech is uttered on an egressive pulmonic airstream (i.e., on the air coming out of the lungs). In many languages there are some sounds which are uttered on other airstreams (notably many Caucasian languages, Indian, Amerindian and African languages). For a description of the operation of these other airstream mechanisms, together with a much more adequate discussion of articulatory phonetics in general, consult the books mentioned in Further Reading at the end of this chapter.[1]

2 Phonology

2.1 Segmental phonology

Phonology is concerned with the description of the systematic speech habits of the speakers of one given language.

One of the aims of a phonological description is to identify the *contrastive* units of the sound system of a language—those units which will distinguish the meaning of words. Whereas there is an infinite number of phonetically varying segments in the speech of any one individual, this infinite number of phonetic segments can be grouped into a small number of items which function linguistically—that is, they serve to distinguish between words. It is suggested that a native speaker will ignore as irrelevant the mass of phonetic variation, and abstract from the acoustic signal the minimum linguistic information necessary to identify a word or a sequence of words. This small number of linguistically functioning units comprises the set of *phonemes* of the language.

Two notions which play an important part in the description of a language are those of *paradigmatic* and *syntagmatic* relations (sometimes called *system* and *structure*). Items which occur in the same paradigm may be said to be in *opposition*. Thus in:

[1] I should like to record my indebtedness in this section to the work of David Abercrombie and other colleagues in Edinburgh. They will find much of their teaching and practice exemplified here.

peep	[pip]
teat	[tit]
cease	[sis]

the initial consonants are in paradigmatic relation with each other, and the final consonants are in paradigmatic relation with each other, but, since they occur in different places in structure, the initial consonants can never be in opposition to the final consonants. The members of the initial set, p_1, t_1, s_1, are said to be in *parallel* distribution with each other— that is they all occur at the same place in structure—but the initial set is in *complementary* distribution with the final set p_2, t_2, s_2.

Suppose we hold the environment the same and simply vary the items in the initial slot:

peat	[pit]
teat	[tit]
seat	[sit]

We can state that the varying of the initial item in each case produces a different English word. These initial items p_1, t_1, s_1, may be said to be in *opposition*, since they all occur in the same paradigm (i.e., they are in parallel distribution) and they distinguish the meanings of words. Suppose now we hold the initial environment the same and vary the last item:

peep	[pip]
peat	[pit]
peace	[pis]

We can state that the varying of the last item produces three different English words. p_2, t_2 and s_2 may be said to be in opposition, since they occur in the same paradigm and distinguish the meaning of words. We have now identified two sets of contrastive items—p_1, t_1, s_1 and p_2, t_2, s_2. Our aim is to group these sets, which are in complementary distribution, into as few phonemes as possible.

There are several reasons for wanting to make this grouping. First, it is generally held in any description that, all other things being equal, the description which utilizes the smallest number of units and makes maximally general statements about these units is to be preferred to one which operates with a larger number of units. This is the criterion of *economy*. (There may be some discussion about the implications of 'other things being equal'.) Another, related, reason is that a phoneme-like concept underlies many writing systems which are based on alphabetic principles. Many orthographies have been devised on this basis during this century (for example by the Summer Institute of Linguistics).

The concept of economy depends not only on the number of symbols required for printing presses, typewriters, etc. (though this is certainly a consideration), but mainly on the fact that native speakers are happy to group a number of phonetically different sounds together and to represent them with the same letter. The criteria we shall apply in grouping our two sets of items p_1 t_1 s_1 and p_2 t_2 s_2 into phonemes are as follows:

(i) the items must be phonetically similar

(ii) the grouping must result in sets of sounds which a native speaker is happy to represent with the same letter.

Returning now to [pip], [tit] and [sis], we see that there are regular phonetic differences between the set p_1, t_1, s_1 and the set p_2, t_2, s_2. In all cases the oral stricture is longer in duration for set_2 than it is for any member of set_1. In all cases, at least in the English accent known as 'R.P.' (Received Pronunciation), the initial sound is more palatalized than the final sound. (This is especially clear in the case of the fricative— prolong the *s* initially and finally and note that the initial *s* is higher in pitch than the final *s*.) The difference between the initial and final stops is even more clearly marked. The stops are aspirated when in initial position (voiceless onset to following vowel) and the aspiration has the quality of the following vowel. In final position they are preceded by glottal closure—if you say 'peep' very slowly, drawing out the vowel, you should hear the abrupt cut-off of voicing before the lips make a complete closure for the final *p*. All the members of set_1 are phonetically different from those of set_2. On the other hand there are clear similarities between p_1 and p_2, t_1 and t_2, s_1 and s_2. Both *p*s are bilabial, voiceless stops. Both *t*s are alveolar, voiceless stops. Both *s*s are alveolar, voiceless fricatives. The phonetic differences between set_1 and set_2 are attributed to their occurring at different places in structure—the pronunciation habits of the English speaker are different in syllable initial position from syllable final position. The phonetic differences between set_1 and set_2 can never serve to distinguish the meanings of words. On the basis of the similarity of articulation between p_1 and p_2, t_1 and t_2, s_1 and s_2 we may group these six items into three phonemes /p/, /t/ and /s/. A native speaker will be happy to accept this analysis—and is conditioned to accept it by English orthography.

So far we have considered the grouping of items which occur in different places of structure and which can never contrast. We must also consider the possibility illustrated in the following paradigm:

1	[kip]	'keep'
2	[kɑp]	'carp'
3	[kup]	'coop'

Here phonetically different *k*s all occur in the same place in structure—in the initial paradigm. k_1 is fronted, k_2 is articulated further back against the velum, k_3 is articulated against the velum and rounded. Despite the fact that these phonetically different *k*s all occur in the same paradigm, it is clear that the articulation is in each case conditioned by that of the following vowel. The *k*s cannot contrast because the articulation of each *k* depends on the following vowel. So, on the basis of phonetic similarity—they are all voiceless velar stops—the three *k*s are grouped into one phoneme, /k/.

The phonetically different variants which are grouped into one phoneme are said to be *allophones* of that phoneme. Thus k_1 and k_2 in 'cook' are both said to be allophones of /k/ just as the initial consonants in 'keep', 'carp', 'coop' are said to be allophones of /k/.

Items which are phonetically dissimilar may not be grouped into one phoneme. A celebrated instance of the impropriety of attempting to make such a grouping on the grounds of complementary distribution alone is that of English *h* and *ŋ*. (*ŋ* is the sound at the end of 'sing'.) *h* occurs only initially in syllables, *ŋ* only finally. These two are therefore in complementary distribution (never in opposition). They are, however, phonetically quite dissimilar and, more important, no native speaker will accept that these may properly be represented by the same letter.

The principles we have examined in setting up the phoneme are exemplified in the following two exercises:

Exercise A

Study the distribution of *l* and *r*. Could *l* and *r* be grouped into one phoneme? Vowels are written phonemically, consonants have appropriate phonetic values. Data from Lugisu, a Bantu language of East Africa.

1	umuserimu	a witch doctor	6	kaluba	a small chicken
2	ßaserimu	witch doctors	7	ßuluba	small chickens
3	umusala	a nurse	8	mulimi	a table
4	ßasala	nurses	9	mirimi	tables
5	luluba	a chicken	10	kalimi	a small table
			11	ßulimi	small tables

Symbol: ß is a voiced bilabial fricative.

This simple exercise illustrates the principle of complementary distribution. Phonetic *r* (a voiced post alveolar, slightly retroflex non-syllabic vocoid) occurs following front vowels *i* and *e*. Phonetic *l* (a voiced alveolar lateral) follows non-front vowels. *r* and *l* are in complementary distribution and so can never contrast. They are accepted as the same functioning entity by speakers of the language (cf. the difficulty Lugisu speakers have in distinguishing English words like 'read' and 'lead'). They may therefore be grouped into one phoneme, /l/, and ɪ can be phonemically written /umuselimu/.

Exercise B

In the following data the stops and fricatives can be grouped into three phonemes. State the distribution of the allophones of these phonemes (*v* should be disregarded). (Restricted data from Tamil supplied by R. E. Asher.)

1	ṭambi	'younger brother'	7	nambu	'trust'
2	aðu	'it'	8	vaːŋgu	'buy'
3	aṇḍa	'that' (adj.)	9	kaːðu	'ear'
4	paːmbu	'snake'	10	maxan	'son'
5	vaṇḍeːn	'I came'	11	iŋgu	'here'
6	axam	'interior'	12	koːßam	'anger'

Symbols: C̣ represents a dental consonant

Vː a long vowel

ð a voiced dental fricative (as in '*th*en')

x a voiceless velar fricative (as in 'Ba*ch*')

ŋ a voiced velar nasal (as in 'si*ng*')

ß a voiced bilabial fricative.

This more complex data illustrates the principle of complementary distribution. Note that the voiceless stop series occurs only word initially, and that in this position *p*, *t* and *k* function to keep words apart, that intervocalically a fricative paradigm occurs which, again, functions to keep words apart, and that following a nasal a voiced stop paradigm occurs. This data is representative of Tamil as a whole—voiceless stops only occur in word initial paradigms, fricatives intervocalically and voiced stops following nasals. On the basis of phonetic similarity nine sounds may be grouped into three phonemes:

the labial set p, ß, b into /p/

the dental set ṭ, ð, ḍ into /t/

the velar set k, x, g into /k/

We can then state as a very general rule that this set of phonemes will be realized as voiceless stops when they occur word initially, as fricatives when they occur intervocalically (voiced for labial and dental, voiceless for velar) and as voiced stops when they occur following nasals.

We have now attained the first object of a phonological description—we have identified the *contrastive* units of the language and we have grouped them together into a minimal number of *phonemes* and made very general statements about the phonetic realization of these phonemes in different environments. It may be noticed that, in these general statements, we have made a silent appeal to the notion of 'natural class'; i.e., the notion that phonetically similar items tend to function in a similar way phonologically.

So far we have considered only one of the aims of phonological description—we have discussed how to identify the contrastive sound units of a language. It is certainly true that a language teacher needs access to a statement of the contrastive units in the mother tongue and in the target language, and that a comparison of the inventories of phonemes in the two languages should help the teacher to predict areas of difficulty. For example, if *l* and *r* appear as separate phonemes in one language (e.g. in English) but as allophones of one phoneme in another (e.g. Japanese, Korean, Luganda) the teacher will expect that a Japanese speaker, for example, will have difficulty in discriminating between English *l* and *r* and that he will fail to produce a consistent contrast. Much very valuable English language teaching material has been produced on this basis.

It is, however, one thing to be able to state the number of contrastive sound units in a language, and to specify in fairly exiguous phonetic terms what the allophonic realization may be in different phonetic environments. It is quite another thing to state what phonetic features may exist in the environment which may enable a native speaker to identify one of the contrasting elements. Let us consider a simple example. English is said to have a set of voiced obstruents (e.g. *b, d, g, v, z*—we will ignore the rest for the moment) which contrasts with a set of voiceless obstruents (*p, t, k, f, s*). The difference between *p* and *b*, the initial consonants in 'pin' and 'bin', is said to lie in the fact that whereas *p* is voiceless, *b* is voiced. (They are both labial stops.) Similarly the difference in the final consonants of 'tap' and 'tab' is said to lie in the difference of voicing. Now let us consider the phonetic realization of these four words:

1 pin   2 bin   3 tap   4 tab

We find that in (1) there is a moment of hold of voiceless bilabial closure which is followed by release into a momentarily voiceless vowel which is then voiced. In (2), in the speech of many southern English speakers, there is a moment of hold of voiceless bilabial closure—which is immediately followed by release into a voiced vowel. In other words, for native English speakers the main distinction between these two sounds lies not in voicing versus voicelessness during the actual closure for the consonant—which is of course implied by the labels 'voiced/voiceless bilabial stop', but in the timing of the onset of voicing in the vowel. It is the aspiration, the moment of voiceless vowel, which distinguishes *p* and *b* in these two words. It is not surprising, then, that English speakers sometimes find it difficult to understand the English of French or West African speakers, where the opposition *p/b* is phonetically realized by voicelessness during the closure for *p* followed immediately by release into a voiced vowel, and by voicing during the closure for *b*. In fact phonetically a French or West African *p* may be much more like an English *b* than it is like an English *p*.

If we now look at the final consonants in (3) and (4) a similar problem arises, though the phonetic facts are different. The most obvious phonetic difference between 'tap' and 'tab', as pronounced by many native speakers, lies in the comparative shortness of the vowel in 'tap' and the fact that the voicing of the vowel is cut off abruptly by a glottal stop immediately preceding the labial closure (or simultaneous with it— the timing relations vary slightly with different speakers) and the much longer vowel in 'tab' with the gradual cessation of voicing during the closure for the *b*. There may be no audible phonetic difference during the labial *closure* for *p* or *b* at all (some speakers may have a dying away of voice during *b*—phonetically 'whisper', cf. Abercrombie 1967, p. 28). This variation in vowel length is characteristic of all syllable final voice/ voiceless distinctions in English. Thus the following pairs are principally distinguished by vowel length:

cease	/sis/	seize	/siz/
leaf	/lif/	leave	/liv/
set	/set/	said	/sed/
smelt	/smelt/	smelled	/smeld/
sent	/sent/	send	/send/

(In the last two pairs, the length of the lateral or nasal is shorter before a syllable final voiceless consonant than it is before a syllable final voiced consonant.) It is difficult in an account of allophonic variation to explain that a contrastive element may in fact be identified by its environment (which may be why this commonplace of English phonology is very often not known to teachers of English). We can state that vowels will be longer before voiced consonants than they are before voiceless consonants. But this is stating the allophone of the vowel, not the allophone of the consonant. (Chomsky 1964 makes this point more formally in an attack on the notion of the phoneme.)

It is clear that a statement of the sort we have just made—that the phonetic realization of initial and final voiceless and voiced obstruents in English may be observed most clearly in their environment—must be part of any phonology which can be of value to a language teacher, since the teacher is concerned not only with listing the contrastive items but with teaching the discrimination and production of words within utterances. This example also illustrates two closely related pitfalls which confront a reader who wants to extract teaching material from a phonological description. One is the danger of supposing that an identical term used to characterize contrastive items in different languages necessarily implies an identical phonetic realization. Compare in the light of the very brief description above, the phonetic realizations of the terms 'voiceless bilabial stop' in English and French. The related danger is, of course, the use of identical symbols in the phonemic inventory of two different languages—the symbols represent a very abstract level of contrast and the phonetic realization which actually carries the distinction may differ considerably between the two languages. It is possible to be misled by a phoneme inventory into supposing that, since a language has the vowel contrasts /i, e, a, o, u/, then at least the vowel in English 'fat' will be consistently produced and recognized. However, since there are no contrasts in this putative language in the central vowel region it is very likely that the phoneme /a/ covers a multitude of phonetic realizations, which may range through the vowels in an English speaker's 'pat', 'putt', 'pert', 'palm', and that this will lead to considerable difficulties in consistent production and recognition.

A statement which describes the phonetic features by which a contrastive item may be identified should be part of a general description of the *timing relation* characteristics (coarticulation habits) of a language. This description should include a statement of voicing habits, such as the degree of voicing, onset and offset of voicing, what happens to voicing at the end of words—does it fade into whisper but have distinctive vowel lengthening, as in English, or disappear completely with no distinctive vowel lengthening, as in German? What happens to a voiced consonant at the end of a word—is the suffix voiced as in English 'rubs' /rʌbz/, 'dogs' /dogz/, or can the voiced consonant be devoiced as in Modern Greek /lambo/, /elampsa/ 'I shine', 'I shone'? What are the habits of voicing assimilation between words? In most accents of English voicelessness/voicing remain distinct even when juxtaposed across word boundaries but in Modern Greek a final voiceless fricative will be voiced when followed by a word initial voiced consonant as in /tus/, /majirus/— /tuzmajirus/ 'the cooks'.

Other areas of timing relations which need to be stated are, for example, the effect of nasal consonants on adjacent vowels, the effect of front vowels and rounded vowels on adjacent consonants, and the effect of syllable structure on the pronunciation of sequences of allophones. Let us briefly consider each of these in turn—here we can only hope to look very briefly upon this very important area. Nasal consonants may always be preceded by nasalized vowels, as in many West African languages. This means that an English word like 'pond' may be pronounced with very marked nasalization on the vowel, and no perceptible nasal consonant at all (a feature which occurs widely in French). This particular habit is widespread in some accents of English, in many American accents for example, but it is comparatively rare in the English of southern England. On the other hand, nasal consonants may be more likely to nasalize the following vowel, as happens in some Bantu languages.

In some languages front vowels have a very marked effect on preceding consonants, especially on velar consonants which may be fronted to the very back of the hard palate as in English 'key', or even fronted onto the hard palate and heavily affricated as in Luganda *kyalo*, 'a village'. A Luganda speaker may well pronounce the English word 'kitchen' with a sound identical to the middle consonant both initially and medially 'chitchen'.

Round vowels may have the effect of rounding the consonant following them or consonants preceding them. 'Round' vowels may not always be rounded however. Where there is some other feature to mark the distinctiveness of vowels—backness in English for example—the round-ness may not be realized in normal speech. Thus in English many vowels, which in citation form are pronounced as back round vowels, may be pronounced in fluent speech with little if any rounding—especially the vowels in 'not', 'go', and 'look'.

The effect of syllable structure on the phonetic realization must also be taken into account. We have already noted that voiceless stops in English tend to be aspirated syllable initially, and pre-glottalized syllable finally. It is well known that in the so-called 'r-less' accents of English, syllable initial *r* is realized, but syllable final *r* is only indicated by the lengthening of a vowel, as in 'tar', 'four' etc., or in a centring diphthong as in 'hear', 'hair' etc. Most textbooks mention the 'clear l' which occurs syllable initially and the 'dark l' which occurs syllable finally. In general when a consonant occurs in the middle of a word it is difficult to decide which syllable it belongs to—thus in 'butter', 'meadow' 'very' which are all stressed on the initial syllable there may be no particularly good reason for assigning the medial consonant to either syllable since the phonetic realization is often quite different from that which occurs initially or finally. The voiceless stop in 'butter' may be neither preglottalized nor aspirated, and possibly not even realized as a stop at all, but as a very brief voiceless fricative—a good deal less high pitched than s would be. Similarly there may be little, if any, lengthening of the vowel before d in 'meadow' (not more than in 'metal' for example) and again the stop may be realized as a voiced fricative—with very little friction. The intervocalic r in 'very' is sometimes pronounced as a voiced tap rather than as a nonsyllabic vocoid.

It is often easier to decide which syllable an intervocalic consonant belongs to when it is followed by a stressed syllable. There is a general tendency to cluster consonants at the beginning of a syllable as in 'wardrobe'—referred to in the furniture trade as ''drobe'. Some difficulties remain—for example in 'petrol' the t may be preglottalized which suggests that it is syllable final, but the r may be voiceless—following the general rule that r, l, j, w are voiceless following syllable *initial* voiceless stops as in 'tray', 'play', 'queue', 'twelve'. (The voicelessness here may be regarded as equivalent to the moment of voiceless vowel which occurs when these consonants are immediately followed by a vowel.)

Clearly the complex constraints governing the pronunciation of consonants in different parts of the syllable in English, where consonants (and consonant clusters) can occur syllable finally as well as syllable initially, would pose many problems for a speaker of a language which allows only CV syllable structure. There is a well-known tendency for people to make the sound sequences of their target language conform to the constraints on sound sequences (structure) of their mother tongue. Thus speakers of CV languages typically insert vowels and elide consonants in their pronunciation of English and we find well-known examples of this like:

'screwdriver'	sikurudireba
'taxi'	takisi
'motorcar'	motokari
'mister'	missa
'electricity'	elitirisiti
'can't come'	kaŋkʌm

Consider also what English has done to foreign words to make them conform to its clustering constraints:

tsetse	typically pronounced	[tetsɪ]
Ptolemy	typically pronounced	[tolǝmɪ]

xylophone	typically pronounced	[zailəfoun]
pneumonia	typically pronounced	[niumouniə]
Nkrumah	typically pronounced	[nəkrumə]/[əŋkrumə]

(In English ŋ occurs syllable finally—native English speakers have this sound as a distinctive sound in their speech but find it difficult to produce it in a place in syllable structure which is not allowed in their own language.)

There are other constraints which ought to be stated as part of the phonological description of a language, but which constitute a relatively unexplored area. For example, many people have stated constraints on consonant sequence in initial and final syllable position in English (e.g., Bloomfield 1933) but a statement of the structure of grammatical morphemes as opposed to lexical morphemes (other than the fact that only grammatical morphemes have ð initially) is lacking. Similarly we know little about constraints on the composition of words—if a word has a complex initial cluster is it less likely to contain a further cluster than one which hasn't? What relation, if any, does stress placement in English words bear to consonant structure (this question begins to be answered in Chomsky and Halle 1968).

A further difficulty which language teachers face is the practice of stating a phonological description in terms of an idealized pronunciation, so that, in all exemplification, the native speaker of a language appears to speak in phonemes—or, if any realization rules are given, in very clearly enunciated allophones. Moreover, in order to teach at all, language teachers tend to enunciate the pattern they wish their students to copy with fierce clarity, but when the student meets native users of his target language he finds that in normal speech they tend to 'swallow their words' —that is, they tend not to speak as though they were standing in front of a public address system. Very many courses of English for foreigners, and no doubt similar courses in other languages, tend to be couched in an extremely formal style—often referred to as 'slow colloquial'—which usually means that the situation in the exercise is a customs house or ticket office or grocer's shop where people tend to speak loudly and clearly in order to be heard above the surrounding noise. In really informal conversation in a small group, every language has characteristic habits of articulation. In English, for example, consonant clusters may be simplified following certain rules, all stops may be pronounced without actually stopping the airstream (unless they are initial in a stressed syllable) and stresses are comparatively rare. A phonological description which is intended for use by language teachers ought to include a statement of the characteristic simplifying habits of informal conversational style. The speaker needs to know where, in his target language spoken at a fairly rapid speed, he can expect to find the features which will characterize the words which compose the message. (This is, regrettably, a question which no one is yet in a position to answer in any complete way.) It is not enough for the student to be able to make himself understood—he must be able to understand what is being said to him. It should be clear from the above that a description which simply enumerates the phonemes of a language, classifies them in terms of phonetic labels which may be differently interpreted in different languages ('voiced bilabial stop' for instance), and states in fairly rudimentary terms the more obvious allophonic variations and their characteristic environments, does not provide enough information for a teacher who actually wants to teach students how to speak the target language. In addition some account of the characteristic vocal habits of the target language is needed, and this may be conveniently divided into three parts: (a) a description of the characteristic articulatory setting of a language in terms of lip posture and protrusion, tongue posture and typical movement, velic opening, etc.; (b) a description of the characteristic timing relations—onset of voicing, nasality, fronting, rounding, etc., type of similitude (including a description of the typical assimilation processes, for example what happens in the stream of speech when a word ending in a vowel is immediately followed by a word beginning with a vowel); (c) an account of structural constraints, preferred syllable structure, typical morpheme and lexical structure and restricted systems at different places in structure.

Exercise C

1 What vowels can precede /ŋ/ in English?

2 What vowels can precede /ð/ in English?

3 What consonants can follow /au/ as in 'south'?

4 What consonants can follow /ou/ as in 'boat'?

5 What consonants can follow /oi/ as in 'boy'?

6 What consonants can follow /s/ in initial clusters?

7 What consonants can precede /w/ and /r/ in initial clusters?

8 What characteristic, if any, do those consonants that cannot precede /w/ have in common?

9 What effect, if any, might these constraints exert on the pronunciation of a native English speaker who is trying to speak a foreign language?

2.2 Rhythm and intonation

Many people would consider that the most important area of phonology as far as language teaching is concerned is that which deals with the so-called 'supra-segmental' features of language. Many courses exist which aim to familiarize students with the characteristic rhythm and intonation of English, as well as with characteristic 'tone of voice' used in specific situations. The chief difficulty with these courses is that they tend to illustrate sentences spoken in isolation, or with a very minimal context. Moreover, the sentences are usually spoken loudly and clearly and, especially with intonation courses, so slowly that they destroy any natural English rhythm and increase any tendency the student may have to utter each syllable with equal clarity. A further difficulty is the fact that in many cases the student may be able to copy a given 'tune' without much difficulty, but he is completely unable to extract any general principles from the examples he has been mimicking, and there is very little carry-over into his normal use of English.

For an interesting discussion of rhythm and intonation the reader is referred to Halliday (1967). In the present section I shall confine myself to making some very general observations which are not to be regarded as part of a systematic description in any sense. The purpose of these remarks is to provoke language teachers into a closer examination of some assumptions which are very common in the field of English language teaching.

2.2.1 RHYTHM

Rhythm in any language is always closely tied up with other muscular rhythms of the body. This is especially noticeable when public speakers are talking, as their gestures tend to be larger than normal life allows. They may wave their arms, nod their heads, shake their fists at the audience or bang on the table—but these actions will always accord with the rhythm of their speech. You can observe the same effect on a smaller scale in private life—most people accompany their speech with small unconscious gestures—tapping with their feet or fingers, twitching their eyebrows, frowning or smiling, and many people will have seen a stammerer trying to beat himself out of a stammer, perhaps rapping on the arm of a chair with his hand, trying to re-establish his speech rhythm by emphasizing another set of bodily rhythms.

The characteristic rhythm of one language may differ considerably from that of another, and striking differences may occur between dialects of the same language. In some languages all syllables tend to be of much the same length and to follow each other at regular intervals of time. These languages are sometimes called 'syllable-timed languages', e.g.

French and many Far Eastern and African languages. In other languages, syllables vary in length but stressed syllables tend to occur at regular intervals, e.g., German, the Scandinavian languages and English.

Stressed syllables in English can be distinguished by two main variables: (i) they stand out in pitch from unstressed syllables (usually the pitch is higher); (ii) they are more clearly articulated than unstressed syllables. Here are some of the most important ways in which articulation differs between stressed and unstressed syllables:

stressed syllables	*unstressed syllables*
a Initially stops are completely closed, voiceless stops are aspirated.	*a* There may be no complete closure, but simply an articulatory gesture towards a closure. Voiceless stops are not aspirated.
b Some friction may be heard in fricatives, especially voiceless fricatives.	*b* Stricture of open, rather than close, approximation for 'fricatives'.
c Vowel quality will be identifiable.	*c* Vowel quality may be difficult to identify. There will be a tendency to centralize vowels.
c Diphthongs will be diphthongized.	*d* No diphthongization: simplification and general obscurity.

Now let us briefly consider the function of stress in English. Stress in English serves to mark the meaningful words in an utterance. In most sentences the meaningful words are nouns, main verbs, adjectives and adverbs. (Perhaps the fact that they *are* meaningful helps us to identify them as stressed.) Since word order is so important in English, it is often possible to decode a message perfectly well even if you are not able to hear the unstressed words. A valuable technique for deciding which words should be stressed is to try to formulate a given message as a telegram. The words you are prepared to pay for are the stressed words.

Consider the following message:

'I'll try to meet you at half-past one outside the post office.'

If telegraphic charges were prohibitive you'd probably choose to send this telegram:

'Meet half-past one outside post office.'

This contains a minimum of information. It may be however that there is a strong possibility of your failing to keep the appointment in which case you'd be prepared to pay to insert the word 'try'. It may be that the post office is a tiny building with only one door in which case the word 'outside' may be unnecessary. If the original agreed time was one o'clock and the telegram is merely delaying the appointment by half an hour it may be unnecessary to repeat 'one'. So that whereas there are certainly some words one would expect to find stressed in this message in any case, 'meet'—'post office'—there may well be different possibilities of stressing some of the words in different contexts, depending on what has gone before, what the post office is like, and so on.

If this message were part of a conversation the same rules would hold— the decision to stress some words rather than others would depend upon the context of the message and what it is the message is trying to convey. The really important words in the message are the ones which will be stressed. In general the grammatical words will be unstressed. (When a grammatical word is stressed it will also bear the intonation contour, so we will discuss that possibility under intonation.)

In any group of people there will be some variation with regard to the words that different individuals have chosen to stress, but there will always be a common core of necessarily stressed words. Moreover, the choice of one stressed word sometimes necessarily implies another stressed word, though the relationship does not always hold in the opposite direction. In other words, it is possible to establish a hierarchy among the words which must be stressed in any given text. Where there is disagreement about stress, this may be due to differences in interpretation of the text, or simply to differences in the tempo of delivery—the faster the delivery, the fewer the stresses.

Normally each word has only one stress when it is spoken in the stream of speech, though individual words may have quite complex patterns when spoken slowly in isolation. The context of the utterance is usually quite sufficient to allow the word to be identified by a single stressed syllable.

Stress in English, then, has the function of identifying the meaningful words—the information units—of a message. Since stress plays this important part in signalling to the native speaker where he has to con- centrate his attention, it is very difficult to understand speech in which stress is wrongly used—in which everything is made to stand out equally, so that nothing stands out at all. Students whose own language is a 'stress-timed' language will have little difficulty with unstressing syllables, but for students who speak 'syllable-timed' languages the problem of unstressing is often a very difficult one. To begin with, there is often a feeling that unstressing represents slipshod speech habits, a feeling regrettably often shared by native English speakers who have never paused to observe their own normal speech habits. For spoken English to be clearly understood (and easily remembered) it is essential that the main units of information should be made to stand out—which means that subordinate words and syllables must be unstressed.

2.2.2 INTONATION

All languages have intonation, in the sense that all languages have phonological groups (which are usually co-extensive with a grammatical constituent), within which main phonological processes occur. The main function of intonation appears to be to delimit information structures—to chop up the stream of speech into message units which have a coherent internal structure and can be decoded as units by the listener.

In English (as in other languages), intonation plays an important part in making clear the structure of an extended discourse. Intonation contours delimit *tone-groups* (message units). The tone-group is normally co-extensive with one of the constituents of a sentence. Consider the following conversation, where // marks tone-group boundaries:

A // and when he first came in // he said it would be all right // if we all went together//

B // but surely the question isn't so much what he said // as whether or not we all want to go together//

It would clearly be possible to divide that conversation up in several different ways. If A, for example, was speaking quite fast, it would be perfectly possible for him to say all he has to say within one tone-group. B, on the other hand, could speak in a much more deliberate way, thus:

//but// surely// the question isn't so much// what he said//

and so on. This example illustrates one general point—the more tone-groups you divide an utterance into, the more weight you are assigning to each part of the utterance. The way utterances are divided up differs very much with the individual and with the mood of the individual. Public speakers who are trying to present a rational front tend to enunciate slowly and to divide their utterance into fairly short tone-groups. Public speakers who want to carry an emotional crowd with them tend to speak more rapidly, in much longer tone-groups, punctuated with short tone-groups from time to time. There is no doubt that a discourse composed of tone-groups of a very even length, whether short, long or medium-sized, tends to be extremely monotonous. The really important point is that the units which form the tone-groups must have some coherent internal structure. Thus if you have a long utterance:

The tall girl standing on the pavement on the other side of the street was waiting for a taxi it would not be divided up like this:

//The tall girl standing // on the pavement on the other// side of the street was// waiting for a taxi//

In this form the utterance is quite possible to understand, but it would be much more readily understood if it was divided up like this:

//The tall girl// standing on the pavement on the other side of the street// was waiting for a taxi//

or as above but no // after girl.

Now how can one recognize a tone-group in the stream of speech? This is not an easy question to answer. There are however some general points to note. One is that there will normally be no pauses within a tone group—but there are very often pauses between tone groups. Another is that many grammatical words have a form which cannot occur before tone group boundaries. Compare

1 //Who's *that* for?//

2 //It's for *John*.//

3 //I don't think he can *go*.//

4 //Ah, but *I* can.//

In 1 'for' is unstressed but has a back rounded vowel; in 2 it is unstressed but has a far more obscure vowel. In 3 'can' is unstressed, with an obscure vowel; in 4 it is unstressed still but the vowel has a much clearer quality. The obscure form cannot occur before a tone group boundary. Another point is that a tone group is frequently characterized by an overall pitch pattern in which there is a recognizable peak with a smooth falling-away on both sides. Most important of all is that each tone group will contain only one *tonic word*—that is only one word which is lengthened and bears a moving tone. This word is the most important of the stressed words in the tone group, it represents the focus of information in this chunk of message. When an utterance is said in isolation, the tonic is usually placed on the last lexical item in the tone group, which is the focal, or tonic, word. Consider the following conversation:

A The meeting's supposed to be at three.

B I suppose Henry will be late.

In A, the first utterance in the conversation, the focus is on the time of the meeting—three. But the complexity of the analysis we are trying to undertake is illustrated in B. It is clear that both speakers know about the meeting and that both speakers know who Henry is. Whether it is 'late' or 'Henry' which gets the tonic in B depends very much on the

c

speaker's attitude to Henry. If Henry is well known to make a habit of being late and people are tired of this habit the remark might be

//I suppose *Henry* // will be *late//*.

If, on the other hand, Henry may reasonably be expected to be delayed but there is no information about anyone else we might find

//I suppose Henry will be *late//*.

And it is this last choice which is regarded as the most neutral intonational choice you can make. This is because the most usual arrangement of the English sentence appears to be to state what is known at the beginning of it and to add the new piece of information at the end of it to move from the known to the unknown. That is a dangerously general statement— but consider the following sentences in the light of it:

This is the girl you met on Tuesday.

She has a certificate of proficiency in swimming.

I bought a trendy black suit.

Peter got up and punched him.

Do you realize what the time is?

In all cases the most neutral reading would put the tonic on the last lexical item—Tuesday, swimming, suit, punched, and time. Notice however what happens if we put one of the sentences in various different contexts:

1 What did you buy?

  I bought a trendy black *suit*.

2 Did you get a dress?

  I bought a trendy black *suit*.

3 You said you were going to get something super but Susan says you've just got an ordinary black suit.

  I've got a *trendy* black suit.

In the first case the reply is to a completely open question. 'Bought' will probably be unstressed, having just been mentioned, as it will in all the other examples. 'Black' will be stressed but 'suit' will not only be stressed but have the tonic curve since this is the word which actually answers the question. Similarly in 2, only here the tonic on 'suit' may be a bigger curving tone in order to point the fact that it is a suit, not a dress. (The same effect may be got with the same intonation as in 1, but with a big smile on 'suit', or by pursing the lips on 'suit', or by 'breathy' voice on 'suit'.) In 3, however, 'suit' is mentioned in the question. It is unlikely then that it will get the tonic in the reply. What does get the tonic is 'trendy' which is pointing the fact that this is not just any ordinary black suit. In general when any lexical word follows the tonic in the same tone group you will find that that lexical word has already been mentioned or is implied by the context. In general when the tonic is not on the last lexical word in the tone group it is possible to see that there is a direct relationship between its placing and what has previously been said in the conversation—as in 3 above.

Occasionally a non-lexical word bears the tonic. In this case the implication is often said to be contrastive or contradictory. We will briefly consider some examples.

I think she's *pretty*.

She *isn't* pretty.

This sort of example, where the tonic moves on to the verbal auxiliary, is a particularly clear illustration of 'contradictory' intonation. Another clear case is

This is the one I want.

Since the function of the tonic is to identify the focal point of information in the message it is essential that the tonic should be made to stand out from its surrounding context. The most usual way to do this (in southern English speech) is to make a *fall* in pitch on the tonic word. This is true whether the utterance is declarative or interrogative. A pervasive myth in English language teaching is that so-called 'yes-no' questions are normally spoken on a rising pitch. Anyone who has studied the speech of native English speakers in their native habitat—i.e., when they are not speaking a peculiar brand of English reserved for teaching foreigners—will attest that this is by no means always the case. And to begin with, at any rate, the fall should be regarded as the primary and basic pattern. In order to make the tonic stand out from the other stressed words in the tone group, any following words (stressed or unstressed) must follow the pattern of the fall established in the tonic. Note that any jump of pitch after the tonic will immediately establish a new tone group and a new information focus. Similarly any words preceding the tonic in the same tone group (stressed or unstressed) must be arranged in a smooth pitch contour and not bounce out of the overall pitch movement.

There are two types of pre-tonic which should be noted. One type of pre-tonic occurs when there are two important points of information within one tone group in a message, for example when a human subject is the actor:

John's gone to the *meeting*

Peter got up and *punched* him

It was the *secretary* who saw him *first*

There is a tendency for the pre-tonic to start high and slide (or step) gradually down until it reaches the tonic. When it reaches the tonic the pitch starts from high again, so the outline of the contour for such a tone group looks like this:

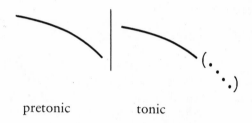

pretonic   tonic

In the above examples prominence is given to two information points—though the tonic, the information *focus*, is still the most prominent. It is important to remember that in such tone-groups there is only one tonic—only one word bearing a moving, curving tone. Another type of pretonic occurs in passive sentences, and in sentences where the subject is already 'given'. In these cases there is a tendency to start low in the pretonic and to slide smoothly up to the tonic, so the contour looks like this:

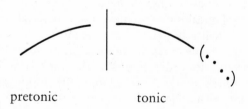

pretonic   tonic

Try saying the following sentences with the second type of contour:

He gave the man the money

It was a good job he was able to come

They said the car was stolen by a man in a mask

They haven't been given their final results yet

3 Teaching pronunciation

Exercise D

The reader may like to consider the following questions before going on to read my comments on them.

1 Suppose you are teaching English to foreign students, on a tight schedule, with no special time for pronunciation teaching. Which of the following problems would you tackle first?

   a discrimination of /θ/ and /ð/

   b elimination of /g/ following /ŋ/ (as in 'sing')

   c confusion between 'not'/'naught', 'can'/'calm', 'pull'/'pool'

   d vowel length before voiced/voiceless consonants

   e stressed v. unstressed syllables.

2 If you were preparing some tapes for use in teaching would you choose as models:

   a native speakers of English using a great deal of current, idiomatic slang

   b non-native speakers of English whose speech represents the educated local brand of English

   c young native English speakers using standard modern English but with traces of regional accents

   d speakers whose speech conforms closely to the 'R.P.' model described by Daniel Jones (1956a).

3 Would you record material to be used as a model:

   a spoken slowly, in complete sentences

   b spoken at normal conversational speed

   c slowly at first hoping to build up to normal conversational speed in time

   d as isolated segments followed by illustrations of each segment in different places in different words.

4 If you were preparing a course in English pronunciation, how could you utilize the following:

   a tapes and records

   b films

   c mirrors, pencils, tissue paper

   d chorus work

   e phonetic transcription.

Discussion of Exercise D

What pronunciation you decide to teach, and how you decide to teach it depends on a large number of variables, many of which may be quite outside your own control. One variable is the age of the students. While it is quite appropriate to try to instil a sense of English rhythm into small children by using nursery rhymes, this might be a less appropriate approach for adults. Another variable is the degree of expertise of the students; are you teaching beginners or trying to correct ingrained habits by remedial teaching? Another variable is the standard you decide (or are required) to teach to, and the number of hours allotted to English pronunciation as distinct from the rest of the English syllabus. Clearly a high standard of pronunciation can be expected from students who are undergoing full-time education in their target language (as happens in Bulgaria for instance), and a somewhat lower standard from students who receive practice irregularly within an English syllabus which allots no special time to pronunciation teaching (a much more common experience).

Possibly, given the latter situation, we can do little for the teacher except sympathize with him. But there are some points the teacher might bear in mind.

(i) When time is short it is probably not worthwhile spending time on teaching θ and δ if the students find them difficult, but be sure that the sounds substituted by the students are f and v sounds which are acoustically similar to θ and δ and bear a low functional load in English (i.e., don't distinguish many words), and not s and z, which are acoustically very different from θ and δ and bear a much higher functional load. It is not worthwhile trying to iron out a g following η (as in 'sing') since this turns up in some native accents of English and never causes confusion, nor is it important to teach 'not'/'naught', 'can'/'calm', 'pull'/'pool' distinctions, since many native English speakers get along very well without them. You would not try to get rid of post-vocalic rs since the majority of native English speakers have them anyway. You would, however, teach aspiration following stressed voiceless stops, shorter vowels before voiceless consonants and longer vowels before voiced consonants and a distinction between l and r—if there is time. If there isn't even this much time, I think the most important thing of all is to teach unstressing.

At a more ambitious level, you might try a fairly sophisticated programme including, for example, θ and δ. But even at this level it is important to consider what constitutes a real, attainable target. In most foreign-language teaching situations it is very unlikely that you are hoping to produce speakers of what sounds like native English. You are more likely to take as your model a very well educated local speaker. This appears to be a more realistic aim, and it is important that everyone concerned feels that it is attainable. Furthermore, it is unlikely that your students really want to sound like native speakers of English. Very few people are prepared to sacrifice their individuality to the point of giving up all trace of their native accent. Most people want to sound like a national of their own country, speaking the target language, fluently but with a perceptible foreign accent. Both these considerations lead to the same conclusion—even in an ambitious teaching programme, with lots of time devoted to spoken English, the target the teacher should have in mind is the best local brand of spoken English.

(ii) Whether the best local brand of spoken English should actually be presented to the students, as a model for them to imitate, is another matter. If you take the best local brand as a teaching model, you may find that by the second generation the model may have altered and may perhaps be less like native English. As the template varies through succeeding generations, you may find that a local variety of English emerges which is as characteristic of its place of origin as, say, the English of Australia, Wales, the southern states of the U.S.A. or southern England. Many people believe that the English spoken in West Africa has already reached this status—that there is a recognizable brand of educated West African English which has fully predictable characteristics. (It is this attribute which allows West African English the status of a dialect of English. It is *not* useful to regard West African English as a highly deviant version of standard southern English studded with common errors.)

A distinct local dialect of English is more likely to emerge where English is the accepted second language which is used in government, broadcasting, etc. Where English is taught as a foreign language and used comparatively little in the day-to-day life of the country, the situation is obviously very different. It seems more appropriate in this latter case to offer students a native brand of English as a teaching model. This does not prevent the teacher from tacitly accepting the best local brand of English as a target for achievement. Where oral examinations are concerned, for example, it would be appropriate to examine to the best local brand rather than some idealized native English ('Received Pronunciation' or General American) which the teacher himself may not speak.

It has been the usual custom in English language teaching to offer a native brand of English as the teaching model. It is to be hoped that adequate descriptions of the best local brand will be provided in countries where English is a second language and that in this type of situation the local variety of English will continue to grow and develop as spoken language normally does. Where English is taught as a foreign language, care must be taken to provide a current English model rather than the sort of English spoken by the grandparents of the present generation.

I do not mean by this that students should be taught current idiomatic expressions, let alone slang, which changes every six months and marks indelibly the vintage of a foreign speaker's English. What I have in mind here is the fact that habits of pronunciation change. If you listen to British films made in the forties and fifties, you will find that it is possible to date these recordings reasonably accurately by means of the pronunciation alone. Older speakers may lament that the English of the younger generation is more 'slipshod' than it was than when they were young. It is true of course that it is different, just as the language habits of people everywhere are different today from what they were thirty years ago.[2] It gives a curious impression to meet a young foreign speaker deliberately articulating a style of speech now appropriate to those drawing their old age pensions.

(iii) Having decided on a target, and teaching model, you will find that the actual methodology of teaching will vary enormously according to the situation. It is impossible here to deal with methodology in any detail, and I shall have to be content with offering a few general hints.

First, you must make sure that any native English demonstrated to your students is spoken at normal speed and with normal intonation. There is a predictable resistance from most teachers to this suggestion. They say that the students will not understand what is being said. Then you must play the same tape or record again and again until they do understand—glossing between sentences if necessary but never disturbing the natural speed and rhythm of English—and this should be done from the very beginning, otherwise students will learn wrong habits from their earliest lessons which you will later spend fruitless hours trying to eradicate. If you play a slowed-down version of English, the syllables that ought to be unstressed, which ought almost to disappear, will have to be slowed down too, and some of them may appear to be stressed as a result. Students copying such models will learn that extraordinary brand of English which is never spoken except to and by foreign learners. If you are choosing a taped course of English, you should choose one which sounds most like rapid conversational English, even if the students find it difficult to understand at first. As a result, if the students ever meet real-life native speakers it is much more likely that they will be able to understand them, and to participate in normal conversation, rather than exchanging laborious, highly stressed sentences, which are difficult to listen to, and to understand.

Secondly, you should not spend long hours teaching individual segments, but encourage your students to look like Englishmen when they

[2] Some of the changes have been described. For example Gimson (1961) describes some striking changes in the realization of R.P. vowels which have taken place during the past thirty years.

are talking. Show a film of some normal English people in close-up, not a film specially made for foreigners but something like a demonstration of a scientific experiment for English schools which will be spoken in fairly slow but normal English. Turn off the sound track and tell the students to watch for some specific mouth movements—perhaps the pronunciation of *f* and *v*, or the movement of the lips during *sh* or *s* or *r*. Ask them to bring pocket mirrors so that they can mimic the lip movements and watch themselves doing it. Then turn on the sound track and consider the characteristics of English *t* and *d*, for example. In this case they may not be able to see much—except perhaps the tongue flapping up after an open vowel. Practise alveolar *t*s and *d*s trying to copy the sound on the film. Only after establishing alveolar stops should you move on to the dental fricatives *θ* and *ð*—these again you should be able to see something of in the film. Draw attention to the aspiration following voiceless stops—the preglottalization of voiceless stops when they are syllable final, the length of vowels before voiced consonants, the degree of rounding on consonants before rounded vowels, the nasalization, if any, of vowels adjacent to nasal consonants, the typical preferred syllable structure, the rhythm, the unstressedness of unstressed syllables. Relate different features of spelling to different types of unstressing. Notice which words get stressed, which words bear the intonation tonic, and how these relate to previous and following sentences.

(iv) The aim in this sort of work is to make students more aware of general articulatory setting and timing relations in the target language, as well as encouraging them to relate the units of structure out of which the message is built, to units of rhythm and intonation. Ideally this sort of work is carried on in small classes with audio-visual aids, but unfortunately such ideal conditions are rare. However, much can be done with simple aids like mirrors, pieces of tissue paper held in front of the mouth which flap when aspiration is produced, pencils stuck between the roof of the mouth and the tongue to feel which piece of the tongue is pressing up, and records of English which are not deliberately slowed down for foreign speakers. It is wise, in large classes, to avoid chanting in chorus if at all possible, unless the piece chanted is strongly rhythmical with a distinctively English rhythm—like a nursery rhyme. Otherwise there is a danger that the mother tongue rhythm may imperceptibly emerge among the chanting throng.

Finally I would like to make one point about the use of phonetic transcription in teaching. Most people prefer not to use phonetic transcription at all for the first few years, and this seems to me very wise. When phonetic transcription is used, I think it is important to stress that symbols mean different things in different contexts. If, for example, you are using a system which differentiates between the vowels of 'bid' and

'bead' with a length mark in the second symbol (e.g., /i/ versus /iː/)
you must make sure that the length mark doesn't lead to undue length
before voiceless consonants, that 'beat' is not pronounced with such a
long vowel that an English speaker would hear it as 'bead'. It is true that
the vowel in 'beat' *is* longer than that in 'bit' but it is certainly no longer
than the vowel in 'bid'. The length mark indicates that the vowel is
relatively longer in an identical environment, not absolutely longer all
the time.

4 Further reading

Abercrombie, D. *Elements of General Phonetics*. Edinburgh: Edinburgh
   University Press and Chicago: Aldine, 1967. (Especially Chapters 2, 3,
   4, 8 and 9).
Halliday, M. A. K. *Intonation and Grammar in British English*. The
   Hague: Mouton, 1967.
Honikman, B. 'Articulatory settings'. In D. Abercrombie, D. B. Fry,
   P. A. D. MacCarthy, N. C. Scott and J. L. M. Trim (eds.), *In Honour
   of Daniel Jones*. London: Longmans, 1964.
Pike, K. L. *Phonemics*. Ann Arbor: University of Michigan Press, 1947.
   (Especially Chapter 1.)

3 Pedagogic Grammar

J. P. B. ALLEN

1 Transformational grammar and language teaching

Since linguists and language teachers are both concerned in different ways with the same language material, it is natural to ask whether a knowledge of linguistic grammars can make any contribution to language teaching methodology, and if so what the nature of the contribution is likely to be. The purpose of this chapter is to investigate the relevance of linguistic grammars for language teaching, with special reference to Chomsky's model of transformational-generative grammar. It should not be assumed that we attribute any unique status to transformational grammar, which is only one among many grammatical models deserving close attention on the part of the language teacher. However, Chomsky's model of grammar is important in that it has had a profound effect on the way in which linguists and psychologists think about language. Moreover, recent work in transformational grammar has led a number of writers to consider afresh the question of whether and to what extent a knowledge of theoretical linguistics can be expected to contribute to successful language teaching. For these reasons transformational grammar provides a useful focal point for the various issues involved in a discussion of pedagogic grammar, though many of the arguments have a wider application and are relevant to any situation in which we aim to utilize formal linguistic insights in the construction of practical teaching materials.

1.1 Formal and pedagogic grammars

In order to investigate the relationship between linguistic knowledge and language teaching methods we must make a clear distinction between scientific or formal grammars on the one hand, and practical or pedagogic grammars on the other. A scientific grammar is concerned with a specification of the formal properties of language, with the 'code' rather than the 'use of the code'. The writer of a scientific grammar aims to give a systematic account of the idealized linguistic knowledge, or competence, which underlies the actual use of language in concrete social situations. A scientific grammar is based on a formal theory of language and it is expected to attain certain standards of descriptive adequacy; for example, it must be as explicit and exact as possible, it must specify all the sentences of a language in terms of the widest possible generalizations, it must be as simple as possible, and it must generate all combinations of elements which are interpretable as sentences of a language, and no others. Most modern linguists have adopted these criteria as a useful standard against which existing grammars may be judged, even though no grammar so far has come anywhere near meeting all the requirements.

A pedagogic grammar has quite different aims from a scientific grammar. The writer of a pedagogic grammar is primarily concerned not to give a systematic account of a native speaker's idealized competence, but to provide a comparatively informal framework of definitions, diagrams, exercises and verbalized rules which may help a learner to acquire knowledge of a language and fluency in its use. A good pedagogic grammar does not depend solely on the personal inspiration of a teacher or textbook writer. In normal circumstances the writer of a pedagogic grammar turns to a scientific grammar (usually more than one) in order to ascertain the linguistic facts or to verify the intuitions that he already has. Once the writer has established a basis of linguistic facts drawn from one or more scientific grammars the next step is to convert the formal linguistic statements into that type of presentation which he knows from experience is most likely to promote quick and efficient learning in the particular group of students he has in mind. Clearly, in devising a classroom presentation of grammatical rules we must take into account many factors—e.g., the age of the students, the skill of the teacher, the aims of the course—which are purely pragmatic and bear no direct relation to the type of consideration involved in the writing of formal linguistic grammars. Consequently a pedagogic grammar is not expected to attain the standards of descriptive adequacy required of a scientific grammar, nor need it be consistent with any one formal theory in order to produce good results in the classroom. A pedagogic grammar is typically eclectic in the sense that the applied linguist must pick and choose among formal statements in the light of his experience as a teacher, and decide what are pedagogically the most appropriate ways of arranging the information that he derives from scientific grammars.

A pedagogic grammar is a collection of material extracted from one or more scientific grammars and used as the basis for language teaching. It is possible to distinguish three stages in the conversion of scientific grammars into practical teaching material, and all three types of operation may be regarded as different aspects of pedagogic grammar. At the first stage we evaluate scientific grammars according to their own (theoretical) terms of reference and extract those features which are potentially useful for language teaching. This stage corresponds to what Halliday, McIntosh and Strevens (1964) call *methodics*: 'the techniques and procedures which cluster round the point where linguistics and classroom teaching fuse together'. At this stage it may be convenient to establish an *interlevel* between scientific grammars and language teaching textbooks, an area of applied linguistics where we aim to establish a pedagogically oriented statement of the linguistic facts as a preliminary to the construction of actual teaching materials (Jarvis 1971). The second and third stages in the conversion process are concerned with specific teaching procedures which do not necessarily require any direct reference to scientific grammars as such, and correspond to what Halliday et al. call *methodology*. At the second stage we draw up an outline of the whole grammatical scheme which we intend to present in a language course. This is often referred to as a *structural syllabus*. At the third stage, using the structural syllabus as a basis, we construct the full array of texts, exercises, diagrams and explanations (with or without pictures, tapes and other audio-visual aids) which constitute the *textbook*, i.e., the actual materials used in language teaching.

Although there is no reason in principle why the arrangement of material in a pedagogic grammar should reflect the content of a scientific grammar in any direct or systematic way, there may sometimes be a fairly close correspondence between the two types of grammar. This is quite likely if the pedagogic presentation is based on a surface structure or taxonomic model of grammar, as is the case with most foreign language teaching material produced since the Second World War in Britain and the United States. The aim of a taxonomic grammar is to present a classification of those elements of sentence structure which can be directly related to the linear arrangement of writing or the temporal flow of speech. The surface structure of a sentence may be represented in the form of a hierarchical bracketing of phrases and subphrases:

> John bought a new car
>
> bought a new car
>
> a new car
>
> new car

A hierarchical bracketing can be collapsed into a slot-and-filler diagram, in which a construction is divided into a number of constituents simultaneously. A pedagogic grammar based on an analysis of surface structure usually consists of a number of slot-and-filler diagrams in which mutually substitutable elements are arranged in columns, e.g.:

John	bought	a new car
Tom and Mary	had to buy	that big house
My old uncle	should have bought	two dozen eggs

Each column or 'slot' represents a unit of grammatical structure. If the slots in the diagram reading from left to right are assigned the labels 'Subject', 'Verb', 'Object', we can describe *John bought a new car, Tom and Mary had to buy that big house*, etc., as examples of a Subject + Verb + Object or S + V + O construction. A surface structure grammar of this type can easily be converted into teaching material since the descriptive framework is conceptually simple and requires comparatively little explanation. Substitution diagrams can be used as the basis for various exercises and drills, and provide a convenient frame of reference for students whose main concern is to achieve fluency in the use of language rather than proficiency in analysing the formal properties of sentences.

So long as language teaching materials were based on a taxonomic model of grammar there was usually no very marked discrepancy between the basic scientific grammar and the type of formulation adopted for classroom use. The last two decades, however, have been noted for the emergency of various generative models in linguistics, of which Chomsky's transformational-generative grammar is the best-known type. Chomsky's grammar is generative in the sense that it constitutes, in principle, a procedure for testing any combination of words and deciding whether it is a sentence in the language. The grammar 'decides' that an utterance is grammatical if an identity relation obtains between the utterance in question and some combination of symbols which is generated by the rules of the grammar. In order to decide automatically which utterances are grammatical and which are not the rules must be fully explicit, i.e., all the information needed for the generation of sentences must be present in the rules themselves and nothing must be left out in the expectation that it will be tacitly 'understood'.

A transformational grammar is highly abstract in the sense that structures underlying sentences are not related in any simple way to material substance, but merely constitute a record of the application of a particular set of rules. Thus a transformational grammar differs from a pedagogic grammar since the aim of the latter is to impart information about the structure of a language by means of simple non-technical statements which as far as possible make immediate sense to the learner without having to be puzzled out or made the subject of lengthy explanations. It follows that we cannot expect any detailed point-by-point correspondence between transformational grammar and an informal pedagogic statement based on it, since highly abstract rules do not lend themselves easily to the straightforward type of grammatical presentation that appears to be necessary in language teaching.

However, in spite of the fact that we cannot expect any close correspondence between the rules of transformational grammar and the contents of a pedagogic grammar, transformational grammar is of particular interest to both linguists and language teachers because it claims to be a formal representation of a native speaker's linguistic competence, i.e., that knowledge which language teachers presumably hope to impart to students during the course of their teaching. The question arises whether a transformational model can be used *indirectly* as the basis for teaching materials and, if so, what is the nature of the relationship between a pedagogic grammar and the scientific grammar on which it is based, where the latter consists of an abstract representation of a native speaker's competence. At present it is far from clear what contribution transformational grammar is likely to make to language teaching methodology. The arguments surrounding this issue are typical of the varied and often contradictory advice which linguists offer to language teachers in the hope of influencing what they do in the classroom.

1.2 How should languages be taught?

Many people are prepared to admit that the study of scientific grammars may provide interesting background information about the subject matter of language teaching, but question whether the contents of a scientific grammar can be directly relevant to classroom activities. Supporters of this view tend to favour a 'natural' teaching method in which language is learned a whole act at a time, in a meaningful social context, with little or no attention to the formal properties of language. Newmark (1964) represents this point of view when he claims that systematic attention to the grammatical form of utterances is neither a necessary condition nor a sufficient one for successful language teaching: 'that it is not necessary is demonstrated by the native learner's success without it; that it is not sufficient is demonstrated by the typical classroom student's lack of success with it'. According to Newmark, 'teaching particularly utterances in contexts which provide meaning and usability to learners is both sufficient (witness the native learner) and necessary (witness the classroom learner)'. The systematic teaching of formal grammatical relations does not reflect 'relationships of meaningful use', and a lesson plan based on an analysis of the formal properties of language is 'incompatible with the only necessary and sufficient method we know has succeeded for every speaker', i.e., the method whereby he learns, as a child, to speak his native language.

Newmark's article constitutes a strong plea for teaching-in-context and the liberation of language teaching from any kind of grammatical theory, but his argument contains three erroneous assumptions. The first is the common assumption that what is true for one teaching situation is necessarily true for all. Newmark makes no attempt to distinguish between different types of student and different teaching situations, and he does not appear to consider the possibility that in some cases we might usefully combine teaching-in-context with the systematic presentation of formal grammatical relations. Newmark's second assumption is that the utilization of grammar rules has an inhibiting effect on the acquisition of fluent language skills, but this must be demonstrated and cannot simply be taken for granted. Thirdly, Newmark's belief that what is true for first language acquisition is also true for second language learning is surely an oversimplification, since most of us would expect to find some difference in learning strategy between an infant acquiring his first language and, say, an adult second language learner who needs English in order to begin advanced studies in pharmacology or engineering.

Newmark's belief that the methods of formal linguistics have no relevance to the solution of practical classroom problems would seem to constitute an unnecessarily negative view of the relationship between linguistics and language teaching. However, a cautious attitude to the claims of linguists is not in itself a bad thing. Far more dangerous are the strong claims of those linguists who advocate a radical change in language teaching practices to correspond to recent developments in linguistic theory. Quite often this attitude finds expression in the view that pattern-practice and other well-established classroom techniques based on stimulus-response psychology no longer have any useful part to play in second language teaching, as a result of the fact that a simple habit-structure theory is no longer regarded as an adequate basis for a theory of human language behaviour.

Jakobovits (1968) appears to believe that concepts established in the study of first language acquisition can be carried over, essentially without modification, into the domain of second language learning. The rationalist point of view adopted by Jakobovits attributes to the child a 'language acquisition device' which guides his discovery of the rules of the language to which he is exposed. According to this theory the learner is endowed with a set of language universals and a hypothesis-forming ability which guides him through the progressive differentiation of grammatical categories to the discovery of the underlying rules. The role of environmental speech is important in this process, but the learner is not merely the passive recipient of environmental stimuli. Using the 'specific innate competences' which he has at his disposal, the learner imposes an interpretation on the random collection of data which he happens to hear. This interpretation is used as the basis for a grammar which is inherently so complex that it could not possibly be acquired by means of a conditioning process dependent solely on the occurrence of external stimuli.

In applying the concepts of first language acquisition to second language learning Jakobovits generalizes without adequate justification. We may agree that 'concept attainment and hypothesis testing are more likely paradigms in child language acquisition than response strength through rote memory and repetition', but there is no reason why this finding should be carried over uncritically into the domain of foreign language learning. Many teachers can testify that pattern practice and reinforcement routines frequently succeed in the classroom, whereas similar routines applied to infants learning their first language would presumably be self-defeating. On the other hand, the fact that children learn their first language orally without the use of written symbols is not necessarily an argument for teaching a foreign language in the same way, since the average student differs from a child learning his first language both in terms of general maturity and in the range of acquired skills that he brings to the task of learning. The nature of the task does not appear to be the same in the two situations, since a child learning his first language begins with single words and word combinations and then proceeds to more elaborate utterances, while an older student is expected to learn complete sentences from the beginning. Corder (1967) suggests that the exploitation of errors has a more useful role to play in second language learning than is commonly assumed, but it is also the case that too many mistakes on the part of the student tend to have a detrimental effect, while this is apparently something that we do not have to worry about in the case of a child learning his first language. Since the two situations are so dissimilar it would seem to be unwise to make too many assumptions about the process of second language learning on the basis of what happens when a child learns his first language.

The articles by Newmark and Jakobovits represent two types of theoretical assumption about second language teaching which do not stand up to close examination. A third questionable assumption is the belief that a model of linguistic competence must necessarily provide the best possible basis for a pedagogic grammar. One of the strongest statements of this point of view is to be found in Saporta's claim that a knowledge of transformational grammar enables textbook writers to base their material on the most adequate description. Saporta argues that because transformational grammar provides the 'best' description from the linguistic point of view, it by definition also provides the best basis for language teaching. No other possibilities need be considered, since 'it is incongruous to argue that some less adequate formulation can be successfully applied when a more adequate one cannot' (Saporta 1966).

According to Saporta, the habit-formation procedures of the audio-lingual method are based on a superficial and inadequate learning theory, since fluency cannot be achieved simply on the basis of rote learning and the memorization of a long list of sentences. This leads Saporta to his first 'paradox of second language learning': 'language is rule-governed behaviour, and learning a language involves internalizing the rules. But the ability or inclination to formulate the rules apparently interferes with the performance which is supposed to lead to making the application of the rules automatic.' Saporta does not attempt to find a solution, but in fact this is unnecessary since the paradox ceases to be relevant as soon as we realize that different methods can be used to induce rule-governed behaviour in a student. As teachers we know that students often succeed in internalizing rules on the basis of pattern practice plus a small amount of explanation, and performance is inhibited only if abstract grammatical analysis is allowed to occupy too much time at the expense of adequate practice. It appears that Saporta's 'paradox' is a theoretical speculation which has little to do with the realities of actual language teaching. In any normal classroom situation learning problems are solved empirically by combining grammar and drill-work in proportions that can be varied indefinitely according to the teacher's assessment of individual needs.

Saporta also believes that 'the best scientific description provides the basis for the best pedagogical drills'. Thus, the relation between *I like amusing stories, I like raising flowers* and *I like entertaining guests* cannot be indicated by manipulating the elements of surface structure. A full understanding of the structure of these sentences involves knowledge of the underlying structure, where the differences are marked. In this case, Saporta suggests a suitable drill might start with an instruction to insert the article *the* at appropriate places, thus yielding *the amusing stories*, but *raising the flowers* and both *the entertaining guests* and *entertaining the guests*. According to Saporta, this leads to a second paradox: an automatic drill 'does not necessarily indicate discrimination of an underlying structure', while a non-automatic drill 'presupposes knowledge of precisely the information it attempts to teach'. The implication seems to be that any attempt to teach a language by means of conventional pattern-practice is doomed to failure. But Saporta fails to take into account the ways in which different types of drill are used in classroom work. Thus, automatic drills are used to provide pronunciation practice and to encourage the establishment of habitual associations such as subject-verb agreement and the fixed tense-forms of verbs, while non-automatic drills are used either as a form of testing or to develop a student's ability to discriminate between structures which have already been learned. In between there are various types of substitution and transformation drills which can be done 'automatically', i.e., without incurring a lot of mistakes, but which if followed through intelligently and with the help of simple explanations can succeed in instilling a knowledge of the relevant grammatical rules. Saporta is merely stating the obvious when he denies the existence of a drill 'which serves as input to a naive student and which is somehow converted into command of precisely the appropriate rule'. In reality few teachers can be under the illusion that such a magic formula exists. We know that even a beginning student has some expectation about the nature of language structure, and therefore cannot be regarded as wholly 'naive'. Moreover, 'command of precisely the appropriate rule' is not an instantaneous event but comes as the result of a long process of trial and error during which the student's imperfect grasp of the rule is gradually extended and made more secure through his developing experience of the target language. The gradual nature of this process suggests that successful language teaching is not a matter of applying any one 'method' but of finding, through practical experience, the most effective combination of a number of different activities, including automatic drills, 'meaningful' drills and simple grammatical explanations.

Learning a language involves acquiring knowledge of the code together with the ability to use that knowledge in producing appropriate utterances and in understanding what is said by other speakers. If we accept that the conventions which govern performance do not stand in any direct or simple relationship to the rules of competence, then we must reject Saporta's argument that a model of linguistic competence necessarily provides the best possible basis for a pedagogic grammar. However, in view of the prevailing uncertainty about the relationship between competence and performance it would be as well to look more closely at the reasons why we cannot maintain that there is any direct connection between the rules in a scientific grammar and the arrangement of material in a pedagogic grammar. In this way we may come to understand more about the nature of pedagogic grammar.

1.3 Formal versus pedagogic criteria

Linguists who believe that transformational grammar has a contribution to make to the design of language teaching materials often attempt to justify this view with reference to the formal properties of comprehensiveness, explicitness and explanatory adequacy. In denying that any of these properties bear directly upon the design of language teaching materials we shall be asserting the independence of methodological decisions from formal linguistic constraints, whether deriving from transformational grammar or any other model. It does not follow from this that transformational grammar is irrelevant for language teaching purposes; it does follow, however, that claims as to the relevance of transformational grammar must be based on pedagogic rather than formal linguistic arguments.

First of all, let us consider the sense in which a set of generative rules can be said to be 'comprehensive'. It is often claimed that transformational grammar provides the most comprehensive treatment of English syntax, as well as indicating the underlying relations between sentences better than other types of grammar. Furthermore, the rules in a transformational grammar are said to be 'complete' in the sense that they can apply without limit to produce an infinite number of well-formed sentences. Every step in the generation of sentences is fully specified, and nothing is left out on the grounds that it will be 'tacitly understood', as was often the case with more traditional grammars. These are important advantages, but it will be apparent that a transformational grammar can be complete in terms of its internal organization, and yet account for only a small part of language structure. For example, the rules of the grammar might be capable of producing an unlimited number of sentences, just so long as all the sentences belong to a relatively restricted set of simple sentence-types. In principle a transformational grammar incorporates the whole of a speaker's knowledge of his language, but it is well known that none of the grammars so far available contain anything like a full description of English. Moreover, it so happens that many of the items that have to be taught at a fairly early stage in a language course (e.g., articles, modals, quantifiers, interrogatives, negatives and adverbials) are precisely those which present serious problems to linguists who attempt to handle them within the framework of modern scientific grammar. Until linguists have succeeded in solving these problems it is inevitable that textbook writers will continue to turn to the compendious, though informal, grammars of the past as a basis for many of their pedagogic statements.

Secondly, transformational grammar is often given credit for an 'explanatory' value which other grammars lack. Here the argument turns on a special meaning of the word 'explanatory' as used in transformational theory. A linguistic theory is said to have explanatory adequacy if it incorporates a principle for selecting the most highly valued set of rules, given two or more possible sets of rules which account for all the relevant data. We might argue further that a set of rules which is part of the most highly-valued grammar is 'explanatory' in the sense that the rules reflect some absolute truth about the structure of language in general, and of one language in particular. However, there is a more general use of the word which is more commonly used in the context of language teaching; i.e., whatever statement about grammar 'makes sense' to a student and helps him to achieve a learning task, is in some important sense explanatory. The informal statements which appeal to students as being insightful and correct undoubtedly have an important part to play in the formation of learning strategies, and as far as the student or teacher is concerned they require no further validation. It is not necessary for language teaching purposes to show that such statements derive from a theoretically powerful grammar. On the contrary, it appears that many of the rules deriving from theoretically powerful grammars are notably lacking in that quality of intuitively felt correctness that is so important to a student, while other insights, deriving from notional and *ad hoc* grammars, are frequently seized upon because they are felt to have the 'explanatory' qualities that the more formal rules may lack. In the context of language teaching 'explanation' tends to be a rather vague concept since it refers to whatever prompts, clues and mnemonic aids a student happens to find helpful in his attempts to master the material. Explanations in this general sense can be derived from a variety of sources, including the comparison of two or more languages, the study of both deep and surface structure and the demonstration of language in context without reference to the formal properties of language.

Thirdly, some writers have suggested that an explicit step-by-step enumeration of rules of the type found in Chomsky's grammar might be incorporated into language teaching material in the form of exercises, so that students have a full set of instructions for producing grammatical sentences in the target language. The suggestion that sets of algorithmic rules might be incorporated into classroom materials brings us up against a problem which has long been familiar in connection with the use of substitution tables. A substitution table is a generative grammar of a simple kind; grammatical sentences can be 'read off' automatically, but there is no guarantee that they mean anything to the student or that he is learning how to use these, or similar, sentences in real-life situations. The result of employing substitution tables or similar mechanisms in the classroom is that we obtain a high degree of control over the output at the cost of providing insufficient scope for the creative intelligence of the student. The question concerns the form of the teaching materials which will be most effective in helping students to internalize the relevant rules. Presumably our aim as language teachers is to devise exercises which maintain an adequate degree of control while providing scope for the student to develop his own linguistic judgement. It is not immediately clear how the manipulation of an automatic sentence-generating device, a kind of robot which makes all the decisions on our behalf, can help a student to develop his own judgement in deciding what is and what is not a sentence in the target language, and how that sentence is appropriately used.

A final point concerns the function of grading in language teaching materials. It has sometimes been suggested (e.g. Newmark 1964) that the ordering of rules in a transformational grammar has implications for the ordering of material in a teaching syllabus which may be different from conventional principles of grading. This view suggests a contrast between a teaching grammar in which the ordering of material is determined by a system of formal rules and a teaching grammar in which grading is formally unmotivated since it is based on an intuitive or empirical notion of the relative complexity of structures. Thus, Newmark assumes that in a teaching grammar based on the rules in *Syntactic Structures* kernel sentences will be taught first, then obligatory transformations, then optional transformations. Accordingly, we would not be able to teach questions, which involve transformations, until after the kernel sentences have been taught. This conflicts with the usual practice, which is to introduce questions at the beginning of a course because of the greater variety of exercises and drills which can then be made available at an early stage. We cannot take this argument seriously, however, since it ignores the existence of an important difference in principle between a scientific grammar and language teaching material based on it. A pedagogic grammar consists of a selection of material drawn from one or more scientific grammars and presented according to principles which are entirely pragmatic and which have nothing to do with the axioms of linguistics. Any question concerning the order of presentation of teaching material must be decided on the basis of the pedagogic grammar, not of the linguistic grammar. It does not necessarily follow that linguistic grammars are totally irrelevant to questions of grading, since work in the field of linguistics may well be a source of useful ideas about the presentation of material in the classroom. However, it must always be the case that these ideas are realized in a manner consistent with the requirements of a particular teaching situation. In other words, the contents of a linguistic grammar may suggest, but not dictate, the arrangement of material in a pedagogic grammar, since the essentially pragmatic considerations of frequency, usefulness, relevance to situation, etc., must be built into any grammar which is intended for teaching purposes.

1.4 The role of grammar in second language teaching

We have examined several cases in which views about the relationship between linguistic theory and language teaching practice are rendered suspect by a tendency on the part of linguists to over-generalize, and to assume that an approach which may be helpful in handling one particular problem must necessarily be valid for all aspects of language and language learning. We must now consider briefly the role of grammar in second language teaching, and the extent to which a conscious knowledge of the rules can be expected to help a student in his attempts to acquire a practical mastery of the language.

According to Chomsky and his followers a simple habit structure view of language is inadequate as the sole basis for a theory of human language behaviour, nor can it be accepted as central to such a theory, since it fails to account for exactly those qualities that make human language behaviour unique, in particular a speaker's ability to produce and understand sentences that he has never seen or heard before. However, the present trend away from a habit structure view of language and in the direction of language as rule-governed behaviour does not mean that teachers must begin to encourage conscious rule-learning in every part of the syllabus. There is no reason why habit-formation theory should not be invoked to account for some features of language, nor is it necessarily the case that the whole of human language behaviour is based on the operation of deep-level rules. For example it is quite true, as Rivers points out, that the 'habitual, automatic associations' operating in certain areas of grammar (e.g. subject-verb agreement, the fixed forms for interrogation and negation, the formal features of tenses) do not always require intellectual analysis, and may be learned 'without more than an occasional word of explanation' (Rivers 1968). In other cases, however, learning may be impossible without a conscious understanding of the rule involved. Thus, a student could perform drills based on the model sentences *I've lived here for two years*, *I've lived here for six months* on the one hand, and *I've lived here since 1965*, *I've lived here since last Christmas* on the other hand, and still produce the erroneous forms **I've lived here for 1965*, **I've lived here since two years*, because he has not perceived the underlying rule that 'since' is used in English for naming time and 'for' is used for counting time. With this type of problem in mind Carroll has suggested that aural-oral methods might be more successful 'if, instead of presenting the student with a fixed, predetermined lesson to be learned, the teacher created a "problem solving" situation in which the student must find . . . the appropriate verbal response for solving the problem'. As a result the student would be forced 'to learn, by a kind of trial-and-error process, to *communicate* rather than merely to utter the speech patterns in the lesson plans' (Carroll 1961).

Rivers (1968) accepts that language is rule-governed behaviour, and that one of the tasks of language teaching is to find ways of helping students to internalize the rules, but how do we teach the grammar of a language? According to Rivers, language use involves both lower-order skills (the manipulation of elements which occur in fixed relationships in clearly defined systems) and higher-order skills, i.e., the level of expression of personal meaning. The pattern practice approach is appropriate at a level where the student is establishing the lower-order skills, but inadequate at a level where he is trying to develop his ability to use the foreign language as a vehicle for personal meaning. A traditional grammar-learning approach may be appropriate at a higher level, especially if the students express an interest in abstract rules, but it would be unwise to extend conscious rule-learning downwards into the beginners' class, where the emphasis should be on establishing strong habitual associations between the elements in a set of basic sentence patterns.

In order to accommodate procedures suitable for both higher-order skills and lower-order skills, Rivers suggests a 'strategy of interplay' between two kinds of language learning: 'There must be a constant interplay in the classroom of learning by analogy and by analysis, of inductive and deductive processes, according to the nature of the operation the student is learning. It is evident that higher-level choices cannot be put into operation with ease if facility has not been developed in the production of the interdependent lower-level elements, and so learning by induction, drill and analogy will be the commonest feature of the early stages. Genuine freedom in language use will, however, develop only as the student gains control of the system as a whole, beyond the mastery of patterns in isolation.' Rivers believes that the process of automatic drill, inductive learning and extension-by-analogy breaks down at the point where the student becomes involved with problems of contextual meaning. When a student has to decide what he wants to say and how he is going to say it he is faced with a more complicated initial choice and needs to know something about the potential of the language system as a whole. At this stage the inter-relationships within the language system may need to be clarified by a systematic grammatical presentation, and 'practice with understanding' in 'real communication situations' should have priority over automatic drills and exercises.

Most of the achievements in the field of language teaching methodology during the past twenty-five years have been associated with the elementary syllabus. It is natural that in developing a new course writers should prefer to start at the beginning, especially since this is the point at which problems of language organizations are at their least intractable. It could be argued, however, that in concentrating all their attention on the needs of beginning students, teachers and textbook writers have brought about a serious neglect of the intermediate and advanced syllabus. In particular there is a danger that teachers will assume that because habit-formation techniques appear to work quite well at an early stage, it necessarily follows that they will continue to work well later on. In fact there is some evidence that the problems of advanced language learning do not simply involve more material but are qualitatively different from those that are encountered at an elementary level, so that a teaching technique which produced good results in the first six months will not necessarily be equally successful at the end of the second·or third year.

It may be the case, for example, that more advanced students need to have access to a grammatical description and a terminology which will enable them to obtain some degree of formal insight into language structure, whereas at an earlier stage it might well be more appropriate for students to acquire their knowledge of grammar by a process of induction based on pattern practice and the observation of language in use. The suggestion is that we may have to correct the present imbalance in favour of the beginning student and introduce conscious rule-learning into the intermediate and advanced syllabus wherever there appears to be a need for it. The purpose of this would be threefold. A conscious knowledge of the rules would give the advanced student some degree of conscious insight into material that he has already learned to use without benefit of grammatical explanation. Furthermore, it would help him to predict the behaviour of phenomena not brought under direct observation in the teaching text, and to achieve discriminating control over the increasingly large quantities of data that he will be called upon to handle as the course proceeds.

2 Exercises and exemplification[1]

In this section we present some rules from a transformational grammar of English in order to illustrate the process of converting a scientific grammar into material which is suitable for language teaching. All the material that follows is drawn from Chomsky's *Syntactic Structures* (1957) or Paul Roberts' *English Syntax* (1964), which is broadly based on *Syntactic Structures*. The theory of transformational grammar underwent substantial modification in *Aspects of the Theory of Syntax* (1965), but the earlier model has been selected here because many teachers feel that it is still of particular relevance as a source of insights for language teaching.

A transformational grammar of the type described by Chomsky in *Syntactic Structures* has three components: phrase structure (or constituent structure) rules, transformational rules and morphophonemic rules. The constituent structure rules apply first and produce a set of phrase structure terminal strings, each with an associated phrase marker. For example, the following phrase marker underlies the sentence *His sister can sing*:

[1] For an explanation of the special symbols used in this section see p. 361.

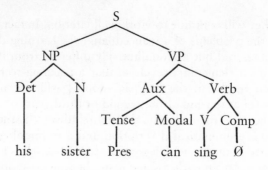

The transformational rules operate on the elementary phrase markers to produce derived phrase markers representing more complex sentence types. The transformational rules yield strings of morpheme symbols which the morphophonemic rules convert into the conventional forms of the written language, or the sound sequences of the spoken language.

The transformational rule that forms yes/no questions from underlying declarative sentences in English states that if the predicate of the underlying structure begins with a modal, some form of *have* or some form of *be*, these elements reverse with the subject to form a yes/no question:

T-yes/no (optional)

NP Tense + Modal	X	⇒ Tense + Modal	NP X	
NP Tense + have	X	⇒ Tense + have	NP X	
NP Tense + be	X	⇒ Tense + be	NP X	
NP Tense	Verb	⇒ Tense	NP Verb	

In T-yes/no the strings to the left of the arrow are called the *structural description* and the operation indicated by the rule is called the *structural change*. The yes/no transformation applies to all strings that are *analysable* in terms of the elements referred to in the structural description. For example, if a string is analysable into three substrings, and these substrings are dominated in the phrase marker associated with the string by the symbols NP, Tense and Modal respectively, then the string satisfies the conditions defined by the structural description, and falls within the domain of the yes/no transformation. X indicates that any element may occur at this point; i.e., this part of the input string does not affect the yes/no transformation and need not be specified in detail.

It is a characteristic of many transformational rules that at least one of the symbols in the structural description functions as a variable which may take as its value any one of the substrings dominated by that symbol in the phrase marker associated with the string. Thus, in the case of T-yes/no, NP is a variable which may take as its value any of the substrings generated by the phrase structure rules and dominated by NP, including *his sister, the girl next door, the wife of the chairman of the committee,* and others potentially without limit. In some cases an informal treatment may give the impression that transformational grammar offers little more than a restatement of the rules of traditional grammar. However, transformational grammar is always far more exact in its statements than traditional grammar, with regard both to the conditions under which transformations operate and to the precise nature of the variables which are incorporated into structural descriptions.

After the application of T-yes/no another transformation is needed:

T-affix (obligatory)

$Af + v \Rightarrow v + Af$

Af stands for any tense, *en* or *ing*, and v stands for any modal, *have, be* or verb. The following diagram shows how T-yes/no and T-affix operate on a string *NP T M Verb* (Noun Phrase + Tense + Modal + Verb). For simplicity we have used lexical items to represent the abstract structures that underlie sentences; strictly speaking, only the terminal string should receive a phonetic or orthographic representation.

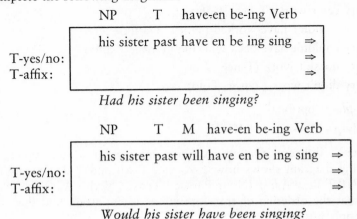

	NP	T	M	Verb

	his sister pres can sing	$\Rightarrow$
T-yes/no:	pres can his sister	sing $\Rightarrow$
T-affix:	can pres his sister	sing $\Rightarrow$

Can his sister sing?

Exercise A

Complete the following diagrams:

	NP	T	have-en	be-ing	Verb

	his sister past have en be ing sing	$\Rightarrow$
T-yes/no:		$\Rightarrow$
T-affix:		$\Rightarrow$

Had his sister been singing?

	NP	T	M	have-en	be-ing	Verb

	his sister past will have en be ing sing	$\Rightarrow$
T-yes/no:		$\Rightarrow$
T-affix:		$\Rightarrow$

Would his sister have been singing?

If T-yes/no moves *Tense* to the front of the sentence, and there is no *M*, *have* or *be* to act as 'carrier' for the tense, then T-do applies obligatorily:

T-do (obligatory)

Tense ⇒ do + Tense

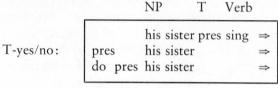

NP   T   Verb

		his sister pres sing	⇒
T-yes/no:	pres	his sister	⇒
	do pres	his sister	⇒

Does his sister sing?

Exercise B

Draw a box diagram like those in Exercise A to show the derivation of *Did his sister sing?*

The negative transformation is as follows:

T-neg (optional)

NP Tense + Modal	X	⇒	NP Tense + Modal not X
NP Tense + have	X	⇒	NP Tense + have not X
NP Tense + be	X	⇒	NP Tense + be not X
NP Tense	Verb	⇒	NP Tense not Verb

Exercise C

Note the similarity between T-neg and T-yes/no. Draw diagrams to show the derivation of the following sentences:

  Henry can't work (T-neg, T-affix)
  Henry couldn't have worked (T-neg, T-affix)
  Henry couldn't have been working (T-neg, T-affix)
  Henry doesn't work (T-neg, T-do)
  Henry didn't work (T-neg, T-do)

T-wh, place (optional)

X + Adv-p + Y ⇒ where + X + Y

X, like Y, indicates that any element may occur at this point. The following diagram shows how T-yes/no, T-wh and T-do operate on a string *NP T Verb Adv-p* (Noun Phrase + Tense + Verb + Adverb of place). Note that the ordering of transformations is important and that T-wh must apply after T-yes/no:

	NP	T	Verb Adv-p	
	his sister	pres	sing at the party	$\Rightarrow$
T-yes/no:		pres	his sister sing at the party	$\Rightarrow$
T-wh:	where	pres	his sister sing	$\Rightarrow$
T-do:	where do	pres	his sister sing	$\Rightarrow$

Where does his sister sing?

T-wh, time (optional)
$X + Adv\text{-}t + Y \Rightarrow when + X + Y$

T-wh, manner (optional)
$X + Adv\text{-}m + Y \Rightarrow how + X + Y$

T-wh frequency (optional)
$X + Adv\text{-}f + Y \Rightarrow how\ often + X + Y$

T-wh, noun phrase (optional)

$X + NP + Y \Rightarrow \begin{Bmatrix} who \\ what \end{Bmatrix} + X + Y$

T-wh, article (optional)

$X + Article + Noun + Y \Rightarrow \begin{Bmatrix} which \\ what \end{Bmatrix} + Noun + X + Y$

T-object
$who \Rightarrow whom$

(obligatory when *who* is preceded by a preposition in surface structure, otherwise optional).

Exercise D

Draw diagrams to show the derivation of the following sentences:

When will his sister have been singing? (T-yes/no, T-wh, T-affix)
How did his sister sing? (T-yes/no, T-wh, T-do)
How often does his sister sing? (T-yes/no, T-wh, T-do)
Who should have married Fiona? (T-yes/no, T-wh, T-affix)
Who(m) should Henry have married? (T-yes/no, T-wh, T-affix, T-obj)
What has scratched the baby? (T-yes/no, T-wh, T-affix)
What has the cat scratched? (T-yes/no, T-wh, T-affix)
Who(m) did the postman give the letter to? (T-yes/no, T-wh, T-do, T-obj)
Which cat has scratched the baby? (T-yes/no, T-wh, T-affix)
Which baby has the cat scratched? (T-yes/no, T-wh, T-affix)

T-passive (optional)

$$NP_1 + Aux + VT + NP_2 \Rightarrow NP_2 + Aux + be + en + VT + (by + NP_1)$$

The subscripts in NP_1, NP_2 serve to distinguish the two Noun Phrases from one another. Aux stands for Auxiliary, which in the following diagram is manifested by Tense (T). VT stands for Verb Transitive and T-del is a deletation transformation:

	NP_1	Aux(T)	VT	NP_2	
	Henry	past	invite	Fiona	
T-pass:		Fiona past is en invite		by Henry	$\Rightarrow$
T-affix:		Fiona is past invite en		by Henry	$\Rightarrow$
T-del:		Fiona is past invite en			$\Rightarrow$

Fiona was invited by Henry

Fiona was invited

The grammar contains the phrase structure rule (1), and consequently the symbol VT in the rule T-passive may take any one of the values (2):

1

$$VT \Rightarrow \begin{cases} Vt_1 \\ Vt_2 + Prt \\ \begin{cases} Vt_3 \\ Vt_{to} \\ Vt_{ing} \end{cases} + Comp \end{cases}$$

2	Vt_1	(discuss)	(NP)
	$Vt_2 + Prt$	(send off)	(NP)
	$Vt_3 + Comp$	(send to London)	(NP)
	$Vt_3 + Comp$	(think beautiful)	(NP)
	$Vt_3 + Comp$	(elect chairman)	(NP)
	$Vt_3 + Comp$	(regard as stupid)	(NP)
	$Vt_3 + Comp$	(put in a drawer)	(NP)
	$Vt_{ing} + Comp$	(found sleeping)	(NP)
	$Vt_{to} + Comp$	(persuaded to come)	(NP)

Note that Vt_3 has a number of subclassifications which have been omitted from (1). The following diagram shows the derivation of a passive sentence from an underlying structure containing $Vt_3 + Comp$:

	NP$_1$	Aux (T)	VT$_3$	Comp	NP$_2$	
	Henry	past	think beautiful Fiona			⇒
T-pass:	Fiona past is en think beautiful				by Henry	⇒
T-affix:	Fiona is past think en beautiful				by Henry	⇒
T-del:	Fiona is past think en beautiful					⇒

Fiona was thought beautiful by Henry
Fiona was thought beautiful

To form active sentences from underlying structures containing VT + Comp or VT + Prt, it is necessary to apply the following transformation:

T-VT

$$VT_x + \begin{Bmatrix} Prt \\ Comp \end{Bmatrix} + NP \Rightarrow VT_x + NP + \begin{Bmatrix} Prt \\ Comp \end{Bmatrix}$$

VT$_x$ refers to all transitive verbs that can be followed by a particle or complement. T-VT is obligatory for complement construction unless the complement is long and complicated (e.g.: *The committee elected chairman the man who happened to know most about regional planning*). T-VT is optional for particle constructions unless the NP is a personal pronoun, in which case it is obligatory: *John put the letter away, John put away the letter, John put it away.*

Exercise E

Draw diagrams to show the derivation of the following passive sentences. The words in brackets are optional.

Mary was regarded as stupid (by our friends).

Henry was sent to London (by the firm).

The money was put in a drawer (by the secretary).

William was elected chairman (by the committee).

Douglas was persuaded to work (by the professor).

The patient was found sleeping (by the nurse).

Exercise F

Draw diagrams to show the derivation of the active sentences corresponding to the above passive sentences.

The above exercises show something of the concise and economical nature of English structure, in particular the way in which transformational rules operating on the output strings of phrase structure grammar succeed in drawing together into a unified whole a great deal of data which might appear to be entirely unrelated from a study of surface structure alone. The derivations for *Had his sister been singing?* and *Would his sister have been singing?* reveal the motivation for a number of apparently arbitrary decisions in setting up the constituents of phrase structure grammar. The fact that *Tense* comes first in the verb group enables *Tense* to move to the front of the sentence with *Modal, have* or *be* when required to do so by T-yes/no. In the derivation of *had his sister been singing* T-yes/no moves *Tense have* to the front of the sentence; T-affix converts *Tense have* to *have Tense*; *Past* is selected to replace *Tense*; and a morphophonemic rule gives *had* as a result of combining *have* and *Past*. The fact that the phrase structure rules set up a sequence *en be ing Verb* enables T-affix (already needed to convert *Tense have* into *have Tense*) to apply twice more, giving the required sequences *be en* (been), *Verb ing* (singing), without our having to add any further rules to the grammar.

We have seen that the effect of T-yes/no is to move *Tense* together with *Modal, have* or *be* to the front of the sentence. T-affix then reverses the order of Tense and whatever element immediately follows to give the first word in such sentences as *Can his sister sing? Had his sister been singing?* and *Was his sister singing?* Notice now what happens if T-yes/no moves *Tense* to the front of the sentence, but there is no *Modal, have* or *be* to act as 'carrier' for the tense. In this case T-do applies obligatorily with the result that *do* acts as a 'carrier' for the tense, *do + Present* becomes *does* and *do + Past* becomes *did*.

The advantages of the present treatment become clearer when we consider the class of negative sentences such as *His sister cannot sing, His sister had not been singing, His sister did not sing.* We can generate all these sentences by means of a transformation T-neg which operates on exactly the same strings as those that appear on the left of the arrow in T-yes/no, but with the following difference: instead of interchanging the first and second segments of these strings as in the case of T-yes/no, T-neg leaves segments 1, 2 and 3 in their original order and inserts the negative element *not* between segments 2 and 3. Apart from the difference in ordering and the presence or absence of the element *not*, T-yes/no and T-neg are shown to be very similar operations. Both transformations operate on the same structures, and involve the use of T-affix and T-do in exactly the same way. In order to describe the negative transformation almost nothing must be added to the grammar, since the subdivision of the sentence and the rule for appearance of *do* were required independently for yes/no questions. In other words, transformational analysis brings out the fact that negatives and yes/no questions have fundamentally the same structure, and we can make use of this fact to simplify the description of English.

Another set of relationships in the deep structure of English is revealed by those transformations which derive 'wh-questions' (e.g., *When will his sister have been singing?*, *How did his sister sing?*) from structures underlying the declarative sentences *His sister sang at the party* and *His sister sang beautifully*, etc., by way of intermediate structures which underlie the yes/no questions *Did his sister sing at the party?*, *Did his sister sing beautifully?*, etc. An informal representation of this process, suitable for language teaching purposes, may be given as follows:

T-wh, time:

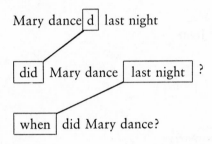

T-wh, manner:

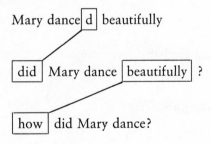

T-wh, frequency:

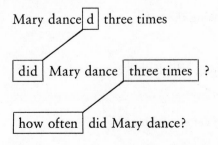

D

T-wh, noun phrase:

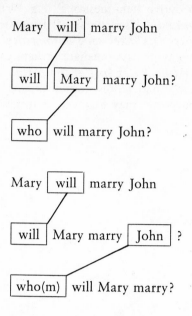

T-wh, article:

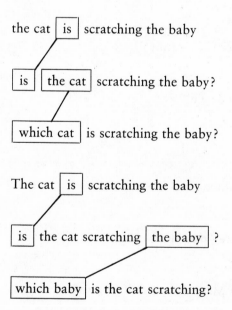

A knowledge of transformational grammar may suggest ways of ordering material in a pedagogic grammar which will not always be obvious from a study of surface structure alone. Thus, in the case of T-passive, we have seen that VT is a variable which may take a number of substrings as its value, enabling us to generate a wide range of sentence-types on the basis of a single rule. A pedagogic treatment of passive sentences based on the rules in *Syntactic Structures* is suggested by the following diagrams. Note, however, that we will not be able to exploit the insights provided by Chomsky's T-passive unless we are prepared to admit into the pedagogic description some reference to underlying structure, in this case represented by 'Henry regarded-as-stupid Fiona', 'Jones sent-to-London Henry', etc.:

T-passive:

Henry   invited Fiona

Fiona was invited   by Henry
Fiona was invited

T-passive with Complement structures:

(i)

  T-VT:

  Henry regarded-as-stupid Fiona

Henry regarded   Fiona as stupid

  T-passive:

  Henry   regarded-as-stupid Fiona

Fiona was regarded as stupid   by Henry
Fiona was regarded as stupid

(ii)

  T-VT:

  Jones sent-to-London Henry

Jones sent   Henry to London

  T-passive:

  Jones   sent-to-London Henry

Henry was sent to London   by Jones
Henry was sent to London

(iii)

T-VT:

Mary put-in-a-box the money

Mary put	the money in a box

T-passive:

Mary   put-in-a-box the money

the money was put in a box	by Mary
the money was put in a box	

3 Four approaches to the teaching of grammar

A review of current language teaching materials suggest that there are three common strategies for providing students with a knowledge of the underlying rules: the situational method, the audiolingual method, and the grammatical explanation method. The aim of situational teaching is to ensure that at all times the language being taught is used meaningfully in close association with the people, objects and actions to which it refers. Followers of this method hope that through the observation and imitation of language in realistic situations students will master the rules inductively without needing to be conscious of them in the form of overtly expressed grammatical generalizations. Both the situational and the audio-lingual method are based on the behaviourist doctrine that language learning consists primarily in establishing a set of habits, that is to say a set of responses conditioned to occur with certain stimuli which may be either situations or words in a syntactic frame. The grammatical explanation method differs from both the audiolingual and the situational methods in that it involves a systematic attempt to provide students with a conscious knowledge of the rules. The justification for this is that some items appear to be taught more efficiently if we utilize the student's powers of reasoning rather than depend exclusively on pattern practice and memorization. Although many theoretical discussions imply that the above methods are mutually exclusive, in fact most teachers have long used a combination of all three techniques. The view adopted here is that successful language teaching depends on a mixture of habit-formation and analytic-deductive procedures, realized in various combinations according to the nature of the learning task and the type of students involved.

3.1 The situational method

A typical procedure designed to help students discover the underlying rules without spending a lot of time 'talking about grammar' is provided by the following instructions from the teachers' book of *Situational English* (Longmans 1966), adapted for general use from *English for Newcomers to Australia*. This material, widely known as the 'Australian situational method', was prepared for the Australian Department of Immigration by a team of writers under the direction of Neile Osman.

(i) *Where, when, how*

Write the following on the board:

Where?	When?	How?
London	June	plane
New York	July	ship
Rome	August	train
Edinburgh	September	car
(some local town)	October	bus

Say: *I want to go for a holiday. Where shall I go?* Answer, pointing to London: *I'll go to London.* Then ask: *When shall I go?* Answer, pointing to June: *I'll go in June.* Then ask: *How shall I go?* Answer: *I'll go by plane.* Write your three questions on the board as part of a substitution table, to be developed further:

Where	shall	I	go?
When			
How			

Repeat the procedure with *we*, and after asking and answering the three questions, add the pronoun to the third column of the substitution table.

(ii) *Simple present + negative*

Write *English* on the board and then in an adjoining column write the names of a number of languages which you do not know, e.g. *German, French, Greek, Dutch, Russian.* Say: *I know English.* Pause, then repeat *I know English* and as you point to *German* add: *but I don't know German.* Write the sentence on the board. Repeat with other languages, varying the presentation by using other verbs, e.g. *read, understand, write.*

Bring a student to the front of the class and say: *You know English, but you don't know Chinese,* etc. Write this on the board and present similarly *We don't know* and *They don't know.*

(iii) *Simple present + question*

Write the following verb series on the board:

I   *stay at home*   on Saturdays.
    read the paper
    watch television
    write letters
          etc.

Read out the verb series, then above it write the word *Questions.* Write a large *Do* to the left of the series and alter the full stop to a question mark. The series should now appear as follows:

Questions

Do   I   *stay at home*   on Saturdays?
         read the paper
         watch television
         write letters

Read out the questions and then introduce in turn *we, you,* and *they* under *I.* With the addition of dividing lines you should eventually have the following substitution table on the board:

Do   I   *stay at home*   on Saturdays?
     we   *read the paper*
     you   *watch television*
     they   *write letters*

The play-acting element in situational teaching, together with the ample opportunities for spontaneous oral assimilation which the method provides, make this approach particularly suitable for children (although *Situational English,* and many similar courses, have been designed for use with adults). The disadvantages of situational teaching are that the method tends to be time-consuming, and the point-by-point presentation of structures makes it difficult for the student to acquire a systematic knowledge of areas of grammar which function as a unified whole in the language system. Moreover, in the absence of any clearly-defined terminological framework there is no way of checking whether the students have internalized the correct rule, a partial rule, or no rule at all. For these reasons situational teaching is less suitable for adult learners, who tend to prefer a more 'rational' approach to language learning and feel happier if they are given some kind of explanation of the point being learned before they start doing drills and exercises.

3.2 Pattern practice

A widely-used course which pays systematic attention to the formal features of sentences (insofar as these can be inferred from surface-structure patterns) is the *Intensive Course in English* produced under the direction of Robert Lado and C.C. Fries at the English Language Institute of the University of Michigan. The materials rest upon the view that 'learning a foreign language consists *not* in learning *about* the language but in developing a new set of habits'. These habits are seen as the behavioural correlates of syntactic and phonological patterns. The aim is to teach grammar, defined as 'the particular system of devices which a language uses to signal one of its various layers of (structural) meaning'. Knowing the grammar for practical use means being able to produce and to respond to the signals of structural meaning, without necessarily having to be consciously aware of the grammatical principles involved. In order to develop such habits the student is provided with a great deal of oral pattern practice, in which the emphasis is on promoting strong habitual associations between words and patterns. There is less insistence on the need to form a direct association between syntactic patterns and the real-life situations to which they refer.

Each lesson in the Lado-Fries material consists of six parts, as follows: (1) an outline consisting of key examples, (2) a frame that contains an attention pointer, the new pattern, and one or more comments which summarize the grammar being taught, (3) a set of illustrative examples which show the new pattern in a variety of environments, (4) pattern practice drills, (5) notes on additional patterns for recognition purposes only, (6) a review of key examples. After the presentation of the key examples orally by the teacher and choral repetition by the class, the authors recommend a short discussion during which the rule being taught is discovered inductively by the class. After the grammar has been discussed, the class begins intensive pattern practice, which takes up 85% of the available time. The whole lesson is conducted orally, as far as possible at normal conversational speed, so that all the students obtain maximum practice in listening and speaking. Written homework consists of writing out the responses to particular exercises performed orally in class.

The following presentation of wh-questions is taken from Lesson 4 of *English Sentence Patterns*, one of the four books which comprise the *Intensive Course in English*. The method of presentation should be compared with Chomsky's rules for wh-questions, outlined on pp. 76–7 above:

Key example: WHAT ARE you STUDYING? Grammar.

Observe the word order in the questions.

Previous pattern:

STATEMENT

We	are	studying	grammar.

New pattern:

QUESTIONS				ANSWERS
	ARE	you	STUDYING grammar?	Yes, I am.
	ARE	you	STUDYING in class?	Yes, I am.
	IS	John	LEARNING English?	Yes, he is.
	IS	he	VISITING a friend?	Yes, he is.
	AM	I	SPEAKING slowly?	Yes, you are.
WHAT	ARE	you	STUDYING?	Grammar.
WHERE	ARE	you	STUDYING?	In class.
WHAT	IS	John	LEARNING?	English.
WHO(M)	IS	he	VISITING?	A friend.
WHAT	IS	he	DOING now?	Studying.

COMMENTS

1 Use ARE, IS, AM before the first Class 1 word (YOU, JOHN, HE, etc.) in these questions with the -ING form.

2 Use WHAT, WHEN, WHERE, WHO(M) before ARE, IS, AM.

It has been claimed (Temperley 1961) that the Lado-Fries grammar is *generative* because the student learns how to construct a set of English sentences by studying the relevant model. Temperley also claims that the grammar is *transformational* because the chief instructional device is to present a previously learned sentence pattern as the basis for a new pattern, with the implication that the two patterns are related by means of underlying transformational rules. It is apparent, however, that neither 'generative' nor 'transformational' is used here in the sense intended by Chomsky. For example, if a student sees the point of a Lado-Fries sentence frame he does so by virtue of some knowledge about language structure that he already possesses, rather than by following out a set of rules which are explicitly stated in the teaching material. Furthermore, it is possible to speak of 'transformations' in the Lado-Fries material only if we understand by this a set of replacement rules performed on surface structures, while Chomsky's transformations operate not on surface structures but on the underlying phrase-markers which are more abstract.

On the other hand it might be argued that if we attempt to convert Chomsky's abstract rules into material which is suitable for language teaching we might very well end up with a type of presentation which closely resembles that of Lado-Fries. One possible difference between the Lado-Fries material and a pedagogic grammar based on Chomsky's rules lies in the use of abstract symbols. Thus, Lado-Fries use no abstract symbols, and base the whole of their grammatical presentation on 'model sentences' (i.e., phonologically realized surface structures or their ortho-graphic representation). By contrast, a pedagogic grammar based on the rules of *Syntactic Structures* might employ various abstract symbols (Pres, Past, have + en, be + ing, etc.) in order to make statements of greater generality which convey more information about the nature of the underlying rules.

3.3 Grammatical explanation

A serious weakness of the Lado-Fries material is the fact that it fails to provide deeper insights into language structure as the student enlarges his experience of English. The authors assume that their materials are equally suitable for beginning, intermediate or advanced students; advanced students simply work through them more quickly. It seems to be the case, however, that predominantly habit-formation materials which work very well at an elementary level often lead to boredom and frustration later on. Advanced students need a more sophisticated treat-ment of grammatical rules which goes beyond the manipulation of surface-structure patterns and which provides some degree of insight into deep structure relationships. This need is particularly urgent in the case of remedial students who wish to improve their knowledge of the language but who understandably resent having to work for the second or third time through materials with which they are already thoroughly familiar. At the present time there are few English language teaching texts designed expressly to meet the needs of more advanced students, but an example is provided by W. E. Rutherford's *Modern English* (Harcourt Brace 1968).

Modern English is a remedial text for intermediate and advanced learners of English, aimed at foreign university students of mixed language backgrounds who are studying in the United States. The linguistic orientation of the work is explicitly that of transformational-generative grammar, and the professed aim is to bridge the gap between the repetitive drills of the elementary syllabus and the development of more complex organizational skills needed for meaningful communication in nonpredictable situations. The author accepts the assumption of transformational theorists that verbal behaviour is the result not of reinforced habit but of the 'internalization' of an intricate set of rules which form the basis of a speaker's creative competence. Rutherford admits that transformational theory as such does not tell us how languages are learned, but it nevertheless reveals many underlying regularities and facts about language structure which appear to have pedagogic relevance, in particular the difference between deep and surface structure which is strikingly revealed by transformational grammar.

The author's method is to combine habit-formation drills with fairly sophisticated grammatical explanations. There are twenty units, each containing five sections: dialogue, pronunciation practice, memorized dialogue, idiomatic phrases, grammar. The grammar sections are arranged as follows: (a) presentation of the new pattern in a frame which contrasts it with a previously learned pattern; (b) 'explication' of grammar rules, including an extensive use of transformational terminology; (c) 'verification', consisting of structural drills.

Rutherford's treatment of the passive (Unit 14, pp. 314–16) is clearly derived from *Syntactic Structures*:

> *Passive* constructions are extremely common in English. The passive transformation (T-passive) can operate on any sentence which contains a transitive verb. The effect of the transformation is:
>
> to replace the actor, as Subject, with the person or thing acted upon
>> *He* followed me.
>> ⇒I was followed (by him).
>
> to introduce a form of *be* between auxiliary and verb. (Thus, *be* mirrors whatever form the verb has before the transformation.)
>> He's *following* me.
>> ⇒I'm *being* followed (by him).
>
> to render the verb a past participle
>> He'll *follow* me.
>> ⇒I'll be *followed* (by him).
>
> optionally to render the original NP subject as *by*+NP, with shift to sentence final position

> *He's* followed me.
> ⇒I've been followed *by him*.

The above formulation would be out of place in an elementary syllabus (except, perhaps, as a guide for the teacher). However, an explicit statement of grammatical rules, together with plenty of practice in the form of drills and dialogues, is an appropriate technique in the case of advanced students who prefer to make use of their reasoning abilities as an aid in furthering the development of spontaneous performance skills.

3.4 The multiple line of approach

Although each of the common methods of teaching grammar (demonstration-in-context, pattern practice based on sentence frames, the overt presentation of abstract grammatical rules) seems to be particularly relevant in certain situations, it should be realized that none of these methods is complete in itself, and that most teaching situations call for a combination of all three approaches. The vital task for the language teacher is to find the right combination of activities for any given set of circumstances. It should be no cause for surprise if we find that the required proportions vary from classroom to classroom and that there is no universally applicable rule. It seems safe to conclude that for the time being at least the insights which we expect to be useful in language teaching will be drawn not from a single 'best' model of grammar but from a number of linguistic models which may differ from one another in various respects. This situation should not discourage us. On the contrary, it enables us to give expression in our teaching to Palmer's 'multiple line of approach' (Palmer 1921). In Palmer's view, the essence of a 'complete' method of teaching is that teachers should be flexible. The opposite of a 'complete' method is a 'special' or 'patent' method which 'claims to prevent or to cure all possible ills ... by repeated applications of one special device or drug'. As teachers we should be prepared to study linguistic grammars of all types, and to select from them whatever seems to contribute, from a teaching point of view, to what Palmer calls a 'complete and homogeneous' system of presentation.

How can transformational insights best be utilized, for example, in a second language textbook? One advantage of transformational grammar is the fact that it is absolutely explicit. The rules constitute a full set of instructions for the derivation of sentences, with none of the details omitted and with no gaps, which have to be filled by guesswork or by appeal to a speaker's intuition. Thus a knowledge of transformational grammar serves as a check on a pedagogic description, and enables the textbook writer to propose relations between sentences in a responsible way. Another advantage of transformational grammar is the fact that the constraints imposed by the theory lead linguists to the discovery of 'deep level generalizations' which serve to draw together in a systematic way a large quantity of superficially unrelated data. In order to exploit these discoveries the teacher and textbook writer have to think in terms of deep structure relations. However, in most teaching materials it is not possible to replace the surface forms of utterances with a more abstract representation without running the risk of seriously confusing the students. The challenge lies in finding some way of incorporating formal linguistic insights into teaching materials without destroying the pedagogic validity of the presentation. One possible solution is to retain a surface structure framework as the basic mode of presentation, but to extend the scope of the pedagogic grammar by incorporating trans- formational insights into it whenever this can be done without incurring too many abstract rules. Bearing in mind the basic difference between a scientific grammar and a pedagogic grammar, we do not expect to find any detailed correspondence between the formal rules and the way in which material is presented in the classroom. It seems likely, however, that transformational grammar will continue to provide teachers with useful insights about language structure, and that it may suggest ways of ordering the material in various subsections of the syllabus, but not over the syllabus as a whole.

4 Further reading

Allen, J. P. B. and van Buren, Paul (eds.). *Chomsky: Selected Readings*. Language and Language Learning Series. London: Oxford University Press, 1971.

Commonwealth Office of Education, Sydney. *Situational English*. London: Longmans, 1967.

Gleason, H. A. Jr. *Linguistics and English Grammar*. New York: Holt, Rinehart, Winston, 1965.

Lado, R. and Fries, C. C. *English Sentence Patterns*. Ann Arbor: University of Michigan Press, 1958.

Lester, Mark (ed.). *Readings in Applied Transformational Grammar*. New York: Holt, Rinehart, Winston, 1970.

Roberts, Paul. *English Syntax*. New York: Harcourt Brace, 1964.

Roulet, E. Grammar models and their application to the teaching of modern languages. Strasbourg: Council of Europe, Committee for Higher Education and Research, 1970.

Rutherford, W. E. *Modern English*. New York: Harcourt Brace, 1968.

Thomas, Owen. *Transformational Grammar and the Teacher of English*. New York: Holt, Rinehart, Winston, 1965.

Wilkins, D. A. *Linguistics in Language Teaching*. London: Arnold, 1972. Chapter 3.

4 Language Laboratory Materials

ANTHONY HOWATT and JULIAN DAKIN

1 General discussion

The purpose of this chapter is to discuss materials that can be used in a language laboratory with individual tape recorders for each pupil and with facilities for the teacher to check the pupils' work. Most of the suggestions for exercises can also be used with a simple tape recorder in class, but listening practice is often more effective when the pupil has his own machine and can listen to the same piece many times.

Tape recorders can be used to help the pupil both to understand and to speak the foreign language he is studying. We shall begin by discussing listening practice because it is probably more suited to the language laboratory than speaking practice.

1.1 Listening

A very simple analysis of listening would give it four headings: understanding a speaker's accent or pronunciation, understanding his grammar, recognizing his vocabulary and being able to grasp the meaning of what he says. As teachers of a foreign language we may then construct exercises to practise each of these aspects of listening one by one. However, effective comprehension depends on our being able to do everything at once and so the learner of a foreign language must also have some chance of natural listening practice that is not directed towards any particular aspect of listening skill but involves them all.

We should not be afraid of giving pupils listening practice to broaden their experience of the language outside the syllabus. They can very often guess unfamiliar words and phrases from the context of each passage. In fact we do this all the time in our own language, and if understanding does fail for a short time, this need not worry the learner too much—unless he feels that he has to account to the teacher all the time. Also, we should remember that comprehension is not a 'passive' occupation. If the listener is interested at all in what he is hearing, he will actively try to make sense out of it. Of course, he can make nonsense as well!

To sum up, we feel that there is a place both for detailed listening practice which is carefully linked to the rest of the work that the pupils are doing in class and at home, and also for freer listening practice where the pupil is concerned primarily with following a story or finding something out from the recording that he is listening to. For reference purposes we might call the first kind of practice *intensive listening* and the second kind *extensive listening*. 'Extensive' and 'intensive' are familiar terms from discussions about the teaching of reading, and we are using them here in a similar way.

1.1.1 EXTENSIVE LISTENING

The teaching purpose of extensive listening practice is to give the learner plenty of opportunity to develop and exercise his listening skills in as natural a way as possible. Extensive listening need not be tested in any detail, but will be done for its own sake. The pupil will be following the meaning of the listening passage, because he is interested in the information in it, or simply because he is enjoying it.

What would extensive listening materials look like? Obviously this depends on the level of learner that they are intended for, but it is very important that they should be varied. Recordings of stories and other texts taken from books or magazines can often be used. But for the more advanced learners, it is rather important to get away from language that has been specially controlled for teaching purposes and that was also written rather than spoken in the first place. Recordings from the radio and television are the obvious sources of spontaneous conversation. Listening materials to give practice in making sense of unscripted language can also be specially made if enough native speakers are available to make recordings. Variety does not only mean many different topics, it also means different kinds of language, different accents and dialects, different styles of talking and so on.

Should the language content of these passages be controlled? Again the answer depends on how advanced in their study of the foreign language the pupils are. Listening texts for beginners are unlikely to be found in sources originally meant for native speakers. They would be too difficult, so special passages would probably have to be constructed for this level. As a course progresses into the more advanced stages, however, the distinction between language for learners and language for native-speakers becomes less and less marked until eventually for all practical purposes it can be disregarded. It is important that extensive listening materials should not slavishly follow the set syllabus of a teaching course —that would defeat the purpose of the exercise. There should be not only familiar words and phrases in new contexts, but also new words and phrases which the pupil has to try to make sense of.

How many new items? In the end the answer depends on the reaction the teacher gets from the pupils. If they fail to follow a passage, it may mean that there are too many new words. But it may not. It may mean only that they have missed one or two of the 'key items' in the text. We shall come back to key items in a moment.

How should extensive listening practice be prepared for? We have suggested that it should be done for its own sake, but this need not mean that the teacher would take no interest in it at all. Ideally, a period of extensive listening, particularly in lower-level classes, would be introduced by familiarizing the pupils with the general context of the listening passage, perhaps by looking at a photograph or a picture with them, asking one or two questions about it and perhaps even making sure that they know the meaning of some of the key items which can be seen in the picture or defined verbally. The purpose of this introductory work, which will not of course take long nor go into great detail, is to put the pupils in the right frame of mind for the listening practice, and in this way make it much easier for them to make sense of the language in the passage.

The term 'key items' is not synonymous with 'useful words in English'. They are items which in a particular passage play a specifically significant role in the structure of the passage, so that a failure to understand them is very likely to lead to a failure to understand a large section of the passage, if not all of it. Either these items must be known before the pupils do the practice, or they must be made very clear from the context, perhaps with the use of sound effects in the recording or the histrionic abilities of the speakers.

The following passage is an extract from John Osborne's *Look Back in Anger*. Clearly a passage like this is for intermediate to advanced learners, but it illustrates fairly well some of the characteristics of language that make for good listening practices at any level.

JIMMY: God, how I hate Sundays! It's always so depressing, always the same. We never seem to get any further, do we? Always the same ritual. Reading the papers, drinking tea, ironing. A few more hours, and another week gone. Our youth is slipping away. Do you know that?

CLIFF: (throws down paper). What's that?

JIMMY: (casually). Oh, nothing, nothing. Damn you, damn both of you, damn them all.

CLIFF: Let's go to the pictures. (To Alison). What do you say, lovely?

ALISON: I don't think I'll be able to. Perhaps Jimmy would like to go. (To Jimmy). Would you like to?

JIMMY: And have my enjoyment ruined by the Sunday night yobs in the front row? No, thank you. (Pause). Did you read Priestley's piece this week?

Why on earth I ask I don't know. I know damned well you haven't. Why do I spend ninepence on that damned paper every week? Nobody reads it except me. Nobody can be bothered. No one can raise themselves out of their delicious sloth. You two will drive me round the bend soon—I know it, as sure as I'm sitting here. I know you're going to drive me mad. Oh heavens, how I long for a little ordinary human enthusiasm. Just enthusiasm—that's all. I want to hear a warm, thrilling voice cry out Hallelujah! (He bangs his breast theatrically). Hallelujah! I'm alive! I've an idea. Why don't we have a little game? Let's pretend that we're human beings, and that we're actually alive. Just for a while. What do you say? Let's pretend we're human. (He looks from one to the other). Oh, brother, it's such a long time since I was with anyone who got enthusiastic about anything.

CLIFF: What did he say?

JIMMY: (Resentful of being dragged away from his pursuit of Alison). What did who say?

CLIFF: Mr. Priestley.

JIMMY: What he always says, I suppose. He's like Daddy—still casting well-fed glances back to the Edwardian twilight from his comfortable wilderness. What the devil have you done to those trousers?

CLIFF: Done?

JIMMY: Are they the ones you bought last week-end? Look at them. Do you see what he's done to those new trousers?

ALISON: You are naughty, Cliff. They look dreadful.

JIMMY: You spend good money on a new pair of trousers, and then sprawl about in them like a savage. What do you think you're going to do when I'm not around to look after you? Well, what are you going to do? Tell me?

CLIFF: (Grinning). I don't know. (To Alison). What am I going to do, lovely?

ALISON: You'd better take them off.

JIMMY: Yes, go on. Take 'em off. And I'll kick your behind for you.

ALISON: I'll give them a press while I've got the iron on.

CLIFF: O.K. (Starts taking them off). I'll just empty the pockets. (Takes out keys, matches, handkerchief).

JIMMY: Give me those matches, will you?

CLIFF: Oh, you're not going to start up that old pipe again, are you? It stinks the place out. (To Alison). Doesn't it smell awful?
(Jimmy grabs the matches, and lights up).

ALISON: I don't mind it. I've got used to it.

JIMMY: She's a great one for getting used to things. If she were to die, and wake up in paradise—after the first five minutes, she'd have got used to it.

CLIFF: (Hands her the trousers). Thank you, lovely. Give me a cigarette, will you?

JIMMY: Don't give him one.

CLIFF: I can't stand the stink of that old pipe any longer. I must have a cigarette.

JIMMY: I thought the doctor said no cigarettes?

CLIFF: Oh, why doesn't he shut up?

JIMMY: All right. They're your ulcers. Go ahead, and have a bellyache, if that's what you want. I give up. I give up. I'm sick of doing things for people. And all for what?

(Alison gives Cliff a cigarette. They both light up, and she goes on with her ironing).
Nobody thinks, nobody cares. No beliefs, no convictions and no enthusiasm. Just another Sunday evening.

(John Osborne: *Look Back in Anger*, Faber, 1957, pp. 14–17.)

We have space in this book only for a very short extract from the play. The pupils would of course be given a longer quotation and it would not be presented totally out of its context. However one or two points about it are worth noting:

(i) It is interesting. Furthermore, it lends itself to a particularly intense and dramatic presentation.

(ii) It is a very effective adaptation of natural conversation. Plays are not examples of natural language, far from it. They would not be good plays if they were. But some playwrights are more concerned than others to achieve a style of written dialogue that both sounds natural and works in the theatre.

(iii) It contains *repetition*. Because repetition provides renewed opportunities for understanding and for remembering, it is an important feature of learning through listening or reading. Stories, rhymes, songs and jingles for young children, television advertisements, poems and songs for older readers all make effective use of devices for repetition to aid understanding and memory. Fairy stories and legends are particularly memorable since they often use a special form of repetition on a 'cyclical' pattern. An example is the story of the old woman in the bottle who demands a series of dwellings each one more splendid than the previous one until she over-reaches herself and ends up back in the bottle. The pattern of language repeats itself over and over again with each turn of the cycle, and children remember it. In listening passages for older learners the devices for repetition have to be more subtle. The extract from *Look Back in Anger* is full of examples of language that is repeated because the characters are frustrated, annoyed, are not paying attention and so on.

(iv) *Look Back in Anger* was a particularly successful play and film. It should not be difficult to find illustrations in order to help the pupils visualize the setting in which it takes place. Many have probably seen it for themselves anyway.

It is unlikely that any of the key items in the extract will be unknown to a learner capable of approaching this piece. There is one phrase which would have to be prepared for: 'Priestley's piece'. This would be incomprehensible without knowing that Priestley is an author, and the next few lines of Jimmy's speech depend on this. Other items that could be called key items should present no difficulty. They would include: 'God, how I hate Sundays!' 'Let's go to the pictures.' 'Did you read Priestley's piece this week?' 'How I long for a little ordinary human enthusiasm.' In fact, in a passage such as this, a key item is a major shift in the direction of the conversation. In simpler pieces for lower-level learners key items may be particular words or phrases, whereas in more advanced passages they are the pointers to new and perhaps unexpected aspects of the whole context.

We have already noted that listening passages may be found in books, magazines, newspapers, from the radio or television and also perhaps specially written by the teacher. There is, however, one further source that is worth mentioning: the pupils themselves. They could be asked to construct passages which they think would interest their fellows, have these corrected and recorded by the teacher and in this way build up a class listening library on the lines of a class reading library.

1.1.2 INTENSIVE LISTENING

Intensive listening exercises can be divided into two types:

A   exercises to train a detailed comprehension of meaning, and

B   exercises which get the learner to listen to particular features of language such as vocabulary, grammar or pronunciation.

It is important that exercises of both kinds should be integrated into the rest of the pupil's work, otherwise they may become pointless.

Type A: Listening for comprehension

Intensive listening for meaning is a fairly obvious language lab activity. The point of this section is to stress that there are many different ways of testing comprehension apart from the straight question. The following dialogue has been written in such a way that many kinds of comprehension test could be used with it:

HENRY: You've got a nice suntan. Where've you been?
CLARE: Spain.
HENRY: Very nice. On the Costa Brava?
CLARE: For some of the time, yes. But we hired a car and drove around a bit, too.
HENRY: Did you hire it there, or drive it out from England?
CLARE: No, we flew to Barcelona and hired it there. We only had a fortnight, you see.

HENRY: Yes. Where did you go?

CLARE: Down the coast from Barcelona as far as Valencia. We drove slowly and took three days to get there.

HENRY: Very nice.

CLARE: And then inland.

HENRY: To Madrid?

CLARE: Yes.

HENRY: It must have been hot.

CLARE: Yes, it was, very.

HENRY: How long did it take?

CLARE: A couple of days, and then we spent three days in Madrid itself. It wasn't really long enough.

HENRY: Then you went south?

CLARE: No, we went right across to Portugal and finished up in Lisbon two days later.

HENRY: Then you drove all the way back again?

CLARE: No, we'd had enough by then. We gave the car back and had a rest. We went back to Madrid to catch the plane home.

HENRY: Quite a trip. But how did you get that suntan if you were sitting in a car all the time?

CLARE: It was a convertible, and we had the roof down most of the time.

Examples of exercises

COMPREHENSION QUESTIONS

(a) Factual

(i) Did Clare spend her whole holiday on the Costa Brava?

(ii) Where did she hire the car?

(iii) Did she drive directly from Barcelona to Madrid?

(iv) How long did she spend in Madrid?

etc.

(b) Inferential

(i) Was Clare alone during her holiday?

(ii) How did Henry know that Clare had had a holiday?

(iii) Why didn't Clare hire the car in England?

(iv) Was Clare tired by the time she reached Lisbon?

etc.

(c) Personal

(i) Have you ever been to Spain?

(ii) Have you ever hired a car?

(iii) Where did you go for your holiday last year?

etc.

Personal questions are probably best suited to classwork where the discussion can be more meaningful than in the lab.

MULTIPLE-CHOICE QUESTIONS

The advantage of setting comprehension questions out in a multiple-choice form is that it is a simpler and speedier way of checking understanding without requiring a constructed answer in the foreign language. However, multiple-choice questions cannot be recorded easily, though they can always be presented to the student in writing. The following are examples of multiple-choice questions based on the Spanish holiday dialogue:

(i) Clare spent   *a* her whole holiday   on the Costa Brava.
              b part of her holiday
              c most of her holiday

(ii) She hired her car   *a* in England.
                b in Portugal.
                c in Spain.

(iii) She drove to Madrid   *a* direct from Barcelona.
etc.   *b* from Barcelona via Valencia.

CORRECTION QUESTIONS

If used sensibly, the technique of asking the pupils to correct mistakes is useful. For example, the pupils could be given a sketch map (see page 101) and be asked whether it is an accurate picture of Clare's trip. They would be required to make the necessary corrections on their maps (which they would have in stencilled form) and could discuss these changes in the follow-up class after the laboratory.

PROJECT QUESTIONS

It is often interesting to ask the pupil to use the information on the tape in order to carry out a small project. Here are three suggestions:

a Draw a sketch map of Clare's holiday journey.
b Here is a list of fares and charges. How much did Clare spend on transport during her holiday (excluding the cost of petrol)?
London—Barcelona by air   £45.00 single.
London—Madrid by air   £48.60 single.
Lisbon—Madrid by train   £20.00 return.
Car hire   £6.00 per day.[1]
c Clare arrived in Spain on July 29th and left on her car trip the following day. Write a diary for each day of her holiday.

[1] The answer is given at the end of the chapter.

55457

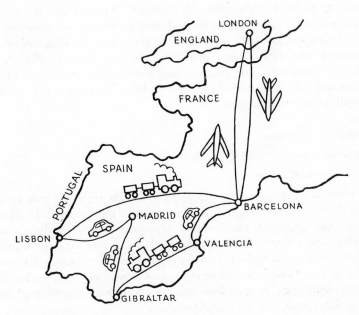

SUMMARY QUESTION

The following question would require a brief summary of the dialogue:
On the last day of her holiday Clare suddenly remembered that she had forgotten to send her parents a postcard. So she quickly bought one and told them very briefly what she had been doing. What did she write?

FOLLOWING INSTRUCTIONS

As it stands the dialogue about the Spanish holiday is unsuitable for this type of exercise. However, if the situation were altered to depict a holiday maker talking to an AA official who was trying to work out the best route to take from London to Dover, the pupils could then follow the instructions of the AA man in making their own route plans.

Type B: Listening for language

As well as testing comprehension, the teacher can also work out listening exercises which get the pupils to notice particular features of language. These may be pronunciation features, or points of grammar or vocabulary. We now turn to detailed exercises with this purpose.

There are three general points to be made about linguistic exercises. Firstly, care should be taken to ensure that the pupils understand what they are listening to before they go on to more detailed work. Secondly, the points chosen for special practice should be well prepared for and followed up in class. Otherwise, they merely 'hang in the air' and the pupil is unable to relate what he is doing in the lab to anything else. Thirdly, linguistic exercises should be related to each other rather than unconnected bits and pieces. Probably the coursebook syllabus will provide the framework for the teaching points, but sometimes there is no such textbook, and special care has to be taken to give the lab work an overall plan and structure.

Examples of exercises
DISCRIMINATION EXERCISES

(a) For pronunciation

Discrimination exercises get the pupil to decide which of two or more sounds, stresses, rhythm patterns or intonation patterns he can hear on the tape. For example, the holiday dialogue contained the question 'Then you went south?' The fact that this remark was a question and not a statement was indicated only by the intonation. To extend this point a little, the pupils could be asked to record on a piece of paper which of the following utterances are questions and which are not, assuming of course that they have been well prepared for this:

> You liked your holiday?
> Clare didn't go to France.
> She was alone?
> She went home by plane?
> etc.

(b) For grammar

Again on the assumption that the point fits into the scheme of work, the pupils could be asked which of the following sentences describe what Tom does every Saturday evening and which describe only what he is doing this Saturday:

> He goes to the pictures.
> He meets his friends in the pub.
> He's doing a crossword puzzle.
> He takes his girl friend out.
> He's listening to his tape recorder.
> He's smoking his pipe.
> He gets a meal at the fish and chip shop.
> etc.

(c) *For vocabulary*

The pupils could be given a stencil with the following drawings on it. While listening to the tape, they could be asked to draw lines between the people and their vehicles following the information the tape gives them:

John's got a bike.
Mary's got a scooter.
Mr. Simpson's got an American car.
Mr. Bell's got a Mini.

For certain classes exercises requiring the pupils to discriminate between correct and incorrect language could also be valuable. For instance, a class of teacher trainees, who eventually will have to be able to hear whether their pupils are right or wrong, could be given recordings of typical learners at different levels in school. The trainees would then have to notice certain errors (for pronunciation, grammar or vocabulary) and as a follow-up exercise after the lab would be asked to construct remedial exercises for the pupil they had been listening to.

HUNTING EXERCISES

Hunting exercises are discrimination exercises in disguise but they provide some variety of activity for the learners. The reader is invited to do the following exercises as a pupil. (Answers on page 120.)

(a) *For pronunciation*

Listen to the following dialogue and then try to answer the questions.

MUM: Henry!
H.:   Yes.
M.:   Breakfast's ready. Are you up yet?
H.:   Well . . . nearly. Where's my jacket?
M.:   On the back of your chair, I expect.
H.:   Oh, yes. Thanks, Mum.
M.:   Quick. Your egg's getting cold.

1 How many words have the sound /a/ in them?

2 How many words have the sound /e/ in them?

3 How many times can you hear the sound /ı/?

(b) *For grammar*

In the next exercise the pupils would be asked to listen for phrases expressing direction. Most such phrases need the preposition 'to', for example 'I drove to a garage'. Some, however, do not require 'to', for example 'I drove home'. In the following exercise write down the phrases like 'I drove to a garage' in one list, and phrases without 'to' like 'I drove home' in another:[2]

JIM: What's the matter with your eye?
BILL: I had a car accident on Saturday.
J.:   Really? A bad one?
B.:   No, it wasn't serious, but I cut my face a bit.
J.:   What happened?
B.:   Well, I was driving home with the family from the seaside and the car ran out of petrol. So I naturally drove to a garage to fill up.
J.:   Yes?
B.:   I was just turning right at the garage exit when this van hit me. Luckily we were both going very slowly.
J.:   Yes, that was lucky.
B.:   The van driver said he didn't see me. You see, the road past the garage runs along the coast for five miles. So you have to drive west directly into the sun before you can turn inland.
J.:   Did you get home all right?
B.:   Oh yes. I had to go to the doctor but he said my eye would be all right in a week or so.

[2] The answers are given at the end of the chapter.

(c) *For vocabulary*

Make a list of the verbs in this story which mean 'go fast'.

Gerald Meredith had to catch the five o'clock plane to London. It was very important because his girl-friend was meeting him and they had planned to spend the evening together. But the customers in his office had kept him talking, so now he was late and he would have to rush. He ran out of his office and tried to get a taxi. Finally, he succeeded and jumped in. 'The airport, please. And could you hurry. I'm rather late.' 'I'll do what I can, sir' said the driver. The taxi went very slowly indeed because there was so much traffic on the road. 'Please could you speed up a bit', begged Gerald. 'There's a speed limit, you know, sir', said the driver rather unhelpfully. At last they arrived at the airport. Gerald raced into the airport building, and tore up to the check-in desk. 'The five o'clock to London', he said out of breath. 'I'm not too late, am I?' 'Oh no, sir,' said the clerk, 'the five o'clock's been cancelled. Fog in London. The next one's at nine.'

DICTATION EXERCISES

(a) *General dictation*

This needs no special comment or example. A normal dictation text is simply recorded for lab use and the pupils' work either corrected in the follow-up class or taken in by the teacher.

(b) *Specific dictation*

By giving the pupils a fill-in stencil to complete, dictation can be used to attract the pupil's attention to a specific linguistic point. For example, the following dialogue would be recorded on tape. The pupils would have the gapped version on an accompanying stencil and they would have to fill in the gaps. The point being practised is obviously the weak forms. 'You're/I'm' against the strong form versions 'You are/I am'. There are examples of each in the dialogue:

Tape	*Written stencil to be filled in*
BOB: You're late, Jim.	BOB: ...... late, Jim.
JIM: No, I'm not. It's only ten o'clock.	JIM: No, ... not. It's only ten o'clock.
BOB: You *are*, you know. The game started at nine.	BOB: ......, you know. The game started at nine.
JIM: Oh, I'm sorry.	JIM: Oh, ... sorry.
BOB: Never mind. Are you staying for lunch?	BOB: Never mind. ...... staying for lunch?
JIM: Yes, I am, thanks.	JIM: Yes, ..., thanks.
BOB: Good.	BOB: Good.

1.2 Speaking

The language laboratory is not so suitable for speaking practice as it is for listening practice. You can listen to and learn from a tape, but you cannot really talk to one. You can only simulate talking. Listening in the language lab can therefore be a real language experience, whereas talking in the lab is only a rehearsal for real conversation. As a result speaking exercises in the lab have a rather limited function which we can discuss under two headings: Type A, Imitation and Type B, Manipulation.

Type A: Imitiation of native speech models

Dialogue exchanges can be recorded to practise the pronunciation of particular sounds, stress and rhythm patterns and intonation. The learner can repeat these models in the privacy of the laboratory as many times as he wants to.

Type B: Manipulation of speech patterns

The pupil cannot practise speaking in a language laboratory, but he can practise using the rules of the foreign language that he will need when he speaks. Exercises or drills for this purpose can be divided into two types—exercises that require substitution and those which require transformation. (The term 'transformation' is being used here in its everyday sense; it has nothing to do with 'transformation' as a technical term in transformational grammar.)

(a) *Substitution drills.* When he is doing a substitution drill, the pupil hears a model sentence, for example:

Does John like tea?

He then hears the word or phrase that he is supposed to substitute into the model sentence. For example: 'Coffee'. He must now produce the sentence:

Does John like coffee?

And he will hear the correct version on the tape, so that he can compare his response with the correct one. On the tape the drill takes this form:

VOICE 1: Does John like tea?
VOICE 2: Coffee

PAUSE—to let the pupil have a go.

VOICE 1: Does John like coffee.

SECOND PAUSE—to let the pupil correct himself.

Drills like this are sometimes called 'four-phase' drills. Phase One: the model sentence along with the substitution item; Phase Two: the pause for the pupil to respond; Phase Three: the correct response recorded ready on the tape; and Phase Four: the second pause for correction. Sometimes the second pause is left out, making a 'three-phase' drill. This may make the drill go more quickly, but if the pupil does not need a chance to have a second go, he probably does not really need the drill anyway.

Our example above, which would be the first of seven or eight, appears to be practising question forms in English which require the use of the verb *do*. Here is the complete drill:

> Does John like tea?
> Coffee.
> Does John like coffee?
> Milk.
> Does John like milk?
> Fish.
> Does John like fish?
> Meat.
> Does John like meat?

However, suppose the pupil were to hear the first three words as one rather long word whose meaning was obscure, for example as 'Derzchonlie', he could still get the responses in the drill right.

If the reader is not convinced that he could, he should try it for himself. In fact the drill we have been looking at does not necessarily practise the question form with *do* at all. It practises only the changes of vocabulary 'tea', 'coffee', etc., and these need not be understood. However, if we ask the pupil to substitute different items instead of 'John', then we do draw some attention to the syntax of the interrogative form, e.g.:

> Does John like tea?
> John and Mary.
> Do John and Mary like tea?
> Susan.
> Does Susan like tea?
> Her parents.
> Do her parents like tea?

In this drill the pupil must notice that there is some syntactic connection between the subject and the verb. The other words can be ignored, however.

In reply to these comments it might be said that the pupil would not be prepared to speak nonsense, and by repeating the same pattern over and over again he is gradually familiarizing himself with it and making it 'automatic'. This may be true, but it means that the pupil is bringing more to the exercise than he is asked to do, and he is practising something which the drill is not itself practising.

To sum up so far, we have seen that there are two kinds of substitution drills: those which require no other changes in the sentence except the substitution (Does John like tea/coffee/milk/ . . . etc.) and those which require a change (Does John like tea?/Do John and Mary like tea? . . . etc.). However, in neither case is the pupil asked to notice the syntax of the whole sentence, and those bits he can ignore need not even be comprehensible.

(b) *Transformation drills.* In order to practise question forms in English, the pupil could be asked to do a drill on this model:

> John likes tea.
> Does John like tea?
> Mary likes milk.
> Does Mary like milk?
> Bill likes onions.
> Does Bill like onions?

In this drill the learner is asked to transform a sentence which is an example of a declarative into a sentence which is an example of an interrogative. He is practising the rules for forming sentences of different types. He is not actually asking questions. In real life we do not ask questions by converting declaratives into interrogatives. We ask questions when we want to find something out. We can now see why it is so important to prepare and follow up language laboratory practice work. In the preparatory work in class the pupil can best learn how different kinds of questions are asked in the foreign language. And it is only in the follow-up work with the teacher that he can ask appropriate questions to which he wants to know the answer. In the lab he is merely practising the rules for forming questions.

(c) *Vocabulary and general knowledge drills.* So far we have been concerned with drills that get the pupil to manipulate syntactic rules. With ingenuity, drills can also practise vocabulary and general knowledge as well.

Picture drills

Using the pictures at the top of p. 109, the pupil could make sentences on the model:

> John likes tea.
> Bill likes ice cream.
> Susan likes cake.
> etc.

It is difficult to use pictures to prompt questions, except by using conventions such as question marks, e.g.:

Sound effect drills

Sound effects on the tape can also be used to guide the student's responses, e.g.:

Can you hear a cuckoo?   (CUCKOO NOISE)
Yes, I can.
Can you hear an owl?   (CUCKOO AGAIN)
No, I can't, but I can hear a cuckoo.

Sound effect drills are a bit limited, but they can be fun.

General knowledge drills. The student's general or local knowledge can also be used to help him in framing answers to questions, e.g.:

> What does Tony Jacklin do?
> He's a golfer.
> And Ann Jones?
> She's a tennis player.
> And Pele?
> He's a footballer.
> And Kip Keino?
> He's a runner.
> etc.

These are usually very interesting drills, but they do not appear very much in commercial courses because they tend to date quickly. They are specially suited to the teacher making up his own drills for a particular class.

Finally, there are drills based on the fact that one sentence can imply another one. For instance:

> The Ganges is longer than the Thames.
> The Thames is shorter than the Ganges.
>
> An aeroplane is faster than a car.
> A car is slower than an aeroplane.
>
> London is bigger than Birmingham.
> Birmingham is smaller than London.
> etc.
>
> I've got toothache.
> You should go and see a dentist.
>
> I've got a pain in my back.
> You should go and see a doctor.
>
> There's something wrong with my eyes.
> You should go and see an oculist.
> etc.

These drills are based on linguistic facts about English. The first drill practises antonyms: 'short' is the opposite of 'long', 'slow' is the opposite of 'fast', etc. In the second drill 'a dentist' is synonymous with 'a man who looks after your teeth'. This is important because it means that there is a correct answer to the drill examples which can be recorded on the tape.

We can also make use of everyday implications and consequences, but these present a problem for lab work because there is usually more than one possible answer. For example:

I've got a toothache.
You should go and see a dentist.

I've got a cold.
You should go to bed.

I've got a sore throat.
You should smoke less.

In this drill it is possible to think up many examples of the type of advice you would give to somebody who had a cold or a sore throat—they should go to bed, wear a thick coat, have a whisky and so on. Such drills should work in the lab if the pupils are warned to expect that their own answers might not be the same as the ones on the tape, but perhaps in the end they are better suited to classwork. However, they do provide variety, and nothing is more welcome in the language laboratory than that.[3]

1.3 Summary

In concluding this discussion of language laboratory materials, we wish to re-emphasize three points. Firstly, the most effective use of the laboratory is likely to be in the training and development of listening skills, although, as we have shown, it can also be used in a more limited way to train speech habits. Secondly, laboratory lessons need to be carefully planned and integrated with classroom work. Thirdly, the laboratory materials themselves need to be interesting as well as relevant, if possible amusing as well as systematic. We have shown a variety of different techniques being applied to a single passage in the section on Intensive Listening. But so far we have not shown how the different techniques of speech practice, or a suitable selection of them, could be integrated to form a coherent approach to a particular language problem in the laboratory. The next section discusses and illustrates in full the material for an actual laboratory lesson.

2 A sample language laboratory lesson

The students for whom this lesson was designed were a group of overseas teacher-trainees at Jordanhill Training College in Glasgow. The vocabulary and grammar of these students was on the whole good, but not unnaturally their pronunciation was in some respects very different from that of native speakers. In particular they sometimes had trouble in controlling the rhythm of English sentences and in making an appropriate use of 'weak forms'. In this particular lesson, which had been preceded

---

[3] The idea of meaningful drills based on semantic relationships rather than structures is discussed at length with a large number of examples in Dakin (1973).

by discussion and preparation in class, the students were being trained to use the weak forms of two different words: 'are' and 'a'. As it happens the two words often have an identical weak form in English which may be represented by the phonetic symbol /ə/.

Step I: Repetition

The students hear, and are made to repeat, a conversational rhyme which contains the weak forms of both words. The tape goes as follows:

(i) *Listen:*

What are you going to be?

What are you going to be?

I shall be a teacher.

That's the life for me.

(ii) *Repeat one line at a time after me*

(each line is recorded separately on the tape with a pause in between for the student's repetition).   ·

(iii) *Now recite the whole rhyme with me*

(the rhyme is repeated without pauses. The student is supposed to speak in time with the voice on the tape).

(iv) *Now recite the rhyme on your own*

(a suitable pause is left on the tape).

The purpose of this first step in the lesson is to give the student a model of how the weak forms should be pronounced, and to give him the chance of imitating this model until he can reproduce it accurately and easily. A rhyme is particularly useful in this case as it sets a strong rhythm to which the student must adhere. The actual sentences of the rhyme, which the student can now reproduce accurately, are going to act as 'models' or substitution frames for the manipulative drills and exercises comprising the rest of the lesson.

Step II: Repetition by substitution

Attention is now concentrated on the use of the weak form of 'are' in a single sentence type. The student is required to change the vocabulary in the sentence, but the real point of the exercise is to get him to use the weak forms and preserve the rhythm unconsciously, in a familiar setting, while concentrating on something else—in this case, the vocabulary substitution. The tape continues as follows:

(v) *Ask a question beginning:*

What are you going to . . .?

Example:

VOICE 1: I've just decided on my career.

VOICE 2: What are you going to be?

Now ask your own questions

1 I've just decided on my career.
   (pause)

   What are you going to be?
   (pause)

2 I'm going shopping.
   (pause)

   What are you going to buy?
   (pause)

3 I'm going to the cinema tonight.
   (pause)

   What are you going to see?
   (pause)

(The reader can perform the rest of this exercise as if he were a student. He will find some suggested responses on page 121.)

4 I've got to prepare the dinner.
   . . . . . .

5 I've got to do an essay for tomorrow.
   . . . . . .

6 I'm giving a talk tomorrow.
   . . . . . .

7 I'm going to a party tonight, but I haven't got any decent clothes.
   . . . . . .

Step III: Contrasting strong and weak forms by substitution

The next step is to get the student to contrast the strong and weak forms of 'are' in an appropriate context. This is again a substitution exercise but the student's questions are prompted by a single word rather than a whole sentence as in the previous exercise. The tape goes as follows:

E

(vi) *Now ask TWO questions in each of the following conversations.*
Your first question must begin:

Are you going to . . .?

Your second question is always the same:

Oh, are you?

Example:

VOICE 1: A picture.
VOICE 2: Are you going to draw a picture?
VOICE 1: Yes, I'm going to draw a lion.
VOICE 2: Oh, *are* you?

Now you ask your questions (again the first three examples are given here, the rest are left for the reader to do as a student).

1 A picture.
(pause)

Are you going to draw a picture?

Yes, I'm going to draw a lion.
(pause)

Oh, *are* you?

2 An essay.
(pause)

Are you going to write an essay?

Yes, I'm going to write about my trip to Stratford.
(pause)

Oh, *are* you?

3 A model.
(pause)

Are you going to make a model?

Yes, I'm going to make a model of my girl-friend.
(pause)

Oh, *are* you?

4 A film.
. . . . . .

Yes, I'm going to make a film about seagulls.
. . . . . .

5 A song.

......

Yes, I'm going to sing 'Old Macdonald had a Farm'.

......

6 The dinner.

......

Yes, I'm going to make scrambled eggs and chips.

......

7 A game.

......

Yes, I'm going to play Monopoly.

......

The important feature of this exercise, apart from the contrast between strong and weak forms, is that it attempts to simulate real conversation by answering the student's questions and thus prompting him to make a further conversational response. The answers he hears are sometimes humorous, the intention being to keep him amused and awake.

Step IV: Contrast of strong and weak forms using general knowledge

The next exercise gets the student to contrast strong and weak forms again in a different context, this time by answering questions from his general or local knowledge. The statements he produces are genuine minimal pairs. The tape continues as follows:

(vii) *Take part in each conversation by using a sentence beginning 'They're' or 'They are'.*

Example:

VOICE 1: Who are those people studying in the library?
VOICE 2: They're students.
VOICE 1: They can't be students!
VOICE 2: They *are* students.

Now try to do the same

1 Who are those people studying in the library?
(pause)
They're students.
They can't be students!
(pause)
They *are* students.

2 Who are those people trying to teach the students?
(pause)

They're teachers.

They can't be teachers!
(pause)

They are teachers.

3 Who are those people marching up and down?
. . . . . .

They can't be soldiers!
. . . . . .

4 Who are those people painting pictures?
. . . . . .

They can't be artists!
. . . . . .

5 Who are those people sitting down in the middle of the street?
. . . . . .

They can't be demonstrators!
. . . . . .

Step V: Repetition by substitution (using implication)

The student is now switched to the weak form of 'a', but once again he is encouraged to use it unconsciously by having his attention concentrated on the vocabulary of the sentences he constructs.

(viii) *Name the occupation of the people in the pictures.*

Example:

VOICE 1: What does John do?
VOICE 2: He's a student.

What does John do?
(pause)
He's a student.
(pause)

2

What does Henry do?
(pause)
He's a painter
(pause)

3

What does George do?
......

4

What does Jane do?
......

5

What does Sally do?
......

6

What does Charles do?
......

7

What does Betty do?
......

(Suggested responses on page 121.)

Step VI: Repetition by substitution using a guessing game

Further practice in the use of the weak form of 'a' is given to the student by getting him to ask questions about the identity of an object on the lines of 'I Spy'.

(ix) *'I'm thinking of something. What is it? Ask me. Begin your question with 'Is it a . . .?'*

Example:
VOICE 1: It begins with C, and people sit on it.
VOICE 2: Is it a chair?
VOICE 1: It's a chair.

Now ask questions in the same way:

1 It begins with C, and people sit on it.
   (pause)
   Is it a chair?
   It's a chair.

2 It begins with W and there are four of them in every room.
   (pause)
   Is it a wall?
   It's a wall.

3 It begins with T and people sit at it.
   . . . . . .
   It's a table.

4 It begins with D and you shut it behind you.
   . . . . . .
   It's a door.

5 It begins with T and it repeats everything you say.
   . . . . . .
   It's a tape recorder.

6 It begins with P and it hangs on the wall.
   . . . . . .
   It's a picture.

The reader will have noticed in the drills for Steps III and IV that the second pause for self-correction has been left out. If the pupils were allowed correction pauses in the middle of the conversations, the feeling of dialogue would be lost.

Step VII: Discriminatory test by dictation

As a final test the student is required to identify the weak forms of 'a' and 'are' when used by a native speaker in a surreptitious set of minimal pairs. This exercise should teach him that in native speech only the context will tell you, in many cases, whether a native speaker actually meant to say 'are' or 'a'.

(x) *Dictation. Write down the following sentences.*

1 What a bore!

2 What are bores?

3 A unicorn is an animal.

4 Are you Cornish?

5 What are you so full of joy for?

6 What a useful exercise!

7 I'll introduce you to a friend of John's.

8 I see you are friends already.

(Each sentence is repeated twice. The student's dictation is then corrected and discussed by the teacher.)

3 Practical work

Extensive listening

Create or choose a set of 3 passages suitable for extensive listening practice for each level of proficiency (beginners, intermediate, advanced). Decide how these passages would be presented to the pupils.

Intensive listening

(i) Select or write passages for intensive listening practice on particular aspects of pronunciation, grammar and vocabulary, and construct exercises to accompany these.

(ii) Make suggestions for a course in comprehension of different varieties of language.

Speaking practice

Design a set of drills to practice a particular learning point, for instance the difference between 'like' and 'would like'. Some examples are given in Appendix I, p. 344.

4 Further reading

Dakin, J. *The Language Laboratory and Language Learning.* London: Longmans, 1973.

Hayes, A. S. *Language Laboratory Facilities.* London: Oxford University Press, 1968.

Nuttall, C. E. (ed.) *English Language Units.* London: Longmans, for the British Council, various dates, 1968–.

Stack, E. M. *The Language Laboratory and Modern Language Teaching.* New York: Oxford University Press, 1960. Published in Language and Language Learning Series, 1969.

Tatham, M. A. A. *English Structure Manipulation Drills.* London: Longmans, 1968.

Turner, J. D. *Programming for the Language Laboratory.* London: London University Press, 1968.

The following are some current courses specially designed to integrate the language laboratory with classroom work:

Abbs, B., Cook, V. and Underwood, M. *Realistic English.* London: Oxford University Press, 1968.

Dickinson, L. and Mackin, R. *Varieties of Spoken English.* London: Oxford University Press, 1969.

Howatt, A., Webb, J. and Knight, M. *A Modern Course in Business English.* London: Oxford University Press, 1967.

Mackin, R. *A Course in Spoken English: Texts, Drills and Tests.* London: Oxford University Press, 1967.

Mackin, R., Webb, J., Scott-Buccleuch, R. L. and McKean, I. R. W., *OPEAC Oral Drills, A, B, and C.* London: Oxford University Press, 1968.

Wakeman, A. *English Fast, 1 and 2.* London: Rupert Hart-Davis, 1967.

Answers to questions in Chapter 4

Page 100: *b* £173.60

Page 104: 1 Three (jacket, back, thanks).

      2 Nine (Henry, yes, breakfast, ready, yet, well, expect, egg, getting).

      3 Seven (Henry, ready, nearly, jacket, expect, quick, getting).

Page 104: *b Phrases with 'to'*
      I naturally drove to a garage
      I had to go to the doctor
      Phrases without 'to'
      I was driving home

I was just turning right
You have to drive west
Before you turn inland
Did you get home all right?
c rush, ran, jumped in, hurry, speed up, raced, tore.

Page 113: 4 What are you going to cook?
5 What are you going to write about?
6 What are you going to talk about?
7 What are you going to wear?

Page 117: 3 He's a butcher
4 She's a secretary
5 She's a nurse
6 He's a doctor
7 She's a traffic warden

5 Error Analysis

S. PIT CORDER

1 General discussion

1.1 Introduction

A learner of a language is progressively changing his language performance to bring it more into line with that of the native speaker. Instability
in the characteristics of his language is thus both to be expected and
desired. If, however, we could say 'stop' for a moment we could regard
the learner's language at that point as a peculiar 'dialect' of the target
language, differing in many crucial aspects from it and perhaps having
some characteristics of his mother tongue. It would possibly be simpler
and more regular, in the sense of being describable by fewer rules, and
probably impoverished, in the sense of not providing the means for
expressing all the messages the learner wished to convey or receive.
This peculiar dialect we shall call his transitional dialect or idiolect.
The fact that in most cases we cannot, on the basis of the limited data
available to us, provided by the learner at any moment in his learning
career, construct a 'grammar' of his language is neither here nor there.
It in no way invalidates the concept of the transitional dialect as a
language, that is, a means of communication however limited. As a
language it will be systematic and, in principle describable, provided we
have the means to interpret it, i.e. know the meaning of its sentences.
A learner's sentences may be deviant, ill-formed, incorrect or erroneous
only in the sense that they are not fully describable in the terms of the
grammar of his mother tongue or the target language. They are, however,
presumably 'well-formed' in terms of the grammar of his own transitional idiolect at that point in time. I shall, however, hereafter use the
term *erroneous* to mean either superficially deviant or inappropriate *in
terms of the target language grammar* as is the usual practice.

1.2 Mistakes, lapses, errors

Native speakers very frequently produce ill-formed utterances. By definition these cannot be the result of an imperfect knowledge of the language

or an imperfect competence. The characteristic of native speakers' errors is that when noticed by speaker or hearer they are usually readily correctable by the speaker. Such errors can be classified as transpositions or substitutions or additions of a speech sound or morpheme, word or complete phrase, or some sort of blend of these. Some ill-formed utterances appear to be false starts or restructurings of what the speaker wants to say. Native speakers' slips of the tongue or 'lapses' are a field of research at the present time since it is believed that they will yield important evidence about how utterances are planned and executed. This is part of the psycho-linguistic and neuro-linguistic research into language performance. Since many of these lapses seem to increase in frequency under conditions of stress, indecision and fatigue, it is to be presumed that the second language learner will demonstrate similar lapses in performance, where all these conditions are likely to be more pronounced. It may not always be easy to distinguish such lapses, slips and mistakes of performance from errors arising from an imperfect competence in the target language. They are, however, of no particular significance otherwise to the language teacher.

1.3 Breaches of the code and errors in the use of the code

If we regard a language as a code, a set of rules for generating syntactically, phonologically and semantically well-formed sentences, then a breach of the code, i.e. a use of wrong rules or a misuse of right rules may, but does not necessarily, result in superficially ill-formed sentences. As we have seen, native speakers do not normally commit such breaches. They may, however, commit errors in the use of the code. By this I mean that they may produce well-formed utterances which are contextually or situationally inappropriate. Linguistics is principally concerned with the nature of the rules of the code; it has not yet developed a well-articulated theory about the use of the code, that is, the relation between language and the world outside. While it is not difficult to identify, in general terms, failures in the use of the code, it is not yet possible to describe them rigorously. Errors of appropriateness may, however, be generally classified into *referential errors*, where the speaker uses a term with the intention of referring to some feature of the world to which it is conventionally inapplicable, i.e. when he calls a *hat* a *cap*; *register errors* where, for example, in a naval context, he refers to a naval *ship* as a *boat*; *social errors*, where he selects forms which are inappropriate to his social relations with his hearer, as when a pupil greets his teacher with: *Well, how are we to-day, old man?*; or *textual errors*, when the speaker does not select the structurally correct form to show the intended relation between two sentences in a discourse, as, for example, in answer to the question: *Who is the man over there? *John is.* This analysis of the typology of error gives us a four way division.

If native speakers make inappropriate use of the code in one or more of these ways, it is certain that learners will also do so. The problem is to what extent we should aim at achieving a native-like ability in this area of communicative competence. This is tied up with the problem of what the social role of a 'foreigner' is in any society. The most we can say is that referential and textual errors interfere most seriously with cognitive communication and require attention. Social and register errors are concerned with a different aspect of communication, e.g. interpersonal relations. Here a greater tolerance is clearly possible. We can summarize this section in this way:

A learner's utterance may be:

superficially well-formed	and	appropriate	erroneous[1] or correct
superficially well-formed	but	inappropriate	erroneous
superficially deviant	but as far as can be judged	appropriate	erroneous
superficially deviant	and as far as can be judged	inappropriate	erroneous

[1] See below for utterances which are 'right by chance'.

In what follows I shall be concerned wholly with what I have called 'breaches of the code' and not at all with 'misuse of the code'.

1.4 Receptive and expressive errors

The errors we most readily notice are those in expressive activity, the utterances of learners in meaningful discourse. But it is clear that errors of comprehension do also occur. These can obviously only be studied indirectly by inference from the learner's linguistic and non-linguistic responses to utterances in the target language, e.g. answers to questions, obedience to orders. The study of expressive performance offers the only direct source of information about the learner's transitional competence. It is generally assumed that a learner's receptive abilities always exceed his expressive abilities. It is difficult to know whether this is necessarily always the case since errors in comprehension will frequently pass unobserved. We can test comprehension in rather general terms, but it is very difficult to assign the cause of failures of comprehension to an inadequate knowledge, for example, of a particular syntactic feature of the misunderstood utterance.

1.5 The errors of groups and individuals

We teach groups but it is individuals who learn. For practical purposes it is the errors of groups which are of interest, since syllabuses and remedial procedures are designed for groups not individuals, and the nature of the errors made by the group are part of the data on which these are devised. However, the study of group errors may only be meaningful if the group is homogeneous, i.e. the members have the same mother tongue and are educationally, socially and intellectually matched. Since some part of the errors made by a learner have some relation to the nature of his mother tongue, a group of learners having different mother tongues will produce a more heterogeneous set of errors than a homogeneous group. This does not necessarily mean that there will be no errors common to the whole group (see below). What is generally of little value is a consolidated list of common errors made by the learners of a particular language whatever their mother tongues, and level of knowledge. The implication of such lists is that there a certain features of the target language which are inherently difficult, i.e. for all learners whatever their mother tongue, intelligence and social and cultural background. Linguistic studies do not support this view. All languages appear to be equally difficult. As proof of the theory of inherent difficulty, it is often put forward that native speakers of two genetically unrelated languages may make similar errors in learning a third language. This, however, could equally well be accounted for by the fact that in respect of one particular linguistic system (e.g. tense or number) the two unrelated languages are more similar to each other than they are to the target language. It is a fallacy to suppose that because languages are genetically related they must in all respects be more similar to each other than to some unrelated third language.

We study the errors of individuals for theoretical reasons. The study of error is part of the investigation of the process of language learning. In this respect it resembles methodologically the study of the acquisition of the mother tongue. It provides us with a picture of the linguistic development of a learner and may give us indications as to the learning strategies. In this respect, error analysis may prove to be one of the central activities in the psycholinguistic study of language learning. If we knew what the natural course of the development of a speaker of language A in the learning of language B was, then we would have some information of cardinal importance for the devising of linguistic syllabuses for teaching language B to speakers of language A.

1.6 The data for error analysis

We have already seen that error analysis is, perforce, largely confined to the study of expressive errors. These may be spoken or written. But from a practical point of view it is clearly easier to make a systematic study of written materials. However, we should be aware that different types of written material may produce a different distribution of error or a different set of error types. Written work produced by learners can be divided into spontaneous (free composition) production and controlled production (translations, précis, paraphrases, retelling of stories). The distinction here is between the learner selecting his own messages and processing already given messages. In the latter case there is also the problem of comprehension of the messages of the original texts. Furthermore, there is always a likelihood, in the latter case, that the learner's text will contain memorized or partly memorized passages. On the other hand, in spontaneous production the learner can deliberately avoid linguistic areas in which he feels uncertain. Like tests, controlled productive material is *error-provoking* whereas spontaneous production is *error-avoiding*.

1.7 Preliminaries to the analysis of errors

There are three stages in error analysis: recognition, description and explanation. These are logically dependent upon each other. Most teachers reckon they can recognize an error when it is committed. They may be wrong, since it is always possible that a well-formed and apparently appropriate utterance has been misinterpreted, i.e. the learner has not meant to say what he appears to say. *Recognition of error is thus crucially dependent upon correct interpretation of the learner's intentions.* Description can only begin when recognition has taken place. It is clear that for the purposes of error analysis a grammar which aims to relate the semantic structure of a sentence to its surface structure by a set of explicit rules is the most appropriate theoretical model for the description of error, since we wish in the process of correction to be able to show the learner in what way he has failed to realize his intended message (c.f. contrastive analysis). Explanation of error can be regarded as a linguistic problem, i.e., a statement of the way in which he has deviated from the realization rules of the target language in the derivation of his sentence, that is, what rules he has broken, substituted or disregarded. Or explanation can be regarded as a psycholinguistic problem, i.e., the reasons why he has broken, disregarded or ignored the rules of the target language.

1.8 Recognition of error

I have already suggested that an apparently well-formed utterance may nevertheless be erroneous. It may be right by chance. The learner may not know all the rules, yet, by random guessing, hit on a well-formed utterance. For example, if the learner did not know the rules for forming plurals, i.e. distinguishing between singular and plural forms of the noun, he might express his meaning correctly half the time. He might have learned a structure as a holophrase and produce it on the appropriate occasion and yet not know the rules for generating that structure. In what sense is such a structure right or wrong? On the other hand, a learner may produce an utterance which is well-formed and such as a native speaker would produce on some appropriate occasion, but which, when taken in its context is not plausibly interpretable at all. Such an utterance is clearly erroneous. It may be that at the other extreme the utterance is such that no native speaker would utter it in that or any context. Such utterances may or may not be plausibly interpretable. This would depend on their degree of incoherence. The apparent grammaticality or ungrammaticality of a learner's utterance is therefore of only partial relevance for error identification, since apparently well-formed utterances may be unsusceptible of plausible interpretation in their context, whilst fairly grossly ungrammatical utterances may readily receive plausible interpretation. Thus all learner's utterances must be presumed erroneous until shown to be otherwise (i.e. shown to mean what their surface structures could mean in the target language; could not would, since surface structures are ambiguous).

The recognition of error, then, depends crucially upon the analyst making a correct interpretation of the learner's intended meaning in the context. We can speak about the learner's utterances as being *overtly* erroneous (i.e. superficially deviant) or being *covertly* erroneous (superficially well-formed but not meaning what the learner intended to mean). The difficulty in identification of error is thus firmly put where it belongs, on interpretation. The problem is: how do we arrive at a knowledge of what the learner intended to say? If he is present we can question him (as we would a native speaker whom we did not understand properly), or ask him in his mother tongue to tell us what he meant to say (if we understand his mother tongue). By these means we can arrive at an *authoritative interpretation* and hence an *authoritative reconstruction* of his utterance, i.e. what a native speaker would have said to convey that message in that context.

When our data is written it may well be that we cannot consult the learner. In that case we must attempt to infer the meaning intended by the learner from the surface structure of his text-sentence in conjunction with the information derived from its context. Clearly, the level of confidence we can achieve in our interpretation is much lower. I shall call such interpretations *plausible interpretations* and the related reconstructions *plausible reconstructions*. The process of recognizing and identifying errors is then one of comparing original utterances with their plausible and authoritative constructions, and identifying the differences. This is the input to the next stage of error analysis. The process is one which experienced teachers perform almost automatically; it is, however, as I have tried to show, a complicated one and involves a number of logically related decisions which can be expressed in the form of an algorithm (see page 129).

1.9 Descriptions of error

The description of error is essentially a comparative process, the data being the original erroneous utterance and the reconstructed utterance. From here on the process is similar to that described in the chapter on Contrastive Analysis. The criteria for decisions as to the grammatical model to adopt are exactly the same. The fact that we may possess descriptions, according to various models, of the target language but of none of the learner's idiosyncratic dialect is irrelevant. Our object in error analysis is to explain error linguistically and psychologically in order to help the learner to learn. Consequently only that description which shows the respects in which the realization rules of the target language differ from those of the learner's dialect is of value. It is obvious that we cannot do this unless we have adequate data. In other words, a single instance of an error is insufficient to establish that there exists a regularity (i.e. a set of rules) in the learner's dialect. It may represent merely a lapse or a mistake or a guess. It is only when we observe the same error occurring regularly that we can begin to talk about the rules the learner appears to be following and attempt a description of his transitional dialect (or that of the class as a whole). It is on the basis of systematic errors that we construct syllabuses and remedial programmes.

Teachers will, of course, know that individual learners may be highly inconsistent in their errors; indeed, inconsistency is often apparently more characteristic of errors than systematicity. This fact requires explanation and will be dealt with in the last section.

1.10 The explanation of error

Whereas description of errors is largely a linguistic activity, explanation is the field of psycholinguistics. It is concerned with accounting for why and how errors come about.

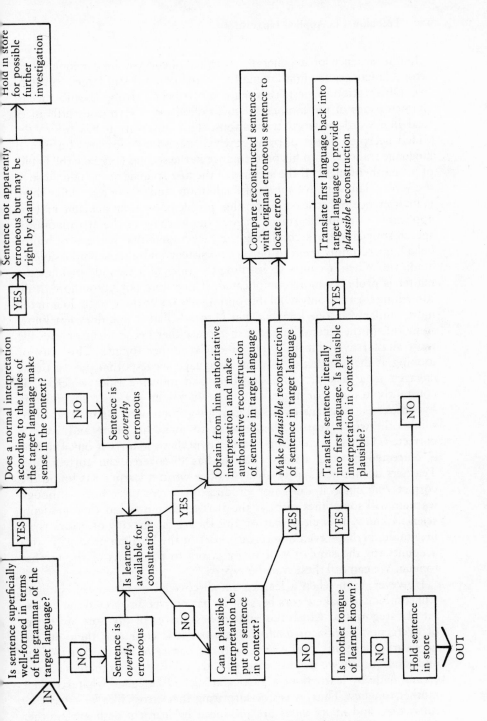

Figure 1: The process of recognizing and identifying errors.

In the absence of a generally accepted theory of how people learn second languages (or first languages), explanation is still largely speculative. Observation suggests that many errors bear a strong resemblance to characteristics of the mother tongue, indeed many erroneous utterances read like word-for-word translations. This observation has led to the widely accepted theory of transfer which states that a learner of a second language transfers into his performance in the second language the habits of his mother tongue. If the systems of the first language resemble those of the second language we speak of facilitation, and where they differ there is interference or, at least, a learning problem. Such an account may be applicable to motor learning, such as the learning of the articulation of speech sounds in the second language, where habitual patterns of motor behaviour certainly seem to be very persistent and almost impossible to eradicate. When it comes to learning the rules of a second language the matter is probably more complicated. If one does not know how to do something then the only available options are not to do it, or to do it in the most similar way one knows. That is to say that if one does not know some rule of the second language then one either keeps silent or uses the most similar available rule, i.e. of one's mother tongue. This way of looking at the learning of a second language suggests that the learner is engaged in a task of processing data and inducing rules which he is constantly testing for their validity. We might say that his starting hypothesis is: language two is like language one until I have reason to think otherwise; 'reason', here, being to make an error and have it corrected. He will then set up another hypothesis and try it out. Until he is corrected he will assume that he has discovered the correct rule. Teachers do not necessarily always notice when a learner has found the correct rule since it does not produce incorrect utterances, although learners will sometimes surprise the alert teacher by what they suddenly seem to know. It is clear that on this theory the making of errors is an inevitable, perhaps even a necessary, part of the learning process. It also accounts for the similarity of many errors to the forms of the mother tongue. We can call these *transfer errors*.

However, even when a learner has discovered a correct rule he may still continue to make errors because he has not yet discovered the precise set of categories to which the rule applies. Errors of this sort are errors of overgeneralization or *analogical errors*. It is clear that these do not necessarily have any connection with the nature of the mother tongue, and consequently we would expect to find (and we do) that there is a set of errors made by learners of a particular second language whatever their mother tongues. Thus, it is not surprising that errors like *he singed, he cans come* and *many mens* are produced by learners with any mother tongue. Analogical errors are inherent in the very learning process.

There is a third type of error which is much more difficult to establish in any particular case, namely, errors arising from the methods or materials used in the teaching. That such exist is now almost impossible to doubt. It is, however, not easy to identify such errors except in conjunction with a close study of the materials and teaching techniques to which the learner has been exposed. This is probably why so little is known about them. Only this class of error, *teaching-induced* error, is avoidable or redundant and represents inefficiency in the learning-teaching process.

1.11 Systematicity of error

It has already been noted that learners often appear inconsistent in their production of errors. They often seem to alternate between getting something wrong and getting it right. We may be able to distinguish three steps in learning as evidenced by the nature and degree of systematicity: (a) *the presystematic stage:* the learner is unaware of the existence of a particular system or rule in the target language. His errors are quite random. He may even occasionally produce a correct form. When asked to correct his sentence he cannot do so nor give any account of why he chose the particular form he did. (b) *The systematic stage:* his errors are regular. He has discovered and is operating a rule of some sort, but the wrong one. When asked to correct his error he cannot do so, but he can give some coherent account of the rule he is following. (c) *The postsystematic stage:* the learner produces correct forms but inconsistently. He has learned the rule but fails through lack of attention or lapse of memory to apply it consistently. This is the practice stage of learning a particular bit of the language. When asked to correct his error he can do so and give a more or less coherent account of the rule. Learners will, of course, be at different stages in respect of any particular system of the language, e.g. postsystematic in the number system, systematically erroneous in the use of articles and presystematic in the use of the perfective aspect.

2 Practical work

2.1 Exercise A: Spelling

The text[2] is the whole of a free composition by a native English-speaking child from a Glasgow school (Age 14½, I.Q. 73). Since she is a native speaker of a dialect of English, the only respect in which there may be

---

[2] Quoted by permission from H. Fraser, *Control and Create*. Longmans, 1967.

evidence of 'transfer' is in connection with her Glasgow accent and dialect forms. In the absence of any information about her social, educational or medical history it would be unwise to attempt any explanation of her spelling errors except insofar as they may relate to her pronunciation.

The interpretation we have was obtained from her teacher after consultation with the learner and is thus presumed to be authoritative, although there are signs that some degree of 'normalization' of her dialect forms may have been undertaken. Superficial inspection shows that the words of the text can, with one or two exceptions, be put into one-to-one correspondence with those of the reconstruction, and that her errors are therefore all at a phonological/graphological level, as one would expect in the case of a native speaker. The omission of one or two necessary words is probably no more than a mistake in writing.

The suggested procedure is to make a word by word comparison of text and reconstruction and to assign the differences found to one or another of a number of categories such as: omissions, errors of selection, sequence or orientation of letters. A single word may show more than one error and appear, therefore, in more than one list. The next step is to seek regularities within each category, e.g. whether any particular letters or sounds are particularly affected. One might notice, for instance, that the only consonant letter the learner doubles is 'l', and this incorrectly in three cases out of four.

We must remember that the pupil is learning the orthographic system of English. Where she has not already learned *the* correct spelling of a particular word as a unit (whether 'regular' in some sense, or not) she will adopt some sort of a strategy for arriving at *a* spelling. While it is clear that she shows some inconsistency (i.e. the same word spelled differently on two occasions), this does not mean that she has not some general strategy for writing words she has not yet learned to spell correctly. What does her strategy appear to be, and how successfully does she apply it? There are a number of items which she gets consistently right. Try listing these in order to see if they have any characteristics in common, grammatical, phonological or statistical.

The text

Last sumer in cevlinog parc I so a alsatian dog was wander adowt parc. After a we will is ran by me. I sat suday wot it was they tod me. That it was ruing adowt the parc for tow weset. They tod me that it eat rats. And exdud trid to cast her dut node did wen they trid to cash hur grow and smapt. Wum day they was a complad the dog. Utill the rangers can dut they were now psup. Utill they calld the plest they sjerst to pot dow a pet of met with a durg in the mit, then they put it dow. The dog eat the met and fate it went unconscious. And they toc the dog away and they adow the pust. and they pust were tanc to hormes. and the alsatian was tran for pelles dog.

Authoritative reconstruction

Last summer in Kelvingrove Park I saw an alsatian dog which was wandering about the park. After a wee while it ran by me. I asked somebody what it was: they told me that it was running about the park for two weeks. They told me that it ate rats. And everybody tried to catch her but nobody did; when they tried to catch her she growled and snapped. One day there was a complaint against the dog. Then the rangers came but there were now pups. Then they called the police. They suggested to put down a piece of meat with a drug in the meat; then they put it down. The dog ate the meat and after it went unconscious. And they took the dog away and they adopted the pups. And the pups were taken to homes. And the alsatian was trained for a police dog.

2.2 Exercise B: Syntax

The passages containing the errors are the answers to an examination question which required advanced learners of English of various nationalities to write a paragraph introducing the following words: *debt, blood, tribe, exact, tribute, parade, contempt, condemn, sworn, lance.* The errors we are to describe and account for are those connected with these items. These are what are often called 'errors of usage'. But what does this mean? Is it simply choosing the wrong word? A 'word' has semantic, syntactic and phonological properties. Errors of usage may be at any or all of these levels.

The first step in the analysis is to arrive, if possible, at some plausible reconstruction of those sentences in which the test item occurs. In some cases we may be in considerable doubt about the adequacy of the reconstruction; in others we may not be able to make any reconstruction at all. Reference to our knowledge of the mother-tongue of the learner may be helpful. The next step is to assign the 'error' to the level of syntax, semantics or phonology/graphology or to several levels at the same time. Where the error occurs at more than one level we usually have difficulty in making a plausible interpretation.

Given the particular situation in which these texts were produced we must bear in mind the possibility of errors of recognition of the test item caused by phonological/graphological similarity to some other item in the target language or even items in the mother-tongue, e.g. in text (*a*) *lanced* for *glanced* with a further source of confusion *lancer un coup d'œil* and text (*c*) *tribed* for *driven*, by confusion perhaps with German *treiben* (= to drive).

Assignment of the error to syntax or semantics normally presents no particular problem, but further description of the error necessarily requires an account of the 'correct' usage of the test items in English. For such an account we go to a dictionary. But is the information given in the dictionary adequate both syntactically and semantically? For example, just what is erroneous about the use of *exact* in text (c)? Is the dictionary classification of *exact* as an adjective sufficiently precise? Sometimes there is neither a clear syntactic nor semantic error and yet the item is inappropriate in the context in some way. Such errors of usage are 'stylistic' in the broadest sense and the inappropriateness of the use gives a feeling of 'foreignness' to the utterance. Here the dictionary is sometimes useful, as when it specifies the register, e.g. nautical, or style, e.g. vulgar, in which the item is used appropriately. In what way is the word *condemn* inappropriately used in such a sentence as: *The judge condemned him to pay a heavy fine?*

The texts

a When I looked into the debt of the valley I saw a man lying and blood all around him. I would have sworn I had seen that man before, I was so contempt and confused that I did not know what to do. Also I had to be back for the parade at the exact time. I lanced at my watch but it was condemned. The tribe of what I saw of the man was terrible to face so I hurried back to the tribute.   (French speaker)

b There was a parade before the king of an African tribe. The soldiers, every one with a shining lance, were sworn to tribute to the freedom of their country with the blood of their young bodies and to pay the debt for their fathers. To condemn aggression of the neighbour tribe was no time, but the wizard, in contempt, gave an explanation of the exact situation.
                                                                          (German speaker)

c Once a year we have a parade in our town, where the children dress up. Most of the little boys are Indians with blood-red patterns on their faces, nicely and exactly painted by their mothers. They swing lances and receive a lot of tribute. Last year something tribed the group of indians into debt of our garden and they robbed the apple trees and left bare branches but were contempted with themselves. My father on seeing them sworn to condemn them.   (German speaker)

d I paid the exact price of my condemn to the king of the tribe, now I only had to pay the tribute of blood and all my debts will be cancelled. My fight with the native warrior will last till the apparition of blood. I remembered I had sworn to fight again but the look of contempt I saw in the parade of natives gave me no other alternatives.   (Spanish speaker)

e The Indian tribe sworn to condemn the white people which had brought blood within the camp. The debt had to be paid and only another war could bring contempt within the population. To lance and war the indians had a good excuse as soon after a white man was seen hunting in their territories and the Indians started the war. The Indians won and they went on parade to pay tribute on the exact spot where they haf won the war and where their chief had died.   (Italian speaker)

2.3 Exercise C: Vocabulary

The passage is a story written by a 12-year-old Indian immigrant child after one year of primary school in England. She had no schooling before her arrival and was then illiterate. The spelling has been corrected but was, in fact, almost faultless. The object of the analysis in this case is to identify, and attempt a description and some explanation of the writer's almost exclusively syntactic errors. The mother-tongue of the learner was Punjabi, but it is not easy to relate the errors in most cases in any direct way to the mother-tongue.

Since the text is very short it is possible to follow the simple procedure of listing exhaustively (a) all noun phrases whatever their function in the sentence and (b) all predicate phrases. By grouping together similar structures, it will be possible to arrive at a complete statement of the limited surface forms the learner uses. Bearing in mind what the learner is trying to say (we have an authoritative interpretation) it will be found that she is inconsistent in her way of doing it. Different structures are assigned the same meaning, e.g. *said*, *is go* and *is sitting* all refer to the past; and the same structure is assigned different meanings, e.g. *the chair*, *a dinner*, *one man* all have unidentified reference. It is in the learner's use of determiners that some influence from her mother-tongue might be detected.

The most interesting problem is her frequent but inconsistent use of *a* within the verb phrase, e.g. *is a sitting*, *is a eat*, etc. This has no counterpart in her mother-tongue and the explanation must be sought elsewhere.

The passage

This is my story one man.
One man is go my home. He is sitting on the chair. He said: 'Very good chair.' I said: 'All right.' He is a fat. Chair is broken. He is a sitting on floor. I said: 'Your chair is a broken.' He said: 'Today is a very cold.' He is a eat a dinner. He broke the plate. I said: 'Your dinner is fall down and your plate is broken.' 'I'm very sorry.'

Authoritative reconstruction

This is my story (about) a certain man. A certain man went (to) my home. He sat on a chair. He said, 'A very good chair.' I said: 'All right.' He was fat. The (afore-mentioned) chair broke. He sat on the floor. I said: 'Your chair has broken.' He said, 'Today is very cold.' He ate some dinner. He broke the plate. I said: 'Your dinner has fallen down and your plate is broken.' 'I am very sorry.'

2.4 Exercise D: Comprehension

The passages are all summaries. The writers were required to 'give the plain meaning' of the passage quoted below in one sentence of not more than 30 words. We are therefore not dealing here with spontaneous expressive use of language, but a situation in which the learner has first to understand some language in an admittedly rather extreme journalistic style, and then reproduce it in a modified and drastically condensed form. There are therefore two possible types of error: receptive and productive. It might be thought that it would be difficult or indeed impossible to assign the resultant errors to failures in reception or production. However a study of the original passage shows that the underlying notions are not inherently complex ones and should not be difficult for an advanced learner to express in simple terms, if he has been able to extract them from the original text in the first place. The assumption upon which the analysis will be carried out then is that we are dealing principally with errors of comprehension.

The first step in this task is to produce a model summary of the original passage of the length specified. This then serves as the authoritative interpretation with which the learners' summaries are to be compared. Naturally we do not expect in this case to have any sort of word-by-word or phrase-by-phrase correspondence. What correspondence we expect may be at clause level and comparison is semantic in a general sense rather than syntactic.

Analysis of the model summary will show that it takes the form of a number of clauses standing in various logical relations to one another, e.g. coordinate: conjunctive, disjunctive; subordinate: conditional, concessive, etc.

The next step is to identify in these clauses the main semantic content points and their function in the clause, e.g. the content of the subject, object, main verb, etc. We thus obtain an account of the principal information items in the model reconstruction and the set of relations in which they stand to one another.

Similar 'content analyses' of the learners' summaries can then be attempted and the points of correspondence between them and the model reconstruction noted. This will give a general measure of the learners' comprehension of the whole passage and an identification of the points where errors of interpretation have taken place.

Apart from the stylistic difficulties of the original passage, it will probably be impossible to explain particular errors of comprehension.

Original passage

Ever since the telly came to claim pride of place in every parlour, prophets of doom have described the corruption of the soul and emasculation of the mind bound to result from exposure to the sights and sounds churned out by the networks. Youth has been named as the prime victim of the persuaders, although I for one, far from fearing for the mental welfare of the modern young, envy them their painless access to vivid information about the world in which they are growing up. I suspect that television, by preparing young minds for the vagaries of mankind, has made the business of cutting apron strings and launching into independence far less traumatic than it was when I was a girl.

Summaries attempted by the students

1 Youngsters of nowadays are victims of corruption and persuaders in the parlour of their own homes, through the television advertisements on propaganda programs preparing youngsters for the vagaries of mankind.

2 Youth, as the victim of education nowadays, tries to build up his own world.

3 The modern world is more accessible to youth. The means of communication such as T.V. or any others, have taught the young people things that they would surely know later, but without being so painful to them.

4 Prophets of doom have told that the networks caused mental corruption and youth has been considered the victim of the persuaders, but the influence of television seems to decrease.

5 Although supposed to be victim of the persuaders, the modern youth are well prepared to any information, specially by television, without fearing for their mental welfare, and get greater independence.

6 There will come an illiteral generation, which will do nothing but sing, and the television instead of leading them will teach them nothing more but to be unusual.

7 It is about the sights and sounds which we have them now in our modern life. Television is suspected for preparing young minds for the vagaries of mankind and independence.

8 Man in order to make publicity doesn't take into account the methods he uses and is damaging youth, although it is preparing it to go into the world.

9 Youth had been named as the most important victim of our society. By means of the television young people are getting idea of how the world is.

10 Since the telly came, prophets began describing the corruption of the soul, the youth their prime victims, and due to television there are less traumatic than it was before.

3 Discussion of exercises

3.1 Discussion of Exercise A

Errors fall into two primary areas: grammar and spelling. There are only seven grammatical 'errors': the omission of *which*, *the* and *she* in the first part, and *against* and *a* in the second; the use of *until* meaning *then*; the choice of tense and aspect in *they told me it was running about the park for two weeks.* The omissions might reasonably be regarded as slips of the pen, the last two 'errors' as dialectal forms. Spelling errors are far more numerous and far less easy to classify. There are two ways we can set about it: classifying the learner's spelling according to (a) how well it corresponds to her pronunciation or (b) how well it corresponds to the conventions of English spelling. To select one or other set of criteria is to prejudge how she is setting about learning English spelling. Therefore the categories we use for classification should include both criteria. Thus 'sound spellings' and 'unnecessary letters' are categories in which the criteria relate to her pronunciation whilst 'omissions', 'inversion' and 'letter shape', relate to the convention of spelling. One should also include a category of 'correct spellings'. It is an important principle in error analysis that what the learner gets right is just as important evidence about the systems and strategies of learning he is using as his errors. Since the same word may be an instance of more than one category (e.g. *suday* for *somebody*, a sound spelling and an omission) there is a good deal of cross-classification involved in the lists which follow:

Sound spellings	*Omissions*	*Inversion*
adowt	a (n)	ce*v*lin (kelvin)
sat (asked)	adow (pted)	*c*ast (catch)
cevlin	ca(t)sh	du*r*g (drug)
cash (catch)	compla(in)d	*f*ate (after)
cam (came)	dow(n)	ps*u*p (pups)
calld	exdud (everybody)	sat (asked)
hur (her)	g(r)o(ve)	to*w* (two)
met⎫(meat)	growl(ed)	tan*c* (taken)
mit⎭	no(bo)de	we*s*et (weeks)
node (nobody)	ru(nn)ing	
parc	su(mbo)day	*Letter shape*
pelles⎫(police)	sjerst(ed)	adowt (a*b*out)
ples⎭	to(l)d	can (ca*m*e)
pot (put)	tran(ed)	dut (*b*ut)
sumer	u(n)till	exdud (every*b*ody)
suday (somebody)	wander(ing)	pet (pie*c*e)
smapt		plest (poli*c*e)
sjerst (suggest)	*Unnecessary letters*	pust (pu*p*s)
so (saw)	hormes	s*m*apt (s*n*apped)
tod (told)		we*s*et (wee*k*s)
they (there)		wu*m* (o*n*e)
toc (took)		

Sound spellings

tanc (taken)
trid (tried)
wot (what)
we (wee)
will (while)
wum (one)

Correct forms

a	*it	were
*after	last	with
and	me	went
away	how	wander(ing)
by	*put	
call(ed)	ran	
dog	rats	
did	they	(* = also incorrectly spelled)
day	that	
for	then	
*her	the	
in	to	
I	was	

The 'systematicity' of the errors

The first column above reveals a general strategy of the pupil. When she cannot copy words from the blackboard (viz. unconscious, rangers, alsatian) and is unsure of the spelling, she spells them as she thinks she pronounces them. It is worth noting that nearly all her 'grammatical' words are correctly spelled, e.g. *a, the, it, for, with, to, and, that, in.* Presumably because of their high frequency she had learned them quicker, although they are not in general any more 'regular' in their sound-spelling relationship than other words. In her strategy of spelling words as she thinks she pronounces them, she appears to be highly consistent (exception: pups, police, catch, put).

Subject to these provisos, the rules she appears to be following are given below. One must always, however, when looking at them, remember that she speaks with some variety of a Glasgow, and not an R.P., accent.[3] The correspondences suggested below are therefore no more than tentative, since in this case we cannot observe the learner direct.

[3] For this reason the symbols used in this section have a different value from those used in the rest of the book.

(i) *Vowels*

Letters may represent either their 'name value' or some phonetically similar grouping of sounds

(a) *Name values*

'i' stands for /ʌi/and/ae/: will (while), trid (tried)
'e' stands for /i/: we (wee), plest (police), met (meat)
'a' stands for /e/: tanc (taken), tran (trained), can (came)
'o' stands for /o/: tod (told), cevlinog (Kelvingrove)

(b) *Phonemic value*

'i' stands for the front close vowels
/ɪ/: did, with, cevlinog (Kelvingrove)
/i/: mit (meat)

'e' stands for the front vowels
/ɛ/: wen (when), cevlinog (Kelvingrove)
/e/: node (nobody)

'a' stands for the open vowel
/a/: parc (park), sat (asked), smapt (snapped)

'o' stands for the back rounded vowels
/ɔ/: so (saw), wot (what)
/u/: toc (took), pot (put)

'u' stands for the central vowel
/ʌ/: sumer (summer), ruing (running), wum (one)
    also hur (her)

'ow' stands for the diphthong
/ʌu/: adowt (about), growl (growled), down

(ii) *Consonants*

'c' stands for /k/: calld (called), parc (park), complad (complained)
'w' stands for /w/ and /hw/: we (wee), will (while), wot (what)
although her speech probably distinguishes /w/ from /hw/

't' and 's':   it appears that when the sounds /s/ and /t/ occur in a cluster, they are regularly represented by 's' and 't' in the correct order: last, rats, sjerst, sat (/ɑst/ = asked). 's' is however also used to represent /ʃ/: cast (catch); and 't' is sometimes used to represent /p/: pust (pups), and /k/: weset (weeks). In such cases, the sounds of the plosive + fricative cluster are liable to be reversed.

'n' and 'm': The distinction is correctly observed in *initial* position: node (nobody), met (meat), but not always in *final* position: wum (one), can (came).

The simplicity of her strategy of sound spelling is confused by several performance factors, apart from the small element of inconsistency already noted.

1 The pupil does not seem to be able to cope with words of more than two syllables (except: Kelvingrove). These are reduced by omitting the endings, e.g. -ed, -ing (*trained, suggested, adopted, wandering* and also *growled*) or in one case by omitting an intermediate syllable (*everybody*). Note that *somebody* and *nobody* may be pronounced by her /sʌm(b)de/ and /nobde/. They may therefore be examples of her general strategy of sound spelling and not cases of inability to cope with words of more than two syllables.

2 She breaks her strategy of sound spelling in her doubling of the letter 'l'. She is evidently aware that this letter at least does occur doubled, but does not yet know where this occurs. No other consonant letters appear doubled.

3 She is uncertain of her left-to-right orientation in the case of the formation of 'b' and 'd' (the only letters which are mirror images in a vertical plane). She uses 'd' in all cases but one for 'b'. This is in one of the 'known' words. It is interesting however that the error is only in one direction, i.e. she never uses 'b' for 'd'. Whether this error arises from visual or auditory perceptual confusion is not clear from the data.

3.2 Discussion of Exercise B

Only certain of the test items have caused trouble of the sort which could fall under the general heading of 'errors of usage'. It is clear that phonological/graphological confusions of the sort *debt* for *depth*, *contempt* for *content*, *tribe* for *drive* and *tribute* for *tribune* are not matters of usage and are an artefact of the test situation: a failure of recognition of some sort. The interesting items are *contempt, condemn, exact* and *tribute*, where the learner has got some part of the meaning right. We can divide up meaning into syntactic and semantic. It is possible to use a word syntactically correctly but semantically wrongly and vice versa, or to use a word incorrectly both syntactically and semantically. If the latter is the case, it is often difficult to place a plausible interpretation upon the sentence in which this occurs, e.g. 'I was so *contempt*'. On the other hand where interpretation can be attempted, it will usually be found that the error is either semantic or syntactic but not both, e.g. 'My watch was *condemned*'. Here the failure is semantic only, since the sentence is superficially well formed but uninterpretable in the context. One would hazard that *condemned* means something like 'out of order'. Similarly where the failure is syntactic as in 'My father *sworn* to condemn them' there is usually no difficulty in interpreting the sentence plausibly. This task is an exercise in description and imposes on us the necessity of being able to give a full account of the correct way to use the test items.

We can now list the 'errors of usage' of each of these words in the various passages, together with an assignment of the error to syntax or semantics or both, and a plausible interpretation of the relevant part of the sentence. Following each analysis is an account of the standard usage of the word, i.e. the sort of information we should have in a dictionary in explicit form, but usually don't.

1 CONTEMPT

Text	Error	Plausible interpretation
a I was contempt and confused	syntactic/semantic	I was so put out and confused
b in contempt	semantic	?
c were contempted with themselves	syntactic/semantic	?
d The look of contempt I saw	semantic	?
e could bring contempt within the population	phonological confusion	bring contentment to the population

(a) *Standard dictionary entry*

contempt: noun   (i) act of despising; *hold, have, show contempt for someone*

               (ii) state of being despised; *bring, fall into contempt*

              (iii) disobedience (legal) *contempt of court*

(b) *Syntax*

Contempt is a suppletive nominalization of *despise*, i.e. it bears the same relation to *despise* as *detestation* does to *detest*.

e.g. John despises Bill ⇒ John's contempt for Bill

cf.   John detests Bill ⇒ John's detestation of Bill

Despise, from which *contempt* 'derives' is a member of that sub-category of verbs which require human subjects and human objects.

e.g. John despises Bill ⇒ John's contempt for Bill

*The table despises Bill ⇒ *The table's contempt for Bill

*John despises the table ⇒ *John's contempt for the table

Note also: John looked at Bill and despised Bill ⇒ John looked at Bill with contempt

*John looked at the table and despised it ⇒ *John looked at the table with contempt.

(c) *Semantic relations*

Synonyms: disdain, disrespect $\Big\}$ (for) Noun Phrase [+Human]
Antonyms: esteem, regard, respect

Superordinate terms: feeling (for), opinion (of), attitude (to)

2 CONDEMN

	Text	Error	Plausible interpretation
a	My watch was condemned	semantic	out of order
b	There was no time to condemn aggression	none	? This was not the time to condemn aggression
c	sworn to condemn them	semantic	? sworn to get them (arrested and) convicted
d	price of my condemn to the king	syntactic/ semantic	? price of my indemnity to the king
e	sworn to condemn the white people	semantic	? to take revenge on the white people

(a) *Standard dictionary entry*

condemn: transitive verb   (i) censure, blame, *condemn someone's behaviour*

(ii) doom, consign to some permanent fate, *condemn to prison, death*

(b) *Syntax*

Condemn requires a human subject and in quasi-legal contexts, a human object and usually an adverbial expressing reason or direction or both.

  e.g. condemn the cottage (to demolition)
  condemn the milk (for being sour)

(c) *Semantics*

Condemn occurs in what we can call quasi-legal and non-legal registers; it does not occur in legal registers, e.g.

  (i) *Quasi-legal* (fiction, religious, moral and anachronizing texts)
  try → judge → *condemn* to death/his fate/eternal punishment/do penance.

  In this register *condemn* will have a human object.

  (ii) *Non-legal*

$$\text{test/examine} \rightarrow \begin{cases} \text{judge} \\ \text{assess} \\ \text{evaluate} \end{cases} \begin{array}{l} \rightarrow \text{commend, praise} \\ \qquad\qquad\text{(for something)} \\ \rightarrow \textit{condemn}\text{, censure, blame} \end{array}$$

  In this register *condemn* may have a non-human object.

Note the equivalent *legal* usage, where *sentence* is the synonym of *condemn*.

$$\text{try} \rightarrow \text{verdict} \rightarrow \text{find} \begin{cases} \text{guilty} \\ \text{innocent} \end{cases} \rightarrow \begin{cases} \text{acquit} \\ \text{pass judgement} \\ \text{convict} \end{cases} \rightarrow \textit{sentence}$$

3 EXACT

	Text	Error	Plausible interpretation
a	at this exact time	syntactic	at the agreed time
b	explanation of the exact situation	syntactic	an exact explanation of the situation
c	exactly painted by them	semantic/ syntactic	carefully painted
d	I paid the exact price	syntactic	I paid the full price
e	the exact spot where	none	

(a) *Standard dictionary entry*

exact: adjective, precise, rigorous, accurate (said of sciences, measurements, description, reports, etc.)

(b) *Syntax*

(i) The dictionary entry only deals with one meaning of *exact*, i.e. its function as a gradable adjective, e.g. *very exact measurement, more exact information*. In this use it is paraphrasable by 'corresponding to the facts'. *Exact* as an adjective is used only as a predicate to nominalized sentence subjects.

e.g. He reported exactly ⇒ His report was exact ⇒ his exact report

(ii) *Exact* has however another function, which we can call 'anaphoric determiner intensifier'. This use is not mentioned in dictionaries, since it is a purely syntactic function. It resembles *own*, *very* syntactically.

e.g. The very day   *A very day   *The day was very
       His own mother   *An own mother   *His mother was own
       The exact sum   *An exact sum   *The sum was exact

(c) *Semantics*

The semantic function of *exact* is to intensify the equivalence between two terms.

e.g. The equivalence between £5 and the sum was exact.
       ⇒ The sum was exactly £5. ⇒ The exact sum was £5.

It therefore occurs only in sentences expressing equivalence or identity, usually in terms of some measurement, time, quantity, place.

e.g. The exact time is 3 p.m. ⇒ The time is exactly 3 p.m.
       *The soldiers arrived at the exact time.

This is ungrammatical since no notion of identity or equivalence is expressed or implied.

4 TRIBUTE

Text	Error	Plausible interpretation
a hurried back to the tribute	phonological ⎫ graphological ⎭ confusion	hurried back to the tribune
b sworn in to tribute to the freedom of their country	syntactic/semantic	to contribute to
c receive a lot of tribute	semantic/syntactic	a lot of contributions
d pay the tribute of blood	none	
e to pay tribute on the exact spot	syntactic/semantic	? to commemorate (their chief) ? to honour (their chief)

F

(a) *Standard dictionary entry*

tribute: noun　(i) money or obligation paid to king, chief, etc. by another in return for protection

(ii) thing done or said as mark of respect

(b) *Syntax*

Tribute is both a countable and uncountable noun.

e.g. The chief received a quantity of tribute from the conquered.
The pianist received many tributes from the audience.

The rule seems to be that *tribute* [uncountable] is confined to 'feudal' contexts and refers to concrete material while *tribute* [countable] is used in non-feudal contexts and refers to abstract things, i.e. respect, honour, praise. Thus in:

He received many tributes

He can only refer to a public figure or artist, whilst in

He received much tribute

He must refer to a feudal overlord. The distinction is neutralized in the fixed phrase (idiom) *to pay tribute to*. Thus

We paid tribute to him

is ambiguous as to possible referents for *him*, cf. *pay homage* where *homage* is neither countable nor uncountable.

*We paid much homage to him.
*We paid homages to him.

Pay tribute requires an explicit indirect object unless the context provides the information about the recipient.

3.3 Discussion of Exercise C[4]

Since the spelling has been corrected—there is one interesting 'sound' spelling of *fat* as *pat*—and there are no vocabulary mistakes, the errors in this passage are entirely grammatical or stylistic. The grammatical errors necessarily fall in one of two areas: development of the *noun phrase* or development of the *predicate phrase*.

(a) *The predicate phrase*

This assumes a variety of surface forms:

(i) is + (a) + Adjective = (is a fat, [is] sorry)
(ii) is + (a) + Past Participle = (is a broken, is broken)
(iii) is + (a) + Present Participle = (is a sitting, is sitting)

[4] The analysis is substantially that made by Julian Dakin.

(iv) is + (a) + Infinitive = (is a eat, is go)
 (v) Verb + Past + Sentence (I said . . .)
(vi) Verb + Past + Noun Phrase (broke the plate)

Leaving aside the question of the 'a' in some of these, all the various predicate constructions except (iv) are superficially grammatical: that is each form taken out of context is acceptable syntactically in English. But all these forms occur in a story about a series of events in the past. Only the direct speech refers to the present (e.g. to-day is very cold). The learner makes no systematic distinction between forms referring to different times. In other words she does not yet show a *tense* system in her language. This does not mean that she does not 'possess' the semantic categories of past and present time, only that she has not yet discovered how these are realized in English. She has a stock of miscellaneous verb phrase forms available between which she makes no systematic distinction. She is evidently at the presystematic stage in this respect. She selects randomly amongst available verb forms not yet having discovered any system at all. Some of her forms are right by chance, e.g. *said, broke.*

(b) *The noun phrase*

This displays a similar profusion of forms:

  (i) one + Noun = (one man)
 (ii) the + Noun = (the chair)
(iii) a + Noun = (a dinner)
 (iv) Possessive + Noun = (my home)
  (v) Ø + Noun = ((on) floor)

Out of context all these forms are acceptable. In context the first, third and fifth are ungrammatical, but merely to say this is to ignore the system which the pupil is following. 'One' denotes a particular individual about whom more is to be said. It is akin to the biblical '*a certain* man'. 'The' is used to mark the first mention of an object that will be talked about again (without benefit of determiner) in the course of the story. 'A' is an unhappy word about which more will be said below. Only the possessive adjective is being consistently used as it would be by a native speaker.

Explanation

The causes of the pupil's errors might be attributed to two factors:

(i) *Previous teaching:* her teacher had drilled her on and off for six months on the form of the present continuous tense. From the very beginning the pupil had wanted to talk (and write) about events in the past as well as in the present. Having only one tense form at her disposal, she readily applied it to both purposes and the result is an apparent confusion of tenses. I say 'apparent' because the pupil knows perfectly well whether she is talking about things in the past or things in the present, but the inadequacy of the material presented to her by the teacher has led her to set up the multi-purpose predicate forms (ii)–(iv). As we have seen these may all contain the indefinite article 'a' immediately after the word 'is'. This again is probably the result of misguided drilling, but see below.

(ii) *Mother-tongue influence:* There is no exact translation equivalent for the English articles in the pupil's mother tongue (Punjabi). There is, however, a word *ek* in Punjabi which is a translation of the English word *one* in some contexts, one of these being the first mention of some thing or person in a story, e.g., 'Once upon a time there was *a man . . .*' This may account for her opening sentence:

This is a my story one man.

But the pupil has noted the occurrence of 'a' and 'the' in the utterances and drills of the teacher. 'The' has been interpreted in the sense noted above. 'A' has received a much more peculiar interpretation. Presumably under the influence of drills like:

This is a book/box/pencil/, etc.

in which no article would be used in Punjabi, the pupil seems to have decided that 'a' is part of the verb *to be* and in particular that it follows 'is'. But she has also observed that it does not always do so, with the result that it sometimes occurs after 'is', and sometimes does not. 'is' and 'is a' are, in other words, free variants of the third person singular of the verb *to be*. The only other perceptible influence of the pupil's mother-tongue is in the narrative sentence 'Chair is broken'. This corresponds in content, but not in word order, to the normal past tense form in Punjabi. Thus this pupil, like the native child whose spelling was investigated above, displays a 'systematic confusion' in her writing. All or nearly all of the errors disappeared after six months, without any further drilling or any formal teaching of grammar.

3.4 Discussion of Exercise D

Précis involves interpreting a passage and then by a process of selection and transformation expressing the meaning of it. Our starting point in this case, then, is the 'authoritative interpretation'. We know what the learner ought to be trying to say. However, since précis involves both interpretation and expression, error may occur in either of these processes. Our suggested assumption is that the failures are mainly those of comprehension.

The first task, as always, is to identify error. Since here we are dealing with a 'discourse' it may be that while the learner can interpret all the parts, he may not be able to interpret the logical connections or relations between the parts. A study of the learners' attempts does, in fact, suggest that this does indeed happen (i.e. where learners succeed in interpreting *d, e* and *f* below, but not *a, b* or *c*).

The following is offered as a model summary of the original passage in 28 words:

Pessimists say that TV has always corrupted people, principally the young. On the contrary, TV informs young people about the world and may help them to become independent.

This can be further condensed into a list of the salient points:

Pessimists say—TV-always-corrupts-youth
But I (author) say (i) TV-informs-youth and (ii) TV-liberates-youth.

The 'logical structure' of the discourse can be drawn in the shape of an informal 'tree diagram' where Σ stands for 'macrosentence' or 'discourse'.

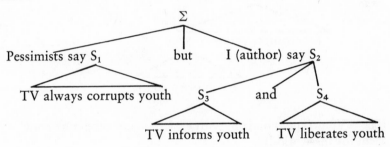

Adequate interpretation involves therefore comprehension of:

a Contrast: someone says S_1 *but* someone else says S_2
b Identification of Subjects of S_1 and S_2: Pessimists, I (author)
c Conjunction of S_3 *and* S_4
d S_1: TV—always—corrupts—youth
e S_3: TV—informs—youth
f S_4: TV—liberates—youth.

By analysing the structure and content of the passage in this way we have a means for identifying failures in comprehension (and perhaps expression) and a means for quantifying this failure. Thus we might give one point for recognizing that the basic structure embodies a contrast: 'Someone says something, but someone else says something else'; two points for identifying the subjects of the contrasting assertions; one point for the conjunction of S_3 and S_4; and ten points for identifying the main content elements of S_1, S_3 and S_4. The nominals may be realized as nouns, pronouns or zero ('TV informs youth and (it) may liberate them'). This gives us 14 points total.

Note that while a scheme of this sort might provide a technique for marking précis tests in an examination, as used here, it takes no account of the relative difficulty of interpretation of each point and is merely a way of checking whether certain elements and relations have been correctly interpreted.

Using this outline, let us now analyse some of the students' summaries.

1. Youngsters of nowadays are victims of corruption and persuaders in the parlour of their own homes, through the television advertisements on propaganda programs preparing youngsters for the vagaries of mankind.

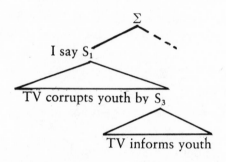

(i.e. 'TV corrupts youth by virtue of the very programs which prepare them for the world.')

a Contrast S_1 but S_2
b pessimists, author
c conjunction $S_3 + S_4$
d TV, always, corrupt, youth
e TV, inform, youth
f TV, liberate, youth

Score: 7

Although 'TV inform youth' is dominated by the wrong node and therefore incorrectly related to the rest of the sentence, we can give points for the correct identification of its basic element. This student, therefore, scores 7.

2. Youth, as the victim of education nowadays, tries to build up his own world.

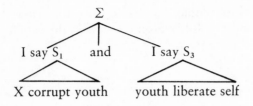

Σ

I say S_1 and   I say S_3

X corrupt youth   youth liberate self

a Contrast S_1 but S_2
b pessimists, author
c conjunction $S_3 + S_4$
d TV, always, corrupt, youth
e TV, inform, youth
f TV, liberate, youth

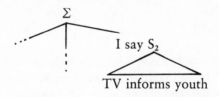

Score: 5

3. The modern world is more accessible to youth. The means of communication such as TV or any others, have taught the young people things that they would surely know later, but without being so painful to them.

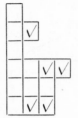

Σ

I say S_2

TV informs youth

The first sentence is not incorporated in the diagram because it does not constitute the first part of the required configuration 'somebody says something unfavourable about TV but I say something favourable'. Rather, the first sentence anticipates what is said in the second sentence ('I say something favourable').

a Contrast S_1 but S_2
b pessimists, author
c conjunction $S_3 + S_4$
d TV, always, corrupt, youth
e TV, inform, youth
f TV, liberate, youth

Score: 4

This student has 'but without being so painful to them' which corresponds to 'far less traumatic' in the original. If we want to give recognition for this, we can expand our outline to include [-shock] or [-shock/pain/hurt] under S_2, in which case the total score would be 5.

4. Prophets of doom have told that the networks caused mental corruption and youth has been considered the victim of the persuaders, but the influence of television seems to decrease.

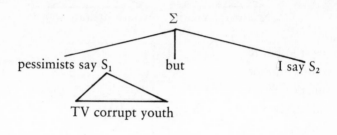

a Contrast S_1 but S_2	✓			
b pessimists, author	✓	✓		
c conjunction $S_3 + S_4$				
d TV, always, corrupt, youth	✓		✓	✓
e TV, inform, youth	✓			
f TV, liberate, youth				Score: 7

This summary seems to contain a large proportion of random copying. Are we justified in assuming that in the student's mind, 'prophets of doom' = pessimists and 'the networks' = TV? One mark was given for 'TV' under 'I say' because the subject is correct, even though the predicate is the opposite of what is required.

5. Although supposed to be victim of the persuaders, the modern youth are well prepared to any information, specially by television, without fearing for their mental welfare, and get greater independence.

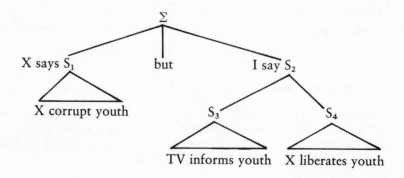

a Contrast S_1 but S_2
b pessimists, author
c conjunction $S_3 + S_4$
d TV, always, corrupt, youth
e TV, inform, youth
f TV, liberate, youth   Score: 10

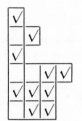

According to our analysis, this is a good interpretation, in spite of the clumsiness in production. 'Supposed to be' is analysed as 'someone (unspecified) says'. 'Persuaders' (copied from the text) is not accepted as a meaningful synonym for TV, and therefore 'X corrupt youth' is analysed as lacking the relevant subject.

6. There will come an illiteral generation, which will do nothing but sing, and the television instead of leading them will teach them nothing more but to be unusual.

(Interpretation: 'We will live to see a generation of illiterate people who will do nothing but sing (pop-songs?), and television instead of setting them a good example, will teach them nothing except how to be unconventional.')

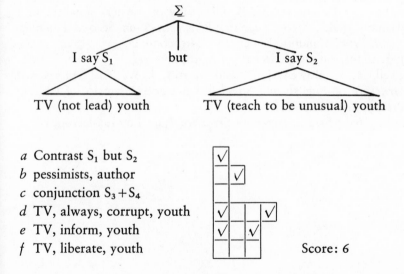

a Contrast S_1 but S_2
b pessimists, author
c conjunction $S_3 + S_4$
d TV, always, corrupt, youth
e TV, inform, youth
f TV, liberate, youth   Score: 6

Again, quite a good score for interpretation, in spite of some very odd features of production. We have not accepted 'not lead' as a substitute for 'corrupt' and we have given no marks for 'teach to be unusual'.

4 Further reading

Corder, S. P. The significance of learners' errors. *IRAL*, 1967, 4, 161–70.

Corder, S. P. Idiosyncratic dialects and error analysis. *IRAL*, 1971, 9, 147–59.

Corder, S. P. Describing the language learner's language. CILT Reports and Papers, 1972, 6, 57–64. London: Centre for Information on Language Teaching.

Corder, S. P. Die Rolle der Interpretation bei der Untersuchen von Schulfehlern. In G. Nickel (ed.), *Fehlerkunde*. Berlin: Cornelsen-Velhagen & Klasing, 1972.

Corder, S. P. The elicitation of interlanguage. Special Issue of *IRAL* on the occasion of Bertil Malmberg's sixtieth birthday, 1973.

Dušková, L. On sources of error in foreign language teaching. *IRAL*, 1969, 7, 11–36.

Nemser, W. Approximative systems of foreign language learners. *IJAL*, 1971, 9, 115–25.

Nickel, G. (ed.). *Fehlerkunde*. Berlin: Cornelsen-Velhagen & Klasing, 1972.

Richards, J. A non-contrastive approach to error analysis. *ELT*, 1971, 25, 204–19.

Richards, J. Error analysis and second language strategies. *Language Sciences*, 1971, 17, 12–22.

Richards, J. and Sampson, G. P. The study of learners' English. In J. Richards (ed.), *Error Analysis: Perspectives on Second Language Acquisition*. London: Longmans (forthcoming).

Selinker, L. Interlanguage. *IRAL*, 1972, 10, 209–31.

Stockwell, R. P., Bowen, J. D. and Martin, J. W. *The Grammatical Structure of English and Spanish*. Chicago: University of Chicago Press, 1965. Chapter II.

Svartvik, J. (ed.) *Errata: Papers in Error Analysis*. Lund: Gleerup, 1973.

6 Reading and Writing

ALAN DAVIES and H. G. WIDDOWSON

1 General discussion

1.1 Introduction

It is a commonplace these days that reading is an activity made up of a large number of skills of both a motor and a cognitive kind. Yet it is as well to bear in mind that for the reader, whether hesitant or fluent, what he is doing is engaging in a single co-ordinated activity. Its composite nature is something which he is no more aware of than is the taxi-driver of the composite nature of car-driving. The analysis of reading skills has been very detailed, but we seem to be a long way from understanding the manner in which different features of the skill relate to form one process. We have had a good deal of analysis but little synthesis.

The way in which people handle written language, whether receptively in reading or productively in writing, is extremely complex and as yet little understood. We make no claim in this chapter to resolve the complexity but merely attempt to bring certain points of this complexity into prominence. Nor do we attempt a comprehensive survey of the problem: our discussion will range over certain aspects of it which seem of particular importance.

1.2 The Reading Ability

In any educational situation there are three factors: the student, the teacher, and the materials. In such a situation, because learning is taking place, there is the fourth factor of time. For reading these four factors can be arranged in the following figure:[1]

		Student	Teaching	Materials
Time	A	Recognition	Initial	Literacy
	B	Structuring	Intermediate	Comprehension (a)
	C	Interpretation	Advanced	Comprehension (b)

[1] The figure is a development of an idea discussed by Dakin (1969).

On the assumption of three arbitrary stages of time (A, B, C), we can fill in the gaps as in the above figure. The student must first (Stage 1) *recognize* written characters for what they are. Venezky (1967) has further subdivided this single stage into three skills, those of a task (the student must be aware of what it is he is about—he isn't drawing pictures), of relating oral language to the printed page (i.e. that there is a systematic connection between the student's own speech and the written language), and of decoding (he must be able to connect the written symbols to what they stand for). This decoding skill takes us on to Stage 2, that of *structuring*. As well as recognizing the written characters (as visual symbols, representing language sounds) the student must combine them to make first words and then sentences. Then, in addition to recognizing and structuring the student must control the third stage, that of *interpretation*. If we wish we may relate these three stages to three linguistic levels, recognition to the phonological, structuring to the syntactic and interpretation to the semantic. There is a good deal of overlap in the linguistic levels; the threefold division is for purposes of analysis and has no necessary psychological reality. Similarly the three stages in the reading process are not discrete; there is overlap here too. What is more, they are not necessarily sequential. Little is known about the actual strategies the learner employs; as we shall see our lack of knowledge about the learning process causes us to impose various taxonomies which vary according to what we think it is like and, as usual, we are influenced in our approach to reading by our psychological or linguistic allegiances. Our lack of knowledge also causes great controversy about the right method of teaching reading to beginners.

And so we come on to column 2 in our figure, the teaching column. We shall consider the controversy about method in our discussion on initial reading. Here we wish only to indicate that while, of course, initial teaching must cope with all three stages of the student, the most important one is that of recognition. Intermediate teaching has passed the recognition stage and can concentrate on the structuring stage (while again moving where necessary into interpretation). Advanced teaching, therefore, can concentrate on interpretation (though there will always be residual problems of recognition; thus we all meet new words for the first time, e.g. *prosoma*, where we may need to shunt right down to the recognition stage); similarly, there are residual problems of structuring, as when we meet an ambiguous sentence (e.g. *He ran through his lines*) where we may need to shunt back to the structuring stage in order to disambiguate at the syntactic level.

Our third column deals with materials: these are normally designed to match columns 1 and 2. Thus what we have called literacy materials are intended for initial teaching at the recognition stage. They will also do some structuring and some interpretation. Comprehension (a) materials are designed for intermediate teaching at the structuring stage and comprehension (b) materials for advanced teaching at the interpretation stage. We further distinguish comprehension (a) and (b) into comprehension in general and speed reading. As Carroll (1964) points out it is only among advanced readers that the positive correlation between comprehension and speed reading ceases to be significant. Among intermediate students speed is artificially held back because of their slowness in general comprehension.

The third column considers materials from the point of view of purpose. We could add a fourth column to subdivide the content of materials. Thus we would have in the A slot, very familiar; in the B slot, familiar; and in the C slot, unfamiliar. Once again there is overlap between times and stages. To the learner very familiar materials will be those from his spoken language environment (family, home, etc.); Familiar materials will have to do with experience that is new (e.g. school) or available only through the written language (stories, the class reader, arithmetic). Unfamiliar materials he will simply not touch. In modern class readers it is usual to provide the learner with saturation in content that comes from the very familiar category. At the other end of the scale, the advanced reader still has all three types of material to cope with. As far as the present writers are concerned, examples of very familiar materials would be letters from home and detective stories (all of which can be skimmed rapidly); familiar materials would be the customary daily newspaper and professional reading matter (which are, as it were, read at the 'normal' rate); unfamiliar materials would be a legal document, e.g., a will or contract, or the reading matter of some other profession (all of which will certainly be read slowly and with uncertain comprehension; and may need expert help to be fully understood.

Three recurrent themes are heard again and again in the recent literature on reading. They will come up again in our present discussion but it is as well to note them here prominently. The first is that the learner, child or student, has to realize the *nature of the reading task*. We are not ourselves clear enough about it to give him an analysis which will be of much help. The best we can do is to provide certain definitions such as: '[reading is] the activity of reconstructing ... a reasonable spoken message from a printed text, and making meaning responses to the reconstructed message that would parallel those that would be made to the spoken message' (Carroll 1964, p. 62), or: 'reading is translating from written symbols to a form of language to which the person already can attach meaning' (Venezky 1968, p. 17). We can point out that the reader's job is to obtain meaning from print, that it is connected with speaking, that it is a cognitive task, and so on. But whatever we can do and however inadequately we are able to do it, the fact is that the learner has to see for himself what it is he is about; and the question to which he seeks the answer may be 'what is it for?' rather than 'what is it made up of?'.

The second theme is concerned with *different types of reading material*. In learning to read it is essential that the learner should realize that he must read different kinds of material at different rates and with different amounts of attention. Otherwise he will always remain at the intermediate stage, always reading everything as if it were new to him in structure. He must learn to follow Bacon's advice and read at different speeds and for different purposes. Reading is, in this, quite unlike other types of learning (except those which are partly parasitic on reading, e.g., playing a musical instrument, knitting) where learning involves overall increase in speed of response up to a plateau and then maintenance of that speed. Thus an experienced pilot controls his instruments at speed but he does not manipulate them differentially according to the terrain of the ground he is flying over, except in emergencies. The fact that he flies at different speeds is irrelevant here.

The third theme is *our ignorance about learning itself*. We know a great deal about the materials and rather less about the teacher; but of the child or student we know almost nothing. Whatever the teaching method, whatever the materials, and whatever the link between them, some 85 per cent of children learn to read. It is sometimes suggested (e.g., Dakin 1969) that they learn in spite of the teaching and materials. But some 15 per cent do not succeed in learning to read. At different periods we tend to blame the child for failure (he is backward, he suffers from specific developmental dyslexia, he comes from an inadequate home), or the teacher (she is not trained) or the materials (they are not well enough grounded linguistically; or they are too much so). It is clear however that a combination of factors is at work, and in different combination for each child. We need to focus more attention on the individual learner and less on the sometimes bizarre explanations about where the difficulty really lies. Young teachers in training need to be taught how to observe their children as well as how to teach them.

1.3 Initial reading

There seems to be agreement that the key to progress in reading comes at the initial reading stage. This is not a very clear argument to maintain because the initial reading stage is as long or as short as one wishes to make it. The argument is therefore self-justifying, in the sense that anyone who has not made progress can be said not to have mastered the initial reading stage. What is really being argued here is that the key which a beginner must find at the initial stage is the ability and interest to work on his own. Initial reading is therefore an attempt to get a child working on his own.

As with all learning there are many factors influencing the child at the initial reading stage. The method of teaching reading may be the key for some children; the medium in which reading is presented (e.g., the alphabet) may be the chief factor for some; a child's teacher may be the main influence on his development; or the child may be suffering from some sort of reading retardation. The last of these—reading retardation, sometimes called specific reading retardation or dyslexia—is very much in dispute and its opponents reckon that it has been invented simply to explain reading failure since everyone agrees that none of the other factors, alone or in combination, provides sufficient explanation.

Given our general ignorance of how learning to read proceeds we are forced to manipulate those factors which we can control. We shall not discuss the medium here; this has been brought into prominence recently through the i.t.a. experiments (see for example Downing 1967). As far as the method is concerned we can examine it from two points of view.

Materials may be controlled *linguistically* or *situationally*, that is, they may be structured according to one of the following criteria:

Linguistic   *a* Alphabetic
              b Phonemic
              c Syntactic

Situational   *a* Whole word   }
               b Whole sentence } 'Look and Say'

Of these the alphabetic, the whole word and the whole sentence are the most widely used methods and between them there is contention. In practice most teaching seems to employ a mixture of methods. Let us briefly consider all five in turn:

Alphabetic: This is not a complete method in itself, though advocated by Bloomfield (Bloomfield and Barnhart 1961). Learners are to be taught the names of the letters and then pronounce the words. This method is usually used in conjunction with one of the others.

Phonemic: The learner is taught to associate the sounds (phonemes) of English with letters or groups of letters. The general belief in the irregularity of the grapheme-phoneme (letter-sound) correspondence has recently been challenged (e.g., Chomsky and Halle 1968). The learner then 'sounds out' the sequence of letters, but because of lack of correspondence it does not always work; however, whatever other strategy the learner may employ he undoubtedly makes use of this phonics strategy as part of his general method. Recent discussion (e.g., Venezky 1967) suggests that if we really knew more about the underlying correspondences between

sounds and letters then we would be in a better position to teach beginners. Wardhaugh (1969) has pointed out that the beginner is troubled by
superficial not underlying irregularity. There is linguistic evidence that
the correspondence is not as irregular as is popularly believed. The
teacher's problem is really how to establish the notion of this correspondence in the first place (Stott 1964).

Syntactic: In opposition to Venezky, Bever (1968) has argued that what
matters are the higher-order syntactic constituents, and though he does
not explicitly say so, it appears that he selects these units on linguistic
rather than situational grounds. Approached linguistically this raises the
problem of just what constitutes syntactic difficulty or complexity, a
problem which Carroll (1964) suggests may be determined by some kind
of transformation count, or operationally by a cloze procedure test. The
situational approach we return to below. In either case there is serious
dispute over procedural questions. Once the student has acquired the
various skills, passed through the various stages, which are generally
agreed on, and has become an intermediate or even an advanced reader,
does he still make use, in however accelerated a form, of the strategies
that he used as a beginner? Hochberg raises this question: 'Reading
skills are acquired in stages, and the techniques and coding procedures and
strategies that are appropriate to one stage are not necessarily used in—
and might even be hindrances at—the later stages' (Hochberg 1968,
p. 84).

Whole word and whole sentence: Since sentences may consist of one
word (e.g. 'Look!' or a proper name) we shall treat these two methods
together. The notion in normal life is that the learner sees and hears
stretches of speech as wholes ('Kids talk in sentences, not single words
and single sounds. Therefore, it seems quite reasonable to predict that
they would learn to read in sentences somewhat more effectively than to
read in individual sounds') (Bever 1968, p. 19). We should, then, as Bever
says, use in a situational approach graded words and sentences. Just as the
'phonics' method has to face the problem of irregularity, so the 'Look and
Say' method has the problem of a multiplicity of rules. No doubt we may
assume that frequent display of the same sentence type (e.g., *John sees
the ball*) may lead to the discovery of a syntactic rule—though since we
are teaching reading not grammar it is difficult to see why this is important. Since the learner is, in any case, only going to meet acceptable
sentences in his reading material the rationale behind this method must
be motivational, i.e., that meaning is more accessible in longer than in
shorter segments, and, since situational grading places it within his
experience, the learner can interpret what he sees and respond to it
readily.

However, with all these methods there remains an unanswered

question, perhaps the most important one: granted that all these methods 'work', (there is sufficient evidence that any method works with most children) the child is forced in all of them at some point to take off on his own, he must proceed by generalization from what he knows to what he does not. Here the linguistic, especially the 'phonics', method is more plausible, because on the basis of what it can teach, the child can generalize, not the whole way, but quite a long way, in order to deal with new words. The situational methods, on the other hand, appear to lead less easily to generalization. There are, of course, morphological regularities which may be generalized (e.g., -*ing*, -*ly*) but these are only of partial help. Quite soon the child is faced with making a guess at a new word. This may be easier than we are making it out to be, because guessing within a known context and a known environment is not so difficult when the material is situationally graded. Any adult who has tried learning a new language which also involves a strange alphabet will know the difficulty of mastering the characters when, in a text, he has no idea what the subject and context are. So it may be that a situationally well-graded reader will allow for and admit of guessing and even facilitate it.

1.4 Intermediate and advanced reading

1.4.1 LANGUAGE SYSTEM AND COMMUNICATION

The problems of initial reading are predominantly those which relate to the levels of recognition and structuring in our representation of the reading process. When the learner begins to learn to read, he has already acquired some degree of competence in the language. In the case of the first language learner, this competence may be quite extensive; in the case of the second language learner it may be very limited. In both cases the competence has developed and is used exclusively through the reception and production of language in its spoken mode. In the early stages, learning to read is very largely a matter of transferring an already acquired competence into a different mode of performance.

Once the initial stage is over and the transfer effected to the extent that the learner's competence can begin to develop within the new medium without reference to speech, somewhat different problems arise. These problems have to do with the fact that written language is not simply a different physical realization of the abstract language system, marks on paper instead of sounds in the air, but is also different in the function it is required to fulfil as a means of communication.

The understanding of language, in either its spoken or its written modes, requires a knowledge of the language system, or competence in the sense of Chomsky and his associates, and a knowledge of the manner in which the system is used for the purposes of communication. The second kind of knowledge, which in recent linguistic discussion has been called communicative competence (Hymes 1970, Lyons 1972) enables the language user to recognize what linguistic elements count as when they are produced in an act of communication. When we speak of someone's 'knowing a language', what we usually mean, in fact, is that he can produce and receive correct linguistic forms in accordance with the rules of combination which constitute the language system, and that he can associate these forms with communicative or rhetorical functions in a way which is recognized as appropriate by the conventions of social usage.

A piece of language, then, is not merely an exemplification of the rules of the language system; essentially it is a use of these rules in the performance of some kind of communicative act. Many of the difficulties which face the language learner at the more advanced stage of reading have to do with the fact that the communicative acts fulfilled by written language do not have exact counterparts to those fulfilled by spoken language.

In the second language situation there is an additional difficulty. Whereas the first language learner has acquired communicative competence in spoken language, the second language learner usually has very little experience of the communicative functioning of language in the spoken mode, insofar as the language being learnt is concerned. He knows how his own language is used in the business of living, but not how the target language is used. It is true that current approaches to second language teaching insist on the importance of speaking, and that oral drills, dialogues, and so on, are widely used to provide practice in the spoken mode. But these are almost always designed to exercise the learner's knowledge of the language system. It is difficult to imagine how a naturally communicative use of speech could possibly be reproduced in classroom conditions, and no matter how realistic and stimulating contrived speech situations are, the learners still recognize them as contrivances, and know perfectly well that they are not using language in normal social communication. How, then, do second language learners ever acquire communicative competence in speech? The answer is that they usually do not acquire it at all. Given the type of learning situation where students rarely, if ever, meet native speakers of the target language, it is difficult to imagine how the students could acquire communicative competence in the spoken mode. On the other hand, whereas it is well nigh impossible to recreate ordinary spoken communication in the classroom, it is easy to provide examples of ordinary written communication. There is a strong case for the teaching of communicative competence through written language since, generally speaking, in second language teaching it is only through the written mode that the way language actually functions as communication can be satisfactorily demonstrated.

1.4.2 THE SOCIAL PURPOSE OF WRITTEN LANGUAGE

Both linguists and language teachers agree in considering spoken language as primary. One of its claims to primacy is that it is used more than written language and has a wider range of functions. We may accept that speaking is a more common activity than writing, and listening to speech more common than reading, but this kind of quantitative statement is not particularly helpful. What we need is some kind of qualitative assessment of the different kinds of function that the two forms of language fulfil.

The first point to make is that the two forms of language are not in free variation. That is, we are seldom faced with a choice between using one or the other. It is true that with the invention of the telephone we may either write someone a note or give them a ring, but in general it is true to say that the situations which call for speaking are not the same as those which call for writing. In short, the two media of communication fulfil different social functions.

What, then, are the kinds of situations which require written language? We may say that they are those situations in which the addressee is not accessible to speech. There are two reasons for inaccessibility: in the first place the addressee may be physically absent and in the second place the writer may not know exactly who the addressee actually is. It is the first situation which calls for personal correspondence and which nowadays provides us with an alternative in the telephone conversation. We know perfectly well who our distant interlocutor is and so our personal writing is closest in function to speech. In the second situation, however, things are rather different. We are further from the speech situation because the addresser does not know who exactly he is addressing. He may know him as a member of a social group, as the filler of a role, as a personage, but not as an individual. We will call the kind of written language which is produced in response to a situation where the addressee is simply absent *personal communication*, and that which is produced in response to a situation where the addressee is both absent and unknown *institutional communication* since its principal purpose is to maintain contact within and between social institutions—economic, administrative, legal and so on. In the present paper we shall be principally concerned with institutional rather than personal communication.

1.4.3 FEATURES OF SPOKEN LANGUAGE

What are those features of written language which derive from the fact that the addressee is absent? Let us approach this question by considering the nature of the normal speech situation.

In spoken communication we rely on two phenomena which complement the actual utterance of language items to a degree that is perhaps not always fully appreciated. To begin with, the actual phonetic realization of language elements is only one component of face-to-face communication. In addition to purely verbal elements, we have non-verbal or paralinguistic elements like 'tone of voice' and gesture. For example, an utterance which can only be represented graphologically as:

He is going

may be spoken in such a way as to carry implications of irony, relief, impatience and so on, and may function as a prediction, a promise, an appeal and so on. The structure itself is neutral as to these different interpretations: it must be provided with some additional paralinguistic feature, an element of what Abercrombie calls 'voice dynamics' (Abercrombie 1967), before it can count as communication.

The first phenomenon associated with speaking, then, is the use of paralinguistic features like voice dynamics and gesture. The second is feedback. In a speech situation there is a constant interchange between the participants, each playing the role of speaker in turn. What the speaker says is controlled by the reactions of the listener expressed either by linguistic or by paralinguistic means, either by what the other says, or by the non-linguistic sounds he makes, or by his gestures and facial expressions. The reactions of the listener provide feedback to the speaker who modifies what he says, and the manner in which he says it, accordingly. In communication by speech there are always two participants actively involved, each monitoring the other.

1.4.4 FEATURES OF WRITTEN LANGUAGE

Whereas in speech the actual realization of linguistic elements is only one component, and by no means always the most important component, of the communication, in written language almost the whole burden of the communication falls on linguistic elements. 'Almost', because there are certain graphological devices which fulfil something of the function of the paralinguistic elements in speech—punctuation, underlining, capitalization and so on—but compared to the resources available to spoken language they are very few, and very limited in communicative capacity. Written language has, therefore, to make use of the language system in such a way as to compensate for the absence of the variety of paralinguistic elements available in speech situations. At the same time, it has to compensate for the fact that the communication is one-sided. There is no interlocutor to tell the writer how well, if at all, he is getting his meaning across. We must consider what devices are used to compensate for these deprivations.

The question then, is: how, in writing, can the language user indicate just how he wishes the linguistic elements he uses to be taken as items of communication? Since, as we have said, the devices must be almost entirely linguistic, they are also, of course, available to speech, and are used in speech for added explicitness; but because of the presence of paralinguistic elements, they do not play such an essential role as they do in writing.

The principal purpose of the paralinguistic elements in speaking is to express the speaker's attitude either to what he is saying or to whom he is saying it: their function is essentially a modal one. In writing, this function has to be fulfilled by linguistic signals. These, therefore, carry more information than they do in speech, and in consequence they tend to be chosen with more precision. One such signal is the modal verb, but this is not the only, nor often the most common means of indicating how a given sentence is to be taken. There are in fact a wide range of modal devices and it is characteristic of writing that it makes use of this range more extensively than does speech. Consider the following:

It may be too late.

The modality expressed here by the modal verb *may* can be expressed by means of the adverb *possibly*:

It is possibly too late.

If one wishes to emphasize the possibility in speech, one would normally stress the modal verb to produce the following utterance:

It *may* be too late.

This device is denied to the written form. (The use of underlining, or italics, is a reflection in writing of the spoken form, and may not always be appropriate.) The alternative is to re-arrange word order to produce something like:

Possibly it is too late

or to select a different surface form, which introduces the modal element in a structure which is separate from that which contains the main propositional content:

It is possible that it is too late.

This type of structure is very common in certain kinds of writing, its function being to make modality explicit while at the same time avoiding reference to the writer himself, such reference being of course unavoidable when modal verbs are used. Expressions like It *is possible that* . . . It *is likely that* . . . It *is necessary that* . . . It *is certain that* . . . and so on may, then, be regarded as explicit modal devices which compensate for the absence of paralinguistic elements in writing.

Let us now consider the second phenomenon of the speech-situation which arises from the active participation of the addressee: feedback. How does writing compensate for its absence? The problem is far less acute in personal communication than in institutional communication, since in the former the writer is familiar with the addressee, his ideas and attitudes and so on, and therefore knows what may be presupposed, and how his communication will be received. In the case of institutional communication, on the other hand, the writer cannot be certain of the knowledge, ideas, attitudes and presuppositions of his addressee. Consequently, in written language of an institutional type we tend to find devices which ensure that the reader is not mistaken about what is being discussed. Hence business letters begin: *With reference to your letter . . .* and within the letters themselves there are constant pointers to what precisely is being discussed: *regarding your proposal . . . in respect of your account . . .* and so on. These expressions are simply used to single out and identify the point to be discussed. University textbooks, again, are frequently broken up into chapters and sections and sub-sections of sections, each of which is given a heading. This serves as an identifying label for the topic to be discussed. Very often the introduction of the topic concentrates on defining terms: initial sentences have a 'metalingual' function of this kind because the writer must be assured that his reader knows what he intends the vocabulary to refer to. This is the reason why so many textbooks begin by giving information which is already familiar to the majority of their readers: the writer must be certain that he can rely on a foundation knowledge before he proceeds. Another way of providing for the absence of feedback is to introduce redundancy in the form of summaries and statements of intention within the body of the text. Thus expressions like *in short, in brief,* and others are signals that a summary is to follow; and expressions like *We may say, then . . . we may conclude by stating . . . in conclusion . . .* are signals that the writer is about to conclude an argument. The function of the following is simply to prepare the reader for what is to follow, to open up the channel of communication, as it were:

> First we shall discuss X, and then consider what implications this has for Y. Finally we shall discuss Z.

The fact, then, that the person or persons to whom a writer addresses his communication is absent and usually unknown results in the use of a wide range of linguistic devices which function in ways other than that of merely communicating information content. We may recognize at least the following functions: the *modal function*, which serves to indicate the writer's attitude towards what he is saying; the *metalingual function*, which serves to define exactly what it is that the writer means his terms to refer to; and the *contact function*, which serves to keep the channel of communication open, to maintain contact with the reader. All three functions play an important part in written communication and reading comprehension depends on the reader recognizing them, just as writing ability depends on the writer being able to control them appropriately.

An efficient reader is adept at recognizing what linguistic elements count as, that is to say what function they fulfil, because he is schooled in the conventions which associate certain linguistic forms with certain communicative functions. The learner at the intermediate and advanced levels of reading has to develop this knowledge of conventions also. In addition to his linguistic competence, in other words, he must acquire the necessary communicative competence. Reading comprehension cannot take place unless the reader understands the meaning of the linguistic forms and the communicative function they fulfil in the text concerned.

1.5 Reading comprehension

In this section we shall be concerned with two related questions: firstly, what it is that we do when we fully comprehend written communication; secondly, how can we develop the ability to do this in the language learner?

A complete answer to the first question would yield a satisfactory theory of reading comprehension, and a complete answer to the second question would provide us with a definite set of pedagogic procedures related to the theory. We are, of course, nowhere near such complete answers: they may, indeed, represent unattainable goals. All that we can hope to do in this section is to suggest some of the factors which appear to be involved in comprehension, and some ways in which these might be accounted for in comprehension exercises.

We shall proceed pragmatically by considering what kinds of comprehension question are most commonly asked and by trying to work out what assumptions lie behind their devising. We shall then give an informal assessment of their adequacy in the light of our discussion on the nature of written communication in the previous section.

1.5.1 TYPES OF COMPREHENSION QUESTION

The questions which are appended to reading texts are devised by reference to some set of assumptions and beliefs, no matter how unconsciously held, and no matter how incapable, or reluctant, the deviser may be of giving them a precise formulation. It is part of the business of applied linguistics to establish the principles which underlie the preparation of teaching materials, so our concern here will be to bring such assumptions and beliefs into the light so that they may be assessed. If we do not thereby resolve any issues, we might at least clarify some.

On p. 157 a distinction was made between 'comprehension in general' and 'speed reading'. We shall focus our attention on the former since it would seem to be the case that speed develops as a function of general comprehension. If, as has been suggested, rapid reading can be developed without loss of understanding or decrease in information intake, then it would seem possible that it involves increasing the speed and efficiency of a process already acquired as general comprehension, and not the development of a new process altogether. This may be said to be borne out by the fact that one can recognize two kinds of speed in reading: speed alone, that is to say how fast you can read anything, and rate; that is to say what your speed is for different kinds of reading material. This suggests that speed relates to the familiarity of the material which is being read and consequently to ease of interpretation. Certainly, in reading speed tests, like the following, we are measuring not only speed but general comprehension as well (indeed it is difficult to see how we could possibly measure speed in any meaningful way without taking comprehension into account).

Test: Read the following passage in one minute, underlining the inserted words:

The length of he time taken is to simple perceive a simple and shape is related to former its size and brightness containing

It may be, of course, that one relaxes the comprehension requirement in the interest of greater speed, but in general it seems reasonable to assume that speed develops from efficient comprehension in the sense that it is a speeding up of an already acquired process. It is this process which we wish to examine in this section.

We will make a rough division of types of comprehension question into four categories which we will call *direct reference, inference, supposition,* and *evaluation.* This is not intended as an exhaustive classification, but a large number of common kinds of question fall into these categories.

(a) *Direct reference*

What we have in mind here are questions which only require of the reader that he recover information directly from the text as an almost automatic procedure. All he needs to do is to refer to that part of the passage to which the question naturally directs him. Consider the following short passage:

Apes get around mainly by swinging with their arms, not by climbing with all four limbs. This made it possible for their hind-limbs to become differentiated as supporting feet. Finally it was necessary for the apes to descend from the trees.

(Julian Huxley: *Evolution in Action,* Penguin 1963, p. 131)

A direct reference question on this passage would be:

What was it finally necessary for apes to do?

This is the simplest kind of direct reference question and its value is, of course, limited. In fact, it does not really relate to comprehension at all, so far as the passage itself is concerned, since all that is required of the reader is that he understand the question, and then look for the sentence which corresponds to it. Direct reference questions of this kind, then, relate to sentences and not to the use to which sentences are put to communicate information.

Essentially, therefore, a direct reference question makes use of the text simply as an exemplification of the language system. It can be answered without the reader needing to recognize how the system is being used. Not all direct reference questions need be as automatic as this. If, for example, a passage refers to somebody wearing a red tie, a direct reference question might be:

What colour was X's tie?

To which the answer would be:

Red.

Again, all the reader needs to know is the relationship between 'colour' and 'red' and this he knows by virtue of his knowledge of the language system. The text is, in a sense, irrelevant.

It would appear, then, that direct reference questions do not so much exercise comprehension as competence in Chomsky's sense. They are therefore related to questions of the following kind:

The word 'rapid' in line 12 means:

a angry   *b* quick   *c* frightened   *d* proud

Questions of this kind can often be answered without reference to the text at all and there may be no need to refer to the line in which the word appears.

(b) *Inference*

Whereas the direct reference question takes the sentence as its limit (the sentence being the largest unit of grammatical description) the inference question is directed towards the discovery of the relationship between sentences and the manner in which they combine in communication. It is concerned with smaller units also, but whereas the direct reference question relates items in the text to their types in the system of the language, the inference question relates items in the text with other items in the text.

An inference question on the passage by Huxley quoted above would be:

How did the ape's hind-limbs come to be used as feet?

In order to answer this question, the reader has to consider how the statement represented by the first sentence in the passage is related to that represented by the second. This relation is mediated by the pronoun 'this', the meaning of which cannot be derived from the language system but only from the context in which it appears. The reader must understand that 'this' refers to 'the fact that apes get around mainly by swinging with their arms not by climbing with all four limbs'.

Inference questions may require the reader to relate two items of language in juxtaposition or two items which are widely separate from each other in the text. The principle remains the same: comprehension occurs when the reader relates the meaning of a language item as an element in the code or system—let us call this the *signification* of the item—to the meaning it acquires by virtue of its being contextualized in a stretch of meaningful discourse—let us call this the *value* of the item.

Inference questions may be very simple. Corresponding to the direct reference question on the meaning of the word 'rapid', for instance, we may have something like the following:

The word 'light' in line 15 means:

a not heavy   *b* not dark   *c* to switch on   *d* a lamp

Here, the meaning can only be discovered by the reader referring to the line mentioned in the text, and he is required to select that meaning which is syntactically and semantically consistent with the context in which the word appears. In the case of homonyms like 'light', 'bank' and so on, the reader has simply to select from a number of code significations that one which corresponds to contextual value. But the task of relating signification and value may not be so easy. When confronted with expressions like 'a light drink' or 'a light meal', or 'a light laugh', or 'a light footstep', the reader has to infer meaning by selecting from one of the significations of the code element 'light' those semantic features which are being set in prominence, that is to say which are being provided with particular value in the context.

The problem of the interpretation of metaphorical expressions comes up for consideration here. When confronted, for example, with expressions like 'an angry sea' or 'the wild wind', the reader has to reconcile the signification of the adjectives, which he will have learnt, let us suppose, in association with words relating to animate objects like 'man' and 'animal' and so on, with the value which is bestowed upon them by virtue of their association with the inanimate nouns 'sea' and 'wind'.

It may be objected that in normal circumstances signification, deriving from the language code, and value, deriving from the context of occurrence, coincide, so that there is usually no interpretation problem. This, however, seems not to be the case. In fact, it would seem to be true that what is abnormal is for language items *not* to be modified in some way by the context. The modification is not, of course, always as obvious as in the case of 'figurative' or 'metaphorical' expressions, though it is worth pointing out that such expressions are far more common than is often realized. We tend to think of them as abnormal and so to be ignored in our language teaching. In fact, what would be abnormal would be an absence of such expressions, and to leave them out of our teaching is in some degree to cut our pupils off from normal language. 'Figurative' or 'metaphorical' language is only a more obvious instance of the modification of code significance by contextual value which is a natural feature of all language use.

So far we have been considering the mutual modification of language items in juxtaposition. Items may, however, be related in different parts of the text. If the passage by Huxley already quoted had run as follows, for example:

Apes get around mainly by swinging with their arms, not by climbing with all four limbs. These animals . . .

the signification and value of the words 'arms' and 'limbs' coincide. In both cases the former is a hyponym of the latter. Consider, however, the relationship in the text of 'apes' and 'animals'. Whereas in the code we have the same relationship of hyponymy between them as between 'arms' and 'limbs', in this context 'animals' is simply a lexical substitution for 'apes' and so has the value of an anaphoric reference. We may say that the signification relationship between 'apes' and 'animals' is one of hyponymy, whereas the value relationship is one of synonymy.

Establishing the value of particular lexical items in context is especially troublesome when the reader has no obvious signification relationship to guide him. Consider the following extract:

Alloys are made by mixing two metals together in the molten state. If the ingredients are copper and zinc, the alloy produced is brass.

The value of the word 'ingredients' here derives from the fact that it refers to the metals mentioned in the first sentence. But although we may say that these two words have the value of synonymy in the text, they do not have the signification of synonymy in the code.

In view of what appears to be involved when the reader infers meaning from context, it would seem reasonable to suggest that the traditional kind of comprehension question illustrated on p. 170:

How did the ape's hind-limbs come to be used, as feet?

might be supplemented by others which develop an awareness in the reader of the devices which are used to signal meaning.

The purpose of comprehension questions, it will be generally agreed, is to develop in the language learner the ability to comprehend *texts*, not to guide him to a comprehension of *a text*. The difficulty is that many comprehension questions are not so much exercises to direct the reader towards a comprehension strategy as tests of whether he has understood a particular text or not. In the case of the question we have cited above, for example, if the reader has understood the passage, he will be able to give an answer. If he has not understood the passage, he will not be able to give an answer, or he may hazard a guess and give an incorrect answer. The question is a test if the text is too difficult for the reader. The belief seems to be that the language learner will gradually learn how to comprehend by being exposed to questions of this kind. This may or may not be true, but at all events it does not seem a very satisfactory approach to the teaching of comprehension.

There seems to be a case, then, for the devising of questions which, as well as being within the reader's grasp, direct his attention to the relationship between language items which give them contextual value, thus leading him to adjust his knowledge of the language system according to how the system is used in actual discourse. Questions of a traditional kind tend to focus on the connection between the content and the manner in which it is expressed. We are not suggesting that tests are extralinguistic and questions intralinguistic; they may, of course, be both. The basic difference between a test and a question is that the test discriminates among readers, the question does not.

What kind of questions might be devised to draw the reader's attention to the way the language system is actually operating in communication? First of all it may be noted that there is no reason why reading comprehension exercises should be always associated with the traditional 'text plus questions' format. If one wished to draw attention to the anaphoric value of lexical items like 'animal', for instance, one might begin by getting the learner to insert a number of items into appropriate spaces:

animals, apes, limbs, arms.
. . . get around by swinging with their . . ., not by climbing with all four . . . These . . . have gradually acquired etc.

This is a simple example, but it is easy to see how the same principle would work with more elaborate passages.

One might train learners to scrutinize texts closely for contextual clues by providing them with alternative words, only one of which has the semantic features which make it an appropriate insertion in a given incomplete passage. For example:

1 It is impossible to carry out experiments in the laboratory without voltmeters, ammeters and other measuring . . .

a tools   *b* machines   *c* instruments   *d* gadgets

2 . . . like the French Revolution and the American Civil War had a powerful effect on the course of history in Europe.

a rebellions   *b* wars   *c* actions   *d* events

These are just two simple examples of a type of exercise which can, of course, be varied in the demands it makes on the learner. Passages may be lengthened, alternatives may range from those among which only one is possible at all, to a set of near synonyms from among which one is more stylistically appropriate than the others. At a later stage, learners could be provided not only with alternative words and phrases but with alternative sentences.

Exercises of this type can be adapted for difficulty, and directed towards instructing the learner in elementary sense relations at one end of the scale, or towards developing in him a sense of stylistic appropriateness at the other. One other advantage of this type of exercise is that its problem-solving character is likely to engage the interest of the learner. This is, of course, of particular importance when one is teaching people whose general level of cognitive ability is not congruous with elementary language teaching procedures.

The purpose of the kind of exercise which we have been discussing is, then, to develop in the reader an awareness of how language items are related in texts in the hope that this will lead him to adopt a sort of 'inferential strategy' when reading, which he will be able to bring to bear on any material he is confronted with. The aim is to get him primed to look for relations, and to get into the way of accumulating semantic clues on the basis of which he may set up his own expectations as to how the text is likely to develop.

The two remaining types of comprehension question which we are reviewing here may be dealt with more briefly. They differ from inference questions in that they require the reader to go outside the text for an answer, to relate what is said in the text to a wider 'context of knowledge'. They typically involve the reader in making some judgement or other about the implication or relevance of what is said.

(c) *Supposition*

What we call here supposition questions are those which require the reader to say what he supposes is implied by certain language items. It is not always easy to distinguish between questions of this type and inference questions. Perhaps we may say that whereas inference questions are contextual and are directed at getting the reader to relate parts of the text, supposition questions are situational and are directed at getting the reader to relate the text to the wider situation of communication. They tend to get the reader to make suppositions of what exactly is intended by certain phrases and this sends him outside the text, to the writer, or to his own knowledge of the world.

A supposition question on the Huxley extract might be something like:

Why does the writer say that it was necessary for the apes to descend from trees?

Although it may not be clear from the extract given, Huxley's theme is the evolution of man from apes. Assuming the reader to know this, he will suppose that it is necessary for the apes to descend from trees in order for them to serve as an evolutionary stage towards man the upright, two-footed animal. At any rate, the purpose of the question is to draw out such a supposition.

Supposition questions are necessary because writers do not always say exactly and fully what they mean. Most writers are not fully explicit, and to understand what a passage really means, the reader has often to supply what is left to be 'understood' from his own knowledge of the world, or his knowledge of the conventions of communication which the writer is using. Writers presuppose shared knowledge of this kind, but the foreign learner often finds himself in difficulties because such knowledge is very often culture dependent, and he does not share it. For example, consider this extract:

Arthur carefully closed all the windows in the kitchen, locked the door, and turned on the gas in the oven.

A first language English reader will have no difficulty here in recognizing a suicide attempt because what is described is a fairly well-known and well-established procedure for suicide in our particular culture. The reader from a different culture, however (one, let us say, that has quite different suicide procedures) is likely to miss the point of Arthur's actions, no matter how well he may know the language. He may well understand perfectly what is said without at all understanding what is implied.

Questions dealing with the writer's 'attitude' might be said to come under this category of supposition. One frequently comes across questions which begin something like:

What is the author's attitude to . . .?

Do you think the author believes so and so/sympathizes with so and so?

The limitation of such questions is the same as that which we have noted when talking about inference type questions. They are tests rather than exercises and do not focus the reader's attention on the devices in the text which indicate what the answer should be. We are concerned, of course, with what we have called in Section 4 the modal function, the use made of language to indicate what the writer thinks or feels about what he is saying. What seems to be needed is a kind of question which will draw the reader's attention to elements of language which carry modality: modal verbs like *may*, adverbs like *possibly, perhaps*, modal phrases like *it may be the case that* . . ., *it is possible that* . . . and so on.

(d) Evaluation

This kind of comprehension is probably only suitable for learners who have already acquired a high degree of sophistication in the language. It typically requires the reader to assess the value of the reading passage and the effectiveness of the way the information in it has been organized and expressed. Questions of this kind can, properly formulated, lead on to literary appreciation, and perhaps provide a way of relating the teaching of language and the teaching of literature in a meaningful way. An investigation of such a relation, and the part that evaluation questions can play in it, is much needed, but outside the scope of the present chapter.

1.5.2 COMPREHENSION AND COMMUNICATIVE COMPETENCE

We have reviewed certain common types of comprehension question and have suggested ways in which they might be developed. The most general criticism that has been made is that existing questions do not sufficiently draw the reader's attention to the way the language is actually operating in context. The most striking omission is a kind of exercise which makes the reader aware of what communicative or rhetorical functions are fulfilled by the sentences in the text. As we pointed out in Section 4, efficient reading depends on communicative competence: the ability to recognize what linguistic forms actually count as in communication. Learners sometimes get tested on whether or not they have grasped modal function in comprehension questions of the supposition type, but this is hardly enough to develop in them a knowledge of the conventions which associate certain linguistic forms with certain modal functions. Metalingual and contact functions are generally completely ignored.

Comprehension questions usually make demands on the reader's ability to separate out essential propositional content without guiding him to recognize those signals which indicate where it is to be found and how it is to be taken. The first task of comprehension exercises would, however, seem to be to get the learner acquainted with the different devices which indicate what communicative functions are being fulfilled by linguistic elements in a given text.

We might begin at an elementary level by getting the learner to recognize obvious indicators of contact function like *In this section we shall first discuss x, then y, then z . . ., To summarize . . ., We may conclude by . . .*, etc. We might draw their attention to those indicators which make explicit what kind of 'rhetorical acts' sentences are meant to count as, like *We define this as . . ., These may be classified as follows . . ., For example . . .*, and so on. One possible exercise might be to ask learners to alter certain statements by deleting such overt indicators, to convert

We define an alloy as a mixture of two metals in the molten state

to

An alloy is a mixture of two metals in the molten state.

Following on from this one might then introduce an exercise which required the learners to do the reverse: to insert overt indicators into given statements. For example:

Metallic materials may be ferrous or non-ferrous.
Metallic materials may be classified as ferrous or non-ferrous.
We classify metallic materials as ferrous and non-ferrous.

We might then proceed to less obvious indicators: *if* indicating that what is to follow is an example, *however* indicating a qualification on what has previously been said, *therefore* indicating a deduction from a previous statement, and so on.

Two principal points have been made in this discussion on comprehension. Firstly, language learners must be taught in some way how to relate the language they have learnt as elements in a language system to the language as it appears in actual discourse, to develop a strategy which involves recognizing the value of language items in context. Secondly, they must somehow acquire those conventions of communication which associate linguistic forms with communicative function. Briefly, they must learn how sentences become utterances and how utterances are used as statements. One of the difficulties which language learners have is to establish the correspondence between these three manifestations of language. Most language teaching concentrates, sometimes exclusively, on the first of them and in consequence the language learner never gets to the point of really comprehending written communication at all.

1.6 Simplified Readers

What we want to do in this section is to consider how simplified readers contribute to the development of the reading ability. Such readers are very widely used and their popularity and value are very widely attested.

Historically, simplified readers derive from an investigation into reading made by Michael West in the 1930s. He outlines the purpose of such readers as follows:

It (the simplified reader) gives extra practice in reading; it reviews and fixes the vocabulary already learned, it 'stretches' that vocabulary so that the learner is enabled to give a greater width of meaning to the words already learned; and lastly, by showing the learner that what he has learned so far really enables him to do something, it encourages him to read matter which is worth reading.

(West 1950)

It is clear from this that the simplified reader is intended not only to reflect what the reader already knows, but to extend this knowledge. It follows that the procedure of simplification involves a compromise between:

a making a given text easier to understand by bringing its contents within the area of language already assumed to be known

b allowing the inclusion of some language items not already known but whose meaning is, presumably, recoverable from the context.

It is clear that the simplification procedure is based on assumptions as to what is involved in reading comprehension. One simplifies in the light of what one understands will be difficult for the learners. On the other hand, if one includes language items which are not already known, one makes assumptions about what controls the ability to infer meaning from context.

The purpose of simplified texts, then, at least according to West, is to practise and develop reading comprehension. What we have to do is to investigate how simplifiers set about doing this, to discover what principles, if any, lie behind their procedures. The exercise on simplification (2.2) is intended to encourage such an enquiry, and the discussion (3.2), partial though it is, is intended to suggest how the evidence might be assessed.

1.7 The teaching of writing

It has often been remarked that writing is the most difficult of the language abilities to acquire. It is less often that any explanation has been offered as to why this should be so.

Let us first consider the different stages of writing. In 1.2 we suggested a division of the reading process into three stages: recognition, structuring and interpretation. We may distinguish three corresponding stages in the production of written language:

Reception	*Production*
Recognition	Manipulation
Structuring	Structuring
Interpretation	Communication

G

We may now proceed to ask: at what stage does writing become difficult? It seems unlikely that it is at the first stage. Second language learners whose first language employs a different writing system will have difficulty manipulating the shapes of English letters and, if the first language system is right-to-left or top-to-bottom, they will have difficulty with the left-to-right ordering of English, but this will only be at the initial stage of learning. With second language learners whose first language makes use of roman script there will, of course, be no difficulty at the manipulative stage at all.

It seems more likely that difficulties occur at the structuring stage, and this appears to be the most common assumption, judging by the number of books that are available on composition at the sentence level. The difficulty with this assumption is that intensive pattern practice and structural drills do not seem to make it much easier for the learner to write anything except sentence patterns. Furthermore, there seems no reason why, given proficiency at the manipulation stage, structuring should be any more difficult in writing than in speech. Yet the failure of many children to learn to write efficiently in their own language is attested by almost every examiner's report, although presumably these children have no difficulty structuring their speech.

It would seem that the real difficulty associated with writing is to be traced to the communication stage, and here we come upon the problem which we have already touched upon. The circumstances in which written communication takes place, and the social purposes which it serves, are not the same as those of spoken communication. And for the language learner this difference between the two modes of communication is crucial.

As already pointed out, one cannot simply say that writing is written speech. There may be some justification for such an assumption from a narrow linguistic point of view, but if language is considered in terms of social communication it makes no sense at all. Writing is a social activity of a rather specialist and restricted kind, and to learn to write is to learn a kind of social behaviour.

What kind of social activity is writing? Perhaps the first thing to note is that it is a reasonably rare one. Most people do little or no writing. The people who do write do so as part of their professional activity. When one considers the matter, most writing is of what we have called the institutional kind. Lawyers, journalists, educators, businessmen and civil servants are regular writers, and bricklayers, bus-drivers, factory-workers and electricians are not. Writing, then, is the activity of the minority, the professional people who write because their professions oblige them to do so as an essential part of their job, and who write in conformity with conventions which belong to their normal professional routines.

Writing is a normal social activity for the professional minority, who produce institutional writing, and for a small number of people who produce the occasional personal writing. For a very large section of society, it is not normal for children to write. It is not for them a natural means of social interaction, any more than it is for the majority of their parents. Speaking is part of the child's world: he does it naturally and without prompting. Once having learnt the mechanics of reading, that too may become part of this world and a natural thing to do. But writing seldom enters naturally into his world.

When we attempt to get children to write at the level of communication, what we are trying to train them to do is something which cannot possibly have any natural social use for them. We are trying to get them to do something which only adult professional people do in the normal run of their everyday activities. But let us notice that the institutional writing which professional people produce is by its nature circumscribed by conventions which serve as a guide to how the writing is to be done. When children, or adults for that matter, are asked to write an 'essay' or pretend to write a letter to a friend, or an account of some incident or other, they have to provide an addressee of their own out of their heads, and find for themselves the kind of social stance which it is appropriate to take with their imagined addressee. Some language learners do, of course, acquire this ability to set up a communication situation (very often based on the conventional educator-student situation such as is found in their text books), but most do not. Most language learners find it very difficult to assume an addressee (even when they are told who to assume) and to persuade themselves that they are engaging in some kind of meaningful social act when everything points to the fact that they are not. The professional writer does not have this difficulty. Institutional writing is usually addressed to roles rather than to persons and is usually conventionalized, in the sense that there is a set of well-established conventions as to how things should be expressed. These conventions represent partially stereotyped routines. In the case of language learners trying to communicate something in a social void there are no such conventions to turn to. There are no recognized routines which can provide a meaningful framework for the kind of essays that they are generally called upon to write.

One possible way of making writing meaningful to the learner is to create a kind of short-circuit communication situation by having him talk to himself, as it were, on paper. A good deal of success has been achieved by taking this approach (generally known as 'creative writing') which encourages the writer to express himself, his own thoughts, ideas, feelings and so on. Although this approach would seem to provide writing with a place in the learner's world which it does not normally have, it has two limitations.

First of all, the kind of writing which results is naturally of a personal kind, but not like the personal writing one would expect in private correspondence. It is, in fact, literature: a form of language use which has no 'practical' social function. Almost all of the examples given to show the effectiveness of the creative writing approach are prose poems and free verse. The question is whether this kind of writing can ultimately lead the learner to produce writing which does have a normal social function. Put another way, does the ability to write poetry lead in any way to an ability to write business letters, reports, applications and so on? Creative writing clearly has a broad educational function in that it helps to develop the child's confidence and to realize his imaginative potential, but it has yet to be shown that it necessarily leads him to an ability to use written language in the ways in which it is normally used. Does the ability to use language in one very specialized form of communication lead to an ability to use language in other forms of communication? If it does, one can accept creative writing as a valuable means while rejecting its value as an end in itself. If it does not, one must assume that such an approach, while making a contribution to general education, has no vocational value whatever.

The second limitation is that the creative writing approach is restricted to first language teaching. The point of the approach is that it makes the learner aware of the ways he can use written language as a natural expression of his personal perceptions, feelings, thoughts and so on. In the case of second language learners, of course, it is the learners' native language which will naturally fulfil such a function: to use the second language would create the kind of artificiality which it is the whole purpose of the creative writing approach to avoid.

In view of these limitations, we might suggest that an alternative approach might be taken which takes into account the two requirements of the teaching of writing which have been stressed in the foregoing discussion:

1 It must in some way make writing a part of the learner's world. It must be a meaningful personal activity.

2 It must in some way relate to the normal social function of written language. It must be, or lead towards, a meaningful social activity.

One way of achieving this might be to relate the teaching of writing closely with the teaching of other subjects on the school curriculum. Learning geography, history, general science and so on are normal school activities and school activities are very much part of the normal lives of children. There seems no reason why writing at the level of communication should not be practised exclusively in association with such subjects. It seems likely that the learner will accept that writing about igneous and sedimentary rocks, the causes of the French Revolution, or the results of laboratory experiments is a much more normal—and therefore a much easier—activity than writing about something which is not associated with school life at all, and which has no value except for the teacher or the examiner. Furthermore, the textbooks in these subjects provide a model of how the writing is to be done, so that there is a possibility of transfer from what is read to what is written.

This brings us to the second requirement. Textbooks are examples of institutional writing, and the writing which would be done with reference to them would approximate to institutional writing. It would use those rhetorical elements of exposition, description, summary and so on, albeit at an elementary level, which are necessary for institutional communication. As we have already pointed out, learning to communicate is not simply a matter of learning to produce correct linguistic structures: it is a matter of learning the rhetorical conventions appropriate to different kinds of discourse. If learners of either a first or a second language are to acquire an ability to communicate in writing, they have to learn not only to write correct sentences, but also how to define, how to classify, how to organize a description, how to relate the statement of a law to a statement which illustrates its working, how to introduce modal modification, how to keep in contact with the reader and so on. We would suggest that the learner would be more likely to develop this communicative competence, this knowledge of rhetorical conventions, if his writing is immediately related to subjects which naturally require such an ability. It is difficult to see how one can learn science, history and so on without learning the kinds of rhetoric which are characteristic of these subjects. One might go further and suggest that if the teaching of writing were to be associated with one, or more than one, of these subjects, it would not only help in the teaching of writing but would also make an important contribution to the teaching of the subjects themselves.

We have mentioned the question of models, suggesting that writing might be guided by reference to textbooks, and this brings us back to points made in the section on reading comprehension. We cannot expect learners to learn to read or to write by simple exposure. The slogan 'Children learn to read by reading, children learn to speak by speaking', etc., which has had such a vogue in recent years is dangerously misleading. It is true that learning is an individual matter, that what is learnt is not necessarily what is taught, that practice improves, even if it does not make perfect. But it is the business of the language teacher to set up conditions which are most favourable for learning—this is essentially what teaching means—and as far as reading and writing is concerned this means that he must devise ways of drawing the learners' attention to how language is used, of making him aware of the features of written communication which were discussed in previous sections of this chapter. It would appear that the most promising way of teaching writing is first to develop in the learner an ability to recognize how written language communicates by means of the kind of comprehension exercise discussed in Section 5. If he knows how he is interpreting texts, this knowledge will provide him with some guidance as to how to communicate himself. If one takes the kind of explicit approach suggested in this chapter, an approach which makes more appeal than is perhaps commonly the case to the cognitive capability of the learners, then reading comprehension can be seen as a preparation for writing and the teaching of the two abilities can be integrated in a principled way.

2 Practical work

2.1 Exercise A: Sound-spelling correspondence

In one experiment Venezky used a set of synthetic (or nonsense) words to study sound-spelling correspondence. Here is a list of 20 items. Test yourself out on their pronunciation and try to find analogies to real English words:

1 DIT	7 CALP	13 CUG
2 CIFE	8 WANG	14 SHIR
3 RAUD	9 VAIT	15 PIGH
4 YIE	10 VARE	16 TIEP
5 BOART	11 THAWL	17 LAR
6 LAIP	12 LOD	18 VIT

19 TENGE   20 JIRE

Which items do you regard as predictable and which non-predictable? Do you find any difference in your success in their pronunciation?

2.2 Exercise B: Simplification

Study these three versions of a passage from *Oliver Twist* by Charles Dickens. The first is the original passage and the other two are simplified versions of it. You are asked to examine in detail what changes have been made in the two simplified versions, and to

a try to establish from the evidence of your examination what principles of simplification are being practised in each

b assess how valid these principles are.

It is suggested that in your analysis you consider how the versions differ in respect of the following:

Situational features: what aspects of the descriptions of events, characters and so on have been omitted or altered.

Lexical features: which vocabulary items have been replaced.

Syntactic features: which syntactic structures have been modified, and in what way, and which have been replaced altogether.

In your assessment of the principles of simplification and their validity, consider the following questions:

1 What standard of difficulty is used by each simplifier—is it based on the word, the phrase, the sentence, or something else?

2 How consistently is the standard applied?

3 How far is there an attempt to keep as close as possible to the original?

4 What is the point of keeping close to the original? How far does simplification follow—and how far does it need to follow—the same principles as translation?

5 What is the purpose of simplification?

   a To make the content of one particular text more accessible to the learner.

   b To develop a comprehension strategy which can be applied to other texts.

   c To provide a model for the reader's own productive use of the language.

6 What is the relationship between simplification and abridgement?

7 Does the simplification of linguistic elements necessarily result in the simplification of a text as a piece of communication?

Several of these questions are, of course, related.

It is suggested that you might like to attempt a simplification of your own in the light of what emerges from your study of the simplified versions presented here.

Version A: Chapman and Hall (CH)

Oliver Twist. Biographical Edition. Chapman and Hall 1902, pp. 10–11.

    The evening arrived; the boys took their places. The master in his cook's uniform, stationed himself at the copper, his pauper assistants ranged themselves behind him; the gruel was served out; and a long grace was said over the short commons. The gruel disappeared; the boys
5 whispered each other, and winked at Oliver; while his next neighbours

nudged him. Child as he was, he was desperate with hunger, and reckless with misery. He rose from the table; and advancing to the master, basin and spoon in hand, said, somewhat alarmed at his own temerity:
'Please, sir, I want some more.'

10   The master was a fat, healthy man; but he turned very pale. He gazed in stupefied astonishment on the small rebel for some seconds, and then clung for support to the copper. The assistants were paralysed with wonder; the boys with fear.

'What!' said the master at length, in a faint voice.

15   'Please, sir,' replied Oliver, 'I want some more.'

The master aimed a blow at Oliver's head with the ladle; pinioned him in his arms; and shrieked aloud for the beadle.

The board were sitting in solemn conclave, when Mr. Bumble rushed into the room in great excitement, and addressing the gentleman in the high
20   chair, said,

'Mr. Limbkins, I beg your pardon, sir! Oliver Twist has asked for more!'

There was a general start. Horror was depicted on every countenance.

'For *more*!' said Mr. Limbkins. 'Compose yourself, Bumble, and answer me distinctly. Do I understand that he asked for more, after he had eaten the
25   supper allotted by the dietary?'

'He did, sir,' replied Bumble.

'That boy will be hung,' said the gentleman in the white waistcoat. 'I know that boy will be hung.'

Nobody controverted the prophetic gentleman's opinion. An animated
30   discussion took place. Oliver was ordered into instant confinement; and a bill was next morning pasted on the outside of the gate, offering a reward of five pounds to anybody who would take Oliver Twist off the hands of the parish. In other words, five pounds and Oliver Twist were offered to any man or woman who wanted an apprentice to any trade, business, or
35   calling.

'I never was more convinced of anything in my life,' said the gentleman in the white waistcoat, as he knocked at the gate and read the bill next morning: 'I never was more convinced of anything in my life, than I am that that boy will come to be hung.'

40   As I propose to show in the sequel whether the white-waistcoated gentleman was right or not, I should perhaps mar the interest of this narrative (supposing it to possess any at all), if I ventured to hint just yet, whether the life of Oliver Twist had this violent termination or no.

Version B: Longmans (L)

Oliver Twist. New Method Supplementary (Reader Stage 4), pp. 4–6, 'Simplified and brought within a vocabulary of 1,400 words' by M. West and M. Maison, Longmans, 1966.

The evening arrived and the boys took their places. The master stood by the pot; the servants stood near him, and the soup was served.

It disappeared quickly. The boys whispered to one another, and made signs to Oliver. His neighbours pushed him. Although he was only a child
5   he was wild with hunger, and this gave him courage.

He rose from the table and went to the master, with his bowl and spoon in his hand. Almost afraid of his own courage, he said, 'Please, sir, I want some more.'

The master was a fat, healthy man, but he turned very white. He looked
10 with surprise at the small boy. The servants were silent with surprise, and
the boys were silent with fear.
'What?' said the master at length in a faint voice.
'Please, sir,' said Oliver, 'I want some more.'
The master hit Oliver with his spoon, then seized him in his arms and
15 cried for help. Mr. Bumble and some of the workhouse officers came rushing
into the room. The master told him what Oliver had said.
'He asked for more!' they cried. 'Do we understand that he wanted more
than his usual supper?'
They could hardly believe it.
20 'That boy will live to be hanged!' cried one of them.
They took Oliver away and shut him up in a dark room. The next morning
a notice appeared on the gate of the workhouse. This notice offered five
pounds to anybody who would take Oliver Twist.
'I am sure that the boy will live to be hanged!' cried one of the workhouse
25 officers again.

Version C: Oxford University Press (OUP)

Oliver Twist. Tales Retold for Easy Reading, pp. 7–8, by Josephine
Page, Oxford University Press, 1947.

The evening came. The master served out the gruel. The gruel disappeared.
The boys whispered to each other and pushed Oliver a little. Oliver was
frightened but very hungry. He got up from the table, and, basin and spoon
in hand, went towards the master and said, tremblingly: 'Please, sir, I
5 want some more!'
The master was a fat, healthy man, but he turned very pale. He couldn't
believe he had heard rightly.
'What!' he said after a pause, in a faint voice.
'Please, sir, I want some more.'
10 The master struck Oliver a blow on the head with his serving spoon, and
caught the boy in his arms and shouted for the beadle.
The Board were sitting solemnly discussing their business, when Mr.
Bumble ran into the room. In great excitement he cried to the gentleman in
the high chair: 'Mr. Limbkins, I beg your pardon, sir, Oliver Twist has asked
15 for more!' Everyone was shocked. On every face was a look of astonishment.
'For more!' said Mr. Limbkins. 'Be calm, Bumble, and answer me plainly.
Do I understand that he asked for more after he had eaten the supper
allowed each boy?'
'He did, sir,' replied Bumble.
20 'That boy will be hanged,' said the gentleman who had called Oliver a
fool. Nobody disagreed with this opinion. A lively discussion took place.
Oliver was ordered to be shut in a room alone. Next morning a notice
was pasted on the outside of the gate, offering a reward of five pounds to
anybody who would take Oliver Twist as an apprentice to any trade or
25 business.

2.3 Exercise C: Reading comprehension

You are asked to devise a set of comprehension questions on the following passage taken from the S.R.A. (Science Research Associates) Reading

Laboratory. The S.R.A. Reading Laboratory is essentially a set of boxes of reading materials. The boxes are sequenced and intended (in four stages) to cover the reading-age range of 6 plus to 15 plus. Each pupil is given a diagnostic test on the basis of which he is assigned a particular set of reading cards known as Power Builders. In addition to the Power Builders, which are intended to practise and develop general comprehension, the Reading Laboratory contains Rate Builders, which are timed by the reader and intended to develop reading speed.

All the cards in any one set are of the same level of difficulty, though between them the cards cover a wide range of topics. The pupil is trained to use a particular reading strategy for getting information from the cards. He selects a card from his set, reads it and answers some comprehension questions. He then goes on to do some vocabulary building exercises based on the reading text. He times his own reading, marks his own work and keeps his own progress chart. When he is scoring over 90 per cent on both kinds of exercise, he is moved on to the next set of cards, which are slightly more difficult. Materials in the Reading Laboratory are graded (or sequenced) very carefully. The result of careful grading, and of a wide choice of materials, is that each pupil is enabled to work on his own, at his own pace, at an appropriate level of difficulty; and, in consequence, to be continuously successful.

The S.R.A. Reading Laboratory has been used with good results in both the first language and the second language situation.

Write a set of comprehension questions on the following passage, which is taken from Stage 2 of the Laboratory. Bear in mind the points raised in 1.5 and 1.6 and try to relate the questions to some definite principles. How many questions you ask, what they ask about, and what form they take should reflect such principles and be justifiable by reference to them.

Reading passage

The stylistic distance between the sterile geometry of the new Seagram Building in New York City and the absurd vulgarity of this year's automobile is a measure of the crisis in American design today. It would be hard to find another period in all history which presented such aesthetic antitheses. For these two objects do not belong even to the same spectrum of design; one is an aristocratic affectation of poverty, the other a *nouveau riche* ostentation of wealth. One draws its forms from Procrustean concepts of mathematical order, the other from the paperback literature of space age warfare. And in between these poles, with no more apparent relation to each other than the constellations of the Milky Way, lie all the other artistic phenomena with which our landscape is littered.

There are some odd and contradictory forces at work among us.

One increasingly popular explanation for this parlous state of affairs is simply that of our wealth; our design is flabby because we are too rich.

To diagnose the sources of our present dilemma in design is, unfortunately, much easier than to prescribe the cure. The accomplishments of our industrial civilization are too real and too profound to relinquish. In the light of modern scientific knowledge, it is clear that the independent artisan cannot adequately feed and clothe and house the world. We cannot very well outlaw new materials or proscribe new techniques; penicillin and spaceships are not produced by peasants. Least of all can we censor art or licence museums, since these are among the noblest accomplishments of our culture.

It is apparently, ourselves that we must change. And to accomplish this, we must educate ourselves—educate so much more profoundly than we presently do that the imagination boggles at the task. But where design is concerned, a few things are already clear. In a world of increasing specialization, the rest of life must be devoted to mastering the broad and general. The deep but limited wisdom which comes from first-hand experience must be supplemented by first-rate theoretical understanding. And if industrialism has ruptured the traditional relationships between artist and audience, artisan and consumer, specialist and layman, then new and improved relations must be evolved to replace them. For an age which has split the atom, this should not be impossible, but a rocket to the moon will seem both simple and unimportant by comparison.

2.4 Exercise D: Writing

In this exercise we present for examination two suggested methods of improving writing. The first is the situational (usually called 'creative', 'free' or 'personal') approach. The second is the linguistic (or 'structural') approach.

Clegg (1964) is a representative example of the 'creative' approach. He distinguishes between two categories of written English, 'personal' and 'recording'. He characterizes the first of these as 'the English which a pupil would use when writing poetry or expressive prose, or when writing about his personal experiences, impressions or imaginings, relying on his own store of words to do so . . .' Of the other category, Clegg remarks: 'His (i.e., the pupil's) "recording" English which may make up nine-tenths of his writing in school, he will use for his history, his geography, science, religious instruction and so on.' Clegg's contention is that pupils who are encouraged to develop 'personal' writing will naturally acquire an ability to handle 'recording' writing. He says that most of his book 'will be devoted to the "personal" writing of children in the belief that those pupils whose personal writing is maintained at a high standard throughout their school life will write well whatever they write.'

Clegg quotes some pieces of written work 'set out in contrasting pairs, each pair having been written by the same child'. The following are examples of such work. You are asked to consider whether they show any evidence of the carry-over that Clegg refers to.

Passage 1 'Personal'

A Stoat

Needle-like fangs are enclosed in a snarling vicious mouth. This ferocious enemy is unwanted by many a hen, rabbit and mouse. Ready to pounce on an unwary animal. Offering a challenge to all his foes. Only swiftness and bite lie between him and starvation. His back is arched in fury. Forelegs are stiff, hind legs bent and ready to pounce, tail low and curved. Tinted brown and grey, not at all like his pure white winter coat. His black shiny eyes glint evilly. Grey whiskers streak backwards, like his stroked fur. Brown, tan, fawn and nut-brown are also colours in his summer coat. How delicate and innocent the teeth may seem, but once they sank into the flesh of a frightened animal. The tiny paws with tooth-pick claws, once carried a living stoat over the countryside.

Passage 2 'Recording'
Ships

The earliest boats were made by the cavemen. They cut down with their stone axes trees, which they hollowed out. These boats were an early form of the dug-out canoe. Later in the Bronze Age, men made basketwork boats, covered with skin, called coracles. The boats were light enough to be carried on men's backs, and are still used in Wales. The Phoenicians built galleys, made of wood. The ships were manned by galley slaves and used for trading. They had one to three rows of oars on each side of the ship . . .   (10 year old boy)

Our second approach is that of Hugh Fraser (1967). Fraser's course, intended for average and below average secondary pupils aims to 'give a firm grounding in basic sentence patterns' and 'to increase the child's confidence, accuracy and resourcefulness in the handling of English'. He suggests an intensive course of five months, the method being to teach writing through grammatical instruction.

Fraser quotes a number of examples of 'before and after' children: 'The first in each pair was written before training in this method had begun, and the second represents the stage reached after the child has worked about one-third of the way through the scheme. They are typical.'

Read the two passages below. The second clearly differs from the first. What has been taught? Is the second passage an improvement on the first?

Passage 3 'Before'
My favourite television programme

My favourite television programme is Bewitched one day she went to see her new house and her mother just waved her hand and there was trees and flowers all over the garden then they went into the house and she moved her nose and it was all furnished but she had married a human and she promised that she would not use her witchcraft again and she would by all her furniture and plant all the plants by seeds.

Passage 4 'After'
Going a walk

One hot summers day I took my dog a long walk up the back road of Logan. When we were going by a farm a car came out of an opening as fast as anything. Out of the car dropped an envelope. I ran up to it and picked it up. It said 'Mr.

Jones' on the front of it and there was two hundred pounds in it. When I saw the money I started to run home as fast as I could. My mother and father ran me to the police station in our car. The police took my name and address and asked me where and when I found it. He said, 'I was in such a hurry that I dint notice it had fell out.' The owner gave me two five pound notes.

(Boy 12 years, I.Q. 90)

3 Discussion of exercises

3.1 Discussion of Exercise A

Here is a list of analogous English words (there are, of course, many possibilities) with the key sounds—i.e., those being tested—in italics. A phoneme equivalent (Received Pronunciation) is also given.

Item	Key sound
1 DIT	hit /ɪ/
2 CIFE	cipher /s/
3 RAUD	laud /ɔ/
4 YIE	tie /ai/
5 BOART	oar /ɔə/
6 LAIP	lain /ei/
7 CALP	calf /k/
8 WANG	sang /aŋ/
9 VAIT	bait /ei/
10 VARE	care /eə/
11 THAWL	shawl /ɔ/
12 LOD	nod /o/
13 CUG	cup /k/
14 SHIR	fir /ɜ/
15 PIGH	sigh /ai/
16 TIEP	brief /i/
17 LAR	far /ɑ/
18 VIT	wit /ɪ/
19 TENGE	Stonehenge /ndʒ/
20 JIRE	fire /aiə/

The predictable sounds seem to be those with:

1 final 'e' (10, 20)

2 initial and medial 'c' (2, 7, 13)

3 vowel monophthongs (1, 12, 14, 17, 18)

No. 14 may give rise to discussion because of the presence of the final 'r'

4 'ng' final or before final 'e' (8, 19)

The non-predictable sounds seem to be all those which are represented by vowel digraphs (3, 4, 5, 6, 9, 11, 15, 16).

Venezky's results as to relative success in predictable and non-predictable items will be of interest. He found that 'good readers (as measured on reading tests) are consistently more likely than poor readers to give appropriate responses to predictable patterns. . . . Good readers agree more consistently on a preferred (i.e., by frequency counts) pronunciation for the unpredictable digraph vowels . . .' A small-scale investigation at Edinburgh in 1969 showed very high success for English native speaking children on these items (average score over 90 per cent). These children had an average age of 10 plus, suggesting that by age 10 the sound-spelling correspondences have been mastered. By implication the readers of this book should be very successful on this exercise. Adequate proficiency in English means, among other things, having internalized these sound-spelling correspondences of the language.

3.2 Discussion of Exercise B[2]

Situational features

The two simplified versions are almost exactly the same length, each being about half as long as the original. In general, the abridgement has been brought about in each case by the omission of descriptive detail rather than of the events of the narrative or of dialogue. We may perhaps say that whereas the original *recreates* the incidents, the simplified versions simply *report* them.

The difference between the recreation of the original (CH) and the reporting of the versions L and OUP can be seen from the following:

CH	OUP
He gazed in stupefied astonishment on the small rebel for some seconds, and then clung for support to the copper. (10–12)[3]	He couldn't believe he had heard rightly. (6–7)

---

[2] Exercise B and the discussion set out here owe a great deal to an original idea by Julian Dakin. The discussion is a reworking of an early draft of his.

[3] Line reference.

CH	L
There was a general start.	They could hardly believe
Horror was depicted on every	it. (19)
countenance. (22)	

OUP and L do not omit the same descriptive passages. Of the two main scenes of the events described, the dining hall and the meeting of the board, L focuses on the first at the expense of the second and OUP focuses on the second at the expense of the first. In fact, in L the two scenes are telescoped into one since the simplifier has Mr Bumble rush into the dining hall rather than into the board meeting and he together with the unspecified 'workhouse officers' are given the original roles of the gentlemen of the board. In this respect OUP is less of a distortion of the original than L.

With reference to Questions 3 and 4 of the exercise, it seems that there is an attempt to keep intact the main facts of the original, but there is a difference of opinion as to which should be placed in prominence and there is a danger of the non-prominent facts being distorted. Whether the choice of focus is made by reference to some literary judgement or to some criterion of difficulty is impossible to decide on the evidence of the two passages we have here, though a close study of the simplified versions in their entirety might yield some answer.

Simplifications, then, seem to follow the principles of synopsis rather than translation: they aim at reporting the gist. There would seem to be no reason, however, why the principles of translation should not apply in the simplification of short texts (stories, for example). A translation type simplification of a novel would of course make the text too long and defeat the object of the exercise. (See West's comments in 1.6).

Lexical features

The following are some examples of lexical alteration:

	CH	L	OUP
1	gruel (3)	soup (2)	gruel (1)
2	rose (7)	rose (6)	got up (3)
3	basin (7)	bowl (6)	basin (3)
4	pale (10)	white (9)	pale (6)
5	at length (14)	at length (12)	after a pause (8)
6	ladle (16)	spoon (14)	serving spoon (10)
7	pinioned him in his arms (16–17)	seized him in his arms (14)	caught the boy in his arms (11)

8 somewhat alarmed at his own temerity (8)	almost afraid of his own courage (7)	tremblingly (4)
9 aimed a blow at Oliver's head (16)	hit Oliver (14)	struck Oliver a blow (10)
10 desperate with hunger and reckless with misery (6–7)	wild with hunger and this gave him courage (5)	frightened but very hungry (3)

In general, it would appear that L simplifies more than OUP, but sometimes OUP simplifies where L does not (2 and 5). It is not clear why the OUP simplifier should regard 'rose' and 'at length' as difficult and 'gruel', 'basin' as not. It may be that the simplifiers are working from different restricted vocabularies, one of which includes 'rise' for example, and one of which does not, but this does not account for the retention of 'gruel' in OUP, which is hardly likely to appear in any restricted vocabulary. It may of course be that this word is glossed in a footnote in OUP. This brings up the question of the use of footnote glosses in simplification. Instead of replacing 'gruel' with 'soup' why not retain it and add a gloss? But then why not do the same with, say, 'ladle' and 'temerity'? This relates to Question 5: What is the purpose of the simplification?

The fact that OUP simplifies less is consistent with the fact that it is a more faithful recording of the facts of the original than L, as we have noted under 'situational features' above. Sometimes, however, for no apparent reason, this version departs from the original whereas L keeps close to it.

We might notice that oddities also arise where the simplification is carried out at word rather than phrase level (7–10). In OUP (7) the verb 'catch' is used in a rather restricted sense which might well puzzle pupils who only know the word in collocations like 'catch-ball' or 'catch-thief', neither of which makes any sense in this context. The difficulty here is one which is inherent in all restricted vocabularies: the simpler and more frequent a word the more likely it is to have multiple meanings, so that to replace a more difficult or less frequent word with a simpler and more frequent one is often to increase rather than reduce the difficulty of a text. This problem will recur in our discussion of syntactic features, but we might notice that it occurs in (10) here as well. The interpretation of the versions of both simplifications depends on understanding the function of just such simple and frequent words as we have been discussing: 'this' in the case of L and 'but' in the case of OUP. The reader has to understand that 'this' refers to the fact that 'he was wild with hunger', whereas he may be accustomed to assuming that 'this' is used to refer directly to simple noun phrases (*This is a book* and so on). 'But' is odd here because in its normal use it presupposes an incompatibility between the two elements it relates as in *beautiful but sad* or *tired but happy*, in which the presupposition is that beauty normally implies happiness and tiredness normally implies its absence. Thus the expressions *ugly but sad, beautiful but happy, tired but sad* are odd. By the same token, *frightened but hungry* implies that the state of being frightened is in some way incompatible with the state of being hungry, and there is clearly no warrant for such an implication. The reader here has to somehow recover from this expression the implication that Oliver was frightened but that his hunger made him desperate, and that it is his desperation, not his hunger, which makes him ask for more.

Syntactic features

Some lexical changes involve syntactic changes, as is the case with (10) above. Other changes seem to be introduced to reduce the syntactic complexity of the original. In the following, for instance, the embeddings of the original sentence are resolved into separate sentences:

CH

He rose from the table, and
advancing to the master, basin
and spoon in hand, said,
somewhat alarmed at his own
temerity . . . (7–8)

L	OUP
He rose from the table and went to the master, with his bowl and spoon in his hand. Almost afraid of his own courage, he said . . . (6–7)	He got up from the table and, basin and spoon in hand, went towards the master and said, tremblingly . . . (3–4)

We might say that what the simplifiers are trying to do here is to adjust surface structure so that it represents more fully the underlying structure of the sentences concerned. But again, it is difficult to trace any consistency in this procedure. The following surface structure complexities, for instance, appear in the simplified versions:

L	OUP
The master told him what Oliver had said. (16) came rushing into the room (16)	He couldn't believe he had heard rightly. (6–7)

L	OUP
That boy will live to be hanged (20 and 24)	Do I understand that he asked for more after he had eaten the supper allowed each boy? (17–18) Oliver was ordered to be shut in a room alone. (22) etc.

The fact that there are more complexities in OUP than L bears out our previous observation that L simplifies in general more than does OUP. One case in which the OUP version simplifies where L retains the original again brings up the point that a linguistic simplification may introduce a difficulty in interpretation. Compare:

L	OUP
That boy will live to be hanged (20 and 24)	That boy will be hanged. (20)

It is not clear in the OUP version whether the sentence is meant to count as a prediction or an order, whereas the L version, like the original, makes it clear that the former is meant. In general it seems to be the case that the simplifier of L is more concerned with how his version will be interpreted than is the simplifier of OUP. This is further borne out by the fact that in one instance L resolves an ambiguity in the original which OUP retains. Compare:

CH	L	OUP
Oliver was ordered into instant confinement (30)	They took Oliver away and shut him up in a dark room (21)	Oliver was ordered to be shut in a room alone (22)

Was Oliver ordered or was someone else ordered? Perhaps the ambiguity does not matter much, but it is interesting that L should nevertheless avoid it.

Finally, we might notice that irregular surface forms are regularized in both versions:

CH	L/OUP
They whispered each other (5)	They whispered to each other (3/2)
be hung (27 and 28)	be hanged (20/20)
a bill was next morning pasted (31)	Next morning ⎱ a notice The next morning ⎰ (21/22)

Question 5 of the exercise comes up for consideration here. It is unlikely that the original would pose very much of a problem in interpretation here—certainly not in the case of the first of these examples. The change would seem, on the face of it, to suggest that the simplifiers have purpose (c) in mind.

3.3 Discussion of Exercise C

The following selection is from S.R.A.'s own set of multiple choice questions on the text (the questions have been renumbered):

1 The new Seagram Building in New York City is criticized as

   A a nouveau riche ostentation of wealth

   B an absurd vulgarity

   C an aristocratic affectation of poverty

   D an abstract-expressionist monstrosity

   E a push-button electronic marvel

2 The new automobile draws its forms from

   A Procrustean concepts of mathematical order

   B the paperback literature of space-age warfare

   C the constellations of the Milky Way

   D artistic phenomena littering our landscapes

   E stylistic spectrums of design

3 One popular explanation says that our design is 'flabby' because we are too

   A vulgar

   B ostentatious

   C contradictory

   D poor

   E rich

4 To solve today's aesthetic dilemma, the author suggests that we

   A disregard the limited wisdom of first-hand experience

   B devote attention to a special field of design

   C master the use of the new materials and new techniques

   D outlaw new materials and proscribe new techniques

   E supplement the wisdom of first-hand experience with first-rate theoretical understanding

5 If our wealth causes our design to be 'flabby', then the corollary is that
  A   our design would improve if we were poorer
  B   social wealth is the enemy of artistic production
  C   social wealth is a guarantee of great art
  D   artistic creativity thrives only with wealth
  E   art thrives with the astringency of wealth

6 The author's purpose is to show that
  A   a rocket to the moon is simple and unimportant
  B   industrialism has ruptured relations between specialist and layman
  C   new and improved relations are needed between artist and audience
  D   our industrial civilization has produced unparalleled social wealth
  E   censoring art is necessary

Questions 1, 2, 3 and 4 are of the inference type and 5 and 6 are of the supposition type. S.R.A. provide no evaluation questions in this exercise. Such questions are not really suitable for use with a multiple choice format.

The purpose of multiple-choice comprehension questions is to control the student's response rather than leaving him free to write down anything that may come into his head, as is the case with open-ended written-answer questions. A multiple-choice question consists of the question itself followed by a number of alternative answers, one of which is correct, the others being 'distractors'. The student's task is to read the passage, read the questions, read all the suggested answers, search through the passage and indicate the correct answer by means of a tick or some other simple device. The process is purely one of comprehension; no writing is involved. As well as locating the problem (i.e., understanding the question) the student has to find the area of answer, analyse the kind of problem it is, and then decide which of the possible answers is the right one. This may fit in with the typical cycle of problem solving behaviour: recognition, search, analysis and attack. There must be something to do at each stage, which may be why the questions start off in sequence and then after number 3 or 4 tend to move randomly. The result is that the student has something to do at the second stage, i.e., search.

It is clear that a multiple-choice question contains factors which are not present in normal reading. For example, the student must read and understand not only the correct answer, but also the distractors which may have been deliberately designed to confuse him. The following is an analysis of the distractors in the first three S.R.A. questions above.

Question 1: (c) is the correct answer. The author is comparing the Seagram Building with the design of this year's automobile, and since (a) and (b) both refer to the automobile there is a logical connection (the one ... the other) with (c). On the other hand, (d) and (e) are irrelevant to the argument. There is no reference to an 'abstract-expressionist monstrosity' or a 'push-button electronic marvel' in the passage.

Question 2: (b) is the correct answer. (a) refers to the Seagram Building so that again we have a logical connection (the one ... the other), but this time the movement is from car to building rather than from building to car, as in Question 1. (c) and (e) have no particular connection with the car, except perhaps physical proximity in the text. (d) has perhaps some connection with the car, since the latter is an artistic phenomenon, but the suggested answer 'The new automobile draws its forms from artistic phenomena littering our landscapes' makes little sense in the context of the passage.

Question 3: (e) is the correct answer and (d) is its opposite. In the case of (c) the proposed answer is meaningless, but *contradictory* is close to *rich* in the text. (a) and (b) are contextually more remote ('vulgar' relates to *the absurd vulgarity of this year's automobile,* 'ostentation' to *a nouveau riche ostentation of wealth*), but both answers accord with the general meaning of the passage.

The reader is invited to select the correct answer, and to consider the nature of the distractors in the remaining three questions.

Since the nature of the distractors can initially affect a student's performance in a multiple-choice comprehension question, it is necessary for the distractors to be designed with great care. It is not good enough to have one correct answer with four irrelevant distractors thrown in at random. In a well-constructed multiple-choice question the distractors should bear some logical relationship to the correct answer, so that even by reading the wrong answers the student is learning something about the semantic and grammatical structure of the language.

3.4 Discussion of Exercise D

(a) *Passages 1 and 2*

Clegg may mean that children who write well write well, i.e., that there is general over-all excellence. Or he may mean that there is a carry-over from one type of writing to the other. Whatever he does mean, since he quotes this pair as an example of 'good' writing and since both passages are by the same person we may possibly expect to find similarities in the two passages. Do we find them? The samples are short and by the same person at the same time in his writing life.

There is no answer to the carry-over question. The extracts are too short and it is not clear, even if we had very much longer passages, what *kind* of judgement we should make. What we really want to know is whether these two performance examples are proper representatives of the child's underlying knowledge of the language. This is a notoriously difficult matter to investigate. If we had examples of systematic errors we might be able to come to some conclusion. But there are very few examples of deviant forms here (e.g. *How . . . but*, which does not recur and which is only deviant if how means *however* and not *how!*).

We can make some kind of comparison between the two passages:

(a) *Semantic structure*

The movement is not identical in the two passages but both follow a whole/part antithesis. (It looks as though (1) is more complete than (2) which prevents a full consideration of this question.)

The first passage begins with a part (*fangs*), goes on to the whole (*enemy*) and then through a series of parts (including colours) to the whole (*living stoat*) at the end.

The second passage discusses three separate topics and treats each of these systematically (whole: part, part). Notice the anaphoric reference, strong in (1) (*this* ferocious enemy) occurring also in (2) (. . . cavemen. *They*).

(b) *Grammatical structure*

(i) *Nominals and embedding:* Both passages have a large number of nominal expressions of all kinds. The writer knows how to nominalize and does it successfully in both passages. Both contain deletions, especially relative deletion. (2) actually contains a relative (*which they hollowed out*) and several obvious deletions (*covered with skin, called coracles, made of wood*, and *used for trading*). (1) has less obvious ones (*ready to pounce, offering a challenge, hind legs bent, tinted brown and grey*).

(ii) *Passives:* Both passages contain passives (e.g. (1): *are enclosed, is unwanted, is arched*; (2): *were made, are used, were manned*).

(c) *Thematic structure*

Clearly, thematic structure is one of the major differences between the two passages. (1) is full of highly stylized themes (*ready to, offering a, forelegs are, tinted brown, how delicate and innocent*) while (2) has none of this 'poetic' material.

(d) *Vocabulary*

Here is the second major difference. (2) has a few necessary technical words (they could have occurred on the board or in a textbook) but (1) has a long list of specialized vocabulary, very appropriate and really quite difficult (*needle-like fangs, snarling, vicious, ferocious, pounce, unwary, challenge, foes, arched, tinted, glint, evilly, streak, stroked, tooth-pick*).

Conclusions

We cannot make any. The child is in control in both passages but there is no evidence that they are by the same writer.

(b) *Passages 3 and 4*

Fraser himself has a number of comments:

'There are no established norms for written English, and it will not be immediately possible to measure in some objective and scientific manner the progress made by this boy at this stage of his training. It is possible, however, to make some non-controversial observations about the way in which his language behaviour has changed:

1 He has learned to punctuate with conventional accuracy.

2 He has started to use subordinate clauses effectively.

3 There is already an increase in his syntactic resources, as exemplified by the new variety of the sentence structure.'

Fraser's method is to teach a simplified version of a phrase structure grammar (deriving from Halliday's systemic grammar). Thus the students are taught the following structures, with examples:

Sentences with one subject plus one verb (S1)
Sentences with one subject plus two verbs (S2)
S1 plus adjunct (in different positions) (S1A or AS1)
S1/S2 plus conditioning clause (C)
Various combinations 'S1C, CS1, etc.'
Participial clause (Ing)
Additioning clause (Wh-)
(etc.)

On Fraser's evidence we cannot really come to any conclusions. It may be worth considering whether it is his symbolization (S1, etc.—all taught) or the repetition of patterns or something else that produces the improvement of which he speaks and which is testified to by numbers of Scottish teachers.

4 Further Reading

Chaplen, F. *Paragraph Writing*. London: Oxford University Press, 1970. A helpful attempt to give practice in paragraph writing.

Dakin, J. 'The teaching of reading'. In H. Fraser and W. R. O'Donnell (eds.), *Applied Linguistics and the Teaching of English*. London: Longmans, 1969. Dakin takes a cool look at the possible connections between linguistics and reading.

Fraser, H. 'The teaching of writing'. In H. Fraser and W. R. O'Donnell (eds.), *Applied Linguistics and the Teaching of English*. London: Longmans, 1969. Fraser's description of his remedial writing scheme (quoted in Exercise D of this chapter).

Gray, W. S. *The Teaching of Reading and Writing*. UNESCO and London: Evans, 1956. Monograph on Fundamental Education, No. 10. Gray's world-wide survey sensibly links reading and writing with the pursuit of literacy. This is a natural link in second language teaching and should be widely encouraged in the first language field.

Huey, E. B. *The Psychology and Pedagogy of Reading*. London: Macmillan, 1908. Also New York: Holt, Rinehart, Winston, 1968. Huey's book has stood the vicissitudes of time well enough to be reissued sixty years later. It is a book whose insights into the process and teaching of reading put it outside the reach of fashion.

Moyle, D. *The Teaching of Reading*. London: Ward Lock Educational, 1968. A comprehensive guide, simply written, to all aspects of the teaching of reading to native speakers. Concentrates on initial and remedial reading, but does look at other aspects.

Smith, F. *Understanding Reading*. New York: Holt, Rinehart, Winston, 1971. For some time it has seemed unsatisfactory that reading should be looked at from one point of view, that of the psychologist for example, or that of the linguist. Smith attempts (successfully) to integrate these two approaches and most helpfully uses the notion of uncertainty reduction to show how reading develops at all levels.

Vernon, M. D. *Reading and Its Difficulties*. London: Cambridge University Press, 1971. An evaluation of recent research evidence relating to reading, with special attention to backwardness and dyslexia.

Wardhaugh, R. *Reading: A Linguistic Perspective*. New York: Harcourt Brace, 1969. Wardhaugh criticizes what is popularly supposed to be the linguistic contribution to reading instruction but which is no more than phonics. He cautiously examines what linguistics does have to offer—and points out that this means knowing some linguistics proper.

Widdowson, H. G. *Language Teaching Texts*. English Studies Series, No. 8. London: Oxford University Press, 1971. (Sections 11 and 41). Widdowson illustrates some of the ways in which second language students may be given higher literacy practice, writing exercises feeding back into and informing their reading.

Supplementary list

All the books and articles in the above list refer directly to teaching. But we are very much aware that there is one important area to which we have not provided any further references: that is, the part of rhetoric which has to do with the relation between form and function and in particular with the ways in which certain rhetorical (rather than grammatical) forms signal certain functions. Applied linguistics is very much in need of materials in this area to make theoretical work available to the general reader. In the meantime we give below the titles of three works which discuss rhetorical function from a theoretical point of view. In addition the reader may wish to refer to similar discussions in Volume 2, in particular to the chapters on Linguistics and Sociolinguistics and the references therein.

Austin, J. L. *How to do Things with Words*. Oxford: The Clarendon Press, 1962. Austin's seminal book on speech acts. Unsatisfactory if used as a guide to the analysis of a text but exciting as theory and full of suggestive insights.

Halliday, M. A. K. Language structure and language function. In J. Lyons (ed.), *New Horizons in Linguistics*. Harmondsworth: Penguin, 1970. Halliday distinguishes three 'language functions' and shows how these are formally recognizable. The first has to do with the cognitive meaning, the second with interpersonal relations (and therefore with modality, etc.) and the third, with stylistic variation.

Open University. *Reading Development Course*. Open University, Walton Hall, Bletchley, Bucks., 1973. A post-experience course, containing correspondence texts and radio and television programmes. It is intended to serve as a practical guide to teachers of reading at all levels but especially in the middle years of schooling.

Searle, J. R. *Speech Acts*. Cambridge: Cambridge University Press, 1969. Searle takes up and develops some of Austin's insights. If we accept that the writer has a number of strategies by which to communicate to his reader the various speech acts he is employing, it is of obvious interest to understand something of the nature of speech acts.

7 Stylistics

H. G. WIDDOWSON

1 An approach to stylistic analysis

The purpose of stylistic analysis is to investigate how the resources of a language code are put to use in the production of actual messages. It is concerned with patterns of use in given texts.

The user of a language acquires two kinds of knowledge: knowledge of the rules of the code and knowledge of the conventions which regulate the use of these rules in the production of messages. The first kind ensures that what he says is grammatical, and the second kind ensures that what he says is appropriate. Both kinds of knowledge are essential if the user of the language is to enter into effective communication with his fellows. Together they provide language with what is generally recognized as its unique feature: its creativity. It has often been wondered at that human beings continually generate utterances which they have never spoken or heard before; what is equally to be wondered at is the fact that these novel utterances are understood. The reason for this is that though they are novel as manifestations of code, they are familiar as messages. The user of a language is creative because the novel linguistic forms he generates function as familiar units of communication: if they did not, he would only generate gibberish.

The impression is sometimes given that only code is systematic, so that the task of textual analysis is to count the occurrence of tokens of the types of unit discovered in the code. But it is clear that messages are produced in accordance with systems of social convention, otherwise they would not be understood; so that units of the message are not simply tokens but types in their own right definable in terms of social communication. Stylistics is concerned with such message types; its purpose is to discover what linguistic units count as in communication and how the effects of different conventions reveal themselves in the way messages are organized in texts.

Stylistics, then, is the study of the social function of language and is a branch of what has come to be called sociolinguistics. It aims to characterize texts as pieces of communication. It is not part of its purpose to provide a means of discovering the different social functions of language: it is technological rather than scientific in that it works on data provided by others. Texts are assumed to be given.

In this chapter we shall confine the scope of stylistics even further to a consideration of literary texts. This should not be taken as an indication of the limited applicability of stylistic analysis, but as an indication of the limited applications that have so far been made. There is as yet no satisfactory heuristic that can be used to extend stylistics to a consideration of all 'varieties' of language, though tentative beginnings have been made. Meanwhile, we focus our attention on literature.

There are two reasons why it is fitting that stylistics should first concern itself with literary texts: one is methodological and relates to the nature of literature as such, and the other is pedagogical and relates to the value stylistic analysis has for the teaching of language.

To take the first reason first: there are certain features about literature as a mode of communication which are unique and which simplify the task of stylistics. In the first place, it does not fit into any conventional communication situation. In all other forms of language use, we have a sender of the message and a receiver, the addresser and the addressee grammatically marked as the first and second person respectively. The third person is incorporated, as it were, as reference within the message itself. Both first and second persons are necessary in the communication situation: whenever we use language we assume a receiver. Now in literature we constantly find that the normally indivisible amalgam of sender/first person and receiver/second person has been split up. Thus the writer is separated from the addresser and the reader from the addressee. As a consequence of this, all kinds of curious participants enter into the communication situation: among addressers for example we find insects (in Gray) a brook (in Tennyson) and among addressees innumerable aspects of nature: mountains, rivers, flowers, birds and so on, as well as a Grecian urn (in Keats) and, of course, McGonegall's immortal 'railway bridge over the silvry Tay'. The first and second person then has, along with the third person, become incorporated into the text. This points to the essential difference between literary and other uses of language: in literature the message is text-contained, and presupposes no wider context so that everything necessary for its interpretation is to be found within the message itself. All other uses of language on the other hand find some place in the general social matrix; they develop from antecedent events and presuppose consequent events; they are contextualized in a social continuity. Clearly, to characterize the messages in a conventional text, some account must be taken of its social environment. It is this which complicates matters and makes stylistic analysis difficult. With literary texts, this problem does not cause such difficulties; generally speaking we can concentrate on the text itself without worrying about distracting social appendages. This is not to say, of course, that there are no problems. As we shall see there are plenty: most of them are corollaries of the unique feature of literature which has just been pointed out. But before turning to these, we must briefly mention the pedagogical reason which lends support to the concentration of stylistics on literary texts. This is important because it justifies the inclusion of stylistics within applied linguistics seen as an area of enquiry which brings the findings of linguistics to bear on the practical problems of language teaching.

By tradition, the study of literature has been regarded as a branch of aesthetics. As such it has been concerned with the total effect of literary texts as artistic wholes. Description has been by reference to artistic value, and the implication is that there are certain 'universals' of art which find expression in different ways according to media but which can be described in the same terms. Thus a poem, a painting and a piano concerto are different arrangements of universal artistic features realized in different media. Though this is not made explicit, literary criticism of the traditional kind makes appeal to a theory of aesthetics which postulates artistic universals. Unfortunately, the absence of explicitness is crucial. If, as seems on the face of it to be likely, it is possible to describe literature by reference to artistic universals, then it would seem to be essential to establish just what these universals are and to devise a metalanguage for their description. Meanwhile, the literary critic assumes that the artistic value of a work is available to intuitive awareness, and he makes use of an impressionistic terminology to communicate this awareness to others. The difficulty with this procedure is that it makes appeal to intuitions which the reader may not share with the critic. This is generally the case with language learners whose knowledge of the language has not reached the point at which they have an intuitive sense of the subtlety of language use. In this case the critic's impressionistic description can find no response. This is where stylistics can make its contribution. Its concern is with the patterning of language in texts and it makes no presupposition as to artistic value. By investigating the way language is used in a text, it can make apparent those linguistic patterns upon which an intuitive awareness of artistic values ultimately depend. It provides a basis for aesthetic appreciation by bringing to the level of conscious awareness features of the text otherwise only accessible to trained intuition. In brief, stylistics takes the language as primary and artistic values are regarded as incidental to linguistic description: literary criticism, on the other hand, takes artistic values as primary and refers to language in so far as it serves as evidence for aesthetic assessments. Stylistics renders an essential service to language learning in that even if the learner does not develop an appreciation of literature as literature, he will have acquired an awareness of the way language functions in at least this form of communication: he will have developed an awareness of literature as language. This indicates how the study of literary texts can be correlated with the study of texts exemplifying other forms of social communication and suggests a means of co-ordinating the teaching of language and the teaching of literature (at present so often undertaken in mutual isolation) in a way which would be beneficial to both.

These then are two reasons which excuse, if they do not justify, the present restriction of stylistic analysis to literary texts. We can now proceed with outlining an approach to the characterization of such texts. We have already noted certain unique features of literary writing. In the following discussion we will follow up the implications of this observation and see where they lead us.

The irregular realization of the addresser/addressee relationship in literary writing is symptomatic of a general non-conformity with normal conventions of communication. As has already been pointed out literary messages do not find a place in the social matrix as do other messages: they presuppose no preceding events and anticipate no future action. They are complete in themselves, and their significance is accordingly enclosed within the limits of the form they take. On the other hand, the significance of normal messages derives in large part from external circumstances, from the social situations in which they occur. But literary messages are not only notable for their somewhat cavalier treatment of context, but also for their idiosyncratic deployment of the resources of the code. It has been frequently pointed out that literature, and in particular poetry, contains a good deal of language which is grammatically and semantically deviant. Furthermore, poetry makes use of one phonological unit—the metrical line—which occurs in no other use of language. Since the forms that literary messages take do not wholly conform to either the conventions of use or the rules of the code, the question arises: how do they manage to convey any meaning at all? And even if they do manage to convey meaning, what kind of meaning is it? The two questions are closely related, and in considering them we shall be defining the task which stylistic analysis must undertake.

Literary messages manage to convey meaning because they organize their deviations from the code into patterns which are discernible in the texts themselves. What happens is that the writer in breaking the rules of the code diminishes the meaning of language and then proceeds to make up for the deficiency by placing the deviant item in a pattern whereby it acquires meaning by relation with other items within the internal context of the message. Thus the relations set up within a text constitute a secondary language system which combines, and so replaces, the separate functions of what would conventionally be distinguished as code and context.

The interpretation of any text involves the recognition of two sets of relations: extra-textual relations between language items and the code from which they derive and intra-textual relations between language items within the context itself. What is unique about literary texts is that typically the two sets of relations do not converge to form one unit of meaning which represents a projection, as it were, from code into context. Instead, they overlap to create a unit of meaning which belongs to neither one nor the other: a hybrid unit which derives from both code and context and yet is a unit of neither of them. An illustration will help to clarify this.

R. B. Lees (1960) points out that the nouns in a language code, as recorded in a dictionary, do not, numerous as they are, supply all our needs for names. We cannot, for instance, simply utter the word 'coffee' on every occasion we wish to refer to this substance. In order to produce appropriate referring expressions we make use of rules in the code which permit us to combine this noun with other language items. Using such rules, we are able to compose phrases like 'The cup of coffee you left in the kitchen', 'A cup of black coffee' and so on, which refer to particular instances or manifestations of the substance coffee. Combinations of words as such, like 'A cup of black coffee', do not, of course, appear in the code: they are composed to meet the contingencies of the context. What we have to notice is that the 'projection'.of items in the code into specific contexts involves no change of reference. The occurrences of the noun 'coffee' in the above phrases are instances of the general reference as registered in the code; instances which have been contextually particularized as units of the message. The change in the environment of a noun which enables it to play its part in contextual reference does not involve a change in its referential meaning, which is bestowed upon it by the code. Recognizing the contextual implications of a word does not involve a revision of the dictionary.

In literary writing, on the other hand, the case is often different. Consider the occurrence of the word 'coffee' in these lines of Alexander Pope:

> She went, to plain-work, and to purling brooks,
> Old fashioned halls, dull aunts, and croaking rooks:
> She went from opera, park, assembly, play,
> To morning walks, and prayers three hours a day;
> To part her time 'twixt reading and bohea;
> To muse, and spill her solitary tea;

Or o'er cold coffee trifle with the spoon,
Count the slow clock, and dine exact at noon ...

(Epistle to Miss Blount, on her leaving the
town after the coronation.)

Now the context in which the word occurs makes it clear that it is meant
to count as something more than a particular instance of a general
reference. 'Cold coffee' here has a significance over and above that which
is recoverable from the code. Trifling with a spoon over cold coffee is
represented as a similar activity to counting the slow clock and dining
exact at noon. Cold coffee is a sign of boredom. This is borne out further
by the phonological relations between 'cold', 'coffee', 'spoon', and
'count', 'slow', 'clock' which associate all these words in a pattern, and
by the words immediately preceding 'cold coffee' which are the ono-
matopoeic representation of a yawn. The intra-textual relations which are
set up between the item 'coffee' and the other items in its immediate
vicinity create a significance, then, beyond that which the item carries in
the code. The recognition of the contextual implications of the word do
involve a revision of its dictionary meaning, in this case in the form of an
extension.

It might be thought that all that we are illustrating here is the familiar
distinction between connotation and denotation, and that the preceding
discussion simply amounts to saying that literature is characteristically
connotative. The point is, however, that literature characteristically
effaces the distinction between these two different types of meaning.
Connotative meaning is generally taken to be a matter of personal
associations, essentially idiosyncratic and unsystematizable. But as we
have seen, contextual meaning within literary texts is a result of the setting
of linguistic items in a system of intra-textual relations. While one may
regard it, therefore, as connotative with reference to the code, one must
regard it as denotative with reference to the secondary language system
established by the regularities of the context. The meaning of 'coffee' in
Pope's lines is both connotative and denotative in a sense; and in a sense,
of course, neither.

Let us look at another example from Pope:

Here files of pins extend their shining rows,
Puffs, powders, patches, bibles, billet-doux.

(The Rape of the Lock)

Here, 'bibles' acquires an additional significance in that it is made a
member of the same class of objects as puffs and powders and other
accoutrements of female vanity. As before, the association of the item

in question with the other items in its environment is strengthened by phonological relations: we note the identical syllabic structure of the immediately preceding items and the fact that their initial consonants differ only in their absence of voice from the initial consonant of 'bibles'. The effect of all this, then, is to attribute to the word an additional significance derived entirely from the context in which it appears. This combines with the significance it has as an item in the code to create a hybrid unit of meaning. Clearly this is not recoverable from the code alone: no dictionary will include cosmetics among the defining features in an entry for 'bible'. Nor is it recoverable from the context alone—if we did not know the established referent for 'bible', of course, the ironic force of the line would be entirely lost. As a result we have objects littering Belinda's dressing table which are bibles, and yet not bibles; recognizably holy writ but somehow the same sort of thing as the trivia of female vanity at the same time.

We have seen how poetry tends to destroy the distinction between denotation and connotation to create hybrid meanings. We might note also that it has a way of blurring another well-established linguistic distinction: that which is commonly referred to as double articulation or duality of patterning. By this is meant that language is structured on two different planes: that of phonology and that of syntax. But as we have seen from our consideration of Pope's lines, phonological structure can, in poetry, operate directly in establishing relations between different words; in this way it takes on some of the function which is normally the prerogative of syntax. It is by compounding linguistic distinctions in this way that literary language is able to express meanings other than those which are communicable by conventional means.

These are, then, very simple illustrations of how literary messages convey meaning, but before we move on to more complex examples we must consider the second and related question: what kind of meaning does a literary message convey?

We can begin by following the implications of the fact that language is essentially a social phenomenon. It serves a social purpose, and to put the matter simply, it does so by codifying those aspects of reality which a society wishes in some way to control. Language, then, can be regarded as a socially sanctioned representation of the external world. Without such a representation, the external world is a chaos beyond human control. In the beginning was the Word. The members of a society accept the codification which their language provides because it gives them a necessary sense of security. Reality is under control because they share a common attitude towards it by sharing a common means of communication. Communication can only take place if there are conventionally accepted ways of looking at the world. But now we come to the important point: because people as members of a society accept a conventional view of reality as a social convenience, it does not follow that as individuals they are not aware of reality beyond that which their language represents. Indeed, the existence of religion and art is evidence that they are very much aware of reality beyond the bounds of common communication and social sanction. Social conventions supply people's needs insofar as they are members of society, but they have needs as individuals which such conventions by their very nature are incapable of satisfying. Every society has some form of art and some form of religion, and these serve as a necessary outlet for individual attitudes whose expression would otherwise disrupt the ordered pattern of reality which society promotes and upon which its survival depends. Art and religion are a recognition that there is other reality apart from that which is, as it were, officially recommended. What, then, is the nature of this reality?

The first thing to notice is that it is both a part of conventional reality and yet apart from it. This will be clear from a brief consideration of religion, which deals in such contradictions on a large scale. Thus gods have human attributes and are both human and non-human at the same time, omnipresent and yet incarnate in particular animate forms: immortal, yet affected by mortal longings: conceived without benefit of natural processes and dying only to be reborn. This other reality, then, is related to that which is conventionally recognized in the same way as literary language is related to the conventional code. What literature, and indeed all art, does is to create patterns out of deviations from normality and these patterns then represent a different reality from that represented by the conventional code. In, so doing, literature gives formal expression to the individual's awareness of a world beyond the reach of communal communication.

Having indicated how literary language conveys meanings, and what kinds of meanings they are which are conveyed, we can now have a closer look at some of the kinds of patterning which occur in literary texts and at the meanings they convey. We shall do this by analysing two texts, both of which will be poems. The reason why poems have been chosen and not pieces of prose is that it is important for our purposes that we should investigate intra-textual relations within one complete message unit and exigencies of space rule complete prose texts out. It is obvious that patterns in a text can only be recognized as such when they are seen as parts of a whole. It is true that there is often a hierarchical arrangement of patterns, smaller ones functioning as constituents in larger ones and so on up to the total complex of patterns which constitute the whole, so it would be possible to exemplify types of patterns by selecting from different constituent levels. But such a procedure would be likely to be a somewhat arid academic exercise, and for an important

H

reason. As will by now be apparent the unique mode of language organization to be found in literary texts is indistinguishable from the significance these texts have as messages. Since the texts create their own systems of language they inevitably create a different reality, and our awareness of one necessarily entails our awareness of the other. No purpose can be served in attempting to distinguish form from meaning. What we shall be concerned with, therefore, is not the exemplification of constituent patterns but the interpretation of complete textual units, that is to say, with messages as units of meaning.

Futility

Move him into the sun—
Gently its touch awoke him once,
At home, whispering of fields unsown.
Always it woke him, even in France,
Until this morning and this snow.
If anything might rouse him now
The kind old sun will know.

Think how it wakes the seeds—
Woke, once, the clays of a cold star.
Are limbs, so dear-achieved, are sides
Full-nerved—still warm—too hard to stir?
Was it for this the clay grew tall?
—O what made fatuous sunbeams toil
To break earth's sleep at all?

Wilfred Owen

How do we first set about discovering the patterns of language and reality which are presented in this poem? There is no rigid order of procedure; the technique is to pick on features in the text which appeal to first impression as unusual or striking in some way and then explore their ramifications.

Here we may begin by noticing that 'sun', an inanimate noun in the code, has been given the attributes of animacy in the context, and more particularly of humanness. Thus it is represented as touching the living sleeper to wake him up and as whispering in his ear. Further, its occurrence in the environment 'The kind old . . . will know' suggests that it is to be equated with 'man' or 'woman' which would be normal collocates here. But we must notice that although the context confers human qualities on the sun, at the same time the word retains the quality of inanimacy which accompanies it from the code. The pronouns, we note, are inanimate. So we have here an example of a hybrid unit created by the overlap of extra-textual relations which link the word with the code and intra-textual relations which link the word with other items of language in the context. The sun here is both inanimate and human, and yet, of course, at the same time, neither. Having made this observation, we may now proceed to investigate how it relates to the rest of the text.

We may notice next that a recurrent theme in the text is the ability of the sun to awaken things—people, seeds, the earth; and that this theme runs throughout the poem, 'awoke', 'woke' and 'rouse' occurring in the first verse, and 'wakes', 'woke', 'stir', 'break . . . sleep' in the second. Since we have established that the sun has both human and inanimate features, we might reasonably ask whether it is in its human or in its inanimate capacity that it performs the action of waking.

At this point we notice that the word 'wake' is used in three different senses in the poem. In the first place, it is used to refer to the action of rousing an already living human being from sleep and here the sun acts in a human capacity. Secondly, it is used to refer to the action of triggering off, as it were, the dormant life of seeds. Here the sun is the inanimate catalyst which stimulates seasonal growth. Thirdly, it is used to refer to the action of actual creation, and here the sun is represented as the elemental life-force which engenders life from the primeval clay. The first of these meanings relates to the diurnal cycle of night and day, the second to the seasonal cycle and the third to the cycle of creation. The three are, of course, commonly conceived as analogues, which accounts for the multiple meanings conventionally attributed to the words 'wake' and 'sleep'.

Now it is clear that the poet is attempting to conflate these different senses: his argument is that since the sun has the capacity to wake, there should be no difficulty in its exercising this capacity on a corpse. But the futility of this argument lies in the fact that the sun as an elemental life-giver has already done its work: the clay has been activated into life already—it is indeed still warm, which is proof of the fact and therefore a reason for the very reverse of hope. If the sun is regarded as a life-force, it has already fulfilled its function: if it is regarded as a kind old person, on the other hand, it has no function to fulfil since it is not a matter of rousing the living sleeper. The sun in its capacity as a stimulant to dormant life is irrelevant since we are concerned with something which has already grown.

What has happened here is that the composite meaning of the hybrid unit 'sun' develops into an internecine conflict between its constituent features of meaning because the word 'wake' and its semantic adherents like 'stir' and 'sleep', with which 'sun' is intra-textually associated, represent three meanings, each of which remains distinct. We can see in the text an attempt to develop a rational argument to counter the facts of reality which gradually assert themselves on the poet's awareness as the poem progresses. The patterns of imposed logic cannot be sustained, but this failure creates other patterns which represent the reality of the poet's experience, and which provide the text with its essential unity. It is to these patterns that we now turn.

The poem begins with an imperative in the first line and this is matched by an imperative in the first line of the second verse. Syntactically the two lines are, on one level, equivalent, and represent a pattern which relates the two verses. The illocutionary force of these two lines, however, is quite different: the first is an order, the second an appeal. Whereas the similarity of these lines links the two verses, the difference between them marks a transition from the confident command of the first to the somewhat wistful appeal of the second. The similarity serves to draw attention to the difference.

This transition can be said to reflect the realization that rationalization will not work, and the reasoning takes on a desperate note as the second verse develops. But this realization is anticipated in the first verse. Consider the line:

Until this morning and this snow.

Here the word 'snow' acquires a contextual significance over and above that which it has in the code by its association with 'morning', appearing as it does in an identical syntactic environment. 'Until this morning' and '(until) this snow' are syntactically equivalent and both function as temporal locatives. The effect of this is to bring 'snow' and 'morning' into semantic association. But in another respect they are diametrically opposed semantically. Extra-textually, 'snow' is related to 'winter' and both extra and intra-textually it is related to 'clays' and 'cold star' by virtue of the common semantic feature of coldness. Now 'winter' corresponds in the seasonal cycle to 'clays of a cold star' in the cycle of creation: both represent lifelessness. 'Morning', on the other hand, represents life in the diurnal cycle. Thus by bringing 'morning' and 'snow' together in a relation of equivalence, the poet realizes the very contradiction upon which his argument founders. What is true of one cycle is not necessarily true of another: morning and snow can co-exist so that waking in one sense does not entail waking in another sense.

·The awareness of the futility of reasoning develops through the second verse. After the initial appeal, the second line produces an echo of the second line of the first verse: 'awoke him once' and 'woke, once', but again the similarity which serves to link these two expressions also draws attention to their difference. The word 'once' is ambiguous and can refer to recurrent or non-recurrent action. 'Awoke him once' might mean 'used to wake him' or 'woke him once and only once' but the context makes the former more likely, and the fourth line, which is again related to it by the occurrence of 'woke', with its placing of 'Always' in initial position and its distinct reveille rhythm, confirms us in this interpretation:

Always it woke him, even in France.

The initial placing of 'Always', in fact has the effect of deliberately—perhaps too deliberately—dispelling any possibility of an alternative interpretation. The second occurrence of 'once', on the other hand, really admits only of the second interpretation; it is more or less imposed upon us by the fact that it is enclosed in commas and contrasts with 'wakes' in the first line, whose tense carries the meaning of recurrent action. All of this suggests that the poet is aware of the ambiguity of the word and is becoming aware of the implications of this in his use of the word with which 'once' is in close association. 'Once' referring to recurrent action necessarily makes 'awoke' in the first verse recurrent too: 'once' referring to non-recurrent action similarly makes 'woke' in the second verse non-recurrent. The two words, for all their similarity of form, do not mean the same thing. The argument now takes on a more desperate tone as if in reaction to this realization.

The last three sentences of the text are interrogative in form and are, therefore, in some degree of syntactic equivalence. As with the two imperative forms we have already discussed, however, their similarity of form disguises a considerable difference in illocutionary force. The first is a genuine question in that it presupposes the possibility of a reply, though it must be added that the question is framed in such a way as to suggest what the reply must be: it is, in fact, a leading question and carries something of the force of an expression like 'Surely these limbs are not too hard to stir'. The second sentence is somewhat different: in fact it is not really so much a question as a challenge or an accusation. It suggests an attitude which might be alternatively expressed as something like: 'So that's all the flesh grew tall for!' The increase in frustration is reflected in the expression 'the clay grew tall', which recalls the reference to seeds in the first line of the verse and represents a convergence of the seasonal and creative cycles referred to in the first and second lines respectively, again bringing out the contradiction which makes the argument essentially futile. This futility is most fully realized in the third interrogative sentence in this verse, which is different again from the other two and has even less of the force of a normal question: it is rather a cry of despair which carries with it the assumption that there can be no answer.

Two final observations might be made about this movement towards despair which is developed through these last three sentences. Firstly, we may notice the syntactic complexity of the holophrastic expressions 'dear-achieved' and 'full-nerved' which are in marked contrast to the simple attributives in the rest of the text. Their compressed complexity might be said to suggest an emotional intensity and a definite shift from the rationally controlled simplicity of the preceding lines. Secondly, the representation of the sun as both a human and an inanimate entity recurs in the last sentence and links the end of the poem with the beginning. The logical inconsistency that is entailed by the concept of an inanimate-human sun does not lead the poet to abandon the concept, but to recognize different implications in it. The sun even in its role as elemental life force in the form of inanimate sunbeams is humanly fatuous and toils to fulfil its primeval task like humans working in 'fields unsown'.

Here

Swerving east, from rich industrial shadows
And traffic all night north; swerving through fields
Too thin and thistled to be called meadows,
And now and then a harsh-named halt, that shields
5 Workmen at dawn; swerving to solitude
Of skies and scarecrows, haystacks, hares and pheasants,
And the widening river's slow presence,
The piled gold clouds, the shining gull-marked mud,

Gathers to the surprise of a large town:
10 Here domes and statues, spires and cranes cluster
Beside grain-scattered streets, barge-crowded water,
And residents from raw estates, brought down
The dead straight miles by stealing flat-faced trolleys,
Push through plate-glass swing doors to their desires—
15 Cheap suits, red kitchen-ware, sharp shoes, iced lollies,
Electric mixers, toasters, washers, driers—

A cut-price crowd, urban yet simple, dwelling
Where only salesmen and relations come
Within a terminate and fishy-smelling
20 Pastoral of ships up streets, the slave museum,
Tattoo-shops, consulates, grim head-scarfed wives;
And out beyond its mortgaged half-built edges
Fast-shadowed wheat-fields, running high as hedges,
Isolate villages, where removed lives

25 Loneliness clarifies. Here silence stands
Like heat. Here leaves unnoticed thicken,
Hidden weeds flower, neglected waters quicken,
Luminously-peopled air ascends;

And past the poppies bluish neutral distance
30 Ends the land suddenly beyond a beach
Of shapes and shingle. Here is unfenced existence:
Facing the sun, untalkative, out of reach.

Philip Larkin

The most striking feature of this poem is the extremely elaborate
patterning of structures which are syntactically equivalent. The entire first
verse consists of three clauses in parallel, each more complex structurally
than the one preceding and each marked as equivalent by the initial
occurrence of the word 'Swerving'. The first problem which confronts us
is to sort out the syntactic structure of this first verse.

When we begin to read, we assume that 'Swerving', etc. is an adverbial
occurring in thematic position at the beginning of a sentence and we suppose that according to the code of the language once it is complete as a
structure we shall meet a noun phrase functioning as a subject: 'Swerving
east . . . the road (+Verb)' or 'Swerving east . . ., the railway (+Verb)'
or something of this kind. Instead, our expectations are denied by the
recurrence of 'Swerving' initiating another clause longer than the first.
Notice that at this point another expectation has been developed in our
minds; one which has been created by the context: at the end of the
second clause we still suppose that a subject is on its way, but at the same
time we are primed by the already repeated pattern of what we assume
to be adverbials to expect another one of the same kind. Expectations
based on the code are joined by those based on the context. The writer's
patterns, in other words, have the effect of both keeping us in suspense,
waiting for the syntactic completion of the structure which he has
arrested, and of leading us to expect the established pattern to be repeated. The expectations created by the context are not disappointed.
Another instance of 'Swerving' comes next introducing yet another
apparent adverbial which is even longer than the previous two. The
increasing length of these structures, of course, contribute to the dulling
of our expectation of the subject and by this time we may well be re-
conciled to further repetition. The context has gained an ascendency over
the code. We reach the end of the verse and move on to the beginning of
the next assuming that the pattern now firmly established will be continued, though not entirely unmindful of the fact that somewhere a subject must be waiting to make its appearance. The first word of the
second verse takes us completely by surprise. It is neither a continuation
of the pattern, nor the long-awaited subject, but a finite verb. Now we can
only conclude from this that there must be a subject somewhere which
we have missed, concealed somewhere in the complex structures of the
first verse. *What* gathers? Search as we may, however, we shall find no

satisfactory candidate; the only ones which might conceivably qualify only do so by stretching a grammatical point or two.

What we have here, then, it appears, is a patterning of language in context which arrests the completion of the syntactic pattern of the code and has the effect of setting up different expectations which co-exist with, and can dominate, the expectations deriving from the code. But then both kinds of expectation are denied by the occurrence of an item which neither continues the contextual pattern, nor completes that of the syntax. There is a breakdown in normal extra-textual relations and, it might appear, a breakdown too in the intra-textual relations. As we shall see, the disturbance of the contextual patterns here is a function of the patterning formed by the relations set up within the text as a whole. Before taking up this point, however, we might notice other instances in the text where contextual patterns do not immediately correspond with those of the code.

In lines 11–13, we appear to have a series of three prepositional phrases functioning as locative adverbials. There is only one occurrence of the preposition itself—'beside'—but it is, of course, quite normal to have the preposition deleted in a series of this type. So it is that we take the three noun phrases 'grain-scattered streets', 'barge-crowded water' and 'residents from raw estates' as equivalent in that they are all noun phrases 'bound' or 'dominated' by the preposition 'beside'. Another reason for supposing this is the occurrence of 'and' which is conventionally required to link the last two (which may be the only two) items in a series of this kind. It is true that the third of these does not have the same internal structure as the previous two, which are structurally equivalent to a very high degree, this equivalence being 'foregrounded' by the unconventional syntactic form of the modifiers. The third differs also by being followed by a deleted form of the non-defining relative. But these are differences at a lower level of constituent structure; at a higher level it would seem that the three phrases are equivalent. Then in line 14 the finite verb 'push' appears, and it becomes apparent that what the contextual patterning would persuade us to believe is an adverbial is in fact a subject. 'And residents from raw estates', etc., is not the continuation of a pattern, but the initiation of a new one. The authority of the code recalls us from the misleading enticement of the context.

In line 29 the reader is likely to take 'the poppies bluish neutral distance' as one noun phrase until he comes upon the finite verb 'ends' when he begins to wonder, as before, whether he might not have overlooked a subject somewhere at the beginning of the following line. Even so he might assume that the poet is making free with his 'poetic licence' and that the subject of this verb is the following noun phrase: 'the land'. This represents an abnormal word order, but one not unknown in poetry. But on closer scrutiny it becomes clear that 'the poppies bluish neutral distance' cannot possibly be one noun phrase bound by the preposition 'past'. In the first place, we now notice that there is no apostrophe in 'poppies'. In the second place, poppies are red, so it is unlikely that they would take on a bluish appearance in the distance. Furthermore, when we come to consider the matter, it is difficult to see what the poppies' bluish distance could possibly mean. In fact, of course, only 'the poppies' occurs as part of the prepositional phrase, and 'bluish neutral distance' is a noun phrase on its own, functioning as the subject of the verb 'ends'. But once again we have to work it out: the contextual pattern is, as it were, out of focus with that of the code.

What are we to make of this? What significance does it have for the interpretation of the text as a whole? We can best approach an answer by first considering what, in general terms, the poem is about. It describes a movement through different kinds of life: from urban to rural to urban and then back again to rural. Whether this movement represents an actual journey by train or road, or whether it takes place only in the mind of the writer is irrelevant. We begin with industry and traffic and move to the edge of the urban world where workmen are still about and where fields are pieces of waste land rather than meadows. Then we move into the solitude of the rural world, return to urban life, and finally pass through this to emerge once more into the countryside. We might say, then, that in general the theme of the poem is the contrast between man-made urban existence, and the existence of nature. We must now consider how these two opposing worlds are represented.

We notice that on its first appearance, the countryside is presented as an inventory of items:

. . . skies and scarecrows, haystacks, hares and pheasants . . . (line 6)

Now if we look at the way urban life is presented after this, we see that it is done so in much the same manner:

Cheap suits, red kitchen-ware, sharp shoes, iced lollies
Electric mixers, toasters, washers, driers . . . (lines 15–16)

This would seem to suggest an equivalence between the two: both kinds of existence are characterized in the form of an inventory. Furthermore, this would appear to be borne out by the parallelism of the following two phrases, the first referring to rural life and the second to urban:

. . . shining gull-marked mud (line 8)
. . . stealing flat-faced trolleys (line 13)

Though this pair are syntactically different in deep structure, that is to say in the code, they are contextual twins in that their surface forms are syntactically identical

All of this suggests that when the countryside is first encountered it is seen as having much the same character as the town: no distinction is drawn between the artefacts of urban life and the natural objects of rural life.

At the end of the third verse we move again to the 'mortgaged half-built edges' of the town, just as before we moved through the waste land of thin and thistled fields, and the countryside confronts us once more. But this time it is seen in quite different terms. The transition from the third to the fourth verse takes the form of a phrase which poses a similar problem of interpretation to those we have already considered:

... where removed lives
Loneliness clarifies ... (lines 24–5)

The end of the verse at line 24 creates a natural pause and holds the completion of the syntactic pattern in suspense. 'Lives' could in consequence be a noun functioning as a subject of a verb yet to come, thus phonologically representable as/laivz/. The occurrence of 'loneliness' at the beginning of the following verse, however, contradicts this supposition and presents us with a possible candidate for the subject of 'lives', now regarded as a verb and phonologically representable as /lɪvz/. Only with the occurrence of the finite verb 'clarifies' is the puzzle resolved. It becomes apparent that this phrase is to be interpreted as follows:

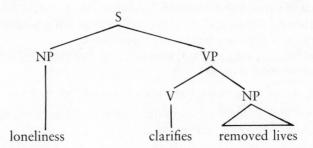

Once again, the code pattern is only established in spite of the contextual pattern. The word 'clarifies' in fact clarifies what is meant: and by so doing marks a transition in the poem which goes beyond the simple linking of the two verses: a transition from complexity to simplicity.

In contrast to the involved complexity of the syntactic patterning of the text up to the appearance of the word 'clarifies', the text following this word develops in a series of short and simple sentences. Whereas up to this point there are only four finite verbs ('gathers', 'cluster', 'push', 'clarifies') around which is constructed the vast superstructure of syntactic elaboration, the following four lines provide us with a sudden plethora of six ('stands', 'thicken', 'flower', 'quicken', 'ascends', 'ends').

It seems that now nature is seen not in terms of a static inventory of items, but of dynamic action, not related to the man-made urban world but remote from it. This remoteness is emphasized. In line 5 nature in its first appearance is associated with solitude, and this separation from the urban world is now stressed repeatedly by the use of the expressions 'unnoticed', 'hidden', 'neglected', 'isolate', 'removed', 'loneliness', 'silence', 'distance', 'out of reach' which occur in the last eight lines of the text. But this physical remoteness is matched by an essential difference in the kind of existence which nature is now shown to have. In the five simple finite structures which occur immediately after the word 'clarifies' there is a reference to all four of the medieval elements: leaves thicken and weeds flower (earth), waters quicken (water), the silence is like heat (fire) and air ascends (air). Remote and hidden from the urban world is an existence where elemental life forces are at work, an essential simplicity apart from the complexity of the immediately perceptible reality of urban life and indeed from the appearance of nature seen in similar terms.

It seems reasonable to suggest that the complexity of the syntactic patterning in the text which creates bafflement in the reader reflects what the writer sees as a confused complexity in perceptible reality. As this yields to a simple vision of elemental natural life, so there is a corresponding simplicity in the patterning of the language. But this awareness of elemental existence is elusive, and ultimately beyond communication —'untalkative, out of reach'. But the very form of the message which draws this conclusion is itself an expression of the other reality which it is beyond the capacity of conventional communication to express.

2 Other approaches

2.1 Halliday, M. A. K. Descriptive linguistics in literary studies. In M. A. K. Halliday and Angus McIntosh, *Patterns of Language, Papers in General, Descriptive and Applied Linguistics.* Longmans, 1966.

Halliday's principal purpose in this paper is to illustrate how the categories and methods of descriptive linguistics can (and should) be applied in the analysis of literary texts as much as in the analysis of any other kind of textual material. His concern is not with the interpretation or the aesthetic evaluation of the literary passages he examines but only with the revelation and precise description of language features which might remain undiscovered by a less exacting and less linguistic investigation. For example, he considers the verbal groups in Yeats' poem 'Leda and the Swan' and tabulates the results of his investigation as follows:

Verbal items in 'Leda and the Swan'

		Items in verbal group (i.e. functioning as 'predicator' in clause structure)			Items in nominal group (i.e. not functioning as predicator)
	I	2 3	4	5	6
a	Inde-pendent	Dependent		Qualifying (rankshifted)	(inapplicable)
b	Finite	Finite	Non-finite	Finite	Non-finite	
	hold push feel engender put on	lie let	drop catch up master		beat (2) caress catch lay	stagger loosen burn break

a Clause class   b Group class

Having made the analysis, Halliday proceeds no further. It is true that he makes the following observation: 'In "Leda", the few verbal items . . . get lexically more powerful as they get grammatically less "verbal": in finite verbal group in free clause we have "hold", "push", "put on", "feel"; while at the other end of the scale, including some not operating in verbal group at all, are "stagger", "loosen" and "caress" ', but he does not go on to discuss how the way the verbal forms are organized relates to other kinds of intra-textual patterning in the poem, and he draws no conclusions as to the relevance of his findings to the interpretation of the poem as a whole.

2.2 Sinclair, J. McH. Taking a poem to pieces. In Roger Fowler (ed.), *Essays on Style and Language*. Routledge and Kegan Paul, 1966.

Sinclair's approach to stylistic analysis is similar to that of Halliday. The purpose of his paper is to anatomize Philip Larkin's poem 'First Sight' by applying Halliday's categories of linguistic description. As in Halliday's paper, the results of his analysis are recorded in tabular form, and any conclusions as to their relevance for interpretation are left to the reader to work out for himself.

Sinclair does, however, mention two aspects of linguistic organization which play an important part in the setting up of intra-textual patterns in literary texts. The first of these he refers to as *arrest*. This occurs when a predictable syntactic pattern is interrupted, its completion being delayed by interposed linguistic units. For example, consider the first lines of the poem that Sinclair investigates in his paper:

> Lambs that learn to walk in snow
> When their bleating clouds the air
> Meet a vast unwelcome . . .

Here the syntactic pattern Noun Phrase (Lambs that learn to walk in snow) + Verb Phrase (meet a vast unwelcome) is interrupted by the interposition of the arresting adverbial: 'When their bleating clouds the air'. The pattern begun by NP is arrested and its completion delayed.

The second kind of contextual organization of language, which Sinclair calls *release*, occurs when a syntactic structure is extended after all grammatical predictions have been fulfilled. In this case there is an accretion of linguistic units on a pattern which is already a syntactic whole. Thus in the following line from 'First Sight':

> They could not grasp it if they knew

the conditional clause is a releasing element since the preceding clause is already grammatically complete.

It is clear that by a use of releasing and arresting elements, a writer can deny the reader a fulfilment of his predictions as derived from his knowledge of the code and replace them with predictions derived from the intra-textual patterns set up in the context of the poem itself. The discussion of Larkin's poem 'Here' in Part 1 indicates how this comes about.

2.3 Leech, Geoffrey. 'This bread I break'—language and interpretation. In *A Review of English Literature*, 1965, Vol. 6, No. 2. Reprinted in Freeman, Donald C. (ed.), *Linguistics and Literary Style*. New York: Holt, Rinehart and Winston, 1970.

Leech's approach to stylistic analysis differs essentially from that of Halliday and Sinclair in that it aims at relating linguistic description with critical interpretation, and at showing how the latter can benefit from the former. He points out that 'a work of literature contains dimensions of meaning additional to those operating in other types of discourse', and he suggests that for this reason descriptive linguistics cannot simply be applied indifferently to literary as to other types of text. He discusses three features of literary expression representing different 'dimensions of meaning' which are not covered by the normal categories of linguistic description, and illustrates them by reference to the poem of Dylan Thomas mentioned in the title of his paper.

1 *Cohesion.* By this is meant the intra-textual relations of a grammatical and lexical kind which knit the parts of a text together into a complete unit of discourse and which, therefore, convey the meaning of the text as a whole. In the poem under consideration, for instance, there is lexical cohesion in the repetition of the words 'oat' and 'break' and in the connection between items which share common semantic features like: *bread-oats-crops, wine-tree-fruit-grape-vine-drink, day-night-summer-sun,* etc. Leech points out that cohesion is not the unique property of poetry but is a feature of all types of text since it is this which combines separate linguistic units into stretches of meaningful discourse.

2 *Foregrounding.* This, on the other hand, is a predominantly literary feature. By foregrounding is meant the deliberate deviation from the rules of the language code or from the accepted conventions of its use which stands out, or is foregrounded, against a background of normal usage. Thus, in the poem under consideration, Thomas uses expressions like 'the oat was merry' in which a noun which normally has the feature of inanimacy is given an animate, and more exactly a human, feature, thereby creating a deviation which is foregrounded against a normal expression like 'the man was merry' 'the farmer was merry' and so on. Again, in the environment 'broke the . . .' a normal choice is restricted to nouns which have the feature of frangibility, for example, 'cup', 'plate', 'clock', etc., but in the poem we have the noun 'sun' which lacks this feature and is therefore a deviant choice which is foregrounded against the background of the normal choices mentioned above. The effect is to bestow upon the sun qualities which we would normally associate with objects like cups, clocks and so on. Foregrounding occurs, therefore, when the semantic features of an item in the code do not correspond with those which are bestowed upon it by the contextual environment in which it appears.

Leech also points out another manifestation of foregrounding. This occurs when the writer instead of exercising a wider choice than is permitted him by the code deliberately renounces his choice and produces uniformity where variety would normally be expected. In the poem, for example, Thomas uses the expression 'Man in the day and wind at night' and so sets up a syntactic equivalence between the two prepositional phrases. A similar syntactic parallelism occurs in the last line of the poem: 'My wine you drink, my bread you snap'. Setting up intra-textual syntactic equivalences, then, is also a feature of foregrounding in that it introduces patterns of language which are not expected in normal use.

3 *Cohesion of foregrounding.* By this is meant the manner in which deviations in a text are related to each other to form intra-textual patterns. Thus, for example, the deviant expression 'broke the sun' is foregrounded against normal usage but takes on a normality in the context of

the poem as a whole, because it is related to deviations of a similar kind like 'broke the grape's joy', 'pulled the wind down' and so on. Similarly, intra-textual patterns are also formed by the cohesion of the fore-grounded expressions 'the oat was merry', 'desolation in the vine' and 'sensual root'.

2.4 Jakobson, Roman. Closing statement: linguistics and poetics. In T. A. Sebeok (ed.), *Style in Language*. M.I.T. Press, 1960.

In this paper, Jakobson discussed the poetic function of language, which he characterizes as a use of language which concentrates on the actual form of the message itself: 'The set (Einstellung) toward the message as such, focus on the message for its own sake, is the poetic function of language.'

In literary writing, unlike other forms of expression, we find language which deliberately draws attention to itself. Foregrounding as discussed by Leech, for example, focuses the reader's attention on the actual form of the message being conveyed. Jakobson expresses the view that it is what Leech refers to as the second kind of foregrounding which is the essential criterion of the poetic function; that is. to say, the setting up of equivalences where equivalences would not normally occur. He refers to the two axes upon which language is organized: the paradigmatic axis or the axis of selection, and the syntagmatic axis or the axis of combination. Items ranged on the former represent alternative choices for any place in a structure and are in this sense equivalent. Thus, for example, the following table shows a number of alternative choices for completing the given structure:

	soaked smothered	in	water mud
A man who had been	lamed cut stung torn	by	stones flints nettles briars

The items ranged vertically in columns are equivalent in that any could be chosen to make up the completed structure, as in the well-known substitution table. If instead of selecting we combine all of the alternatives, we thereby project the principle of equivalence from the axis of selection, where it normally functions, to the axis of combination, where it does not normally function, and so produce the following passage of Dickens:

A man who had been soaked in water, and smothered in mud, and lamed by stones, and cut by flints, and stung by nettles, and torn by briars . . .

It is this setting up of intra-textual equivalences which Jakobson regards as the defining feature of the poetic function of language: 'The poetic function projects the principle of equivalence from the axis of selection into the axis of combination.' 'Measure of sequences is a device which, outside of poetic function, finds no application in language.'

Notice that intra-textual equivalences occur at the phonological and semantic as well as the syntactic levels.

2.5 Levin, Samuel R. *Linguistic Structures in Poetry*. Mouton, 1964.

In this book, Levin develops the notion of equivalence as outlined by Jakobson and shows how it operates at the phonological, syntactic and semantic levels to create structural features which distinguish poetry from other kinds of discourse. Just as Sinclair with his arrest and release and Leech with his cohesion, foregrounding and cohesion of foregrounding find it necessary to postulate descriptive categories other than those of descriptive linguistics to account for the features of literary discourse, so Levin too postulates special types of linguistic patterning.

He distinguishes two types of equivalence. The first, which he calls *Type I or positional equivalence*, is said to obtain between elements which share the same potentiality of occurrence in a given environment. Thus the prefixes *di-*, *re-*, *per-*, *ad-*, *in-*, *sub-*, and *con-* are all said to be positionally equivalent because they may each occur in front of the stem *-vert*. Similarly, all the items which can occur in the environment 'I saw him at'—are said to belong to the same Type I equivalence class: examples would be 'night', 'seven', 'your house', 'at the end of last semester', etc.

The second type of equivalence, which Levin calls *Type II or natural equivalence*, is said to obtain between elements which share common semantic or phonological features. Two elements are said to have natural semantic equivalence when they 'overlap in cutting up the general "thought-mass" '. That is to say, items which are connected by the systems of sense relations in the language would be counted as belonging to the same natural equivalence class, whether the items are in a relation of synonymy like 'happy' and 'gay', antonymy like 'happy' and 'sad' or hyponymy like 'emotion' and 'sadness'. Words which constitute semantic fields would also be members of the same equivalence class: for example 'names of animals, sets of abstract terms, or even a group of words like "moon", "star", "sea", "time" and "sun", between which semantic affinities may be said to exist'.

Natural equivalence of a phonological kind is said to exist between elements which 'overlap in cutting up the phonetico-physiological continuum'. That is to say, for example, that elements having the same syllable structure would be counted equivalent, as would elements sharing certain distinctive phonological features like nasality, voice, plosion, etc. Thus in the following line of Shakespeare

Full fathom five thy father lies

the first three words and the fifth word have naturally equivalent initial consonants and the third, fourth and sixth word have naturally equivalent medial vowels. The word 'fathom' and 'father' belong to the same natural equivalence class because they have the same syllable structure and the first and second syllables have the same initial segment in each case. These words are not naturally equivalent from the semantic point of view of course.

Apart from postulating these two types of equivalence, positional and natural, Levin introduces a third notion: that of coupling. This is said to occur when one type of equivalence converges with another to produce 'the structure wherein naturally equivalent forms occur in equivalent positions'. For example in Pope's line

A soul as full of worth as void of pride

the phrases 'full of worth' and 'void of pride' are positionally equivalent, both modifying 'soul', and are at the same time phonologically equivalent to the extent that they have the same rhythmic structure. The positional equivalence converges with the natural phonological equivalence to form a coupling. Furthermore, this coupling is reinforced by the fact that 'full' and 'void', which are positionally equivalent in that they share exactly the same environment, are naturally equivalent semantically in that they are antonyms, and phonologically in that they are monosyllables. Notice that the occurrence of the words 'worth' and 'pride' in equivalent environments which are couplings has the effect of establishing a relation of antonymy between them. This is an example of intra-textual patterns of the context bestowing meaning on words over and above that recorded in the code.

Levin illustrates his notion of coupling by an analysis of Shakespeare's sonnet 'When to the sessions of sweet silent thought'. Unlike Leech, however, he does not apply his analysis to the interpretation of the poem: he is interested only in revealing how the language in the poem is patterned: 'The analysis is therefore not an attempt at a full-scale interpretation; it is an attempt to reveal the role that couplings play in the total organization of the poem.' In this respect, Levin's approach to stylistic analysis is similar to that of Halliday and Sinclair.

2.6 Thorne, J. P. 'Stylistics and generative grammars.' In *Journal of Linguistics*, 1965, Vol. 1, No. 1. Reprinted in Freeman, Donald C. (ed.), *Linguistics and Literary Style*. New York: Holt, Rinehart and Winston, 1970.

In this paper, Thorne is concerned with the problem of accounting for the kind of deviant sentences which commonly occur in poetry within a grammar of a language. The difficulty is that a grammar as a device for generating all and only the well-formed sentences of a language will not be capable of assigning analyses to deviant sentences and that to extend the capacity of a grammar so that it does generate those deviant sentences which are actually attested in poetic texts will inevitably involve the generation of innumerable 'unwanted' deviant sentences which are not so attested. Thus, if we modify a grammar of English so that it generates E. E. Cummings' line: 'He danced his did' we would also have to accept that it would generate sentences like 'We thumped their hads' and so on. Or, to take an example from the poem of Dylan Thomas discussed by Leech, if the rules of a grammar of English were altered so as to generate sentences in the poem like 'The oat was merry', these rules would also generate sentences like 'The potato was joyful', 'The barley was disconsolate', 'The maize was amazed' and so on—sentences which are 'unwanted' in the sense that they are deviant without the justification of being observed as significant units of meaning in the context of a poem or other literary text.

The solution that Thorne proposes to this dilemma is that a poem should be thought of as being a sample of a different language from Standard English (or whichever standard language the poem is most nearly related to in lexis and phonology). The task of stylistics is then seen to be the writing of a grammar which will describe the structure of this unique language. In effect, what Thorne proposes is that the extra-textual relations which obtain between the language as represented in the context and that as represented in the code should be ignored, and attention directed exclusively to intra-textual relations, which are regarded as representing a separate code altogether.

One difficulty about this procedure is that a single text provides very little data from which the rules of the grammar can be induced, and Thorne acknowledges that the approach he suggests relies a great deal on intuition. What significance to attribute to the various syntactic features in the text depends on the analyst's intuitive sense of what the poem as a whole is about: 'This approach sets a high premium on intuition. Reading a poem, it is suggested, is often like learning a language. When we learn a language we develop the capacity to have intuitions about its structures. A grammar is a special kind of statement about these intuitions.'

Thorne illustrates his approach by applying it to E. E. Cummings' poem 'anyone lived in a pretty how town', a poem which shows a very high degree of deviance from the standard language, but he claims that his approach can also be applied to texts which reveal a high degree of grammaticalness. He considers, for example, Donne's poem 'A nocturnal upon S. Lucies day' and points out that a grammar for this text would have to include rules quite contrary to those of Standard English by which normally inanimate nouns are given the feature of animacy and the reverse. The grammar for this text would therefore generate sentences like 'yea plants, yea stones detest and love' and reject 'I laugh' or 'You love' as ungrammatical. Furthermore, 'It would also reveal the interesting point that in this language the sentence "Were I a man", which occurs in stanza four of the poem, is equivalent to "Were I a stone" in Standard English.'

3 Practical work

Exercise A

Point out how (a) Sinclair's notions of arrest and release (2.2) and (b) Levin's notion of coupling (2.5) are exemplified in the following texts. How far do these notions provide an insight into the literary 'effect' of passages of this kind?

(i) . . . The sounding cataract
Haunted me like a passion: the tall rock,
The mountain, and the deep and gloomy wood,
Their colours and their forms, were then to me
An appetite; a feeling and a love,
That had no need of a remoter charm,
By thought supplied, nor any interest
Unborrowed from the eye.—That time is past,
And all its aching joys are now no more,
And all its dizzy raptures. Not for this
Faint I, nor mourn nor murmur; other gifts
Have followed; for such loss, I would believe,
Abundant recompence. For I have learned
To look on nature, not as in the hour
Of thoughtless youth; but hearing often-times
The still, sad music of humanity,
Nor harsh nor grating, though of ample power
To chasten and subdue. And I have felt
A presence that disturbs me with the joy
Of elevated thoughts; a sense sublime

Of something far more deeply interfused,
Whose dwelling is the light of setting suns,
And the round ocean and the living air,
And the blue sky, and in the mind of man:
A motion and a spirit, that impels
All thinking things, all objects of all thought,
And rolls through all things. . . .   (Wordsworth)

(ii) She wanted to get out of this fixed, leaping, forward-travelling movement, to rise from it as a bird rising with wet, limp feet from the sea, to lift herself as a bird lifts its breast and thrusts its body from the pulse and heave of a sea that bears it forward to an unwilling conclusion, tear herself away like a bird on wings, and in the open space where there is clarity rise up above the fixed, surcharged motion, separate speck that hangs suspended, moves this way and that, seeing and answering before it sinks again, having chosen or found the direction in which it shall be carried forward.   (D. H. Lawrence)

(iii)   See how the world its veterans rewards!
A youth of frolics, an old age of cards;
Fair to no purpose, artful to no end,
Young without lovers, old without a friend;
A fop their passion but their prize a sot;
Alive, ridiculous, and dead, forgot!   (Pope)

(iv) Is not a patron, my lord, one who looks with unconcern on a man struggling for life in the water and when he has reached ground encumbers him with help? The notice which you have been pleased to take of my labours, had it been early, had been kind; but it has been delayed till I am indifferent, and cannot enjoy it; till I am solitary, and cannot impart it; till I am known, and do not want it.   (Samuel Johnson)

Exercise B

The text of the poem referred to in 2.3 is as follows:

This bread I break was once the oat,
This wine upon a foreign tree
Plunged in its fruit;
Man in the day or wind at night
Laid the crops low, broke the grape's joy.

Once in this wind the summer blood
Knocked in the flesh that decked the vine,
Once in this bread
The oat was merry in the wind;
Man broke the sun, pulled the wind down.

This flesh you break, this blood you let
Make desolation in the vein,
Were oat and grape
Born of the sensual root and sap;
My wine you drink, my bread you snap.

a Extend the analysis of the poem along the lines indicated in 2.3 by providing a complete exemplification of the features of cohesion, foregrounding, and cohesion of foregrounding.

b Apply Thorne's approach to the poem (2.6) by suggesting rules which would have to be postulated in a grammar based on the text to account for deviations.

c Suggest an interpretation of the poem in the light of your solutions to (a) and (b) and consider which approach provided you with the clearer insight into the meaning of the text.

Exercise C
The text of 'Leda and the Swan' referred to in 2.1 is as follows:

A sudden blow: the great wings beating still
Above the staggering girl, her thighs caressed
By the dark webs, her nape caught in his bill,
He holds her helpless breast upon his breast.

How can those terrified vague fingers push
The feathered glory from her loosening thighs?
And how can body, laid in that white rush,
But feel the strange heart beating where it lies?

A shudder in the loins engenders there
The broken wall, the burning roof and tower
And Agamemnon dead.
                                Being so caught up,
So mastered by the brute blood of the air,
Did she put on his knowledge with his power
Before the indifferent beak could let her drop?

a Extend the analysis of this text along the lines suggested by Halliday by considering areas of language other than the verbal group.

b Suggest what implications your findings, and those of Halliday, have for the interpretation of the text as a complete poem.

c Use the text to illustrate aspects of the other approaches to stylistic analysis outlined in Part 2.

d Attempt a complete analytic interpretation of the poem on the model of the interpretations of 'Futility' and 'Here' in Part 1.

Exercise D

Assess the practical value of stylistic analysis in the teaching of language and literature by devising lesson plans based on the analyses of Part 1 and the analysis resulting from your answer to problem 3(*d*) above. In particular, consider the validity of the following claims for stylistic analysis made in Part 1:

(i) By investigating the way language is used in a text, it can make apparent those linguistic patterns upon which an intuitive awareness of artistic values ultimately depend. It provides a basis for aesthetic appreciation by bringing to the level of conscious awareness features of the text otherwise only accessible to trained intuition.

(ii) Stylistics renders an essential service to language learning in that even if the learner does not develop an appreciation of literature as literature, he will have acquired an awareness of the way language functions in at least this form of communication: he will have developed an awareness of literature as language. This indicates how the study of literary texts can be correlated with the study of texts exemplifying other forms of social communication.

4 Further reading

A *Literary stylistics*

Introductions

Enkvist, N. E., Spencer, John and Gregory, M. J. *Linguistics and Style.* London: Oxford University Press, 1965.

Hough, Graham. *Style and Stylistics.* London: Routledge & Kegan Paul, 1969.

Leech, G. N. *A Linguistic Guide to English Poetry.* London: Longmans, 1969.

Collections of papers

Chatman, Seymour (ed.). *Literary Style: A Symposium.* London: Oxford University Press, 1972.

Chatman, Seymour and Levin, Samuel (eds.). *Essays on the Language of Literature.* Boston: Houghton Mifflin, 1967.

Fowler, Roger (ed.). *Essays on Style and Language.* London: Routledge & Kegan Paul, 1966.

Freeman, D. C. (ed.). *Linguistics and Literary Style.* New York: Holt, Rinehart, Winston, 1970.

Halliday, M. A. K. and McIntosh, Angus. *Patterns in Language: Papers in General, Descriptive and Applied Linguistics.* London: Longmans, 1966.

Sebeok, T. E. (ed.). *Style in Language*. Cambridge, Mass.: M.I.T. Press, 1960.

Individual papers

Gregory, M. J. Old Bailey speech in 'A Tale of Two Cities'. *A Review of English Literature*, 1965, 6, No. 2, 42–55.

Hendricks, W. O. Three models for the description of poetry. *Journal of Linguistics*, 1969, 5, No. 1, 1–22.

Thorne, J. P. Generative grammar and stylistic analysis. In John Lyons (ed.), *New Horizons in Linguistics*. Harmondsworth: Penguin, 1970.

Thorne, J. P. The grammar of jealousy: a note on the character of Leontes. In A. J. Aitken, Angus McIntosh and Hermann Palsson (eds.), *Edinburgh Studies in English and Scots*. London: Longmans, 1971.

B *Literary stylistics and the teaching of literature*

Doughty, P. S. *Linguistics and the Teaching of Literature*. Nuffield Programme in Linguistics and English Teaching, Paper 5. London: Longmans, 1968.

Edwards, Paul. Meaning and context: an exercise in practical stylistics. In *English Language Teaching*, 1968, 22, No. 3, 272–7.

Rodger, Alexander. Linguistics and the teaching of literature. In Hugh Fraser and W. R. O'Donnell, *Applied Linguistics and the Teaching of English*. London: Longmans, 1969.

Widdowson, H. G. *Literature and Language*. Listen and Teach Series. Mimeo, English by Radio and Television, B.B.C., London, 1970.

Widdowson, H. G. Stylistic analysis and literary interpretation. *The Use of English*, 1972, 24, No. 1, 28–33.

ANTHONY HOWATT
8 Programmed Instruction

1 The principles underlying programmed instruction

The principles which underlie programmed instruction are not in themselves very new. What is unfamiliar, however, is the way in which these principles have been applied in creating teaching materials. This chapter will, therefore, contain a number of examples so that the reader may see for himself the kind of materials that programming ideas have provoked. First, however, we should briefly summarize these ideas.

The dominating principle of programmed learning is the need to encourage the pupil's active participation at every step in his learning. In the traditional classroom, most pupils are silent most of the time. If the teacher asks a question, only one pupil is called upon to answer it. The others are supposed to be 'following the lesson'. That is to say, they are meant to think of an answer to the teacher's question and to measure it against the answer which the teacher actually accepts as correct. If there are 40 other pupils in the class, nobody has much opportunity of participating actively in the lesson. The traditional system works up to a point, but programmed learning enthusiasts believe that learning would be much improved if every pupil had a chance of answering all the teacher's questions. This need to provoke an active response from each pupil is the cornerstone of programmed learning, though the form which these responses take may vary considerably between one programme and another.

If the idea of active responding is developed a little, it is clear that a way must be found of telling the pupils whether they are right or wrong. The usual technical label for the information given to the pupils about their answers is *knowledge of results*. Different approaches to programming take different views about the best way of providing this knowledge of results, and about the psychological effects on pupils of being told that they are wrong. However, there is no disagreement on the necessity for giving the learner some kind of feedback on his attempts to solve the problems which he has been confronted with.

So far, then, we have seen that a programme sets the pupil a series of problems to solve and then provides him with information about the correct solutions. If learning is to be efficient and effective, it is obviously very important that the problems should be related to each other so that the pupil is led gradually to an understanding of the major point which the programme is trying to teach. This means that a teacher writing a programme must break down the major teaching point into a number of related smaller points and then construct a series of problems which will take the pupil step by step towards the final goal. This process is sometimes described technically as *analysing the desired terminal behaviour*. Obviously, we must also take into account what the pupil already knows about the topic, his so-called *entry behaviour*.

In outline, then, programmed teaching materials have a clear enough aim. They seek to take the learner from his supposed entry behaviour to the desired terminal behaviour by asking him to solve a series of intermediate problems. This is essentially what teaching has always been about. The special characteristic of programmed instruction is that each pupil is supposed to answer every intermediate problem. Clearly, this cannot be done properly by using traditional teaching techniques or materials. The alternative is to devise materials which the pupils can use individually. Fast learners will work through these materials quickly, slow learners will take longer, but each pupil will work at his own pace. In a sense this is what a traditional textbook is supposed to do. But traditional textbooks do not ask questions. Admittedly, most textbooks have a set of practice examples or test questions at the end of a chapter. But both exercises and tests assume that the major point of the lesson has already been learnt. Programmes set out to teach by asking questions.

Programmes are, therefore, intended to be self-instructional. But, unlike traditional textbooks, programmes set the learner a series of problems to solve. This raises an obvious difficulty. If a pupil is to work through a set of problems on his own, he must either get the answers right or have a way of finding the correct answers easily. If a learner makes mistakes which he cannot correct for himself, he will lose interest in his work. It is, therefore, a firm principle of programming that *errors should be kept to a minimum*. This immediately causes a headache for the programmer— how can you write a self-instructional programme which all the pupils in a class will be able to work through without making too many mistakes, and at the same time avoid boring the faster learners? One solution is to restrict the application of programming to specially selected areas of learning difficulty. In this way, no programme will be particularly long, and the difference in time needed by slow and fast learners will not be too marked. In general, this aim of attending closely to a specially chosen problem in the subject matter, rather than attempting to programme everything, is likely to be the most useful application of programming to foreign language teaching.

There is considerable disagreement about the psychological effect of making mistakes, and this disagreement lies behind the two different types of programmes that have been developed. One view holds that mistakes should be avoided altogether. Programmes should be written so that the pupils get all the answers to all the problems right. The effect of this view is to encourage the programmer to make his questions easy enough for all the pupils to succeed, and ask rather a lot of related questions, so that no question is too much of a jump from the one before. This type of programming, which was developed from the theoretical work of the American psychologist B. F. Skinner, has been labelled *linear* programming. In a linear programme, each pupil is expected to answer each question in the programme one after the other 'in a straight line'. The alternative concept is that different pupils should answer different questions, depending on how well they are doing. We shall come back to this so-called *branching* technique in a moment.

Linear, or Skinnerian, programming rests on the theory that people learn best when they are required to make a large number of active responses, each of which is *reinforced*. Reinforcement is a technical term which means, more or less, reward. If animals are learning a new bit of behaviour, they need to be reinforced by food or a pat on the head or something of the kind. Of course, the reinforcement is only effective if they actually want food or attention. If they are not hungry, they will not learn very well. With people, however, success at getting answers right is reckoned to be reinforcing. Again, this assumes that the pupils want to be successful in the first place. So, in order to provide as many opportunities for reinforcement as possible, a linear programme will tend to ask rather a lot of questions. These should be constructed so that the pupils are correct, and therefore, reinforced. In very general terms, this is an intuitively reasonable way of looking at learning, but it neglects a rather important feature, that is, learning from one's mistakes.

If you make a mistake, it may be a small slip, or it may be evidence of a more serious misunderstanding. If it is the former, you can probably put yourself right, once the error has been pointed out to you. A linear programme can often cope with mistakes of this kind simply by letting the pupils know what the correct answers are. However, if the mistake is more serious, a linear programme will not be able to help because it does nothing more than tell the pupil what the right answer ought to be. A different kind of programme is needed to explain the misunderstanding. This is a branching programme where the pupil is given two or three alternative answers and asked to choose the right one. If he chooses wrongly, his mistake can be explained to him. If he chooses correctly, he can go on to the next problem. Of course, it is important that each alternative answer should represent a possible source of genuine confusion.

2 An illustration of programming techniques

In order to illustrate the different effects of linear and branching programmes, two excerpts are presented below which put the reader in the position of a beginner in a foreign language course. In order to have a learnable language which no reader would already know, one has been invented for the purpose. It is called Novish, and its main characteristic is that the vocabulary is similar to English, but the grammar is not. Both programme excerpts teach short-form answers in Novish and they differ in three respects. The first programme is linear, it avoids translation into the mother-tongue (i.e., into English), and it does not explain the grammar of the foreign language. The second, on the other hand, is branching, it translates the Novish into English, and it explains the grammatical rules. These excerpts come from programmes which have been used experimentally. There seems to be little evidence that one is better than the other, though the first one can produce somewhat erratic results.

The only Novish you are expected to know (your assumed entry behaviour) is that a sentence like *Sademane min* means *This is a man* (*sademane* = *this is*, *min* = *man*).

Programme Excerpt 1—Linear

The answers are in the right-hand margin, one step, or *frame*, to use the technical term, below the questions.

Short form answers in Novish (1)

ANSWERS

1		Ki poi sademane?—Ye, gru	
2		Ki min sademane?—Ye, gr- .	
3		Ki weimin sademane?— , .	gru.
4		Ki pooni sademane?— , gru.	Ye, gru.

		ANSWERS
5	Ki min sademane?— , .	Ye
	Ki weimin sademane?— ,	
	Ki pooni sademane?— , .	
6	Ki tre sademane?— , gru.	Ye, gru. Ye, gru. Ye, gru.
7	Ki tavl sademane?—Ye, stil.	Ye
8	Ki bukh sademane?—Ye, s- .	
9	Ki pokit sademane?—Ye, .	stil.
10	Ki tavl sademane?— , .	stil.
	Ki bukh sademane?— , .	
	Ki pokit sademane?— , .	
11	Ki min sademane?— , .	Ye, stil. Ye, stil. Ye, stil
	Ki tavl sademane?— ,	
	Ki tre sademane?— ,	
	Ki pooni sademane?— , .	

12		Ki tavl sademane? nu, gru.	Ye, gru Ye, stil Ye, gru Ye, gru
13		Ki bukh sademane?—　　　, g-　.	
14		Ki pokit sademane?—　　　,	Nu, gru.
15		Ki poi sademane?—Nu, stil.	Nu, gru.
16		Ki weimin sademane?—Nu, st-　.	
17		Ki pooni sademane?—　　　, 　.	Nu, stil.
18		Ki pokit sademane?—Nu, 　.	Nu, stil.
		Ki poi sademane?—Nu, 　.	
		Ki tavl sademane?—Nu,	
		Ki tre sademane?—Nu, 　.	
			gru. stil. gru. stil.

Programme Excerpt 2—Branching
Short form answers in Novish (2)

1 There are two classes of nouns in Novish—'gru' nouns and 'stil' nouns. 'Gru' nouns are the names of growing things, and 'stil' nouns are the names of things which don't grow. (Please notice that 'stil' is spelt with only *one* 'l' in Novish.) In this programme we shall look at short form answers in Novish, and we shall have to bear the 'gru'/'stil' distinction firmly in mind.

2 Look at this Novish question:

 Ki min sademane?—Ye, gru.

The answer to the question 'Ki min sademane?' (which means more or less 'Is this a man?') is 'Ye, gru' (which means 'Yes, the object you are asking about is a growing thing like a man'). Bearing this in mind, what will the answer to this question be:

 Ki poi sademane?

a Ye, gru. Look at paragraph 8.

b Ye, stil. Look at paragraph 5.

3 Trees are growing things in Novish, so 'Ye, gru' is correct. Things needn't be animals in order to grow. Plants and vegetables are also 'gru' things.

Now continue to the next paragraph.

4 We shall now look at the answer to another question:

 Ki tavl sademane?—Ye, stil.

Why is the answer 'Ye, stil'? Because of course a table is not a growing thing. Notice however, that it is not enough in Novish merely to answer questions of the kind we have been looking at with 'ye' or 'nu' alone. You must be more explicit. Which of the following two statements is true:

a You needn't say whether things are 'gru' or 'stil'. Look at paragraph 6.

b You must always say whether things are 'gru' or 'stil'. Look at paragraph 12.

5 'Poi' is the Novish word for 'boy'. A boy is a growing object in Novish, as in English. So the answer cannot be 'Ye, stil'; it must be 'ye, *gru*'.

Now go to paragraph 9 and continue the programme.

6 In all the examples you have seen, the answers have had two words: 'Ye, *gru*' or 'Ye, *stil*' and the second word tells us whether the object is growing or not. 'Ye' or 'nu' by itself would be ungrammatical.

Now continue with the programme at paragraph 13.

7 You have made a common error for English-speaking learners of Novish. You have forgotten that trees are growing things, so 'tre' must be a 'gru' word in Novish. Things needn't be animals to be 'gru' words; vegetables and plants also grow.

Now continue the programme at paragraph 4.

8 Yes, the answer to 'Ki poi sademane?' must be 'Ye, gru' because the object in the picture is a boy, i.e. a growing thing.

Now go to the next paragraph.

9 Let's have another example. What's the answer to this question:

 Ki tre sademane?

a Ye, gru. Look at paragraph 3.
b Ye, stil. Look at paragraph 7.

10 Right. You must make it clear that the object you are talking about is a 'gru' thing or a 'stil' thing.

Now continue with the programme in the next paragraph.

11 Here are 4 questions. What are the answers?

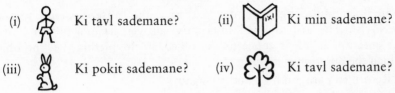

(i) Ki tavl sademane? (ii) Ki min sademane?

(iii) Ki pokit sademane? (iv) Ki tavl sademane?

a (i) Nu, gru (ii) Nu, stil (iii) Nu, gru (iv) Nu, stil. Look at para. 15.
b (i) Nu, stil (ii) Nu, gru (iii) Nu, stil (iv) Nu, stil. Look at para. 14.
c (i) Nu, gru (ii) Nu, stil (iii) Nu, gru (iv) Nu, gru. Look at para. 17.

12 Right. The examples you have seen make it quite clear that you must say 'Ye, *gru*' or 'Ye, *stil*'. 'Ye' or 'nu' by itself would be ungrammatical.

Now continue with the programme in the next paragraph.

13 Let's move on now to negative answers. Here are three examples:

 Ki min sademane?—Nu, stil.

 Ki poi sademane?—Nu, stil.

 Ki pokit sademane?—Nu, gru.

So, when the answer in Novish is 'nu', you must add whether the object is 'gru' or 'stil'. But to what does the 'gru' or the 'stil' refer?

a It refers to the object in the picture. Look at paragraph 10.

b It refers to the object in the question. Look at paragraph 16.

14 You have got everything the wrong way round. It is the object in the *picture* (NOT the object in the question) that you must think about. For example:

 Ki tavl sademane? Nu, *gru*.

Literally, the answer means: '*No, (a boy is not a still thing like a table) a boy is a growing thing.*

Go back to paragraph 13 once again and revise negative answers.

15 Nearly right. But I think you have forgotten that trees are growing things. When you have corrected your answer to number (iv), continue with the programme at paragraph 18.

16 Be careful. This misunderstanding is the cause of many mistakes in Novish. The 'gru' and 'stil' in negative answers has nothing to do with the question at all. It concerns the object in the picture, i.e. the object which the question is *about*.

Return to paragraph 13 and try again.

17 Good. You had to say whether the objects in the pictures were 'gru' objects or 'stil' objects, and you correctly classified 'poi', 'pooni' and 'tre' as growing things and 'bukh' as a still thing.

It should be pointed out that this programme was originally presented in the form of a booklet which is much more convenient and does not give away the right answer so easily.

It is a little unfair that the excerpt from Programme 1 implies that linear programmes cannot explain things. Of course they can, but this excerpt was chosen to illustrate that linear programmes can be used in circumstances where it is impossible to use the pupils' mother-tongue for explanatory purposes. To work properly, branching programmes need a language in which to describe and explain problems. If the programmer cannot use the learners' native language, then he cannot use branching techniques with beginners but must wait until the pupils have learnt enough of the foreign language for this purpose.

Now let us look more closely at what the programmes were teaching:

(i) There is a *conceptual* distinction in Novish between growing things expressed by *gru*, and non-growing things expressed by *stil*. This is similar to the English distinction between animate and inanimate nouns, except that plants are inanimate in English but *gru* words in Novish.

(ii) There is a *formal* pattern to short form answers in Novish which is governed by certain rules. It must be stated explicitly whether the object being talked about is a *gru*-class object or a *stil*-class object, and the verb-form is deleted, i.e. *Ye, sademane gru* is ungrammatical. These rules have some similarity to the rules in English for *Yes, he does*. The speaker must know whether the (singular) subject is masculine, feminine or neuter and he must not repeat the lexical element in the verb. To the question *Does John like beer*, the answer *Yes, he does like* is ungrammatical.

The Novish learning problems are, therefore, parallel to those in real-life learning. The pupil must see, and master for himself, the rules which are responsible for the patterns of the foreign language. These rules may be merely formal, but are much more likely to be controlled by the meaning. In English for example, the difference between the grammatical sentence *John always makes mistakes* and the ungrammatical *John makes always mistakes* is a matter of formal rules of word-order. But the distinction between *John always makes mistakes* and *John's always making mistakes* is controlled by what the speaker means to say.

It is always hazardous to generalize, but it seems likely that linear programming is better suited to the presentation and practice of formal patterns. Branching is rather clumsy in this respect. For example, if you were teaching the distinction between *has* and *have* in English, a series of linear frames would seem to be more convenient and perhaps less confusing than branching sequences:

1

Linear

John	a new Mini.	
The Browns	a new Ford.	has
		have

Branching

a John have a new Mini. Look at page 6.

b John has a new Mini. Look at page 9.

On page 6 the programmer would have to explain why *have* is wrong and it is difficult to provide very many practice examples if each one has to be explained in detail. However, at some point the programmer will want to test whether the learner has grasped the rule governing the different patterns, and a branching question would be a very good way of doing this. If the pupil passed the test, he could go on with the programme, but if he did not, he would have some more practice or explanation. The sample programme on *since* and *for* below mixes linear and branching techniques in this way.

3　A sample programme

Below is a sample programme which may, perhaps, be taken as a model for other programmes. It deals with a specific learning problem for foreign students of English and, as such, might take its place in a library of short programmes on common learning difficulties. Programmes take quite a long time to construct and they also tend to be lengthy. It would seem sensible, therefore, to apply programming techniques fairly selectively to problems which the majority of learners experience.

A programme must have *an objective* and *a plan* for achieving it in accordance with *a general strategy* of language teaching.

General strategy

It is natural that opinions on general strategy should vary, but the following four points sum up the overall viewpoint which the programme exemplifies:

1 The learner of a foreign language experiences stretches of language which he tries to make sense of.

2 To do this successfully, he must see that there are regular patterns in what he experiences.

3 In addition, he must recognize that these patterns are governed by linguistic rules, or stylistic conventions, which involve pronunciation, spelling, grammar, vocabulary and meaning.

4 Finally, in order to produce language of his own, the learner must operate these rules and conventions properly, i.e. like a native speaker.

These points assume that the ability to understand a foreign language logically precedes the ability to produce it correctly. Furthermore, they emphasize that learning general rules which control language patterns is more important than learning patterns in isolation. The programmer must, therefore, ask himself: 'What exactly is controlling the rules that native speakers use in their language?'

Rules may be controlled by pronunciation. The most obvious example in English is the choice between *a* and *an* in sentences like *I've got a new car* and *I've got an old car*. Secondly, they may be controlled by grammar. For example, the choice of *has* rather than *have* in the sentence *John has just bought a new boat* depends on the rules of concord in English. Similarly, the position of *often* in the sentence *I go often to the pictures on a Saturday night* is incorrect because the grammatical order of words ought to be *I often go to the pictures on a Saturday night*.

However, the most difficult learning problems are those where patterns are chosen for semantic reasons. For example, *I read 'Oliver Twist' once* is quite different in meaning from *I've read 'Oliver Twist' once* and the pupils must learn the semantic rules which govern the choice of tenses. Of course, to be perfect, the pupil must try to get everything right— pronunciation (or spelling), grammar and meaning. The rules which govern all these aspects of language are involved whenever he produces a sentence. But in teaching we must be clear in our minds what particular kind of rule we are interested in at any one time, and if we want the pupils to distinguish between *I read* (past) and *I've read* (perfect) as well as between *once* (at some time in the past) and *once* (one time), then we are concerned with semantic rules.

Finally, the choice between patterns may be controlled by conventions rather than rules. These can be found only in a study of the context in which a sentence is uttered. For instance, *Would you mind not being late in the future?* means the same semantically as *Be on time in future, will you?* and both obviously follow the syntactic rules of English. However, the former is more acceptable according to the normal conventions of polite social behaviour than the latter.

In the sample programme, we are concerned with semantics, and it is necessary now to look at the learning objective in some detail.

The objective

The sample programme sets out to teach the native-speaker's choice of *since* and *for* in sentences such as:

(i) I've been here since Sunday

(ii) I've been here for two days.

There are four main points:

1 Sentences of both type (i) and type (ii) describe events or continuous states occurring during an interval of time in the past.

2 In sentences of type (i), the interval of time is looked upon as having begun at a definite, named time (Sunday, in our case).

3 In sentences of type (ii), the interval of time is looked upon as extending over a period of time whose length may be described as a definite number (e.g. *for a week, for three hours*, etc.) or it may be indefinite (e.g. *for some time, for ages*, etc.).

4 If the native speaker can both name the time when the interval began and compute the length of time that has elapsed, he has a free choice between a time expression with *since* and one with *for*. This synonymity is a fundamental cause of difficulty to a foreign learner.

So, we have a discrimination learning problem controlled by the way in which a time interval is viewed by a native speaker. And he may have a free choice between two synonymous time-phrases with which to express this time interval.

The sample programme deals only with this semantic distinction. It does not deal with other aspects of the problem such as the choice of verb-forms. Furthermore, it only deals with the *basic* distinction between *since* and *for*, i.e. between using *since* with the names of time (e.g. *since Sunday*) and *for* with explicitly counted periods of time (e.g. *for two hours*).

The plan

The following six-point plan should be useful for application to many language teaching problems. It derives from the general strategy above.

1 *Exemplify the learning problem in a suitable context*. In the sample programme below *since* and *for* have been exemplified separately in Steps 1 and 2. The learner is given one example as a model and asked to search for others.

2 *Isolate the learning problem for the pupil's attention and describe it briefly*. This is done in Steps 3 and 4 of the sample. The description should be as simple as possible. In the sample, it says only that intervals of time may be expressed by phrases using *since* or phrases using *for* which may be synonymous in certain contexts.

3 *Get the learner to search for the rule(s)*. In the sample programme, the whole point is to teach the pupil what is controlling the choice between

time phrases with *since* and those with *for*. The pupil is asked if he can see a rule from the examples he has been given. At this point the programme branches. If the pupil thinks he can see a rule, he is asked to apply it in a test at Step 5. If he is 100% successful in this test, he is permitted to skip to Step 12 where his rule is tested again, and in Step 13 he is given an opportunity to go back if he was wrong. In order to find the correct rule he must go through Steps 7, 8, 9, 10 and 11. This branch is the most complex part of the programme, and the diagram below may be of some help.

4 *State and test the learner's comprehension of the rule(s).* See Steps 12 and 13 of the sample.

5 *Exemplify the rule(s) again in a new context and get the learner to apply them.* The sample programme follows this part of the plan in Steps 14, 15 and 16.

6 *Re-state and re-test the rules(s).* See Step 17 in the sample.

In addition, the sample programme looks forward to the next programme in the sequence on *since* and *for* by setting the pupils a test. If they get over 70% on this test, they are permitted to skip the next programme altogether.

When reading the sample programme, notice the variety of ways in which the learner can be asked to respond: he is asked to search for examples which follow a given model, deduce a general rule from a set of examples, transform one sentence into another according to a general instruction, answer direct questions, fill in blanks, and construct sentences of his own following a model example. Also notice how the general scheme of the programme follows the plan: Examples—Rules—Examples—Rules. In the literature on programming, the sequence of Examples—Rules is sometimes referred to as the EGRUL system, i.e. inductive learning. The corresponding RULEG (Rules followed by Examples) is obviously a deductive learning system. In foreign language teaching the best plan is probably to get the pupil to search for rules in the examples of language he has been given (EGRUL) and then apply these rules to a new set of examples (RULEG). Then the rules can be revised after the pupil has actually used them (EGRUL again). This gives the whole scheme of EGRUL, RULEG, EGRUL.

Below is a diagram of the sample programme which may make its construction a bit clearer:

$$[1] \to [2] \to [3] \to [4] \to [5] \to [6] \quad\longrightarrow\quad [12] \to [13] \to [14] \to [15] \to [16] \to [17] \to [18] \to [19]$$
$$[7] \to [8] \to [9] \to [10] \to [11]$$

Steps 7 to 11 describe the rules slowly. Notice that a learner can enter this sequence at *three* different points in the programme, i.e. after Steps 4, 6 and 13 in case he skips the slow sequence and then finds out that he should have done it.

Programme on the use of 'since' and 'for' in English

Try to answer the question, or questions, in each step before looking at the answers, which are at the beginning of the following step. Sometimes you may be sent to a different step altogether. Don't be surprised, but just follow the instructions. Now begin:

1 Molly and Bill are on holiday in Brighton. Like everybody else, they like to send postcards to their friends. Here is their card to Jane.

                                        Brighton,
                                        Saturday
Dear Jane,

   We've been here since Monday, and are having a super time. The weather was terrible at first, but it's been sunny every afternoon since Wednesday. George was late. His car broke down on the way. But he's been with us since Thursday morning and sends his best wishes.

                                        Love,
                                          Molly & Bill

This programme is about how to use *since* and *for* in English. How many examples of *since* can you find in Molly and Bill's postcard? Here is the first one:

   We've been here since Monday.

Now try to find the others and write them down:

....
....
....
....

Now look at Step 2 for the right answers.

2 Here are the other sentences with *since* in the postcard:

   It's been sunny every afternoon since Wednesday.
   He's been with us since Thursday morning.

On the same day, Saturday, George wrote to a girl-friend of his called Anne.

Brighton,
Saturday

Dear Anne,

My car broke down on the way here! But I've been here for two days now. The weather's marvellous, but Molly and Bill say that it's only been good for three days. They've been here for nearly a week, and it was raining when they came. So I'm lucky!

Good wishes from all,
George

George uses some sentences with *for* in his postcard. Here is one of them:

But I've been here for two days now.

Can you find the others? Write them down:

. . . .
. . . .
. . . .
. . . .

Now look at Step 3 for the answers.

3 Here are the other sentences with *for*:

It's only been good for three days.
They've been here for nearly a week.

Have you noticed that sentences with *since* can mean the same as sentences with *for*? Here is an example. Remember the postcards were written on Saturday.

George has been in Brighton *since Thursday morning*.
George has been in Brighton *for two days*.

Now can you write sentences in Columns A and B that mean the same.

Remember that today is Saturday

Column A	Column B
Bill's been here since Monday.	Bill's been here for five days.
Molly's been here since Monday, too.	. . . .
. . . .	George's been here for two days.
The weather's been good since Wednesday.	. . . .

4	*Column A*	*Column B*

Bill's been here since Monday.   Bill's been here for five days.
Molly's been here since Monday,   *Molly's been here for five days,*
too.   *too.*
George's been here since Thursday.   George's been here for two days.
The weather's been good since   *The weather's been good for*
Wednesday.   *three days.*

So, in English we sometimes use *since* to talk about an interval of time
And we sometimes use *for*. What is the difference between *since* and *for*?
We shall now try to find out. Look at these examples. Can you see a rule?

Since	*For*
I've been here since Friday.	I've been here for six months.
since August.	for five years.
since Christmas.	for three weeks.
since the winter.	for two hours.
since six o'clock.	for a week.
since 1967.	for twenty minutes.

Can you see a rule for using *since* and *for*?

a Yes, I think so. If this is your answer, look at Step 5.
b No, I don't think so. If this is your answer, look at Step 7.

5 You think you can see a rule for using *since* and *for*. Good. Now
try to test your rule by filling in the right prepositions in these examples:

I've been in London . . . . Tuesday.
. . . . June.
. . . . three months.
. . . . 1968.
. . . . two years.
. . . . last summer.
. . . . a fortnight.
. . . . nearly twenty-four hours.

Now look at Step 6 for the right answers.

6   I've been in London since Tuesday.
since June.
for three months.
since 1968.
for two years.
since last summer.
for a fortnight.
for nearly twenty-four hours.

If you have got *all* the answers right, look at Step 12.
If you haven't, look at Step 7 for some more help.

7 You are not sure whether you know the rule for using *since* and *for*.
Let us look at some of the examples with *since* again:

> I've been here since Friday.
> since August.
> since 1967.

Now, what is the word *Friday*? It is the name of a day of the week.
What is the word *August*? It is the n-.... of a m-.....

8 August is the name of a month.
What is the phrase 1967? It is the .... of a y-....

9 1967 is the name of a year.
Now look at the other sentences with *since* again:

> I've been here since Christmas.
> since the winter.
> since six o'clock.

Christmas, *the winter* and *six o'clock* are all names, too. Christmas is
the name of a special time of the year. The winter is the name of a season.
Six o'clock is the name of a particular time during the day or night.

Now let's look at some of the examples with *for*:

> I've been here for six months.
> for five years.
> for three weeks.

Six, *five* and *three* are not names. What are they?
They are ....

10 Six, five and three are *numbers*. You use numbers when you *count*.
So, when you count the time, you must use *for*. Look at the other
examples:

> I've been here for two hours.
> for a week.
> for twenty minutes.

All these sentences tell you the *number* of hours, weeks or minutes that
have gone by. (Remember that *a week* is the same as *one week*.)
You know that the special word in English for *two weeks* is *a fortnight*.
So, can you complete this sentence:

> John and I have been in Brighton .... a fortnight.

11 John and I have been in Brighton *for a fortnight.*

Now go on to Step 12.

12 You seem to understand the rule for using *since* and *for* to talk about intervals of time.

Can you put *since* and *for* correctly in these two rules:

Rule 1: You use .... when you count the number of days, months, years, and so on which have gone by in the interval of time.

Rule 2: You use .... when you give the name of the day, month, year and so on when the interval of time began.

13

Rule 1: You use FOR when you count the number of days, months, years, and so on which have gone by in the interval of time.

Rule 2: You use SINCE when you give the name of the day, month, year and so on when the interval of time began.

Now say what you think:

a I think I understand these rules. Look at Step 14.

b I'm not sure that I understand these rules. Look at Step 7.

14 Now see if you can use the rules about *since* and *for* in a new situation.

In Britain cars have number-plates which look like this:

| TWS 799 A | | PSY 534 B | | HSC 412 C | etc. |

Look carefully at the letters *after* the numbers.

These letters tell you how old a car is. A car with the letter A was built in 1962. A car with the letter B was built in 1963. And so on.

Here is a complete list of letters and dates:

A	1962
B	1963
C	1964
D	1965
E	1966
F	1967
G	1968
H	1969

It is now 1970
Here are two car number-plates:

| TLC 432 B | This car has been on the road since . . . .

| AVX 645 F | This car has been on the road for . . . .

15 TLC 432 B   This car has been on the road *since 1963*.
   AVX 645 F   This car has been on the road *for three years*.

| BSC 136 | John's had his car . . . . five years.

This is the number of John's car.
Can you complete it?

| BHD 312 | Jane's had her car . . . . 1966.

This is the number of Jane's car.
Can you complete it?

16 BSC 136 D   John's had his car *for* five years.
   BHD 312 E   Jane's had her car *since 1966*.
   Now can you write four sentences like the example:

| KLD 796 F | Tom's had his car for three years since
                1967
The number of Tom's car.

| ASY 215 G | . . . .
The number of Margaret's car.   . . . .

| RFS 281 A | . . . .
The number of Paul's car.   . . . .

| ASX 265 D | . . . .
The number of Betty's car.   . . . .

| PSG 732 H | . . . .
The number of Tony's car.   . . . .

17 KLD 796 F   Tom's had his car for three years since 1967.
   ASY 215 G   Margaret's had her car for two years since 1968.
   RFS 281 A   Paul's had his car for eight years since 1962.
   ASX 265 D   Betty's had her car for five years since 1965.
   PSG 732 H   Tony's had his car for a year since 1969.

In the last example you could also say *for one year*, but *for a year* is better English. You could also say *since last year* instead of *since 1969* because *last year* is another name for 1969. Remember this is 1970.

Can you remember the rules for using *since* and *for*?

Rule 1: You use .... when you count the .... of days, months, years, and so on that have gone by in the interval of time.

Rule 2: You use .... when you give the .... of the day, month, year and so on when the interval of time began.

18

Rule 1: You use FOR when you count the NUMBER of days, months, years and so on that have gone by in the interval of time.

Rule 2: You use SINCE when you give the NAME of the day, month, year and so on when the interval of time began.

In this programme we have used easy examples. In the next programme we must practise more difficult ones where it is not easy to see whether you are talking about a name or a number.

As a test, see if you can fill in these examples correctly. Do not worry if you make some mistakes:

a I've lived in Birmingham .... some years.
b John's been waiting for you .... yesterday.
c Mary's been queueing .... a long time.
d They've been standing outside the cinema .... a few minutes.
e I've had nothing to eat .... the day before yesterday.
f My father's been ill .... many months now.
g He's been drinking .... a very long time.
h I've been in the house .... some time.
i I've been trying to phone you .... last week.
j I haven't seen you .... ages.

19 Here are the answers:

a I've been in Birmingham *for* some years.
b John's been waiting for you *since* yesterday.
c Mary's been queueing *for* a long time.
d They've been standing outside the cinema *for* a few minutes.
e I've had nothing to eat *since* the day before yesterday.
f My father's been ill *for* many months now.
g He's been drinking *for* a very long time.
h I've been in the house *for* some time.
i I've been trying to phone you *since* last week.
j I haven't seen you *for* ages.

If you got more than 7 answers right, you need not do the next programme.

If you made more than 2 mistakes, do not worry. The next programme will give you more practice.

4 The use of programmes in language teaching

Programmes have not been widely used in foreign language teaching up to the present time. There are a number of reasons for this. Firstly, programmes did not seem to perform a function that was not already reasonably well performed by other types of teaching material. That is to say, the traditional teaching methods were rather too teacher-centred for self-instructional techniques, and the more recent methods were too drill-centred for an approach to language teaching that involved explanation as well as practice. Programmes fell between the two proverbial stools. Secondly, programmes of the type we have been concerned with are written rather than spoken. The emphasis on the need for speech practice in the last ten years or so has favoured the development of language laboratory materials rather than programmes. (The term 'programme' has sometimes been applied to language laboratory work but this is rather misleading since programmes and language laboratory exercises have little in common except that both are self-instructional.) Finally, programmes take a long time to construct and tend to become lengthy. The effort required to create them did not always seem to match the use to which they were put, and some of the rather ambitious early efforts in applying programming to language teaching were awesome in size.

These reasons are pointers to a possible use for written programmes in foreign language teaching. In the first place they should be limited in their aims and attempt to deal only with one specific learning problem (or aspect of a learning problem) at one time. In addition, this problem should be common to a wide range of learners so that the materials can be used by a large number of pupils over a longish period of time. Secondly, programmes should complement more traditional drill and exercise techniques and not attempt to compete with them. This implies that the most suitable learning problems for programming are those which cannot effectively be dealt with by practice alone but which require discussion and explanation as well. For instance, it would be rather wasteful to write programmes to drill the irregular past tense forms of the strong verbs in English (*went, came, bought*, etc.). There is no general rule which will allow the learner to produce these forms, they have to be learned by rote. Traditional exercise techniques are quite adequate for this purpose. However, if you want the learner to see the difference in meaning between, say, the past tense and the imperfect, you have a very different kind of teaching problem and one which is particularly suited to the advantages of programmes. In practical terms, what I am suggesting is a library of short explanatory programmes dealing with common learning difficulties encountered by pupils when they reach the intermediate stage of a foreign language course.

5 Practical work

The above sample programme on *since* and *for* is intended as the first of a series to teach the learner to discriminate between two concepts of time. A comparable set of problems arises when you want to teach the difference in meaning between tense forms in English, for example between the simple present and the progressive. Try to construct a programme which will distinguish between:

a the use of the simple present when the speaker is making a general statement of fact, e.g. *John plays football on Saturdays,* and

b the use of the progressive present when the speaker is describing an event actually taking place at the time of speaking, e.g. *Look, it's raining again.*

You should assume that both these tense-forms have been met with previously. You are concerned with the intermediate learner who wants to understand the difference between the forms, not with the beginner learning them for the first time.

A suggestion for such a programme will be found in Appendix I, p. 348.

6 Further reading

Goodman, R. *Programmed Learning and Teaching Machines.* London: English University Press, 1963.

Howatt, A. P. R. *Programmed Learning and the Language Teacher.* London: Longmans, 1969.

Kay, H., Dodd, B. and Sime, M. *Teaching Machines and Programmed Instruction.* Harmondsworth: Penguin, 1968.

Leedham, J. and Unwin, D. *Programmed Learning in the Schools.* London: Longmans, 1965.

Lumsdaine, A. A. and Glaser, E. (eds.). *Teaching Machines and Programmed Learning.* New York: N.E.A., 1960.

Markle, S. M. *Good Frames and Bad.* New York: Wiley, 1964.

9 Audio-Visual Materials in Language Teaching

ANDREW WRIGHT

1 Introduction

When a teacher holds up a book or points to a picture of one (Figure 1) and asks, 'What is it?' he is, in fact, not asking the pupil if he can recognize the object but if he can remember the word for it in the language being taught. When the pupil sees Figure 2 or Figure 3 and is asked, 'What is it?' he is being challenged to work out what the picture represents and to submit his answer in the foreign language.[1] The pupil will care about his idea and will thus be made to care about the language as a vehicle for ideas.

Figure 1

Figure 2

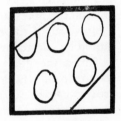

Figure 3

Sound recordings may be used in a similar way, e.g., the sound of a dog barking, of a man walking or some noise more puzzling to identify and to describe. In this case it would be particularly interesting for the students if they made the recordings themselves and questioned each other.

I would like to thank Mr. Michael Buckby and Mr. Jeremy Fox for their help and advice. I am grateful to the following for permission to reproduce the illustrations mentioned: Longman Group *What Do You Think Book I* by Byme and Wright (Figure 5); Nuffield Foundation and E. J. Arnold *En Avant* (Figures 8, 9 and 10); Schools Council and E. J. Arnold *Schools Council French Course* (Figure 11).

[1] A book, a cup, a giraffe passing a window.

These are only small instances of the rich potential offered by audio-visual materials in language teaching. Audio-visual materials can be used to interest and involve the learner; he reacts, the people around him react and they communicate their ideas and opinions. And this interest, reaction and wish to communicate can occur at the earliest stages of language learning.

The first steps in the learning of a new language item very often tend to be mechanical, artificial and boring to the learner. The examples above show that this need not be the case. The later stages of language learning, i.e., when the learner should be attempting full production, can also be made richer and more varied through the use of thoughtfully prepared audio-visual material. Unfortunately, full production is rarely attempted in the classroom, although this is the declared goal of most language teaching. The following extract from a recent CILT publication on examinations shows concern at this lack:

> The transition in group or class work from stereotyped drills, dialogue, and role playing to freer exchange is very difficult to make, but has to be made if the language is to become a genuine means of communication. (CILT 1970, Report No. 4.)

One reason for the lack of a smooth transition from stereotyped drills to a freer exchange is the fact that many teachers do not know how to arouse the desire to communicate in their students. For both the early and the later steps in the learning sequence, audio-visual materials can provide the necessary data, experience and stimulus.

However, if the materials are to make their fullest contribution they should be selected with a particular step of the learning sequence in mind. In Part 2 the stages through which a learner must pass in order to acquire productive mastery of the target language are defined. As the process can be seen from both the learner's and the teacher's point of view, the term teaching/learning sequence, abbreviated to T/L sequence, will be used throughout.

The idea that teachers should select audio-visual materials *for specific steps in the T/L sequence* is rarely given prominence by writers on the subject. This chapter is written in the belief that wherever possible materials should be selected with some specific teaching aim in mind. It would be as well to admit that a teacher's time is limited, and that he cannot be expected to make a new set of visuals for every item in the syllabus. In many cases the teacher will be obliged to do without visuals altogether; in other cases he will compromise and use one piece of material on several occasions. The present chapter should serve to warn teachers of the difficulties which might arise from the multiple use of audio-visual materials.

Lack of space here makes it necessary to discuss the use of audio-visual materials mainly from the point of view of the oral production skills. It should not be assumed from this that there is no scope for audio-visual aids in teaching reading and writing.

2 Audio-visual materials and the teaching/learning sequence

It is convenient to distinguish five stages in the T/L sequence.

At the *recognition* stage, the pupils must first recognize the new item as different from other, similar, items. They must also associate each item with its correct meaning.

At the *repetition* stage the learner says the new item for the first time and he bases his utterances as closely as possible on a model which he has just heard, e.g. the tape or the teacher.

At the *reproduction* stage the learner says a word or phrase he has previously heard and repeated. He now says it, however, without an immediate model, basing his utterances on memory.

At the *manipulation* stage the learner makes new combinations of known items in closely structured situations.

The *production* stage is the ultimate goal for the language learner. He exploits his ability to manipulate and re-combine known items to produce sentences or utterances which he has not previously experienced, but now in a more natural conversational situation, where the emphasis is on the ideas expressed rather than on the forms, words or structures used.

The T/L sequence will now be discussed in more detail with examples of the use of audio-visual material. It should be noted that the choice of audio-visual materials in the following examples was not decided solely by reference to the T/L sequence. It was necessary to take into consideration the age of the learner and the other factors listed in the chart on p. 267. For example, figurines may not be suitable for all types of learner, learning environment and teacher. On the other hand, there is no reason why figurines should not be used for T/L steps other than repetition.

The first stage: recognition

This is the first time the pupil will meet the new language item. If the teacher does not use translation, the situational and linguistic context in which the new item appears must indicate its meaning. There are two points to note here: firstly, it is the context as a whole which will indicate the meaning; secondly, it may not be possible to indicate the precise meaning straight away.

Audio-visual materials used at the recognition stage can help to contextualize the body of language in which the new item appears. The visuals and the dramatic effect of sound recording present an experience to the learner which he understands and to which he can relate the language he hears or reads. The use of known language and audio-visual materials together indicate the meaning of the new language item.

The presentation of single new vocabulary items does not constitute a problem if the words are concrete and easily demonstrable. However, many vocabulary items need a context if the meaning is to be made clear. The meaning of 'elephant' can be demonstrated unambiguously by one picture, but in order to teach the meaning of 'animal' we would need a larger context and, indeed, several contexts.

The meaning of grammatical structures can rarely be conveyed except by being presented in a context. This context might, for example, be a narrative passage, a dialogue or a play in which the language is already known for the most part and the meaning of which as a whole can be heightened by the visual and aural presentation.

The choice of audio-visual material for the recognition stage will depend on many factors (see Part 3). Clearly, however, one factor will be the degree of complexity in terms of context which the teacher or course-writer thinks necessary for the presentation of new items.

EXAMPLES OF AUDIO-VISUAL MATERIAL FOR THE RECOGNITION STAGE

(a) *Visual material*

1 *Filmstrip.* The presentation of new words and structures for younger children is often accomplished by means of a dramatically presented story (see Figure 8). The audio-visual medium together with the use of language which is already known to the children serves to indicate the meaning of new words and structures. Thus, no single visual is expected to convey unambiguous meaning. The filmstrip from which Figure 8 is reproduced is not intended for exploitation and development, but for recognition of new items and as a basis for enjoyable listening comprehension.

2 *Flash card.* Sometimes a structure can be unambiguously presented by means of a single visual, e.g. 'She's drinking', 'He's happy,' etc. Flash cards provide isolated depictions of single concepts. They are usually printed on stiff card for easy handling and measure approximately 4 in. × 8 in.

(b) *Audial material*

The teacher might want the learner to meet the new item in a context which might occur in the foreign country. With this aim in mind, an interview with a native speaker could be recorded and played to the learners. The interview should be on a subject or with a person likely to interest the students. For example, the Schools Council German Project has interviewed Uwe Seeler, the famous footballer, and Freddy Quinn, a singer who has sold 20 million of his records in Germany. Each of the Schools Council projects has interviewed foreign children who are the same age as the learners and talked to them about aspects of their life which might be of interest to the English pupils.

There are a variety of ways of presenting material of this type. Since there is rarely time to present an entire unedited interview, the usual procedure is to edit the tape, selecting points of interest and controlling the level of language. More control is gained by writing an interview based on a real-life recording but heightening interest, simplifying the language, increasing the frequency of occurrence of new teaching items, and reducing the distractors.

Interviews with 'ordinary' native speakers should not be beyond the scope of a teacher who does not wish to buy published material. The interviews can be made during visits to the foreign country, or with the help of native speakers who happen to be visiting the students' home district. It is highly motivating for the students if they can capture a tourist and record him! If the interview is planned beforehand, it should prove possible to ask questions which will elicit the structures that the teacher wants to present in class. If possible, some sort of visual record should be made, since this will make the interview more credible.

It is perhaps advisable not to use 'real-life presentations' as a basis for detailed question-and-answer work. This very common habit tends to disillusion the learner. He feels he was just being interested to be penalized later. Real-life recordings, dramatic dialogues, etc., should be used mainly for listening comprehension or simply for the sake of the fun that they provide. In this type of material questions and answers should be used only to check that the students have got the gist of what is going on. For a discussion of exercise work see below.

The second stage: repetition

Because the learner must concentrate on imitating what he has heard, he should be presented with the minimum of visual distraction. On the other hand the repetition of language items out of context can be counterproductive by leading to boredom. If audio-visual materials are used for the repetition stage they should be simple in design and directly relevant to the language that is being developed.

EXAMPLES OF AUDIO-VISUAL MATERIAL FOR THE
REPETITION STAGE

(a) Visual material

1 *Flash cards.* The nature of the flash card means that it is well adapted to serve as a stimulus for oral repetition work. The scope of visualization on a flash card is too limited for the meaningful presentation of most language items, but once the items are basically grasped, the flash card can act as a symbolic reference to them. The cards are easy to handle, enabling the teacher to keep up essential pace.

In repetition work the teacher may hold up a picture of a man with a rod and say 'He's fishing.' The picture reminds the pupils what this phrase means.

Teacher: He's fishing.
Pupil: He's fishing.

In reproduction work the picture provides a non-verbal stimulus to particular words.

Teacher: What is he doing?
Pupil: He's fishing.

The answer could not have been elicited without the visual.

For repetition work involving two contrasting structures flash cards are again useful, for example:

Picture 1: The cat is eating a fish.
Picture 2: The cat has eaten a fish.

Flash cards can easily be made by the teacher. It doesn't matter if the drawings are crude so long as they are easily recognizable. Photographs cut from magazines can also be used, providing they are not too complicated and do not have too many distractors.

2 *Figurines* (see Figure 4). Figurines (i.e., cut-out figures) provide a degree of simplification and concentration on a limited language situation which is often necessary at the repetition stage.

Articulated figurines (i.e., the position of legs and arms can be changed) give both teacher and pupils the chance to make up their own situations. If a magnet board is available, chalk sketching can also be used.

3 *Matchstick men* can be drawn by the teacher or the pupils. This often proves to be one of the most compelling events that can take place in a language class. Often the very crudeness and limitation of the figures and the teacher's obvious incompetence in drawing combine to arouse

Figure 4

the pupils and make them alive and sparkling. This type of visual is ideal for the repetition and reproduction stages, where the aim is to concentrate on single concepts without losing the interest of the students.

(b) *Audial material*

Audial material is particularly useful at the oral repetition stage. A taped recording of a native speaker gives an authentic and untiring model for the student to copy. The use of repetition exercises need not mean that the student produces his responses automatically with no concern for the meaning of what he hears and says. One way of ensuring that the student thinks about what he is doing is to call for responses on a 'true or false' basis. For example, the student must only repeat the sentence if it is true:

A ship is an animal
A sheep is an animal (repeated by student)

The third stage: reproduction

There are not likely to be any marked differences between the type of audio-visual material used at the reproduction stage and that which is intended for repetition work. In both cases the essential requirements are simplicity, limitation and relevance to the structures or words being learnt.

The fourth stage: manipulation

Now the student is asked to combine the language he has been 'reproducing' with other language which he has previously learnt. At this stage we must ensure that the student experiences the new language in a variety of contexts to avoid the danger that he will come to associate it with one context only.

Although the aim here is to make new combinations with known language the teacher will have a particular structure in mind which he wants the student to use. Thus, audio-visual materials used for manipulation work will usually refer only to the new structure, and in this respect they will be similar to material used for the repetition and reproduction stage. However, at the manipulation stage a number of instances of the new structure must be given. This can be done in two ways:

a by representing a number of examples in the same material, e.g., a large wall picture with various actions describable in the present continuous tense, e.g., 'He's fishing', 'She's climbing', 'They're running', etc.

b by having a number of different materials, each one giving an example of the structure in question, e.g., a number of flash cards each showing one action.

EXAMPLES OF AUDIO-VISUAL MATERIAL FOR THE MANIPULATION STAGE

(a) *Visual material*

1 Pupils' book or overhead projector: 'Compare the two pictures. The artist has made ten mistakes in the second picture. Can you find them?' This well-known game provides opportunities for the practice of There is/isn't, There are/aren't, etc. Examples can often be found in newspapers and magazines.

2 Pupils' book or overhead projector: 'I have lost my cigarettes. Where are they?' Picture shows someone looking for a number of articles 'hidden' in, on, under or behind various objects. This exercise will provide practice in the use of possessive adjectives and prepositions of place.

Both the above games will interest young children or adults, but they are less likely to appeal to teenagers.

(b) *Audial material*

A short and chatty radio interview might be played. This could be either a real interview carefully edited or a scripted interview presented by actors. In either case the aim would be to restrict the language used in order to give prominence to the new structures.

The interview, although heavily loaded with one type of structure, need not necessarily be boring. For example, a man might be interviewed about his collection of pets, in which case the manipulative work for the student might involve the use of the structure 'have got':

TEACHER: He's got an anteater. Have you got a pet, John?
STUDENT: Yes.
TEACHER: Have you got an anteater?
STUDENT: No.
TEACHER: What sort of pet have you got?
STUDENT: I've got a budgie.

The fifth stage: production

At this stage the learner is expected to concentrate on conveying his own ideas, opinions, feelings, etc., by means of the language at his disposal. This is the test of whether the preceding stages have worked. As already pointed out, although production is the final aim of most language teaching, in practice this stage is usually omitted altogether. Teachers tend to stop after satisfactory reproduction has been accomplished, or at most after a little manipulation of the new structures. This widespread failure must be due to the difficulty of creating, in the classroom, a situation in which the learner has something to say and wants to say it. It is not enough to show the students a picture and say, 'Tell me something about it!' Arousing people to think and to wish to say something of their own is a highly skilled task, one aspect of the professionalism of teaching.

Once more, audio-visual materials can provide both the source of the idea and the stimulus and once more the materials should be designed specifically for this stage and not adapted from other stages. The materials should aim to provoke individual responses. It is an advantage if the materials suggest different interpretations so that individual opinions can be formed and opposed to the opinion of others.

Although the aim is to create a situation which approximates to a real-life situation, the teacher must be careful not to evoke ideas which are totally beyond the pupils' power to express in the target language.

EXAMPLES OF AUDIO-VISUAL MATERIAL FOR THE PRODUCTION STAGE

(a) *Visual material*

1 Pupils' book: a picture sequence showing a man waking up, getting dressed, joining in a snowball fight, skiing with a girl, a falling girl, the man helping the girl, etc. The following quotation is from a teacher's report concerning the teaching of German:

The visuals were presented without the accompanying tape recording and the pupils invited to improvise their own dialogues to fit the pictures. For this exercise (which was always enormously popular) the pupils were normally divided into pairs and all of them 'prepared' their improvisation together for a few minutes before individual pairs volunteered to come out in front of the class and act it out. This 'preparation' involved very little English. It was really a matter of establishing roles and exploring the possibilities in German. (Law 1970.)

It probably helps the student to be able to see all the pictures together, since this enables him to run his eyes continually through the sequence, while building up an idea of what might happen next. This is not possible if the sequence of pictures is in the form of a filmstrip. On the other hand, filmstrip has the advantage of full colour, and a more realistic image. Take your pick!

2 Pupils' book

Figure 5

In the picture-sequence example above the amount of visual information may be restricted with the result that the language used by the students is still more or less controlled. Figure 5 is different in that it stimulates the student but leaves him to supply his own idea. The teacher will not know what the student is going to say, and so language is really being used to communicate ideas. Single visuals which are open to multiple interpretation can easily be found by the teacher in newspapers and magazines and used as a starting point for discussion at this all-important stage of language learning.

(b) *Audial material*

1 Odd man out. The student hears several words (e.g., *cat, cow, crow, bus*) and is asked which word is the 'odd man out' and why.

2 A sequence of noises is played to the student, for example: a bus stops, drives away, one pair of footsteps becomes identifiable, a gate opens, a key turns quietly in a lock, quiet footsteps on the stairs . . . then: a gasp! Students describe what they think has happened and what is going to happen, or several students can make up a play using the recording as a starting point.

Five stages in the T/L sequence have been described. Two further features must now be mentioned: Statement of principle and testing.

Statement of principle

At some stage in the T/L sequence (early, middle or late) the teacher will probably want the learner to become consciously aware of the grammatical principle behind the new language being learnt. Audio-visual materials can help here in a variety of ways. The following is an example of visual material used for a statement of principle:

The cat is eating the fish.   The cat has eaten the fish.

Figure 6

The above drawings are intended to direct the learner's attention and to make him consciously aware of the difference between the present continuous tense and the present perfect tense in English. They are intended for use after the learner has been introduced to the two tenses and has shown that he is able to handle them.

Testing

The following is an example of visual material used for testing:

What did he ask his father?

Figure 7

The purpose of Figure 7 is to test the student's ability to respond to the question (an appropriate response would be 'He asked his father whether he could go and play football'). Notice that this visual is unambiguous only if the student knows the relevant patterns. It would not be suitable for the presentation of new language material.

3 Factors influencing the choice of audio-visual materials

Many teachers may have no access to film, many learners might not be of the right age to enjoy games. Every teacher has such factors to consider and every teacher is in a unique teaching situation. On p. 267 a checklist is provided which indicates many of the factors which have to be taken into consideration when a teacher or course-organizer attempts to identify the type of audio-visual material which is most suitable for his needs. When the teacher really feels he knows his students, the potentials and limitations of the place of learning, and the exact stage in the T/L sequence he is aiming at, then he will be able to choose the appropriate medium and decide on how it should be used. The following examples show how some of the factors listed in the chart may influence the choice of medium and the design of audio-visual materials.

CHART 1. FACTORS INFLUENCING THE CHOICE OF AUDIO-VISUAL MATERIALS

1 Each of the following factors should be considered before the teacher makes a choice of audio-visual aids:

T/L SITUATION				T/L AIMS AND OBJECTIVES		T/L STRATEGY
Pupil	Environment	Teacher	Economics	General Aims	Sequence Objective	T/L Steps
Age Socio-cultural Sex Character Motivation Previous experience: a of the language b of the course b of media	Technical Physical conditions	Attitude Abilities Methods	Cost: to design to buy	Linguistic Cultural	1 Productive or receptive skills: Speaking Listening Reading Writing 2 Cultural	Recognition Repetition Reproduction Manipulation Production Presentation (general or selective context) Statement of Principle Mnemonics and reinforcement Testing
All these factors affect design/choice/use of audio-visual aids						The specific T/L step affects design/choice/use of audio-visual aids

CHART 2. MEDIA AND DESIGN

Having considered all the above factors, the teacher is in a position to make a choice of audio-visual aids:

BASIC PHYSICAL REQUIREMENTS	WHICH ANSWER?	1 Medium	2 Pictorial Conventions	3 Audial Type of Presentation
Visual big image/small image for long range/short range use single visual or part of sequence degree of ambiguity permitted quantity of redundant material permitted adaptable to various T/L steps or not technical ease of use movement 3-dimensional form colour, tone, line composition, layout, stylistic character **Audial** degree of dramatic quality number of voices quantity of sound effects need for interaction by pupil	1 Which medium? 2 Which visual convention? 3 Which audial type of presentation?	Computer visual display T.V. (incl. videotape) Film (16 mm, 8 mm loop) Radiovision Filmstrip Slides Overhead Projector Teaching Machines Posters Charts Flashcards Figurines Readers Workbooks Grammar Exercise Books Project Books Kits Project Cards Games Cards Puppets Realia Duplicator Radio Records Tape Language Laboratory	High Realism Selective Realism (simplified, expressive) Stylization Cartoon Stereotype Pictograph Typeface	Dramatic play with sound effects Dramatic dialogue Interview Monologue—Narration Song—Poem Monologue and/or dialogue with fill-in spaces

Clearly, the *age of the students* and the things they like to do must influence the choice of materials. For example, young children at primary school tend to move about and to touch and manipulate things. Consequently figurines are ideal for this age group. The use of filmstrip, on the other hand, would force the children to keep to their places, and the teacher would tend to be lost in the semi-darkness.

Young children find it difficult to grasp the overall structure of a film or a long dialogue. Faced with a filmstrip, they tend to concentrate on minor pictorial details rather than on the development of the story as a whole. A sequence of printed pictures is more suitable for use with young children, since in this case the pictures can be shown one by one or displayed together in sequence on the wall, thus enabling the teacher to obtain maximum control over the presentation of the story.

Many commercial language courses are advertised as suitable for a wide age range. The teacher must judge for himself at which points the materials happen to coincide with the needs of his pupils.

Various *socio-cultural* factors must be taken into account in the choice of audio-visual materials. For example, people in various parts of the world differ widely in their ability to understand the conventions of the film maker: cutting, panning, flash backs, etc. The stylistic conventions of drawing are easy to take for granted, but when language courses are marketed internationally it is impossible to anticipate how students from very different cultural backgrounds will react. This was the case when Ghurka soldiers learning English in Malaya were confused because they interpreted the line shading convention on faces as caste marks.

These, then, are some reasons why the teacher should buy or make as many materials as he can specifically for the needs of his own pupils.

The experience and personal inclinations of the *teacher* should quite properly influence the choice of audio-visual materials. A keen teacher expects to try out materials and ideas which are unfamiliar to him, but it would be unwise to plunge into a method of teaching which is quite new and for which he is unprepared. If the teacher is not a specialist in the language that he happens to be teaching, it is perhaps an advantage if the audio-visual materials are closely integrated. A filmstrip, for example, presents a fixed sequence of pictures which the teacher can do little to change. The inflexible sequence of the filmstrip is also an advantage when it is intended for self-instruction. For the specialist or more experienced teacher, on the other hand, it is an advantage if materials are designed for flexibility in use. Slides are a flexible medium since they permit the teacher to make any combination to suit his own purposes. It is also possible to mix new and old, bought and self-made stock.

Finally, since most teachers have to work on a tight budget the question of *cost* is one of the most important factors limiting the choice of audio-visual materials. Here the best advice we can give the teacher is that he should shop around. For example, the 131 colour posters of Stage 2 of the Nuffield French Course 'En Avant' (Figure 9) cost only £5.00 owing to the cheap method of colour reproduction used. Other posters printed with more colours are currently advertised at 10 for £10.00, while 131 pictures reproduced on filmstrip would cost approximately £2.50.

None of the factors listed in the chart will be unfamiliar to the teacher; none are the product of the ivory tower academic invented to keep him in work! If only some of them *were* fictitious! Listing the factors in this stark way serves to show how complex each teaching situation really is. Clearly, generalizations such as 'Filmstrips are better than slides', or 'Cartoons are the best type of illustration' are quite useless.

4 Media and design

Having taken into account all the factors listed in the chart under *situation, aims and objectives* and *strategy*, the teacher will be in a position to decide on *basic physical requirements*, and *pictorial conventions*. Each of these topics will be briefly discussed below.

4.1 Basic physical requirements

A front projected image can be huge, a rear projected image is likely to be very small; flat, bright colours in contrasting juxtaposition carry well down the length of a classroom but seen close to, in a book for example, they may well seem crude and unsubtle. On the other hand, a sketchy artist's style suitable for some book illustration might be inappropriate for long distance viewing.

Is the material integrated with other materials and, if so, how much does its usefulness depend on these other materials? Must the visual represent as unambiguously as possible the language intended to be used with it, or is a visual required which will provide a variety of practice at the production stage, stimulating a number of possible reactions on the part of the observer and drawing his attention simultaneously to several different situations or events?

For audial material the teacher must decide on his requirements with respect to the degree of 'realism' or relation to real life, the number of speakers involved, the use of sound effects, etc.

4.2 Media

A selection of media is given in this section. For a more detailed description of media used in language teaching the reader is referred to the books by Coppen, Coppen and Lee, Dale, Erickson and Wright in the Further Reading section at the end of the chapter.

The use of *computers* in language teaching is in the research phase. But as with television this expensive technical device may be increasingly used for mass teaching with the possibility of considerable adaptation to the needs of the individual learner.

Videotape is a sound and vision recording for television.

Radiovision: filmstrips and other visual material are supplied for use in conjunction with a radio language teaching programme.

An *overhead projector* is a device used to project a large picture on to a screen or wall. The pictures are supplied in the form of transparencies measuring 8 in. × 10 in.

Project cards contain a text together with problems based on the information given. This type of material is increasingly common and there is considerable scope for its use in language teaching. The S.R.A. Language Laboratory (see Chapter 6) is a good example of the use of project cards.

Kits contain information in the form of facsimiles, realia, etc., together with comments calculated to encourage further investigation on the part of students.

4.3 Pictorial conventions

Various pictorial conventions can be used for the visual representation of real-life experience, e.g., *high realism, selective realism, simplified style, expressive style* or *cartoons.* Any of these conventions can be used with any of the media listed in the chart on p. 268. Each convention will have advantages and disadvantages according to the needs of the T/L situation. For the purposes of this discussion we have classified the pictorial conventions according to the amount of visual information they convey.

High realism

This is a method of representing life by means of movement, colour, tone, shape, texture, detail and passage of time, in such a way that the maximum amount of visual information is conveyed. Movie film and television are particularly well equipped for conveying this richest form of realism, although film and television often incorporate quite different conventions (cartoons, for example). High realism has a greater dramatic potential than any other audio-visual convention. In the audial rather than the visual mode it is excellent for listening comprehension when the students are already familiar with the language being used.

High realism in the classroom has a number of important advantages. It enables the teacher to present new items in a real-life setting or dramatic context; it encourages students to communicate their reactions, thus helping to carry the learning sequence into the oral production stage; it is very often the most satisfactory way of conveying cultural information, since materials containing only expressionistic drawing, stereotypes or cartoons are rather limited for this purpose. It must not be assumed, however, that high realism is the answer to every classroom problem. For example, high realism is not a suitable level of pictorial convention for concentrated work on new language material, since (a) it incorporates too many distracting elements and (b) a natural 'documentary' type of presentation takes the focus away from the teacher and prevents him from interacting quickly and easily with the students.

Selective realism

Figure 8

Figure 8 is an example of *selective realism*, an appropriate convention when the aim is to give emphasis and to reduce the amount of visual information. Slides, filmstrips and artists' 'realistic' pictures (which might themselves be on a filmstrip) can all convey a natural setting for dialogues, stories, dramatic episodes, etc. Selective realism does not allow physical movement to be shown, but a sequence of events can be depicted through a number of different pictures. The convention provides sufficient realism for most language teaching purposes. Materials of this type have the great advantage that they can be controlled to suit the pace of the learner, and manipulated to direct his attention.

Simplified style

Figure 9

Simplified style (Figure 9) is a representation in which basic elements only are depicted, the visual information consequently being much reduced. This style is useful for giving clarity over a long viewing distance and for providing impact and emphasis in a memorable way.

Expressive style

Figure 10

Various 'expressive' styles are available in which the artist emphasizes certain qualities of colour, tone, shape, etc., to heighten the *feeling* associated with the event or situation depicted. This is often helpful in

K

increasing motivation and in clarifying the meaning of more abstract concepts.

Expressive style is a convention which is more likely to be of use for long dramatic contexts, whether these are dramatic episodes for class presentation and listening comprehension or in the form of readers. For short working passages and exercises an expressive style would probably be distracting and out of place.

Cartoons

2. Le lion a fini son repas.

Figure 11

Cartoons are a familiar feature of everyday life, but it is perhaps less well known that there are a number of distinct cartoon styles, each one being appropriate for a certain type of humorous or satirical situation. Too many language courses use the cartoon style, the stereotype or the pictograph for nearly every function. One reason is the fact that artists can produce such styles quickly and economically, another is the short-sighted premise that 'people like funny drawings'.

When and when not to use a cartoon style is a common sense rather than an artistic decision. Texts which are humorous or satirical can be illustrated with humorous or satirical drawings. Texts concerning ordinary, everyday affairs are not made more acceptable by cartoon drawing and would be more appropriately illustrated by an ordinary, informative style (which does not necessarily mean that such qualities as charm and immediacy have to be excluded!).

Jokes illustrated by cartoon drawings are particularly useful when the teacher wants to show a structure in a very limited context. Rarely should a joke context be used to introduce a new language item; cartoon jokes are better used as mnemonic aids or as illustrations accompanying a statement of grammatical principle.

4.4 Types of audial presentation

We can also distinguish between various types of recorded material according to the quantity and type of information conveyed. The equivalent of *high realism* in terms of recorded sound would include any unedited chunk of life noise, e.g., conversations recorded in a street or factory, full of incidental comments, interruptions, coughs, hesitation phenomena and background noises.

A 'high realism' recording could be used in a variety of ways. For example, a recording could be made in a shop. There will be considerable background noise, but the terms used in shopping would have a high frequency of occurrence. Such a recording, perhaps in conjunction with slides projected on to a screen, would be a good way of introducing the learner to the vocabulary of shopping. Students are asked to speculate about the meaning of the language used and asked to identify the shopping terms. Repetition and reproduction exercises follow, in which the shopping terms are repeated by the student, possibly with the help of artist pictures designed to isolate the relevant actions. Towards the end of the T/L sequence another recording from a different type of shop could be made. The learners are asked to establish what sort of shop it is, and what is being bought.

High realism recordings are a source of great interest in the language class. Students enjoy 'hearing the real thing' and respond well to the challenge of picking out significant features and noting their frequency of occurrence. A high realism recording used towards the end of the T/L sequence serves to demonstrate the new language items in a different situation, thus leading the students to be adaptable and to recognize the new items in various contexts and in several different guises.

An enjoyable game could be based on the supposed recording of a group of criminals at their meeting place in a cafe discussing their next crime. The teacher explains that the table was bugged and that this recording is the result. The class listens carefully and selects from the mass of noise and idle chatter any information relating to the proposed crime.

Simplified realism

Simplified realism is a category commonly used in audial material at all stages in the T/L process. In this type of presentation the number of voices is restricted, incidental noise does not occur (though some studio sound effects might be introduced) and the amount and type of language used is strictly controlled. Simplified realism is normally used for the dialogues which provide the context for language laboratory drills. Some examples of the use of simplified realism are given below.

1 A monologue is heard giving personal information. The student fills

in an official form for the person described, thus exercising listening comprehension and writing skills.

2 A weather forecast is given for the week. Students note down with a previously agreed symbol the weather for each day.

3 A short dialogue is played. The students are asked to say where the speakers are and who they are.

4 A number of statements are made, and the students are asked to say whether the statements are true or false.

Low realism

In this type of presentation the quantity of audial information is minimal. Background noises, if used at all, are isolated and occur infrequently. Speech is presented in the form of short utterances without context, and there is not necessarily any thematic connection between utterances. In other words, there is no attempt to give the impression to the learner that he is listening to a real-life recording. This low degree of realism is frequently used for pattern practice, particularly in the language laboratory. A simple example is as follows:

1 (Visual of a book)   TAPE: This is a book.

2 (Visual of a chair)   STUDENT: . . . .

The learner listens to the pattern of (1) and, with the aid of the visual, repeats the pattern with a new vocabulary item.

There is a need for this uncontextualized type of exercise but it is important that the student should move on quickly to exercises set in a richer context which have more chance of being meaningful to him, of arousing his interest and presenting a real challenge.

5 Conclusion

The aim of this chapter has been (a) to convince the reader that audio-visual materials can make an important contribution to language learning, and (b) to show how to decide what type of material to use. It is hoped that the analysis will be relevant for the evaluation of courses and published materials, and that it will serve as a guide for the teacher who wishes to make his own audio-visual materials.

It is impossible in a short paper such as this to make allowance for all the practical considerations which can influence the choice of audio-visual materials in different teaching situations. Theoretical discussions may inform, but they can never replace a teacher's professional experience. In the final analysis it is the teacher's creative imagination which leads to the right material for himself and his students.

6 Practical work

1 A publisher is considering a plan for a secondary-school English course for West Africa, and has asked for your advice about the scope for audio-visual aids. You have not had time to investigate the background in detail, but you must prepare some preliminary comments for a meeting.

Drawing upon your general knowledge and/or professional experience, summarize the probable teaching situation, and the aims and objectives of the course. Using this as a basis, list the basic physical requirements for audio-visual aids, the media likely to be used and the scope you envisage for the use of various pictorial conventions and audial types of presentation. Make brief notes only, and consult the chart on p. 267 for your descriptive framework.

Repeat the exercise for the following:

a a course for immigrant children in Great Britain
b a refresher course for Polish teachers of English
c a basic course in business English for the Common Market.

2 Choose any teaching/learning situation in which you have been the *learner*. Define the situation according to the first part of the chart, and assess the way in which audio-visual materials were used. If you think that audio-visual materials could have been used more effectively, say what improvements you recommend.

7 Further reading

Arnheim, R. *Art and Visual Perception*. London: Faber, 1967.

Coppen, H. *Aids to Teaching and Learning*. Oxford: Pergamon, 1969.

Coppen, H. and Lee, W. R. *Simple Audio-Visual Aids to Foreign Language Teaching*. London: Oxford University Press, 1964.

Corder, S. P. *The Visual Element in Language Teaching*. London: Longmans, 1966.

Dale, E. *Audio-Visual Methods in Teaching*. New York: Holt, Rinehart, Winston, 1954.

Erickson, C. W. H. *Fundamentals of Teaching with Audiovisual Technology*. London: Collier-Macmillan, 1965.

Jones, J. G. *Teaching with Tape*. London: The Focal Press, 1962.

Mialaret, G. *The Psychology of the Use of Audio-Visual Aids in Primary Education*. Harrap/UNESCO, 1966.

Woodman, H. *The Dramatape Guide*. London: The Focal Press, 1962.

Wright, A. The Role of the Artist in the Production of Visual Materials for Language Teaching. *Educational Sciences*, Vol. 1, No. 3. Oxford: Pergamon, 1967.

Wright, A. *Designing for Visual Aids*. London: Studio Vista, 1970.

Wright, A. *Visual Materials for the Language Teacher*. London: Longmans, 1973.

The periodical *Visual Education* and a great many useful booklets on audio-visual media may be obtained from:

National Committee for Audio-Visual Aids in Education,
33, Queen Anne Street,
London, W.1.

10 Contrastive Analysis

PAUL VAN BUREN

1 Introduction

This chapter is based on the assumption that contrastive analysis should convey as many insights as possible into the differences or similarities between the languages being compared. What we mean by 'insight' should become clearer as the argument develops. For the time being, let us assume that an insight involves some kind of explanation. For example, a linguist or language teacher would like to be able to answer questions such as the following: How is it that an English sentence containing noun phrases with definite articles can be translated into, say, a Chinese sentence which contains no articles? Or what is it that enables the simple present tense in French to perform the same function as the present progressive perfect tense in English under certain conditions?

The justification for contrastive analysis is to be found in its explanatory power. If a contrastive study fails to explain anything about the nature of the language data it scarcely seems worth the time and labour that has been expended on it. But this does not mean that earlier contrastive studies which did not attempt explanations have nothing to contribute to our knowledge of language structure and of the relations which obtain between different language systems. Much time has to be spent analysing and classifying data before we can begin to formulate an explanatory hypothesis, and those linguists who are now venturing to seek explanations can do so only because others have made the data available. We do claim, however, that explanatory power should be the ultimate goal of all contrastive linguists, even if the circumstances are such that explanatory insights are difficult to attain.

Given this aim, a crucial question concerns the choice of a linguistic theory to serve as the basis for contrastive statements. The aim of this chapter is, firstly, to examine a number of linguistic theories which may serve as a basis for contrastive analysis and, secondly, to provide a method for evaluating the theories so that we can select the best one for our purpose. Finally, we shall discuss in some detail a problem in the contrastive analysis of English and Chinese in order to show the type of statements we shall have to make if our basic assumptions are followed to their logical conclusion.

A further question concerns the ways in which the results of contrastive analysis can be made available to the language learner. I shall not attempt to answer this question in any detail here, since the establishment of an adequate theoretical foundation for contrastive analysis must precede any attempt to show how the results of such analysis might be applied in the foreign language classroom. It seems certain, however, that the chain of connections between contrastive linguistic theory and what happens in the classroom will be rather complex, and that it must contain at least three major links: the highly technical analysis itself, the conversion of this analysis into a form which can be easily understood by non-specialists and, finally, the conversion of the simplified statement into materials that can be used in the classroom.

2 Some approaches to contrastive analysis

In his book *Linguistics Across Cultures* (1957), Robert Lado presents the following propositions:

a In the comparison between native and foreign language lies the key to ease or difficulty in foreign language learning.

b The most effective language teaching materials are those that are based upon a scientific description of the language to be learned, carefully compared with a parallel description of the native language of the learner.

c The teacher who has made a comparison of the foreign language with the native language of the students will know better what the real learning problems are and can better provide for teaching them.

The above statements have been accepted without question by many language teachers, but on closer inspection they are found to conceal fundamental problems of contrastive analysis. In this chapter we shall examine critically some of the assumptions which underlie Lado's statements and which are implicit elsewhere in his work. First, what do we mean by 'a scientific description of language?' Secondly, what exactly is involved in the process of comparing two (or more) languages? And lastly, how do we 'locate the best structural description of the languages involved' given a plurality of grammatical models?

Perhaps the best way into these problems is to start with an everyday example. Suppose a teacher of English to French students wishes to compare the English sentence (1) with the French sentence (2):

1 I've been waiting for six hours.

2 J'attends depuis six heures.

The French sentence is ambiguous, since it could mean either 'I've been waiting for six hours' or 'I've been waiting since six o'clock'. We will return to this point presently. Assuming for the time being the interpretation given in (1), why should we want to compare (1) and (2)? Suppose the answer is that we want to illustrate a specific feature of English grammar (traditionally known as 'tense') by comparing it with a corresponding feature of French grammar. This sounds straightforward enough, but if we examine the argument more closely we find that it is based on two axioms and a conclusion as follows:

a there is tense in English

b there is tense in French

c therefore tense in English can be compared with tense in French.

The important point about this set of propositions is that it contains two axioms which state that both English and French can be analysed in terms of a concept 'tense'. It might be objected that rather than being axiomatic 'tense' is a fact in English and French. However, the only facts at our disposal are the two utterances in English and French. The concept 'tense' belongs to the realm of theoretical terms which should be sharply distinguished from the realm of facts.

This should not be taken to imply that there are no correspondences between theoretical terms and facts in linguistics. But it should be emphasized that these correspondences may be of an extremely complicated nature since they hold between linguistic entities (i.e., theoretical terms) and extra-linguistic phenomena which ultimately must involve the native speakers of a language. Suppose we use the term 'adverb of past time' in a description of English and suppose the word 'yesterday' is a realization of this theoretical term. Is it a fact that 'yesterday' is an adverb of past time? A careful answer to this seemingly straightforward question reveals a surprising number of assumptions: the theoretical term 'adverb of past time' is explicitly defined in our language system in relation to other theoretical terms, say, verb, noun, adverb of time, etc.; there is an explicit link in the system between theoretical terms and their realizations; the output of the system is well-defined (that is, we can show what belongs to the output of the system and what does not); the output of the system is non-arbitrary, in other words it is linked to observable facts; the observable facts are judgements by native speakers of English; we know what constitutes a native speaker of English; we know what we mean by 'English'; native speakers' judgements concerning the output of the system coincide with the actual output; and so on. Unless these assumptions have been tested we have, strictly speaking, no right to state that 'yesterday' is an adverb of past time.

So far the discussion has been about non-comparative grammatical statements but clearly a description involving two languages and the contrasts or similarities that hold between them presupposes a good many additional assumptions. In attempting to describe the relation between the languages we have entered the realm of 'postulated linguistic universals', or 'common categories'. Without being aware of this fact we cannot hope to set up satisfactory contrastive procedures. It is logically impossible to engage in contrastive analysis without postulating common categories of one sort or another since, more generally, it is logically impossible to compare any two entities without using the same frame of reference. The interesting question of the precise nature of these common categories will be discussed below. Suffice it to say for the moment that in order to compare, for example, interrogative structures in French and Swahili we must be able to give a coherent definition of interrogative structure and this necessarily entails the notion of question asking, that is, a semantic concept. Whether this is a necessary condition for all common categories (or universals) is a hotly debated issue in linguistic theory at the present time. Ironically, many 'structural' linguists who champion the cause of contrastive analysis fail to acknowledge the logical necessity of common categories (or, a fortiori, universals). This failure may have been due to the characteristically structuralist assumption that each language is a self-sufficient system in that every element has a 'value' which is uniquely determined by the structural relations of that system. Clearly, a descriptive technique which is confined to an analysis of the internal relationships of a single language is, strictly speaking, incompatible with the notion of comparison between two or more languages.

Returning to (1) and (2) on page 281, we saw that an answer to the question why one might wish to compare these two sentences involved certain important assumptions about contrastive analysis. Let us look at these sentences again to see what other assumptions might have to be made. Evidently the assumption that there is such a thing as tense in English and French is insufficient. We need to know what kind of tense is manifested by each of the two sentences. In traditional terms we would say that the English sentence illustrates a grammatical phenomenon called the 'perfect continuous tense' whereas the French sentence contains the 'present tense'. Actually the term 'perfect continuous tense' is something of a misnomer since it involves reference to two grammatical categories rather than one, i.e., tense and verbal aspect, but however we label the concepts involved our statement is clearly a contrastive one. In the case of (1) and (2) our contrastive statement is of extremely low generality, being restricted to two sentences only. Moreover, it concerns two sentences which 'have the same meaning', i.e. they are translation equivalents.[1] But suppose we wanted to examine the problems of tense and aspect in French and English in more general terms by comparing two substitution frames in which NP, VERB, TIME, etc., refer to elements of surface structure:

3 *English:* NP + have + been + VERB(ing) + for + TIME

4 *French:* NP + VERB(pres) + depuis + TIME

Each of the substitution frames (3) and (4) contains a statement which is in principle generative (in the sense of 'predictive' rather than 'explicit', see Lyons 1968) since we can produce a large if not infinite number of sentences on the basis of it. But as is nearly always the case with implicit generative statements, (3) and (4) are inadequate as they stand because they express an overgeneralization. In other words the statements are too powerful. To illustrate this suppose we wished to translate the French sentence

J'attends depuis Noel

into English on the basis of frames (3) and (4). This would force us to give as a translation equivalent

I've been waiting for Christmas

which is clearly wrong, the proper equivalent being

I've been waiting since Christmas.

If we change frame (3) to

$$\text{NP} + \text{have} + \text{been} + \text{VERB(ing)} + \begin{Bmatrix} \text{for} \\ \text{since} \end{Bmatrix} + \text{TIME}$$

where the curly brackets indicate an either/or choice, again this leads to the wrong results since among other things it produces the ungrammatical sentence

I've been waiting since six hours.

The difficulty is that frame (3) does not state the correct selectional restrictions holding between the prepositions 'for' and 'since' and their prepositional objects. That is, 'for' must be followed by a time phrase which expresses a *period* of time whereas 'since' goes with a phrase expressing a *point* in time. Incorporating these restrictions into the frame would mean that we are well on our way to a generative grammar in the sense of Chomsky (1965). Let us see how such a grammar might handle sentences (1) and (2).

[1] The important question of whether any two sentences in different languages can ever 'have the same meaning' is ignored here. For a discussion see Catford (1965).

Grammar I

Relevant branching rules for English[2]

E1   S → NP + PP

E2   PP → Aux + VP (Place) (Time)

E3   VP → V (NP)

E4   Aux → Tense (Modal) (Perfective) (Progressive)

E5   Time → $\left\{ \begin{array}{l} \text{Point} \\ \text{Duration} \end{array} \right\}$

E6   Point → Prep + NP

E7   Duration → Prep + NP

E8   Place → Prep + NP

E9   Tense → $\left\{ \begin{array}{l} \text{Past} \\ \text{Present} \end{array} \right\}$

E10 NP → Det + N

E11 V → CS

E12 N → CS

E13 Prep → CS

Relevant subcategorization rules for English

E14 [+ N] → [± Time]

E15 [+ Time] → [± Duration]

Relevant lexicon for English

E16 *Christmas* [+ N, + [− Duration]]

E17 *for* $\left[+ \text{Prep}, + \left\{ \begin{array}{l} \text{Perfective} \\ \text{Perfective} + \text{Progressive} \\ \text{Past} \end{array} \right\} \text{——} [+ \text{Duration}] \right]$

E18 *hour* [+ N, + [Duration]]

E19 *since* $\left[+ \text{Prep}, + \left\{ \begin{array}{l} \text{Perfective} \\ \text{Perfective} + \text{Progressive} \end{array} \right\} \text{——} [− \text{Duration}] \right]$

Grammar II

Relevant branching rules for French

All rules as for English example except for

F4   Aux → Tense (Perfective) (Modal)

Relevant subcategorization rules for French

All rules as for English example.

---

[2] For an explanation of the special symbols used in this chapter see p. 361. See also Chomsky (1965), Chapter 2.

Relevant lexicon for French

heure, as 'hour'

Noel, as 'Christmas'

depuis [+Prep, +Tense ——— Time]

A phrase structure grammar of the type that Chomsky has made familiar is a system of generative rules drawn up in such a way that they explicitly assign the correct constituent structure to a sentence. The rules can be described as a concatenating rewrite system, i.e. they are of the type A → B+C+D, interpreted as an instruction to replace, or 'rewrite', the symbol A with the symbol B followed by C followed by D, etc., strictly in that order. The following abbreviatory conventions are used in rules E1–E13:

(i) $A \rightarrow \begin{Bmatrix} B \\ C \end{Bmatrix}$

(ii) X → Y(Z)

In (i) the braces indicate an alternative choice: A may be rewritten as either B or C. In (ii) the brackets indicate an optional choice; X may be rewritten as either Y or Y+Z. The following rewrite rules are relevant to the present discussion:

E1 (and F1)   S → NP+PP

E2 (and F2)   PP → Aux+VP (Place) (Time)

E4 (and F4)   Aux → Tense (Modal) (Perfective) (Progressive)

Subcategorization rules such as E14, E15 further subclassify syntactic features (which are always given in square brackets). Rule E14 asserts that any lexical category which has the feature [+N], i.e. which is a noun, can be subclassified into those categories which 'express' time and those which do not. E15 asserts that all time nouns can be further subclassified into those which express duration and those which do not. (By implication [−Duration] expresses a point in time here.)

The selection of lexical items is governed by the following rule: a terminal string of the base grammar is derived from a preterminal string by the insertion of lexical items in just those cases where a complex symbol (i.e., a set of syntactic features dominated by the appropriate category symbol, say N), in the preterminal string matches the set of syntactic features contained in a lexical entry. The lexicon of English contains the entries E16–E19 of which E16 and E18 are [+N] that is nouns (*Christmas, hour*). Taking the lexical entry for *Christmas* as an example we obtain the following information: the lexical item *Christmas* can replace a complex symbol in a phrase structure tree (i.e., can be inserted as a lexical item) provided that the complex symbol is dominated by the category N and contains the syntactic feature [−Duration].[3]

Two further points should be made about Grammar I and Grammar II. First, since only the base components of these grammars are relevant to our present argument, a satisfactory transformational component is presupposed. Secondly, as they stand these base components are grossly inadequate as grammars of English and French since only the rules relevant to the argument have been included. Moreover, these rules express only a very restricted number of generalizations about tense and aspect in French and English. However, disregarding irrelevancies, they do account for the following set of phenomena (starred forms are ungrammatical):

The boy has waited for six hours

The boy has been waiting for six hours

*The boy is waiting for six hours

The boy waited for six hours

The boy has waited since Christmas

The boy has been waiting since Christmas

*The boy is waiting since Christmas

*The boy waited since Christmas

Le garçon attend ici depuis six heures

Le garçon attend ici depuis Noel

*Le garçon a attendu ici depuis six heures

*Le garçon a attendu ici depuis Noel

In spite of their inadequacies our two partial sets of rules illustrate a point about grammars in general and about contrastive analysis in particular. The central difference between Grammar I and Grammar II lies in the respective Auxiliary expansion rules. That is, our contrastive statement resides essentially in the difference between the two rules E4 and F4 plus the various selectional restrictions expressed in the lexicon.

Ever since the publication of Katz and Postal's *An Integrated Theory of Linguistic Descriptions* (1964) it has been a central requirement of transformational-generative theory that all semantic interpretation is

---

[3] In fact, it seems to be the case that *Christmas* is neutral with regard to [±Duration] since it is possible to say *He stayed for Christmas, He was there during Christmas,* as well as *I've been waiting since Christmas.* One solution might be to regard *He stayed for Christmas, He was there during Christmas* as surface forms of *He stayed for the period of time (called) Christmas.* There is a case for stating that no time nouns are inherently marked for [±Duration]. This would complicate the formalization of the selectional restrictions on p. 284. We will disregard problems of this sort since it is not our purpose to give a full description of English or French syntax, but rather to make some general points about the nature of contrastive analysis.

carried out relative to the base component of a grammar, and that all elements in the base grammar must be submitted for semantic interpretation.[4] It follows that with regard to the two grammars under discussion the difference between the two Auxiliary expansion rules could lead to different semantic interpretations for the two sentences

I've been waiting since Christmas
and
J'attends depuis Noel
since the one contains the progressive form whereas the other does not. This conclusion is on the face of it paradoxical because it implies that although on independent (extra-linguistic) grounds the two sentences under consideration are translation equivalents they are different in meaning. It might be argued that this conclusion is not really paradoxical since in any case translation equivalents never have the same meaning. However, whatever the exact meaning of the English sentence is to a native speaker of English or of the French sentence to a native speaker of French the two sentences are undoubtedly equivalent in meaning. The crucial question is: given the requirement of a transformational-generative theory of language that all elements in the base component of a grammar should be relevant to semantic interpretation and therefore semantically non-redundant, do statements about tense and aspect belong in deep structure, or should they be derived from some other source in deep structure?

Consider the ungrammatical string

*I go yesterday

and the grammatical sentence

I went yesterday.

How can we account for the fact that both could be meaningful and unambiguous? Presumably we can do so only on the assumption that what is relevant to the semantic interpretation of the sentence *I went yesterday* is not the past tense form 'went' but the notion of past time implied in the word 'yesterday'.

Consider now the sentence

He leaves on Monday

where we have present tense but future time. As many scholars have observed (see Crystal 1966 for a thorough discussion) tense often seems to be irrelevant or redundant for the expression of semantic time in English. Many sentences without overt time adverbials such as *He left* might seem to be counter-examples to the claim that the selection of a

---

[4] This requirement has since been modified (see Chomsky 1965) but this does not affect our argument.

particular tense form is not in itself semantically relevant in English. However the hypothesis is saved if we stipulate that all sentences (except 'timeless' sentences such as *Cats are animals*) have underlying time adverbials in deep structure which may be deleted. As this seems to represent part of our competence as speakers ('Action must take place at some time') and as there are numerous precedents in transformational grammars for postulating deleted deep constituents (e.g., resulting in agentless passives as in *The boy was beaten* which presupposes that somebody performed the action) we may conclude that this proposal constitutes a natural addition to the base component of transformational grammars.

The problem of whether aspect belongs in the base component is somewhat more complicated. Consider the ungrammatical string

*I wait for six hours (now)

The reason why we are able to interpret this unambiguously as *I've been waiting for six hours* again lies in the information contained in the time adverbial. But what precisely is the information conveyed by the time adverbial? In order to answer this question let us first paraphrase the sentence *I've been waiting for six hours* and try to extract the relevant parameters (or 'features') concerning its aspectual properties.

We may regard the compound sentence

. I started waiting six hours ago and I'm still waiting

as a possible paraphrase of *I've been waiting for six hours*. From this paraphrase we may extract the following information concerning the speaker's orientation as well as the beginning, continuation and end of the action:

1 The speaker's orientation is the present. If it had been the past or the future we would have said respectively *I had been waiting for six hours* or *I shall have been waiting for six hours*.
2 The beginning of the action is a definite point in the past, i.e., six hours ago.
3 The action is still continuing at the time of utterance.
4 The precise time of the beginning of the action can be inferred by counting backwards from the point of orientation. If the speaker had intended to name the time of the beginning of the action he would have said, say, *I've been waiting since three o'clock*.

Four important points emerge from a consideration of these parameters. First, the parameters are semantic in nature. They concern, in other words, the meaning of utterances. Secondly, they are common to both languages under consideration. In fact they may well be universal but it is not necessary to make such a strong claim when our purpose is to compare two languages only. Thirdly, the parameters are implicit in the utterance. None of the concepts employed (i.e., orientation, beginning, continuation, end, time-counting, time-naming or past) are overtly realized in the utterance, but it is an interesting fact about language in general that we can 'spell out' these implicit concepts by the device of paraphrase if the necessity should arise. Finally, the possible permutations of the common categories are coded differently for English and French, resulting in different syntactic categories on the surface. For example the following permutation

Orientation of speaker: present

Beginning of action: in past

Time point: named

Continuation of action: in present

produces for English the combination of present tense and perfective continuous aspect plus the preposition *since* but for French the present tense plus *depuis*.

To illustrate the possibilities of this approach in somewhat greater detail we give below a numbered list of English and French translation equivalents followed by a 'grid' of common categories against which the data may be plotted. Since we are only concerned here with a statement of principles the list does not by any means exhaust the possible permutations either for French or for English. Following the diagram we give some specimen permutations and their corresponding realizations as syntactic categories and/or lexical items for English and French.

1 I started waiting five hours ago
  J'ai commencé à attendre il y a cinq heures

2 I stopped waiting five hours ago
  J'ai fini d'attendre il y a cinq heures

3 I started waiting at five o'clock
  J'ai commencé à attendre à cinq heures

4 I stopped waiting at five o'clock
  J'ai arrêté d'attendre à cinq heures

5 I'm waiting (for the bus)
  J'attends (l'autobus)

6 I've been waiting for you (for some time)
  Je t'attends (depuis un moment)

7 I've been waiting since five o'clock
  J'attends depuis cinq heures

8 I've been waiting for five hours
   J'attends depuis cinq heures

9 I waited (but he didn't turn up)
   J'ai attendu (mais il n'est pas venu)

10 I waited from three onwards
   J'ai attendu à partir de trois heures

11 I waited for six hours (but he didn't come)
   J'ai attendu (pendant) six heures (mais il n'est pas venu)

12 I waited for six hours (and he finally came)
   J'ai attendu (pendant) six heures (et il est enfin arrivé)

13 I waited for six hours (before he came)
   J'ai attendu six heures (avant qu'il n'arrive)

14 I waited from three until five
   J'ai attendu de trois heures à cinq

15 I've waited since five o'clock
   J'attends depuis cinq heures
   (more commonly: Ça fait depuis cinq heures que j'attends)

16 I've waited for six hours
   J'attends depuis six heures

17 I had waited since five (when he finally came)
   J'attendais depuis cinq heures (quand enfin il est arrivé)

18 I had waited for six hours (before he finally came)
   J'avais attendu six heures (avant qu'il ne se présente)

19 I'd been waiting since five (when he came)
   J'attendais depuis cinq heures (lorsqu'il est arrivé)

20 I'd been waiting for six hours (before he came)
   J'avais attendu six heures (avant qu'il n'arrive)

The following are ungrammatical with reference to the permutations permitted in Figure 1:

*I'm waiting for five hours (= permutation no. 8)

*J'ai attendu depuis cinq heures (= permutation no. 8)

*I waited for six hours (when he came) (= permutation no. 13)

*J'avais attendu depuis six heures (= permutation no. 18)

*I'd been waiting since five o'clock (before he came) (= permutation no. 17)

*J'ai attendu depuis cinq heures (= permutation no. 11)

	START			CONTINUING		STOP			ORIENTATION			
	Past specified					Past specified			In Past			
	Point inferred	Point named	Past unspecified (but relevant)	Past	Present	Point inferred	Point named	Past unspecified	Time specified	Event specified	Event unspecified	In present
	1	2	3	4	5	6	7	8	9	10	11	12
1	X											X
2						X						
3		X										
4							X					
5					X							X
6			X									X
7		X										X
8	X											X
9				X				X			X	
10		X						X				
11			X			X					X	
12			X							X		
13			X									
14		X		X			X		X			
15		X			X							X
16	X											X
17		X						X		X		
18	X							X		X		
19		X						X				
20	X							X	X			

Figure 1: specimen grid

Notes on Figure 1

Most column headings are self-explanatory. The third heading 'Past unspecified (but relevant)' concerns the difference between (5) *I'm waiting* and (6) *I've been waiting*. Note the inappropriateness of the question *How long for?* when applied to (5) but not when applied to (6). In other words in (5) the beginning of the action is not only unspecified but it is also irrelevant to the proposition.

Columns 10 and 11 define the speaker's point of orientation as an event rather than a point in time. For example in sentence 12 the event which specifies the point of orientation is expressed (in brackets) as 'and he finally came'.

The morphological categories and lexical items which correspond to the various permutations of the semantic parameters are

for English	*for French*
Preterite	Preterite
(HAVE + Past Participle)	AVOIR + Past Participle
(BE + ing)	[+ depuis, + pendant], etc.
[+ for, + since], etc.	

To give an example illustrating these correspondences, the permutation of column-headings $2 \times 4 \times 8 \times 10$ yields for English either *I had waited since five* = [+ Preterite, + (HAVE + Past Participle), + since] or *I had been waiting since five* = [+ Preterite, + (HAVE + Past Participle), + (BE + ing), + since] whereas for French it yields *J'attendais depuis cinq heures* = [+ Preterite, + depuis].

On the basis of the analysis provided by Figure 1 it seems perfectly feasible to regard verbal aspect as a superficial phenomenon which has its origin in semantic relations of a rather intricate kind. There are several points about this type of analysis which should be borne in mind. The most important consideration is that the representation of aspectual parameters given in the specimen grid does not constitute a grammar in the strict sense of the word, since there are no rules which explicitly derive the syntactic categories from the semantic ones. However, there is no reason to suppose that the grid is not in principle capable of being formalized as part of a grammar. In recent years considerable interest has been shown in the proposal that semantic representations should form the basis of a grammar. A number of linguists have attempted to formalize various 'semantically based' models of grammar (see Lakoff 1969, Chafe 1970). Moreover, notional grids are heuristically useful in that they force the investigator to produce data against which he can check the various categories and their permutations. In other words the grid possesses at least one of the properties of generative grammars—it is 'predictive' in the sense that it establishes as grammatical not only those sentences which are attested in the data, but also potential sentences which are implied by the data but not actually present in it (see Lyons 1968, p. 155).

As a result, semi-explicit notional grammars of the type discussed here may create insights into a language (or more than one language when the emphasis is on contrastive analysis). Moreover, since the grammar concentrates on meaning as well as on syntax it attains a certain measure of explanatory power which is clearly of importance in language teaching. For example, it enables us to explain why the French and English examples are translation equivalents in spite of their different structural properties or why under certain conditions an otherwise grammatical sentence is inappropriate or what the difference is between *depuis* and *pendant*.

In order to conclude this section let us sum up the main points that have arisen out of the discussion. We have compared three approaches to contrastive analysis, namely a slot-in-frame technique based on a structuralist approach to language, a transformational-generative account following Chomsky (1965) and lastly what may be loosely termed a 'notional' view of contrastive analysis. It should be emphasized that these three approaches were discussed in relation to one area of grammar only (tense and aspect in English and French). Consequently it would be premature to conclude that any one of the three approaches is superior to the others for contrastive analysis in general: we must allow for the possibility that different jobs may require different tools. However, it is fair to conclude that at the 'deepest' level of analysis we need a theory which distinguishes explicitly between deep and surface phenomena. Since the structuralist view of language lacks this distinction it must be considered inadequate in principle for investigating problems at any except the lowest level of generalization.[5]

Chomsky (1965) distinguishes between deep and surface structure but the disadvantage of his approach is that by implication the deep grammars of any two languages are regarded as similar rather than identical. According to Chomsky the deep component of a grammar is basically one which formalizes constituency relations. It is clear, then, why he assumes a similarity condition on base-components (as opposed to an identity condition) since the identity condition would involve a drastic

---

[5] We should not overlook the great achievements of the structuralist school in both theoretical and applied linguistics, in particular the work of Zellig Harris (see Further Reading section). Shortage of space prevents us from describing the structuralist approach to contrastive analysis in more detail, given the principal objectives of this chapter.

change in the formalism. For example, it is difficult to see how the categories featuring in our notional grid could be incorporated in the type of grammar described by Chomsky (1965) without changing the theoretical foundation of the grammar considerably. The disadvantage of the similarity condition is that the notion of substantive universals (or 'common categories' for our purpose) becomes incoherent. For example, we have seen that the Auxiliary expansion rule is different for English and French. Do we conclude that Auxiliary is a common category or not? If Auxiliary is not a common category then the common label is highly misleading and if it is we should like to have some cross-linguistic reasons for its existence. As far as contrastive analysis is concerned, experience has shown that this type of grammar is not very useful heuristically (in other words its format is not particularly conducive to the production of ideas) nor is it as explanatory or descriptively adequate as one would hope. A notional approach, on the other hand, does reflect the identity condition on deep components and consequently may provide a set of useful 'heuristic constraints' on contrastive statements. It obliges the investigator to search for primary and secondary categories and thus forces him to think rather more deeply about the languages being compared.

3 Some aspects of yes/no interrogatives in English and Chinese

In this section an attempt is made to carry the identity condition on base components to its logical conclusion given a specific problem of analysis. A sharp distinction is made between primary categories of grammar and secondary or dependent categories. The primary or 'common' categories carry semantic information, whereas the secondary categories are dependent on the existence of the primary categories and are therefore semantically redundant. It is argued that, given the data, a viable contrastive grammar based on this distinction must involve a new type of grammatical component which we call a 'grafting' component. The rules of the grafting component, which are unique to each language, specify the conditions under which secondary categories can be 'grafted on to' the primary categories and thus constitute an explicit link between the common base and the individual transformational components.

Before proceeding to examine the data the following points should be made about the purpose of the analysis.

(1) We insist on a certain degree of formalization in the analysis because of its heuristic value. That is, by forcing ourselves to be explicit we expect to gain insights into the data which we might not otherwise obtain. Formalization in linguistics involves establishing a chain of arguments in which each link must be empirically falsifiable if the end

product is to be valid. In other words, formalization forces the investigator to 'think empirically' at every stage of the analysis and obliges him to establish connections between different parts of the data which might otherwise go unnoticed. When we have succeeded in establishing a connection of this type we say that we have 'had an insight about the data'. This does not mean that, in the present state of linguistics, we can be explicit in the analysis of every contrastive problem, or indeed that we shall ever be able to be completely explicit. For example, given the requirement of explanatory power discussed above (p. 279), a full contrastive analysis of the determiner systems of two languages cannot be carried out with the tools that general linguistic theory has available at the present time. This situation, of course, is very much to be regretted. It does not follow, however, that we should not attempt to do our best with the tools that have been made available by recent developments in linguistic theory.

(2) The model for analysis presented here should be regarded as an experiment in applied linguistics rather than as a contribution to theoretical linguistics. The data are not in any way comprehensive and represent only one aspect of the description of interrogatives for the languages concerned. It is suggested, however, that the analysis has two practical merits: it allows us to be explicit, and it incorporates an explanatory distinction between primary and secondary categories. The principle which we have adopted is that any model possessing these characteristics can be used for contrastive analysis.

(3) Inevitably, the data analysed here is highly restricted. Moreover, we are not examining linguistic systems but a list of selected translation equivalents. But one of the main tasks in contrastive analysis is the study of parallel systems. The reason for keeping the data simple is that it allows a detailed discussion of the theoretical issues raised in section 2 of this chapter, without going too deeply into the complexities of the interrogative systems in English and Chinese. Perhaps the apparent discrepancy between the simplicity of the data and the complexity of the description will serve as a reminder of the size of the task that confronts us in contrastive analysis.

3.1 The data

One of the fundamental tasks in any type of linguistic analysis is to find data (that is, both grammatical and ungrammatical sentences) which are relevant to a particular problem or hypothesis ('The data aren't given but taken'). Below is given a set of instructions which constitute one possible approach to this problem of heuristics, followed by a final list of restricted data and problems emerging from the data.

Instructions

1 Start with one or more simple sentences in the first language and their translation equivalent in the second language. Create a data list of relevant sentences and non-sentences.

2 State the problems which emerge from the data.

3 List the problems that have emerged from the data for later reference.

4 With reference to the sentences resulting from instruction 1, consider alternative ways of expressing the same meaning in both languages. That is, find synonymous expressions with different structural properties.

5 Reconsider the original simple sentences and examine their grammatical properties. Think up more sentences with different grammatical properties and observe how they behave under interrogative conditions. Add all these forms to the data list and note the problems.

List of data

Chinese	*English*
C1 Ta gao (he-tall)	E1 He's tall
C2 Ta gao ma? (he-tall-Q)	E2 Is he tall?
C3 Ta gao bu gao? (he-tall-not-tall)	E2 Is he tall?
C4 *Ta gao bu gao ma	
C5 Ta shi Yingguo ren (he-be-Englishman)	E3 He is an Englishman
C6 *Ta Yingguo ren	
C7 *Ta shi gao	
C8 Ta shi Yingguo ren ma?	E4 Is he an Englishman?
C9 Ta shi bu shi Yingguo ren (He-be-not-be-Englishman)	E4 Is he an Englishman?
C10 Ta shi Yingguo ren bu shi? (he-be-Englishman-not-be)	E4 Is he an Englishman?
C11 Ta mai shu (he-buy-book)	E5 He bought a book
C12 Ta mai shu ma?	E6 Did he buy a book?
C13 Ta mai bu mai shu?	E6 Did he buy a book?
C14 Ta mai shu bu mai?	E6 Did he buy a book?

C15 Ta hui mai shu (he-can-buy-book)	E7 He can buy a book
C16 Ta hui mai shu ma?	E8 Can he buy a book?
C17 Ta hui bu hui mai shu?	E8 Can he buy a book?
C18 Ta hui mai shu bu hui?	E8 Can he buy a book?
C19 Ta yao mai shu	E9 He wants to buy a book
C20 Ta yao mai shu ma?	E10 Does he want to buy a book?
C21 Ta yao bu yao mai shu?	E10 Does he want to buy a book?
C22 Ta yao mai shu bu yao?	E10 Does he want to buy a book?
C23 Ta bu X ma? (where X is any verbal predicate)	
C24 *Ta bu X bu bu X?	

List of problems

1 Interrogativeness in Chinese is sometimes marked by a particle (ma), sometimes by 'disjunction' (X—bu—X).

2 There is no copula in Chinese with non-nominal predicates.

3 The copula in English 'carries' tense and number.

4 There are no overt markers for tense and number agreement in Chinese.

5 There are no articles in Chinese.

6 Auxiliary *do* occurs in English interrogatives where there is no *have*, *be* or modal.

7 Pre-verbs occur immediately before the main verb in Chinese.

8 *To* in English is an automatic consequence of the complex predicate with *want*.

9 In Chinese *ma* is the only interrogative marker for negative predicates.

3.2 Writing a contrastive grammar for the data

At this point we have to ask what grammatical model should be adopted for our contrastive statement. The answer naturally depends on our basic assumptions about the nature of contrastive analysis. It was argued in the general introduction that the most fruitful assumption in contrastive analysis is the one which was named the 'identity condition' on base components. If we adopt this strong assumption for our present purposes we shall find that no version of any grammatical model in existence (with the possible exception of 'generative semantics' which is still at an early stage of development) is adequate to describe the data.

Unfortunately the lack of a theoretical model of grammar which is adequate for the performance of some practical task is a common situation in applied linguistics.

Given this situation, two courses are open to us: we either drop the identity condition on base components or we change one of the existing grammatical models. We have everything to gain from being adventurous, so let us adopt the second course. However, we must not be unduly adventurous. We need some sort of check on our procedures so that we know what we are doing at every stage. Such a guarantee exists as part of the general notion of generative (in the sense of explicit) grammar. Let us therefore adopt explicitness as our second condition for selecting a grammatical model for contrastive analysis. Given the conditions of identity on base components and explicitness, what existing model shall we choose for modification? The natural choice is a transformational-generative model, since this incorporates the notions of base component (which presupposes transformations) and explicitness (which is partly implied by 'generative'). Of the three types of transformational-generative grammar described by Chomsky, the 1965 version seems most suitable for our present purposes. The reason for this choice will become apparent during the course of the following discussion. The problem is how to modify the model in order to accommodate both the data under examination and the identity condition on base components. Let us illustrate the problem by examining the first Chinese sentence on the data list, i.e., (C1) *Ta gao* (he-tall) and its English equivalent (E1) *He is tall.*

If we applied the model without modification the phrase structure part of a contrastive grammar generating C1 would have to be different from the one generating E1 since C1 and E1 would have different underlying structures over and above the fact that the lexical items contained in them are different. That is, E1 contains a copula which 'carries' tense (and number) whereas C1 does not. So assuming that NP and VP are necessary constituents in Chinese and English (by no means an uncontroversial assumption) a phrase structure grammar generating C1 would contain rules (1i–iii), while a phrase structure grammar for English might contain rules (2i–iv).[6]

Phrase structure grammar for Chinese (PSC)

1 (i) $S \rightarrow \# NP + VP \#$
   (ii) $VP \rightarrow Adj$
   (iii) $NP \rightarrow Pron$
         (etc.)

---

[6] These rules are essentially Chomsky's. The two grammars are of course partial phrase structure grammars, relevant only to sentences such as E1 and C1. In order to generate C1 and E1 a satisfactory transformational component is presupposed. We shall disregard transformations for the moment.

Phrase structure grammar for English (PSE)

2 (i) $S \rightarrow \# NP + VP \#$

(ii) $VP \rightarrow Aux + Cop + Adj$

(iii) $Aux \rightarrow Tense$

(iv) $Tense \rightarrow \begin{Bmatrix} Past \\ Present \end{Bmatrix}$

(etc.)

There are three ways in which PSC and PSE could be related to the notion of a common base (called 'the base') so as to meet our identity condition on base components: (a) let PSC be the base, (b) let PSE be the base, (c) let neither PSC nor PSE be the base. The first possibility (with PSC as the base) will yield a terminal string (call it b_x) which underlies both C1 and E1. It follows from the rules of PSC that b_x does not contain a copula or tense. In order to generate the English sentence E1 we must derive these categories 'elsewhere'. This crucial implication will be discussed shortly.

The second possibility (with PSE as the base) will yield a terminal string (call it b_y) which underlies both C1 and E1 and which does contain a copula and tense. Certain transformations will subsequently delete the categories Copula and Tense in order to arrive at the surface structure associated with the Chinese sentence C1. On the face of it, the second possibility (with PSE as the base) seems unwarranted. Why should we generate syntactic categories in the base which are never realized on the surface in Chinese? On the other hand, if we adopt the first solution, why should we not generate syntactic categories in the base which are realized on the surface in English? It will become clear that if we can give a satisfactory answer to the second question we shall have answered the first one by implication.

There are many precedents in transformational theory for not generating all surface categories in the base. To give one example, the category of complementizers is never generated in the base. Examples of complementizers are *that* in *He discovered that Mary left early* or *to* in *She wants to read a book*. Categories such as these are not generated in the base because they are perfectly automatic consequences of certain syntactic operations in English involving other categories present in the base. For example the word *that* in *He discovered that Mary left* is an automatic consequence in English of having this particular combination of main clause and subordinate clause. One further important characteristic of purely surface categories such as complementizers is that they are usually devoid of any semantic significance. There are two reasons, then, why certain syntactic categories are not generated in the base: (a) they are dependent on other categories or combinations of categories present in the base and (b) they have no semantic import. The lack of semantic relevance mentioned in (b) is a consequence of the dependency referred to in (a).

Let us now formulate a principle of contrastive analysis as follows: the identity condition on base components is to be equated with the condition that *all and only the categories generated in the base component shall be semantically relevant*. A corollary to this condition is that no categories shall be generated in the base which are dependent on the existence of other categories in the base. Let us call those categories that should be generated in the base *primary categories* and those that should not *secondary categories*.

Restricting ourselves to the data in hand it follows that if we can show that the categories Tense and Copula (in English) are in any way dependent on other categories they should not be generated in the base (that is, they should be designated as secondary categories). It is impossible here to investigate fully the hypothesis that tenses and copulas are indeed dependent on other categories in English but, considering tense first, the following data seem to lend support to such a hypothesis:

5   He bought a book yesterday.

6   *He buys a book yesterday.

7   If I were a bird, I'd fly away.

8   *If I'm a bird, I'd fly away.

9   A defining characteristic of cats is that they are animals.

10   *A defining characteristic of cats is that they were animals.

If tense were independent of the associated semantic categories such as time (past in this case), condition (counterfactual) or 'genericness' we would not be able to account for the ungrammaticalness of (6), (8) and (10).

These are only a few examples of the very intricate relationships that exist between certain semantically relevant categories on the one hand and tense on the other. The point of our hypothesis is that this relationship consists in a one-way dependency between the semantically relevant categories and tense and that as a consequence Tense should not be generated in the base.

The existence of the copula in English is directly related to the existence of tense in English. All sentences in English are in either the past or the present tense. In verbal predicates the tense marker is without exception part of the first verbal element in the verb phrase. Tense is never attached to 'non-verbal' elements in English, e.g. *He talled, *He Englishmanned. Since tense must be expressed in English it follows that there must be a category whose function it is to carry the obligatory tense marker in the absence of verbal elements. This is the category Copula. Tense-carrying is not the only function of the copula. It also incorporates person and number. The copula, then, is dependent on the existence of at least one category (which is in turn dependent on other categories) and should therefore not be generated in the base.

Turning to Chinese we now have a tentative explanation for the absence of tense markers in Chinese. The general tendency in Chinese is towards economy. This manifests itself in a general absence of semantically irrelevant secondary categories on the surface. Since both Tense and Copula are secondary categories they are not part of the Chinese system. Note incidentally that Chinese does have a copula in constructions such a *Ta shi Yingguo ren* (He-be-Englishman). A very tentative explanation for its existence might be that if the copula did not exist disjunctive questions involving nominal predicates could become rather cumbersome, e.g. *Ta Yingguo ren bu Yingguo ren* instead of *Ta shi Yingguo ren bu shi* (or *Ta shi bu shi Yingguo ren*). In other words a simplification in one part of the system would lead to a complication in another part of the system. Indeed in some perfectly normal expressions the absence of a copula in Chinese does lead to circumlocutions. For example, the Chinese equivalent of the sentence *He wants to be rich* is *Ta yao zuo ige youqiande ren* (He want act-as one rich man). This shows that the notion of economy in language systems is by no means a straightforward one.

Thus it seems that PSC is much nearer to the requirement of a common deep component than PSE. However, PSC does not include the category which determines the generation of tense in English, i.e., the semantically relevant category Time, and we must incorporate this category in the base. But there is a complication. If we simply state Time as an obligatory category in the base component we will generate odd sentences such as *He was tall last month* or *Cats were animals in 1957*. That is, there are sentence types, so-called generic sentences, which constitute 'timeless' propositions. (Note that timelessness generally entails the use of the present tense in English.) There are various ways in which this information could be expressed in the base component but given our restricted data we shall present Time as an optional constituent. A fully adequate analysis would presumably involve representing generic and non-generic sentences as distinct sentence types.

Restricting ourselves as far as possible to the data and keeping in mind the conditions assumed for contrastive analysis, a possible common base is the following (for a detailed discussion of these rules see Appendix II, p. 354):

Common base for English and Chinese data

$$\text{I} \quad S \rightarrow \# \begin{Bmatrix} Q \\ \text{Decl} \end{Bmatrix} (\text{Neg}) \text{ Nucleus } \#$$

2 Nucleus → NP + VP (Time)

3 VP → $\begin{Bmatrix} \text{Adj} \\ \text{Pred Nom} \\ \text{(Modal) V + NP} \end{Bmatrix}$

4 Pred Nom → NP

5 NP → $\begin{Bmatrix} \text{N} \\ \# \text{ S } \# \\ \text{Pron} \end{Bmatrix}$

6 Adj → CS

7 V → CS

8 N → CS

9 Time → [± Pro]

10 Time → [± Past]

11 Pron → [± Sing]

12 Pron → [± 3]

Lexicon

ta/he [+ Pron, + [+ 3], . . .]

gao/tall [+ Adj, + —— #, . . .]

yao/want [+ V, + —— # S #, + —— N, . . .]

mai/buy [+ V, + —— N, . . .]

hui/can [+ Modal, . . .]

Yingguo ren/Englishman

The optional constituent Q in rule 1 and the optional Neg are terminal symbols which, when chosen, 'trigger off' the interrogative transformation(s) and the negative incorporation transformation respectively. (For a discussion of these symbols see Katz and Postal 1964.) Although no negative sentences are part of the data, Neg is needed for the formulation of the disjunctive interrogative transformation in Chinese. The optional constituent Time (rule 2) marks the distinction between generic and non-generic sentences and may subsequently be deleted in condition that the feature [+ Pro] is attached to it. Note that articles are absent in the Noun Phrase. This is a good example of the heuristic value of the identity condition on base components in contrastive analysis. It forces us to regard articles as secondary categories in English because articles do not exist in Chinese. An interesting question concerns the nature of the primary categories with which articles are associated. It is doubtful whether there is a fully adequate answer to this question at the present time, but one thing seems certain: 'definiteness' and 'indefiniteness' may be functions of the whole sentence rather than of the Noun Phrase only. (See also Appendix II.)

The rules of the base component obviously do not generate well-formed sentences in either Chinese or English as they stand, and additional rules are needed. In transformational-generative theory such rules are stated in the transformational component, but this division of the syntactic component into two parts (i.e. phrase structure rules plus transformation rules) cannot be adopted without modification for contrastive analysis given the identity condition on base components plus the requirement,.on any type of grammar, that the grammar should express true generalizations. To give an example illustrating this difficulty suppose the base component generates the following base string and its structural description (we have omitted all features which are not directly relevant to the argument):

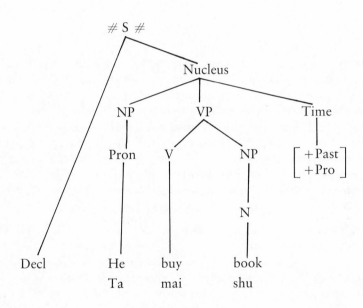

Figure 2

How, with particular reference to the constituents Tense and Article, do we eventually arrive at the syntactic representation given in Figure 2? The following tree, after the application of morphophonemic and phonological rules, will eventually develop into the phonetic representation [hɪ bɔt ə bʊk]:

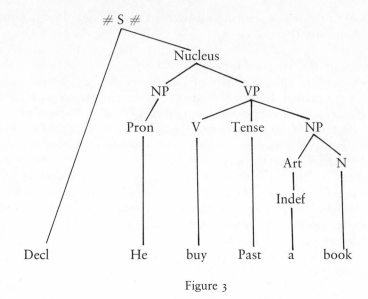

Figure 3

How, in other words, shall we generate the secondary categories such as the auxiliaries (tense only in this case), copulas and articles required for the generation of English sentences? To do this simply by transformation would be either undesirable in that we would lose all the valuable syntactic generalizations which transformational linguists have formulated for these categories in English, or technically impossible because non-terminal constituents such as Auxiliary or Determiner can neither be introduced nor rewritten by transformation. To make this clear let us formulate, very roughly, the following adjunction transformation:

$$X - V - Y - \text{Time} \, [+ \text{Past}] \Rightarrow X - V + \text{Past} - \text{Time} \, [+ \text{Past}]$$

The above transformation adjoins the secondary category Past Tense to the Verb on condition that the primary category Time [+Past] is present in deep structure, in accordance with the conditions on contrastive analysis formulated earlier. A similar transformation would have to be devised for the adjunction of Present Tense. The difficulty with this procedure is not only that we have lost the generalization that Past and Present are instances of the category Tense but also that Tense belongs to a set of Auxiliary constituents about which powerful syntactic generalizations can be made in English (See Chomsky 1957 for some remarkable examples of such generalizations). Similarly, we come up against difficulties if we introduce a constituent Tense by adjunction transformation as follows:

$$X - V - Y - \text{Time} \Rightarrow X - V + \text{Tense} - Y - \text{Time}$$

There is now no way of expressing the fact that Tense may be either Past or Present since constituents cannot be further developed by transformation.

We must conclude that the traditional division of a transformational grammar into a base and a transformational component is inadequate for contrastive statements of the kind envisaged. What seems to be required is an additional component whose categories would be unique to each of the languages being compared and which would act as a link between the common deep component and the individual transformational components. More specifically such a component would create constituents for the secondary categories, expand those constituents and finally 'graft' the resulting branches on to the trees generated by the base component, given certain conditions. The trees resulting from this grafting operation would subsequently act as input to the transformational component.

Let us illustrate how such a grafting component might work in practice by developing the base structure (11) into the intermediate structure (12):

11 $\text{He} + \text{buy} + \text{book} + \text{Time} \begin{bmatrix} +\text{Past} \\ +\text{Pro} \end{bmatrix}$

12 $\text{He} + \text{buy} + \text{Preterite} + \text{a} + \text{book}.$

We will use the term Preterite as a label for the morphological category 'past tense' so as not to create confusion with the semantic category 'past (time)'.

The procedure which converts the base structure (11) into the intermediate structure (12) consists of a set of grafting operations and a set of 'ordinary' transformations as stated below (for a detailed explanation of these rules, see Appendix III):

Grafting component (English)

1 Tense $\rightarrow \begin{Bmatrix} \text{Preterite} \\ \text{Present} \end{Bmatrix}$

2 Art $\rightarrow \begin{Bmatrix} \text{Def} \\ \text{Indef} \end{Bmatrix}$

3 *T-graft* (obligatory)

$\quad \text{X} - \text{VP} - \text{Y} \Rightarrow \text{X} - \text{Tense} + \text{VP} - \text{Y}$

$\quad$ Conditions: a Preterite $\Big/ \begin{matrix} 1 & \text{Time } [+\text{Past}] \\ 2 & ***^7 \end{matrix}$

$\quad\quad\quad\quad\quad\quad b$ Present $\Big/ \begin{matrix} 1 & -\text{Time} \\ 2 & *** \end{matrix}$

[7] The stars indicate that the conditions have not yet been fully investigated.

L

4 *T-graft* (obligatory)

$$X + N \Rightarrow Art + X + N$$

Conditions: *a* Indef/***
               b Def/***

5 Create intervening nodes if necessary

Transformational component (English)

6 *T-suffixation*

$$X - Af - v - Y \Rightarrow X - v + Af - Y$$

(where Af in this example is either Preterite or Present and v is V, i.e. *buy*)

7 *T-delete-Time* (optional)

$$X - Time [+Pro] - Y \Rightarrow X - Y$$

8 Rearrange and/or delete nodes.

The rules (1)–(8) will transform the base string He + buy + book + Time $\begin{bmatrix} +Pro \\ +Past \end{bmatrix}$ into the derived string He + buy + Preterite + a + book. They suggest the following schematic organization for a contrastive grammar involving two languages X and Y. The arrows indicate input-output relations:

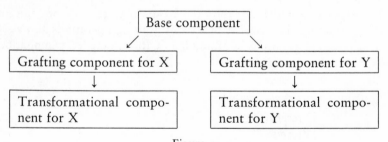

Figure 4

To conclude this section a full contrastive grammar for the data is given below. For convenience explanatory remarks, where needed, immediately follow individual rules.

3.3 A contrastive grammar for English and Chinese data

Base component

This is as stated on page 302. (The reservations concerning the base expressed on page 303 still stand.)

Grafting component for Chinese

No grafting rules are necessary for the Chinese data. This does not imply that no such rules will be needed for a more detailed contrastive grammar involving Chinese.

Transformational component for Chinese

1 *T-shi-incorporation* (obligatory)

$$\# \text{ NP} + \text{NP } \# \Rightarrow \# \text{ NP} + shi + \text{NP } \#$$

This rule transforms the base string *Ta Yingguo ren* (he Englishman) into *Ta shi Yingguo ren*. Note that *shi* is treated by implication as being devoid of lexical content and consequently it does not appear in the lexicon (compare *be* in English). As it stands the rule is too general. In Chinese the copula *shi* cannot occur in certain embedded sentences. For example the Chinese equivalent of the English sentence *He wants to be an Englishman* is not **Ta yao ta shi Yingguo ren* nor (with subsequent equi-NP deletion, see rule 5 below) **Ta yao shi Yingguo ren* but rather *Ta yao zuo ige Yingguo ren* (He want act-as one Englishman). On the other hand one can say in Chinese *Ta shuo ta shi Yingguo ren* (He says he is an Englishman) which also involves recursion. In other words *shi*-incorporation is by no means as unconstrained as the rule implies. However we shall not attempt to formulate these constraints.

2 *T-interrogative 1* (obligatory if rule 3 is not chosen)

$$\# \text{ Q} + \text{X} - \text{Nucleus } \# \Rightarrow \# \text{ X} + \text{Nucleus } \# \text{ ma } \#$$

According to the conventions on cover symbols (see Chomsky 1957) X may be anything including 'null'. It follows from rule 1 of the base grammar that X may be Neg. So the transformation correctly allows for *ma* to be attached to negative questions (See also rule 3). The condition on the application of rule 2 is that rules 2 and 3 form a pair from which one alternative must be chosen if the base tree contains the symbol Q. Note that Q is deleted.

3 *T-interrogative 2* (obligatory if rule 2 is not chosen)

$$\# \text{ Q} - \text{Nucleus } \# \Rightarrow \# \text{ Nucleus } \# \text{ Neg} - \text{Nucleus } \# \#$$
$$ 1 \qquad 2 \qquad\qquad\quad 3 \qquad 4 \quad 5 \qquad\quad 6$$
$$\text{where } 2 \equiv 3 \equiv 6$$

The condition 'where $2 \equiv 3 \equiv 6$' expresses the requirement (by means of the equivalence sign $\equiv$) that the three occurrences of Nucleus are 'the same' (i.e. Nucleus dominates identical trees and lexical items in all cases). This type of recursion, which is indicated by the internal sentence boundary preceding Neg involves no change of meaning. It merely 'spells out' the Q constituent which is thereby deleted.

T-interrogative 2 provides a single underlying form for all disjunctive interrogatives of the kind discussed here. More precisely it asserts that the two alternative forms *Ta mai shu bu mai* (He buy book not buy = Is he buying a book) and *Ta mai bu mai shu* derive from the same hypothetical source, namely **Ta mai shu bu ta mai shu* (He buy book not he buy book). This intermediate structure subsequently serves 'as input to a very general type of transformation which deletes equivalent NP's, in this case either the first or second occurrence of *shu* and subsequently the second occurrence of *ta* (See rules 4 and 5 below). This treatment of disjunctive interrogatives in Chinese is superior to simply listing the possibilities (as is usually the case in traditional and structuralist grammars of Chinese) for two reasons: (a) it formalizes the intuition that in disjunctive interrogatives one both 'adds something' to the main proposition (i.e., the negated form of the preposition) and deletes something as well (i.e., the equivalent NP's mentioned earlier), (b) it is far more general.

4 *T-equi-NP deletion 1* (optional)

$$W + NP + X \; \# \; Y + NP + Z \Rightarrow W + X \; \# \; Y + NP + Z$$
$$1 \quad 2 \quad 3 \; 4 \; 5 \quad 6 \quad 7$$

where *a* W and Y are not null

b NP ≡ NP
$$2 \quad 6$$

This transformation is connected with rule 5 in carrying out the necessary deletion operations across sentence boundaries on structures produced by rule 3. It deletes the first occurrence of a pair of identical object NP's. The fact that it must be the object and not the subject NP is ensured by the condition that W and Y may not be null (as would be the case for subject NP's). To illustrate, it transforms NP_1 mai NP_2 # Neg NP_1 mai NP_2 into NP_1 mai # Neg NP_1 mai NP_2. The transformation holds for all transitive and equative sentences in Chinese including nominalized objects such as NP_1 yao NP_2 # Neg NP_1 yao NP_2. Fully spelled out this structure yields

Ta yao # ta mai shu # # Neg ta yao # ta mai shu #

Note that this transformation is optional. If it is not chosen, then rule 5 must be. This captures the fact that there are two possibilities for disjunctive interrogatives: either we delete the first identical object or the second (but not both and not neither), generating either NP_1 mai # Neg NP_1 mai NP_2 or NP_1 mai NP_2 # Neg NP_1 mai. The first possibility is expressed by T-equi-NP deletion 1. The second possibility, where the second object equi-NP is deleted, need not be expressed separately since, as a formal operation, it is identical to the deletion of the subject equi-NP which in Chinese (and English) can affect only the second occurrence of the subject NP (compare *He wants to go* but not *Wants he to go*).

5 *T-equi-NP deletion 2* (obligatory; re-apply where necessary)

$$W + NP + X \; \# \; Y + NP + Z \Rightarrow W + NP + X \; \# \; Y + Z$$

$$\text{I} \qquad 2 \qquad 3 \; 4 \; 5 \qquad 6 \qquad 7$$

where *a* W ≠ Y

b W and Y must be either both null or both not null

c NP ≡ NP
  2   6

This transformation deletes all second equi-NP's which occur across sentence boundaries, i.e., all subject NP's in second position and, if rule 4 is not chosen, all object NP's in second position. The transformation operates not only on disjunctive interrogatives but also on all structures containing equi-NP's across sentence boundaries, e.g. Ta yao # ta mai shu ⇒ Ta yao # mai shu. Interestingly this transformation also applies to English (with slightly changed conditions) and produces He want # go from He want # he go.

6 *T-delete Time* (optional)

$$X - \text{Time} \; [+\text{Pro}] - Y \Rightarrow X - Y$$

The following derivation illustrates the operation and application of the rules just formulated.

Sentence:	Ta yao bu yao mai shu
Base string:	Q ta yao # ta mai shu #
By rule 3:	Ta yao # ta mai shu # # Neg ta yao # ta mai shu
By rule 4:	Ta yao # Neg ta yao # ta mai shu
By rule 5:	Ta yao # Neg yao # mai shu

All that remains is to delete the internal sentence boundaries and to realize Neg by the word *bu*.

Grafting component for English

1 *a* Aux → Tense (Modal) (have + en) (be + ing)

b Tense → $\begin{cases} \text{Preterite} \\ \text{Present} \end{cases}$

2 Art → $\begin{cases} \text{Def} \\ \text{Indef} \end{cases}$

3 *T-graft-Aux* (obligatory)

$$X - VP - Y \Rightarrow X - Aux + VP - Y$$

where X is not Y $\neq$ Z

Conditions: *a* Preterite $\Big/ \begin{matrix} \text{1 Time} + \text{Past} \\ \text{2 } {*}{*}{*} \end{matrix}$

             b Present $\Big/ \begin{matrix} \text{1} - \text{Time} \\ \text{2 } {*}{*}{*} \end{matrix}$

             c Modal/***

             d have + en/***

             e be + ing/***

The condition 'where X is not Y $\neq$ Z' is an instruction not to graft Aux on to a base tree which contains a nominalized object. It is meant to apply to strings such as *He want $\neq$ he buy book*. There is obviously no sense in grafting Aux on to the second VP (i.e. *buy book*) if it must not appear on the surface (Compare **He wants to went*). The condition is too general as it stands, since there are many cases in English where auxiliaries are part of a recursive object, e.g. *He realized that his position was/ is hopeless* or *He wanted to have bought a book*. However, even in these cases the grafting is not unconstrained.

4 *T-graft-Art*

$$X + N \Rightarrow Art + X + N$$

Conditions: *a* Indef/***

              b Def/***

5 Create intervening nodes if necessary.

Transformational component for English

The following transformations are needed. They are not specified in detail here since a full account is given in Chomsky (1957 and 1965).

6 *T-BE-incorporation*

7 *T-number-agreement*

8 *T-interrogative-yes/no*

9 *T-verbal-suffixation*

10 *T-word-boundary*

11 *T-do-insertion*

12 *T-equi-NP-deletion*

13 *T-to-complementization*

14 *T-delete-Pro-Time* (optional)

15 etc. Various morphophonemic rules

4 Conclusion

In conclusion, the following general remarks may be made. First, a comparison of the Chinese rules with the English rules shows that the description of the English data is very much more complex; six rules for Chinese against 14 formulated rules plus a number of unspecified morphophonemic rules for English. Secondly, the requirements for an adequate contrastive statement are reasonably well met, since (a) the rules are explicit, (b) the difference between deep and surface structure is established, (c) there is an identity condition on deep components in the grammar, (d) an attempt is made to establish valid syntactic generalizations for each of the languages being compared. It should not be assumed that the type of analysis proposed for the above data will necessarily be appropriate for all contrastive problems. In many cases a different type of semantic base has to be devised in order to meet the identity condition, and it is not yet clear in what ways a different choice of base will affect the postulated grafting component.

A semantically based contrastive analysis might be expected to throw light on problems of grading in language teaching. If the contrastive analysis of two or more languages is to be used as a measure of ease or difficulty in foreign language learning, then the identity condition provides us in principle with an empirical definition of what is common between two languages. Moreover, the form of a semantically-based grammar may provide us with a basis for making certain decisions in grading. For example, in a semantically-based grammar the lexical item *remind* might, for one of its meanings, be derived from the lexical item *remember* (more accurately, from a configuration of semantic properties associated with remember) by analysing *remind* as 'cause to remember'. The implication for learning theory is that we would not expect a learner of English to comprehend the full meaning of *remind* without first knowing the meaning of *remember*, but that he would have no difficulty in learning these lexical items the other way round. It should be remembered, however, that although a semantically-based contrastive analysis provides a rich source of speculation about the nature of the learning process, contrastive analysis in itself cannot provide sufficient conditions for a system of grading. There are many factors that a teacher must take into consideration when deciding the order of presentation for language teaching materials, and contrastive analysis does not constitute the sole criterion.

5 Further reading

Dinneen, F. P. (ed.). Monograph Series on Languages and Linguistics, No. 21 (Papers on Contrastive Analysis). Washington: Georgetown University Press, 1968.

Halliday, M. A. K., McIntosh, A. and Strevens, P. *The Linguistic Sciences and Language Teaching.* London: Longmans, 1964. (Chapter 5.)

Harris, Zellig S. Transfer grammar. In *International Journal of American Linguistics*, 1954, Vol. 20, No. 4.

Lado, R. *Linguistics across Cultures.* Ann Arbor: University of Michigan Press, 1957.

Mackey, W. F. *Language Teaching Analysis.* London: Longmans, 1965. (Chapter 3.)

Nickel, G. (ed.). *Papers in Contrastive Linguistics.* London: Cambridge University Press, 1971.

Weinreich, U. *Languages in Contact.* Publications of the Linguistic Society of New York, 1953, No. 1.

11 ELISABETH INGRAM
Language Testing

1 Definition of a test

Tests, like examinations, invite candidates to display their knowledge or skills in a concentrated fashion, so that the results can be graded, and inferences made from the standard of performance in the test about the general standard of performance that can be expected from the candidate, either at the time of the test or at some future time.

The difference between tests and examinations is in the marking. The marker of an examination must use his judgment, whereas the marking of a test is not dependent on the judgment of any individual. However, as Pilliner (1968) points out, the only objective thing about 'objective' tests is the marking; the compiling and the answering of a test is necessarily just as subjective as the setting and answering of examinations.

A test is a measuring device which we use when we want to compare an individual with other individuals who belong to the same group. If we want to compare people for height, we use a yardstick; if we want to compare them in terms of their command of a foreign language, we may use a language test.

2 Requirements of a test

Any measuring device must meet several requirements. It must discriminate. It must be reliable. It must be valid.

Discrimination. If we wanted to measure the height of pre-school children it would be no good using a measuring stand made for the Armed Forces and not calibrated below four feet. The average height of five-year-old English children is about 3 ft 6½ ins (Ellis, 1966). This measuring device would fail to discriminate between the majority of individuals in the pre-school population; all the information one would get would be that the vast majority of them are less than four feet in height.

Reliability. A measuring device should give the same results every time it is used on the same objects or individuals, regardless of who is giving and marking it. If one marked off inches and feet on a piece of elastic and proceeded to measure the floor of one's bedroom, one would be unlikely to get the same result twice, and not one of the results would be reliable. No results are reliable unless they are *stable*. The stability of a test is measured by giving the test to a group of people, giving it to them again a short time later and then *correlating* the scores. *Correlation* is a statistical technique for comparing two sets of scores to see how far they correspond to each other. In this case we would have a *test re-test* or *stability* correlation of reliability.

Statisticians operate also with another kind of reliability, the reliability of *equivalence*. The notion here is that the results one gets from one kind of measuring device should be closely comparable to the results one would have got if one had used another, equivalent, measuring device. The simplest kind of equivalence is having several copies of the same prototype. Ten different yardsticks wielded by ten different drapers should give you the same amount of material, and a hundred cyclostyled copies of the same test should be equally legible. In language testing the problem of simple equivalence is particularly acute in the field of spoken language. All tapes, all replaying facilities and all listening conditions should be identical. In practice, the best one can do is to ensure the best conditions possible, but the lack of reliability of tests using spoken stimuli is notorious.

Simple equivalence of this sort is only a special case of the basic concept, which is based on the theory of sampling. The idea is that there is a large number of items that could have been included in a test of English as a foreign language, and another large number of items that could be included in a test of arithmetic and so on. Any particular test is going to include only a small proportion of these—the items actually included is a *sample* of the *population* of possible items. A particular test is judged to show equivalence reliability if there is a high probability that the scores based on the items that were included are closely similar to the scores that would have been obtained by the same people from a selection of the other items that might have been included but weren't.

The idea of a test re-test or stability reliability is fairly easy to see, but in order to calculate it one needs to test students twice, which can be quite difficult to arrange. The idea of equivalence reliability is more complicated, but it is invaluable in practice, because one can calculate equivalence reliability without having to re-test.

Validity. A test measuring device should actually measure what it is intended to measure. In the early days of intelligence tests—tests which predict the learning ability of schoolchildren—some people thought that reaction times would be useful. The reaction time of an individual is the time between perceiving a stimulus and responding to it in some way, for instance by pressing a key. It can be measured extremely reliably, by means of an electric circuit which incorporates a light bulb, a clock and a Morse key. When the tester closes the circuit the light flashes and the clock starts. The subject presses the key as quickly as he can and that breaks the circuit and stops the clock. The time measured on the clock shows the reaction time. The measurement of the reaction time is reliable, but it is not valid for the purposes of predicting school performance. Validity, like reliability, is estimated by the statistical technique of correlation.

The most obvious way of achieving validity is to arrange for a job sample. If you want to know how good a person is at writing essays, you ask him to write an essay, if you want to know how fluent he is in a foreign language, you ask him to talk to you. The trouble is that validity is limited by reliability; no test or examination can be any more valid than it is reliable. So if it turns out that the reliability of marking essays or of rating command of spoken language is low, then the validity of the marks or ratings must be correspondingly low. It has been known for some considerable time that essay marking is unreliable. There have been many demonstrations of this. In one study by Finlayson (1951) six experienced teachers who received the same instructions marked about 200 essays written by 12-year-old children on a scale ranging from 20 to 0. When the 200 marks awarded by each marker were averaged separately for each marker it was found that there was a discrepancy of nearly 4 points—20% of the scale—between the average mark of the strictest and that of the most lenient marker. While this does not necessarily make any difference to the order of merit in which the essays are arranged, it will make a considerable difference to a child whether his essay is given a mark two points over the passmark, or two points below. In addition to discrepancies between markers, there can also be considerable variation in the marks allotted to the same scripts by the same examiner when he re-marks the scripts after a month or two.

Question (i) A class of 20 was given a test of arithmetic with twenty questions. One mark was given for each correct answer. Fifteen children got 20 marks, three children got 19, one child got 15 and one got 11. Did the test discriminate among the children in the class?

Answer (i) The answer is obviously 'no'.

In less obvious cases a graphic representation may be helpful (see Figure 1). This kind of graphic representation is called a *histogram*. The histogram is one way of representing the *frequency distribution*. The frequency distribution can also be set out in tabular form (see Table 1). ('Frequency' refers to the number of times each mark is obtained by a child).

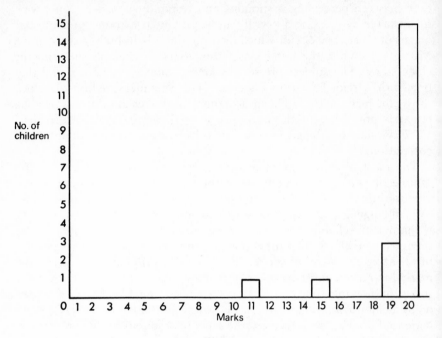

Figure 1

MARKS	FREQUENCY
20	15
19	3
18	—
17	—
16	—
15	1
14	—
13	—
12	—
11	1
	—
	TOTAL 20

Table 1

Question (*ii*) The distribution of a set of scores is set out in the following table:

MARKS	FREQUENCY
10	1
9	3
8	3
7	5
6	9
5	8
4	4
3	1
2	0
1	0
	TOTAL 34

Table 2

Does it look as if this test discriminated reasonably among the children in this class?

Answer (*ii*) Well, yes and no. On the one hand it is very common to find that the greatest frequency is in the middle. In other words, one usually finds that average values occur more often than very low or very high values. On the other hand, when exactly half the children (9 + 8) share 2 marks between them, the discrimination in the middle cannot be said to be very good.

If we draw the distribution, smoothing out the blocks of the histogram, we get:

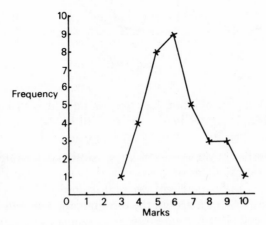

Figure 2

A curve which is entirely symmetrical with the top in the centre and the curve neither too tall nor too flat is known as the *normal curve* describing a *normal distribution*:

Figure 3

It is known that many human characteristics are distributed approximately according to the normal curve. So if a large number of test scores seem to show an approximately normal distribution, this is taken to be a good thing, provided we believe that what is being tested is normally distributed in the population. But we must have a really large number of scores, running at least into hundreds before we can even begin to make inferences from the obtained distribution. On the other hand a test yielding scores which show an approximately normal distribution does not discriminate as well in the middle ranges as it does towards either extreme.

Question (iii) If a test were to discriminate equally well at all levels, would the distribution look like (*a*) or (*b*) or (*c*)?

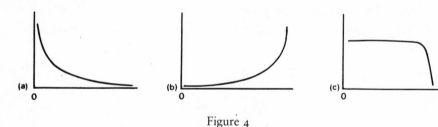

Figure 4

Answer (iii) (*c*) would not represent a normal distribution but the spread of people would be the same at all levels. In (*a*) there is most spread at the top, in (*b*) there is most spread at the bottom.

The distribution of the scores of a test is often deliberately altered, by putting in more easy items or more difficult items, so that the discrimination of the test can be increased where it is needed. If it is a question of picking the top 10% of a group, the discrimination should be best at the most difficult end; if it is a question of assigning every testee accurately then a flat distribution is better

Question (iv) Which type of assessment would you expect to be more reliable:

　a Experienced teachers of music giving marks for excellence in playing the violin, after listening to young violinists performing

　b Researchers in an acoustic laboratory, scoring the ability of students to distinguish notes that are in tune from notes that are sharp or flat.

Question (v) Of the two types of assessment in Question (iv), (*a*) playing skill and (*b*) pitch discrimination, which would you guess was intrinsically more valid for selecting students for a school of music, (*a*) or (*b*)?

Answer (iv) (*b*). Notes could be classified as in tune or out of tune either by determining their physical characteristics by the aid of machines, or by asking people who are known to be good at it, like piano tuners.

Answer (v) (*a*). Having a good ear is obviously only one component of a complex talent. One way of improving the reliability of judging talent, and therefore of improving the functional validity, is to have several markers judging independently.

3 Types of test item

The search for 'objective' testing methods is the direct outcome of dissatisfaction with the unreliability of the marking of traditional examinations. Tests are set up so as to eliminate any differences in results due to variations between different markers, or due to variations in the judgment of one marker at different times. There are basically two formats: open-ended items and multiple choice items.

(a) *Open-ended*

The candidate writes his own answer, which is often a single word, never more than a sentence, in the space provided.

Examples:

　1 Write down in a few words the meaning of each of the following words as has been done for the first word:

　　1 Connect....Link up................

　　2 Support ....

　2 Re-write the underlined portion of the following sentences to produce better English:

　　The thesis developed here shares with Whorf emphasizing the importance of 'frames of consistency'.

3 Change the following sentences into negative sentences:
   1 She sings well.....................
   2 Does he own a car? ....

4 Complete the following sentences by filling in the blanks:
   .... do you live?
   I live on High Street.

5 Insert the correct form of the verb given in brackets:
   (donner)........-moi le canif.

6 Insert the word missing from the brackets:

   | fee | (tip) | end |
   | dance | (......) | sphere |

Examples 1 and 2 differ from the rest in that some element of judgment is required from the marker. In open-ended vocabulary tests like 1 the practice is to supply the tester with a list of acceptable answers, all other answers being marked incorrect. With so-called interlinear items like 2 acceptable answers are again provided, but it is difficult to foresee all variations, so the marker will have to rely on his own judgment at times. This format is not used very often. Examples 3–6 are formulated so that there is only one possible answer.

(b) *Multiple choice*

In multiple choice formats a range of answers is provided, and the candidate has to choose one of them.

Examples:

7 In each group of six words below underline the word which means the same as the word above the group:

   CONTINUE

clash	clutter
tilt	keep on
read	bewail

8 Each sentence has four underlined parts, marked A, B, C and D. You are to identify the one underlined part which would not be accepted in formal, written English.

   | A | | B | C |

   At first the old woman seemed unwilling to accept anything that

D

was offered by my friends and I.

A ( )
B ( )
C ( )
D ( )

9 What do you need if you want to buy a hat?

   a ( ) money   *b* ( ) a coat   *c* ( ) a book   *d* ( ) rain

10 Choose the correct form of the verb:

Elle a ...... toutes les fenêtres

   a ( ) ouvrit   *b* ( ) ouvris   *c* ( ) ouvert   *d* ( ) ouverte
   e ( ) ouvertes

11 Choose the most likely alternative to complete the passage:

We have at least another week to finish our essays.

We........ work tonight. Let's go to a film instead.

   a ( ) musn't   *b* ( ) needn't   *c* ( ) cannot
   d ( ) may not

The number of alternative choices varies, the smallest possible is two:

12 Read the following sentences. If you think a statement is true, mark the box under TRUE, if you think it is false, mark the box under FALSE.

	TRUE	FALSE
1 Viele Deutsche trinken Bier	( )	( )

13 Some of the sentences below are written in good English and some are not. Mark the box under CORRECT for each correct sentence, mark the box under WRONG for each sentence with an error.

	CORRECT	WRONG
1 I am very fond of to swim	( )	( )
2 I am better than you at dancing	( )	( )

14 Listen to the following pairs of words, decide whether they are the SAME or DIFFERENT, and mark the boxes accordingly.

		SAME	DIFFERENT
1 (on tape): watch	wash	( )	( )
2 (on tape): hid	heed	( )	( )

Any open-ended item can be turned into a multiple choice item by providing a range of alternative answers, and any multiple choice item can be turned into an open-ended item by removing the alternative answers (and giving more precise instructions, if necessary).

Question (vi) Example 1 is an open-ended item testing vocabulary. Find the multiple choice item which also tests vocabulary.

Question (vii) Write 11 as an open-ended item. Omit the alternative answers and rewrite the instructions.

Answer (vi) 7

Answer (vii) The instructions must specify that the blank must be filled by a modal verb plus negative. Any formulation will do as long as the candidates understand what they are supposed to do.

Question (viii) Various statements have been made about the respective advantages of open-ended and multiple choice formats. Check the following statements against the examples given above, and see how far you agree with each of them.

Advantages of open-ended items

    a There is no possibility of anybody getting the right answer by chance.

    b Open-ended items test productive skills. Multiple-choice items test receptive skills only.

    c Open-ended items do not present the learner with errors, and so do not risk teaching the wrong thing.

Advantages of multiple-choice items

    d They are much quicker and more convenient to mark.

    e They are independent of the judgement of the marker, in contrast with open-ended items.

    f They provide more diagnostic information, because the candidate is forced to decide among a particular set of choices.

Discussion of Question (viii)

Statement (a) (correct answers by chance). This is obviously true. In a test consisting of one hundred multiple choice items, each with four alternatives, one would on the average expect a quarter of the items to be answered correctly by chance, so that the baseline of scoring would not be zero, but 25. Some testers compensate for the chance element by subtracting for errors according to various formulae, others choose the much simpler expedient of accepting that the range of possible marks is narrowed.

Statement (*b*) (productive/receptive skills). Many people agree with this statement wholeheartedly. I have some reservations. Compare 5 and 10:

5 (donner)......-moi le canif.

10 Elle a ...... toutes les fenêtres.

　　a ( ) ouvrit　　*b* ( ) ouvris　　*c* ( ) ouvert
　　d ( ) ouverte　　*e* ( ) ouvertes

I find it very difficult to see that 5 tests anything very different from 10. On the other hand, though both 2 and 13 involve the recognition of errors, only 2 requires actual sentence construction on the part of the candidate.

Statement (*c*) (teaching errors). Here testers find themselves in flat opposition to most teachers, in distinguishing sharply between a learning situation and a discrimination situation. In the learning situation the student may have a mental set to absorb everything that is presented to him, but in a discrimination or testing situation, he has a mental set to discriminate between right and wrong answers.

Statement (*d*) (ease of marking). Obviously true. But random errors creep into automatic marking, so all marking must be done twice.

Statement (*e*) (objective marking). It is true that all multiple-choice items are independent of the judgement of the marker. But there are many types of open-ended items which are equally objective, in fact all the examples except 1 and 2.

Statement (*f*) (diagnostic information). This may or may not be so. If the alternatives do not include the particular error the candidate would have made if he had been left to construct his own answer, then the information from a multiple-choice item could be positively misleading.

The standard advice given to budding test constructors is to write a test first with open-ended items, give it to a group of people of the sort he wishes to test ultimately, and then use the wrong answers he gets which are common and plausible as distractors for the same items written in a multiple-choice format.

4 The testing of tests

A test is always tested to find out if it is any good. That means trying out several drafts, before one can use a test to draw conclusions or make decisions on the basis of the test scores.

The first step in the testing of a test is to carry out an *item analysis* to

324 Techniques in Applied Linguistics

determine the degree to which each individual item discriminates in the same direction as the whole test. The basic idea is that the whole test, however bad, is bound to be better than any single item. An item analysis has two parts, first to establish the *facility value* of an item—how easy or difficult it is—and secondly to establish how well it discriminates. The *method of thirds*, also called the E_{1-3} (ee-one-three), is a simple way of working out the item analysis.

The scripts from the tryout group are ranked according to the total score and divided into three subgroups with an equal number of scripts in each. Then, for each item one counts the number of people in the upper third who passed the item, the number of people in the middle and the number of people in the lower third. The number of correct answers in each subgroup is then added to give the total number of correct answers for the whole group. The facility value is obtained by expressing the actual number of correct answers as a percentage of the maximum possible number of correct answers.

Each item should be passed by more people from the upper third than from the lower third. The amount of agreement between the answer pattern of each item and the whole test is expressed as a *discrimination index*, which varies from $+1$ to -1. If the discrimination index is $+1$, this indicates total agreement, all the people in the top third passed the item and none in the lower third. Any value between 0 and -1 shows that more people from the lower third passed the item than people from the top third. This indicates that the item is pulling in a different direction from the test as a whole. Professional testers require an average discrimination index of $+0.40$ or more. In practice one retains for the next draft one's best items, and discards or writes those items which have the lowest discrimination indices. With listening discrimination tests one may have to accept rather low values.

Question (ix) The first draft of a test was given to 36 students. The tally below shows how many people in the upper, middle and lower thirds answered the first item correctly (the maximum possible for each third is 12).

Item	Upper Third	Middle Third	Lower Third	Total Pass
1	11	8	5	24
2	6	6	6	18
3	3	4	5	12

a Which item has a positive discrimination index?
b Which item has a negative discrimination index?
c What do you think the discrimination index for item 2 is?
d Which item has the lowest facility value (i.e. which is the hardest)?

Answer (ix) (*a*) Item 1.　　(*b*) Item 3.　　(*c*) Zero.　　(*d*) Item 3.

(Formulae and methods for working the statistical tests referred to are given in most elementary textbooks, and also in Volume 4. For a more detailed description of item analysis, see Ingram 1968b).

Correlation is the other chief tool of a tester when he is finding out how good his test is. There are various kinds of correlations, and one uses one kind or another depending on what assumptions one can make about the data. What all types of correlation have in common is that they express the degree of correspondence between two sets of figures which refer to the same people. The degree of correspondence is expressed by a correlation co-efficient, which varies from +1.00 for perfect correspondence, and −1.00 for perfect correspondence in opposite directions. A total lack of any common trend between two sets of figures gives a correlation co-efficient of zero.

Question (x) Before Christmas six boys were given two tests of arithmetic and after Christmas the same six boys were given another two tests. Their scores for each pair of tests are given below:

	Before Christmas			After Christmas	
	Test i	Test ii		Test i	Test ii
Johnny	8	8	Johnny	8	10
Bill	7	7	Bill	7	9
Sam	6	6	Sam	6	8
David	4	4	David	4	6
Jack	3	3	Jack	3	5
Tim	2	2	Tim	2	4
	Table 3			Table 4	

a What is the correlation between the two tests before Christmas?

b Do you think the correlation coefficient of the two sets of figures after Christmas is +1.00?

Answer (x)

a Since the figures are identical, there must be perfect correspondence, so the correlation co-efficient must be +1.00.

b Probably unexpectedly, the answer is yes. We do not need to have identical scores in order to show perfect correspondence. The two tests differentiate between the six boys in exactly the same way, the relative standing of each boy with respect to the other five is exactly the same for each test. So the correlation coefficient for the two tests after Christmas is also +1.00.

Question (xi)

	Test i	Test ii		Test i	Test ii
Johnny	8	4	Johnny	8	6
Bill	7	5	Bill	7	7
Sam	6	6	Sam	6	10
David	4	8	David	4	4
Jack	3	9	Jack	3	7
Tim	2	10	Tim	2	8

Table 5   Table 6

If the results of two tests were as shown in Tables 5 and 6, would you expect the correlation for Table 5 to be +1.00, or 0, or −1.00? What would you expect the correlation to be for Table 6?

Answer (xi) The correlation for Table 5 is −1.00; the figures show perfect correspondence, but in the opposite direction. The correlation for Table 6 is zero; one cannot see any trend or connection between the scores for the two tests. In practice one hardly ever gets such extreme values; there is usually a connection between two sets of scores which varies from not very much to quite a lot, short of absolute correspondence.

The method of correlation which is used for preference whenever it is possible is called the product-moment, or Pearson correlation. (The symbol for the product-moment correlation index is r). This method can be used, provided one can assume two things:

a that the test on which the scores were made is calibrated, so that a difference of 5 points or one place on the scale represents the same distance as a difference of 5 points or another place on the scale, and so on (in technical terms, that the test measures on the equal-interval scale).

b that the characteristic which is measured has a normal distribution in the population.

It is important to remember that correlations are not a kind of percentage. It is true that a correlation coefficient of +1.00 means 100% correspondence, and that a correlation coefficient of 0 means 0% correspondence, but it is not true that, for instance, a correlation coefficient of +0.80 means that there is an 80% correspondence. Correlations are used to predict from one set of scores to another set of scores. This prediction is quite random if r = 0, and perfect when r = +1.00, but in practice there is always some error. Statisticians have worked out by how much one can expect to improve prediction, in comparison with random procedures, as the correlation coefficient increases from 0 to +1. They express this in terms of the reduction of error of prediction, in comparison with the error of random prediction.

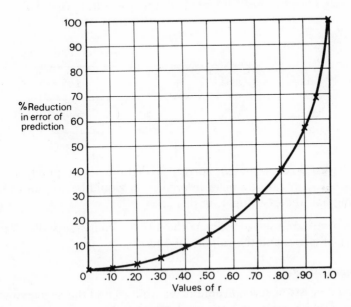

Figure 5.

The figure shows that quite high values of r are needed before the amount of error in the prediction is smaller than the error one would get if one picked out of a hat. When the error is reduced, the efficiency of the prediction is increased. The correlation must come into the 0.70s before efficiency is increased by one third, and it must be almost 0.95 before it is increased by two-thirds.

Question (xii)

    a according to Figure 5, by how much is the efficiency of the prediction increased compared with random prediction, when r = 0.60?

    b What value of r corresponds to an increase in efficiency of 40%?

Answer (xii) (*a*) 20%   (*b*) 0.80.

It is important to remember that the efficiency of prediction increases hardly at all until one comes to the high values of r, but at the same time it should be remembered that the baseline for successful prediction is not zero. If one had to make a decision about admitting or rejecting students for a course in which the pass rate was usually 50 per cent, and there were twice as many applicants as places, the most frequent outcome of selecting at random would be that one would make the correct decision in about half the cases. One would accept half and reject half. Half the acceptances would pass, half would fail. Similarly, half the rejects would have passed had they been accepted, and half would have failed.

	Pass	Fail
Accept	25%	25%
Reject	25%	25%

The shaded boxes represent correct predictions, by a purely random procedure. So any improvement in prediction would be an improvement on getting half the cases right, in this case.

Correlations are used to estimate the internal consistency of a test, the reliability of a test, and the validity of a test.

Internal consistency

If a test consists of several subtests we want to find the degree to which the subtest scores agree with the total scores. Subtests that correlate very highly with the total test discriminate in the same way as the total. The argument is the same as for test items discriminating in the same way as the total; the whole, however imperfect, is bound to be a better measure of actual capacity than any part.

We also want to find the correlations between subtests. Here we do not want very high correlations; if two subtests correlate very highly, they are doing the same job and one of them is superfluous. It sounds strange that subtests may inter-correlate say in the range +0.30 to +0.60 and yet correlate highly with the total, say +0.70 upwards, but this occurs regularly in good tests.

A subtest which has a great many items is likely to correlate more highly with the total than a subtest which has only a few items. This is both because a subtest with many items contributes more to the total score than a subtest with few items, and also to some extent because a subtest with a large number of items is likely to be a 'better' test (i.e., is likely to be more discriminating, reliable and valid) than a subtest with only a few items.

Reliability

The test retest or stability reliability of a test is assessed by correlating the scores for each individual on the first testing with their scores on the second testing by the product-moment method, if appropriate. The scores on the first testing are often a little higher than the scores on the second testing because of improvement with practice but that does not matter, because what we are after is not identity, but correspondence.

Equivalence reliability is estimated by another correlation method. One of the formulae used for assessing equivalence reliability is the Kuder Richardson. This formula is based not on the scores obtained by each person, but on the pass/fail distribution of each item.

The equivalence estimate gives the lower limit of the reliability correlation, i.e., it tends to be slightly lower than the stability estimate. Professional testers demand a reliability coefficient of at least 0.95 from their tests. This refers to stability reliability; one may or may not accept a fractionally lower equivalence reliability. Individual subtests may have lower values.

Validity

The validity of a test or subtest is established by correlating test scores with a criterion, that is, with some other estimate which one believes to be valid and accurate. This is of course often difficult to obtain. The method used is either the product-moment correlation or the rank order correlation, depending on the nature of the observations. Professional testers are unhappy about validity coefficients lower than the 0.70s and tend to prefer them even higher. This is for test totals; subtests may have lower values.

The validity we have discussed so far is empirical validity. A test is a sample of the candidate's behaviour, and from the standard of this sample is inferred the standard of his general performance in a subject. The validity of the inference is assessed by comparing the outcome of the test with some independent estimate of the learner's general standard.

Tests which predict future performance in a subject are called aptitude tests. Tests from which one makes inferences about the candidate's general performance at the time of testing are called attainment tests.

Empirical validity for both aptitude and attainment tests is estimated by correlating test scores with a criterion. The criterion can be an examination, or another test, or teachers' marks or estimates. Since any criterion is likely to be less than perfectly reliable and valid, it is easy to see that achieving true empirical validity is a laborious and uncertain business. In view of the difficulties in demonstrating true empirical ability, appeals are made to the concepts of *content validity* and *construct validity*. If a test samples adequately the 'content' of a subject, for instance as defined by a syllabus or a textbook, it has content validity. If a test is constructed in accordance with a relevant theory, then it has construct validity. The immediate question is whether the contents of a book or a course are a representative sample of the subject as a whole, and whether the theory from which the test is constructed is itself valid. It seems to me that content and construct validity complement empirical validity, rather than substitute for it. One is unlikely to achieve empirical validity (1) unless the test has been written in accordance with some respectable theory of the subject—a language test is inevitably written with some linguistic theory in mind and also, but perhaps less explicitly, according to some theoretical notions of language behaviour; and (2) unless the subject matter and the desired skills have been sampled adequately. On the other hand having theories in mind and doing a little intuitive sampling is no guarantee of the validity of the inferences one makes from the scores as to the general standards of performance. The validity has to be demonstrated by comparison with a criterion.

The best criterion for a language test is teachers' ratings. An experienced teacher who has known her class for some months can rank students in order of merit for command of spoken language, for command of written language, for overall command, etc. She may be slightly uncertain about relative positions in the middle, but by repeated comparison of different pairs of students a very stable and valid ranking can be achieved, as Vernon has shown (1957). The two sets of figures which are correlated are the rank orders based on the test scores, and the rank order provided by the teacher.

The product-moment method of correlation is not appropriate for correlating sets of ranks. One uses the rank order method of correlation.

Question (xiii) When we use the rank order formula of correlation do we correlate

   a the teacher's estimate of rank order with test scores, or

   b the teacher's estimate of rank order with the rank order based on the test scores?

Answer (xiii) (b)

Question (xiv) When we have one set of figures which are ranks and another set of figures which are test scores, do we use the product-moment formula of correlation?

Answer (xiv) No. The product-moment formula can only be used between two sets of scores, provided both tests are calibrated and provided one may assume a normal distribution in the population.

5 Language testing exercises

Language aptitude tests have been discussed by Pimsleur and Davies (Davies 1968). Language attainment tests and the general problem of sampling language behaviour have been discussed by Ingram (Davies 1968).

Recently the terms 'language behaviour' and 'language-like behaviour' have gained some currency. Language behaviour is mainly the behaviour of communicating through language, the creating and comprehension of meaningful utterances in context. Language-like behaviour is any behaviour involving language other than this, for instance drills, substitution exercises, vocabulary matching, pronunciation exercises, discrimination of phonological units, sentence completion, discussing grammatical constituency, learning grammatical rules, and, of course, selecting multiple-choice alternatives.

It is obvious that the aim of language teaching is for learners to acquire proficiency in language behaviour rather than in language-like behaviour. It does not necessarily follow that teaching—and testing—practices should consist exclusively of samples of the desired terminal behaviour. This is not the place to discuss teaching practices, but in testing we come back to the problem of job samples, which are likely to have high intrinsic validity but are unlikely to be working at their true validity because of their poor reliability.

The choice between job sample items and the more artificial or language-like items depends on how much the test writer relies on construct and content validity, in preference to empirical reliability. If the writer relies on content and construct validity, he is likely to use predominantly job-sample items, if he relies primarily on empirical reliability, he will use any kind of item, including job samples which can be shown to have good discrimination, high reliability and satisfactory correlations with a criterion which estimates language behaviour directly, reliably and validly.

Question (xv) Looking at the examples of test items on pp. 319–21, which ones would you say were job samples in the sense that they demand language behaviour rather than language-like behaviour from the candidate?

Answer (xv)

1 This item matches vocabulary, not in context. Language-like.

2 What is demanded here is reconstruction of a sentence, to make it grammatical and make the meaning clear. Language.

3 Depending on one's theory of language, this could well be called language. This item exemplifies the relevance of construct validity. According to some psycholinguistic theories, negative sentences

are formed from affirmative sentences in actual sentence production. According to this theory, item 3 demands language behaviour.

4, 5, 6 and all the multiple-choice items: Language-like.

Section 3 of this chapter contains examples of some common item formats for language tests. More are given in Ingram (1968a), Mackey (1965), Valette (1968), Lado (1961) and in the practice test handouts of TOEFL and the Michigan Proficiency Test.

We will now look at some summaries of testing exercises carried out by a number of students in Edinburgh. The first example is included to show that one must look out for things that can go wrong through no fault of the tester. The other examples illustrate some less usual test formats.

Francesco Recchini gave a test to 33 young Italian learners of English. There were three subtests, as follows:

(i) listening phoneme discrimination (30 items). A native speaker of English read out three words, two of which were the same, and the students had to mark which of the three words were identical.

Example:

(spoken)	beat	beat	bit
Answer sheet:	(X)	(X)	( )

(ii) Grammar, multiple choice (20 items). Exàmple:

1 I am tired (of—with—for) you

2 I (have written—had written—wrote) a letter yesterday.

(iii) Vocabulary test (misleading cognates) (20 items). Example:

1 ACTUALLY = now—in fact—perhaps—rationally

2 NOTICE = whim—news—announcement—nuance

Comment. With ordinary luck, this could be the beginning of a useful test. But there was extensive cheating during the testing, and as Recchini emphasized this made the whole exercise more or less useless. The effect of the cheating showed up in various ways:

(a) Lower than chance correct score on certain items. For example, given the test item 'I am surprised (at—on—for) you' only one person chose the correct answer *at*; the rest were equally divided between *on* and *for*. Usually, fewer-than-chance choice of the correct answer can be attributed to a false but powerful hypothesis. This would be the likely explanation for the fact that only one person chose *in fact* for *actually*, and the rest chose *now* (Italian *attualmente* = at present). But there is no obvious reason for students to reject *at*; it looks more like the result of copying.

(b) Some of the statistical results are a little odd. Not too much weight should be attached to this, for with only 70 items and 33 people, the results can only be suggestive:

Subtest	No. of items	mean	standard deviation	equivalence reliability
i	30	27.4	1.62	0.31
ii	20	11.2	2.34	0.21
iii	20	6.7	2.04	0.83
Total	70	44.5	3.81	0.39

The two unusual features are as follows:

(a) The standard deviations are very small in relation to the means. This means that the scores are very bunched, there is not much difference between the best and the worst students, so the discrimination is poor. The lack of discrimination also shows up in the many items with poor discrimination values, but this is so common in all first test tryouts, that nothing can be inferred from it.

(b) The equivalence reliability is very low. This could be due to other factors, or it could be due to chance, but it is a little unusual to have a correlation for the total test as low as 0.39.

Elizabeth Wilson wanted to try to test knowledge of cultural background in two ways: (a) by asking for links between vocabulary items, through knowledge of the French world; and (b) by asking for recognition of certain set expressions which are obligatory in their context.

Examples of (a)

Maintenant je vais vous dire une phrase et vous demander ou vous pourriez entendre ou le dire.

1 'Un jeton, s'il vous plaît.' Où êtes-vous?
   A Vous êtes à la pâtisserie.
   B Vous êtes au spectacle.
   C Vous êtes à la mercerie.
   D Vous êtes à la poste.

2 'Passez à la caisse.' Où êtes-vous?
   A Vous êtes en classe.
   B Vous êtes dans un magasin.
   C Vous êtes dans le métro.
   D Vous êtes dans le car.

Examples of (b)

Maintenant je vais vous décrire une *situation*, et vous demander ce qui se dit dans cette situation.

   1 Vous avez une cigarette mais pas d'allumettes. Que dites-vous?

     A 'Vous avez une flamme, s'il vous plaît?'

     B 'Veuillez m'illuminer.'

     C 'Avez-vous de la lumière, s'il vous plaît?'

     D 'Vous avez du feu, s'il vous plaît?'

   2 Vous heurtez une personne dans la rue, et lui dites, 'Oh, pardon, excusez-moi!' Quelle réponse fait-elle?

     A 'Il ne faut pas.'

     B 'Je vous en prie.'

     C 'S'il vous plaît.'

     D 'Merci beaucoup.'

The test was given as a listening test, the instructions and the stimulus part of each item was spoken, the alternatives were written. The tryout group consisted of 14 housewives attending an advanced conversation class at the French Institute. The answer pattern is variable, though it is more or less meaningless with such a small group:

Item	Upper Third	Middle Third	Lower Third	Discrimination Index
(a) 6	4	3	3	0.2
(a) 7	2	3	4	−0.4
(b) 1	4	4	4	0
(b) 3	5	3	3	0.4

Comment. This is an interesting idea, which obviously needs very careful working out and pretesting on a much larger group. Giving the instructions in French has its dangers; any failure may be the result of failure to understand the instructions rather than failure to deal with the items, but in a listening test it is probably better to give instructions in the language which is being tested, so that the listeners can get used to the sound of the speakers' voices and accents. To compensate, one must be very careful to give enough examples for each type of item. The item analysis is not to be trusted, but it is interesting all the same that the second item goes the wrong way. Looking at the item, one could guess that some people have simply misheard one of the two words caisse/classe.

A. D. Sproule wanted to test the ability of Scots children to supply the appropriate tenses of the verb in a continuous piece of prose. The test sheet began like this:

Rewrite the following passage using the correct tense of the verbs given in the brackets, and placing the adverbs in the correct position.

Everyday I see him walking past my house. He (stop, never), (look, even, never) in my direction. He (very, slowly, walk), carefully, as if his shoes (be) full of pebbles. Only once (look) in my direction, I (forget, never) it . . .

The key for this fragment is:

1 he never stops	2 never even looks
3 walks very slowly	4 were
5 did he look	6 shall never forget

Twenty-four children aged about 11 to 12 took the test. The item analysis for the six items shown here was:

Item	Upper Third	Middle Third	Lower Third	Total Correct	Discrimination Index
1	4	4	4	12	0
2	7	4	3	14	0.5
3	7	5	3	15	0.5
4	4	3	3	10	0.125
5	1	1	0	2	0.125
6	1	1	0	2	0.125

Comment. In his own comments, Sproule points out that the instructions were far too difficult for the children who did not know the meaning of *tense, verb* and *adverb*, so a lot of time was needed to explain what they had to do. If examples had been provided, this might not have been so serious. This point is underlined by Sproule's discovery that there is a high correlation between scores on the test and intelligence. The six top scores were made by children who all had IQs above 115, the eight lowest scores—the whole of the lower group—were made by children with IQs below 90

Items 5 and 6 were far too difficult for this group. Inspecting item 5 it is easy to see why: the child had to supply the pronoun *he* as well as the difficult emphatic *do* construction. The most frequent rendering was 'Only once he looked . . .' The scoring would be laborious if the number of scripts was very large, but Sproule's open-ended format allows one to discover in a controlled way where children have difficulties with intra-textual verbal relationships.

Deborah Mansergh wanted to see if learners of French could supply the necessary prepositions, conjunctions and sentence adverbs to make sense of a passage with blanks. In order to limit the possible number of answers, the passage was a paraphrase of a complete passage. The pupils were told that they would read a review of the film *Fifi la Plume* followed by a paraphrase of this review which they must complete so that the passage made sense. Only the first paragraph of each passage is included:

Connaissez-vous le cinéaste français Albert Lamorisse? Un charmant petit film intitulé *Le Ballon Rouge* l'a rendu célèbre. Lamorisse s'efforce de divertir les enfants aussi bien que les adultes. Les histoires qu'il raconte sont amusantes et malicieuses.

On parle encore une fois du cinéaste Albert Lamorisse, qui est devenu célèbre (1) . . . un charmant petit film *Le Ballon Rouge*. Il vient de réaliser un nouveau film *Fifi la Plume*. Dans ce film (2) . . . dans *Le Ballon Rouge*, il essaie de divertir (3) . . . les enfants, mais aussi les adultes.

Key: 1 grâce à/à cause de

2 comme/ainsi que

3 non seulement

Only ten people took the test, which makes any item analysis quite useless. The frequency distribution was:

Score	Frequency
16	1
14	1
13	1
11	2
10	2
9	1
8	1
7	1

The correlation with marks for an essay in French plus a recognition test of 50 propositions, conjunctions and sentence adverbs gave $r = +0.82$.

Comment. This is an interesting attempt to test the ability to recall the correct function words in context. The test is rather laborious to construct. The paraphrase must be checked by a native or near-native speaker both for accuracy of paraphrase and correctness and completeness of key. As far as it goes, the frequency distribution suggests that Miss Mansergh has found the right difficulty level for her group—but she does not tell us who the pupils were. The very high correlation with the criterion also suggests that the format is valid, though the number of people involved is far too small to be sure.

Ian Pearson wanted to find out whether teachers of English in an African country commanded the 'patterns' of the first ten lessons of Lado and Fries' *English Pattern Practice*. He wrote 126 multiple choice grammar items, with three alternatives, of which 100 directly sampled the patterns of the first ten lessons. Examples of items (note that in some items, the choice is between complete sentences, in others, the choice is between parts of sentences):

```
 1   a (  )  Is John coming?
     b (  )  Is coming John?    Yes, he is
     c (  )  John is coming?

15              a (  )  means 'exist'?
         What   b (  )  'exist' means?
                c (  )  does 'exist' mean?

31              a (  )  much
  There is not  b (  )  many    news in the paper
                c (  )  much of

45              a (  )  correctly English
  I try to speak b (  )  English correctly
                c (  )  English in class correctly

60              a (  )  for getting
  I've come     b (  )  to get       the money
                c (  )  for get

75              a (  )  same as
  This book costs b (  ) the same as   that one
                c (  )  the same like
```

Forty-six teachers who came for a remedial course were tested. The item analysis for the 126 items can be set out as a frequency distribution:

M

Value of Discrimination
Index in Intervals   *Frequency*

−0.40 ... −0.21	1
−0.20 ... −0.01	11
0 ... +0.19	48
+0.20 ... +0.39	44
+0.40 ... +0.59	19
+0.60 ... +0.79	3

Total   126

Pearson picked out the 66 items which had a discrimination value of +0.20 or more, and rescored the scripts for these 66 items only. Then he correlated the rank order obtained on the basis of counting all 126 items, with the rank order obtained when counting only the 66 items with a discrimination index of +0.20 or more.

Problem (xvi) Should Pearson use the product moment formula or the rank order formula of correlation?

Answer (xvi) Rank order, obviously. Pearson obtained rho = 0.959 between the ranking based on the 126 items and the ranking obtained on the 66 items with discrimination at +0.20 or more.

Pearson also calculated the reliability of his test, on a formula estimating the equivalence reliability.

For the 126 items reliability r = 0.96
For the 66 items reliability r = 0.91.

Comment. This is an example of a real testing job, as distinct from an exercise that students undertake to gain practice. No real test has less than 100 items, and no real first tryout group should be less than about 50, even for amateurs. Professional testers will write 300 items if they want to retain 100, and will not use a tryout group of less than about 300. Pearson, sensibly, decided to accept his best items, even if his limit for discrimination had to be less than for a fully professional job, and retained for inclusion in a second draft all items above +0.20. His item analysis and calculation of reliability on the basis of the shortened test demonstrate vividly the uselessness of retaining items which do not discriminate. The short test is just as good as the long original test, and will take about half the time to administer. The time saved can be used to try out additional items, and about half of these additional items will probably turn out to be good ones.

Problem (xvii) Looking at the alternatives for Item 1 in Pearson's test, can you see anything wrong?

Answer (xvii) The candidates may not know it, but it is perfectly possible to ask a question in English by using Subject—Verb order and a rising intonation. The rising intonation is signalled in print by a question mark. Therefore there are two correct answers to this item, which is a grave sin.

Richard Allwright wanted to test whether Scots children regarded *might* and *could* as synonymous in certain contexts, and whether they preferred one over the other and also whether they preferred *would* to *should* where these are synonymous. This is his description of the try-out situation:

The Sample
School: ******
Standard: VII
Average age: 11 yrs 7½ mths, age range 10.10 to 12.3
Number of subjects: 26
Girls: 9
Boys: 17
Date: 22.1.68
General comments: children described, by teacher, as coming from 'poor homes', and so not expected to be very clever (by teacher). Children took this test immediately after two other student tests, but did not appear to be bored, angry or tired by this.

These are Allwright's test instructions for the first part of the test:

1 Hand out Section A.
2 Write on board: MIGHT   COULD
                       SHOULD   WOULD
3 Read and explain instructions to subjects:
   Write name and age in top right corner
   Listen while instructions are read
   Ask questions if necessary
4 Write first example on board:
   Mr. Thomas is very ill. He . . . be in bed.
5 Establish answer *should*. Write it on the board and tell subjects to write it in on their sheets.
6 Write second example on board:
   I am sure you . . . like my dog. He is very friendly.
7 Establish answer *would*. Write it in on the board and tell subjects to write it in on their sheets.
8 Write example three on board.
   David is so strong he . . . lift a horse.
9 Establish answer *could*. Write it in on board and tell subjects to write it in on their sheets.
10 Leave all examples on board and tell subjects to start
11 Collect in sheets after 10 minutes.

The examples illustrate the type of item used in the first part of the test, where Allwright is trying to establish that the children can use modal verbs appropriately. Section B of the test tries to elicit preferences, in this way:

Again I want you to put these words into gaps in sentences, but this time there may often be more than one of them that you think makes very good sense. When that happens I want you to write in the word you think is used most *often*.

1 The sky looks very black. I think it . . . rain.
2 If John could learn French in one year, so . . . his brother.
3 Michael said Peter . . . borrow the car, if he promised to drive carefully.
9 The telephone . . . ring while I am out. If it does, please answer it for me.

Having established that most of the children could supply correctly the appropriate modal verb for most of the items in Section A—the overall percentage of correct answers was 81%—Allwright had a basis for drawing conclusions from the answers the same children gave in Section B:

a The results gave no definite indication for preference between *would* and *should*, in contexts where they are felt to be synonymous.

b Where the choice was between *could* and *might*, in eight items there was no overall preference for either, which could be just a sampling artefact. But there was an overwhelming preference for *could* in the context of (i) permission (item 3); and (ii) hypothetical logical consequence (item 2), and an overwhelming preference for *might* in the context of a common or concrete situation involving guesswork or common sense rather than more formal logical thinking (items 1 and 9).

Comment. The presentation of information is a model of its kind. One does not have to hunt around to find what the purpose of the test was, who the subjects were, what the testing situation was, or what the results and conclusions were.

This is an example of using a test for experimental purposes. Allwright wanted to know if children had preferences for one modal over another in various contexts. It might appear that all he had to do was to present Section B, but any finding from Section B could not have been interpreted, if we had not known that the children could handle modals in contexts where only one choice is possible.

It is possible to criticize the experiment on the grounds that the results of the first tryout of the test were used not only to provide the information to evaluate the test itself, but also and at the same time to provide the information concerning the abilities of the children. This is an error of experimental design, but it so happened that all the items in Section A, except the first, discriminated as well as they could, given that all the items were easy. That is, all the mistakes were made by children in the middle and lower groups. None of the children in the upper group made any mistakes at all, except in the first item. So, by skill or by chance, Allwright had written a test which fulfilled the first requirement of a good test, i.e., that it should discriminate, and he was entitled to use the information about the children that he got from it.

6 Practical work

1 The statement that tests must discriminate (p. 313) rests on the assumption that the individuals in the test population actually differ among themselves with respect to the characteristic tested. This is obviously true when one is measuring height. Would you expect it to be true for degree of command of a second language in most cases? Can you think of instances when it might not be true? For instance, what do you think would happen if the test population consisted of advanced learners of English and we tested for ability to use the 'do' construction, in negative and interrogative sentences?

2 Which of the following ways of measuring would you expect to be more reliable:

   a Timing a sprint by the second hand of a wristwatch or by a stop-watch. (What about using electronic equipment as against a man with a stop-watch?)

   b Estimating by metronome or by ear the duration that a pianist gives to each bar when playing a piece of music.

   c Pooling the marks of three markers on a set of essays, as against the marks of a single marker.

   d A language test with spoken stimuli, as against a test with written items. (The question is about reliability, not validity. Refer to the discussion on stability reliability, p. 314.)

   e A test with 15 items as against a test with 150 items. (Refer to the discussion on equivalence reliability, p. 314.)

3 Which of the following ways of measuring would you think likely to be more valid:

   a Estimating the quality of figure skating by the time the skater takes to get through the programme or by the subjective assessment of the judges. (What about the subjective assessment of television reporters as against the subjective judgement of the official judges?)

   b Judging the quality of the playing of a piece of music intuitively, or by whether the player has adhered to the metronome marking.

   c Judging a learner's ability to express himself in English by general impression, or by counting mistakes in spelling and punctuation.

   d Judging whether the general standard of English as a second language in a given country has deteriorated or improved over a period of ten years, by the subjective impression of teachers or employers, or by comparing results obtained on a test used at the beginning and at the end of the period.

   e Assessing ability to write a second language by the mark awarded for one long essay, or by marks awarded for several short essays.

4 Here are some statements which may be true or false. Note what you think and check against the text.

   a Objective tests and traditional examinations are distinguished by having different purposes.

   b A test consisting of 50 items was given to 80 students. The tabulation of scores did not approximate to the normal distribution. This shows that the test was no good.

   c It is always preferable to use an objective test rather than a traditional method, e.g., essay writing.

   d An open-ended format is not necessarily more valid than a multiple choice format.

   e A multiple choice format is not necessarily more diagnostic than an open-ended format.

   f Item analysis establishes the reliability of individual items.

   g Item analysis should be carried out before the test is tried on a sample of the intended test population.

   h A correlation value indicates the degree of correspondence between two sets of figures.

   i The amount of correspondence indicated can be roughly interpreted as a percentage, e.g., r = 0.67 means 67% correspondence.

5 The chapter gives six examples of tests constructed as exercises by Applied Linguistics students at the University of Edinburgh.

   a Which test writer disregarded his test result and why?

   b Which test writer(s) constructed a realistic number of items, i.e., a number large enough for the test to be taken seriously?

   c Which test writer(s) examined the 'competence' of native speakers of English?

d What information should be included when we state the circumstances of the try-out situation?

e Which test writer(s) based their items on a continuous text, and which based theirs on discrete items?

6 How do you decide whether a test item is probably a good one? Break the answer down into consecutive steps. Refer to this chapter and to Ingram (1968b).

7 Further reading

Davies, Alan (ed.). *Language Testing Symposium*. London: Oxford University Press, 1968.
Lado, Robert. *Language Testing*. London: Longmans, 1961.
Valette, Rebecca. *Modern Language Testing: A Handbook*. New York: Harcourt Brace, 1968.
Vernon, P. E. *The Measurement of Abilities*. London: University of London Press, 1956.

For a discussion of norm-referenced versus criterion-referenced testing, see the chapter on Testing in Volume 4.

Language tests

Lado, R. *English Language Test for Foreign Students*. Ann Arbor, Michigan: G. Wahr & Co., 1951–60.
Michigan Test of English Language Proficiency. Ann Arbor: University of Michigan, English Language Institute, 1961–.
TOEFL: Test of English as a Foreign Language. Princeton, New Jersey: Educational Testing Service.
Ingram, Elisabeth. *ELBA: English Language Battery*. London: Oxford University Press. (In press).
EPTB: English Proficiency Test Battery. London: British Council and Foundation for National Educational Research, 1964.

Appendix I: Suggestions for a language laboratory lesson and for programmed materials

(A) A language laboratory lesson on the difference between 'like' and 'would like'

The following examples are intended to show how some of the types of drill discussed in Chapter 4 could be applied to a particular problem (teaching the difference between 'like' and 'would like'). The reader might consider what aspects of this problem each drill is exercising and how many drills of each type would be included in a language laboratory lesson.

I *Dialogue*—to present the language point in context

JOHN: Hullo, Mary. What would you like to do this evening?

MARY: Well, the weather's not very nice, is it? I think I'd like to go to the pictures.

JOHN: Fine. I like going to the cinema.

II *Repetition of dialogue*—to practise pronunciation and learn dialogue by heart

JOHN: Hullo, Mary
(pause)
this evening
(pause)
What would you like?
(pause)
What would you like to do?
(pause)
What would you like to do this evening?
(pause)

(Repetition continued in this way until the whole dialogue has been practised thoroughly. Hence, need for very short dialogues.)

III *Substitution drill*—a four-phase drill

1 Would you like to go to the pictures tonight?—The theatre.
Would you like to go to the theatre tonight?
Would you like to go to the theatre tonight?
Would you like to go to the theatre tonight?

2 the ice rink
(pause)
Would you like to go to the ice rink tonight?
(pause)

3 a football match
(pause)
Would you like to go to a football match tonight?
(pause)

4 a barbecue
(pause)
Would you like to go to a barbecue tonight?
(pause)

5 the dance hall
(pause)
Would you like to go to the dance hall tonight?
(pause)
etc.

IV *Substitution drill*—also involving grammatical changes to preserve
concord

1 What do you like doing at the weekends?—John
What does John like doing at the weekends?
What does John like doing at the weekends?
What does John like doing at the weekends?

2 John and Mary
(pause)
What do John and Mary like doing at the weekends?
(pause)

3 your girl-friend
(pause)
What does your girl-friend like doing at the weekends?
(pause)
etc.

V *Transformation drill*

1 I like going to the pictures on Saturdays.
Would you like to go this Saturday then?
Would you like to go this Saturday then?
Would you like to go this Saturday then?

2 I like going to the theatre on Saturdays.
(pause)
Would you like to go this Saturday then?
(pause)

3 John likes playing tennis on Saturdays.
(pause)
Would he like to play this Saturday then?
(pause)

4 We like having a swim on Saturdays.
(pause)
Would you like to have a swim this Saturday then?
(pause)

5 My parents like playing bridge on Saturdays.
(pause)
Would they like to play this Saturday then?
(pause)
etc.

VI *Collocation drill*

1 There's a good play on at the Lyceum.
I'd like to see it.
I'd like to see it.
I'd like to see it.

2 There's an interesting programme on TV this evening.
(pause)
I'd like to watch it.
(pause)

3 This is a wonderful book, you know.
(pause)
I'd like to read it
(pause)

4 Mr Robinson's a very amusing speaker.
(pause)

I'd like to hear him.
(pause)

5 Mabel's a very attractive girl.
(pause)
I'd like to meet her.
(pause)
etc.

VII *Contextualized drill*

1 JILL: What are you doing at the moment, John?
 JOHN: Studying at an engineering college.

 What would John like to be?
 He'd like to be an engineer.

 He'd like to be an engineer.
 He'd like to be an engineer.

2 SARAH: What are you doing, Bob?
 BOB: Looking at a Spanish travel brochure.

 What would Bob like to do next summer?
 (pause)
 He'd like to go to Spain for a holiday.
 (pause)

3 TOM: What are you doing, Jim?
 JIM: Trying to understand this book.
 TOM: What's the matter with it?
 JIM: It's in Hungarian.

 What would Jim like to be able to do?
 (pause)
 He'd like to be able to understand Hungarian.
 (pause)

4 MARY: What are you doing, Fred?
 FRED: Trying to work out a route map from London to John
         O'Groats.

 Where would Fred like to go next summer?
 (pause)
 He'd like to go to Scotland.
 (pause)

5 What would *you* like to be?
 (pause)

6 Where would *you* like to go next summer?
 (pause)

This last drill permits more than one response to each question. This should not cause difficulty, provided the pupils are forewarned. Also, examples 5 and 6 are open-ended and the pupils' responses cannot therefore be confirmed. Again, if open-ended questions are a regular feature of their laboratory work, this should not worry them.

(B) An introductory programme on the simple present and the progressive present tenses in English

(See 'practical work', Chapter 8.)

1 In this programme we shall look at the meaning of sentences like:

John plays football on Saturday afternoons.

and

Look, Robert's playing football!

The verb *play* can be seen in both these sentences. But in the first sentence it has the form ...... and in the second sentence it has the form ....

2 In the first sentence it has the form *plays* and in the second sentence it has the form *'s playing* (the short form of *is playing*).

As you probably know, the form *plays* is part of the Simple Present Tense in English. But when is this tense used?

Let us look at some more examples:

```
                    APPLICATION FORM

        Surname ..............HUNT...........................

        First name(s) ......JOHN............................

        Address .......5  MOUNT  ROAD....................
                ..............YORK.............................

        Married/single

        Wife's first name(s) ........ALISON...............

        Children ...........2........... Ages ..5 + 7........

        Present post ......TEACHER OF HISTORY..........
                ..........YORK HIGH SCHOOL.............
```

So, what do we know about John Hunt? We know that he lives in York with his wife Alison and their two children aged 5 and 7. We also know that he works at York High School as a teacher and that he teaches history.

How many examples of the Simple Present Tense are there in the above paragraph? ......

3 You should have found 7 examples of the Simple Present Tense. Here are three of them again:

John Hunt lives in York.

He works at York High School.

He teaches history.

What do these three sentences tell us about John?

a They tell us what he has been doing today. Look at 4.

b They tell us certain facts about John's life. Look at 5.

4 Clearly, if you say *John lives in York,* this tells us nothing about John's actions today. It is a fact which we know about John. But what about the other two sentences? *He works at York High School.* This is also a fact which we know about John's life. It may of course be true that he went to work today, but it may not. For example, you might say *John works at York High School, but he isn't working today because it's Sunday.* Similarly, *He teaches history* is a fact about his life. Whether it is true today or not we don't know. For example, you might say *He teaches history but today he's teaching English because the English teacher's ill.*

So the Simple Present Tense tells us certain facts which are generally true. This is why it is *impossible* to say *John's liking coffee but not tea,* because either he likes coffee or he doesn't. Liking coffee is not something which only lasts a short time. ·

Now look at 6 for some more practice of the Progressive Tense.

5 The Simple Present Tense tells us certain facts about John's life. This is correct. We know that John lives in York, works as a teacher and teaches history. We do not know anything about his actions today. We know only some information about his life.

Of course, it is possible for John to leave York, work in a different school or take another job. But as far as we know at the moment, his life as a history teacher in York is permanent. So the Simple Present Tense is necessary when we are describing these facts about him.

Now look at 6 for some practice of the Progressive Present Tense.

6 Look at these pictures:

Robert's a teacher, too.
He's on his way to school.
He's waiting for the bus.

This is his first lesson.
He's teaching arithmetic.

It's lunch time and he's
having a sandwich in the
staff room.

He's teaching history now.

It's 4 o'clock and
he's going home.

How many examples of the Progressive Present Tense can you find?

7 There are 5 examples of the Progressive Present Tense.

Why is it necessary to use the Progressive Present when you are describing the pictures in Step 6?

a Because the pictures tell us facts about Robert's life. Look at 8.

b Because the pictures describe particular actions which Robert is doing at a particular time. Look at 9.

8 Careful. We don't know whether Robert waits for the bus every day or teaches arithmetic every day or has a sandwich for lunch or teaches history every afternoon or even if he goes home at 4 o'clock every day. The pictures don't tell us any facts about Robert's everyday life. They only tell us particular things which he did at one particular time. Now look at 10.

9 The pictures describe particular actions, or particular events, which are actually taking place at particular times. We do not know from the pictures if these actions happen every day or not. So pictures cannot tell us facts about somebody's life.

So, you are quite correct. The Progressive Present is used when you describe a particular action or event which you can see or hear. Now go to 10.

10 Look at this picture:

Now which of these sentences is grammatical:

a Bill's swimming. Look at 11.

b Bill swims. Look at 12.

c They are both grammatical. Look at 13.

11 *Bill's swimming* is grammatical. Yes, this sentence describes the event in the picture. Go on to 14.

12 *Bill swims* is ungrammatical because *Bill swims* means that swimming is Bill's hobby. If skating is Jane's hobby and boxing is Fred's hobby, you could say *Jane skates and Fred boxes*. But if you look at the picture you do not know whether swimming is Bill's hobby or not. You know only that he is swimming at the particular moment when the picture is taken. Go on to 14.

13 You think that both sentences are grammatical. This is incorrect. *Bill swims* cannot be grammatical. For an explanation, look at 12.

14 Now can you complete these two statements?

(i) If you want to describe the weather which you see when you look out of the window one morning, you will use the . . . . Present Tense.

(ii) If you want to describe the British climate, you will use the . . . . Present Tense.

15 (i) Progressive

(ii) Simple

Let us apply this idea. Try to complete the following text.

The climate in Britain is very changeable. It is warm and wet one minute and cold the next. 'You'll need your umbrella this morning, dear,' said Jane to her husband at breakfast, 'it . . . . (rain) very heavily.' A few minutes later, her husband looked up from his newspaper, 'I won't, you know,' he said. 'You won't what?' asked his wife. 'I won't need my umbrella. The rain . . . . (stop) and the sun . . . . (come out).' 'Yes,' said his wife, 'but it hasn't stopped completely yet, and who knows what this afternoon may be like.' 'All right, you win. I'll take it.'

This is typically British weather. It often . . . . (rain) for a short time and then the sun . . . . (come out) and by the afternoon it is wet again. In the winter it sometimes . . . . (snow) all day but in the evening it . . . . (stop) and by the next morning the snow has disappeared altogether.

16 It *is raining* very heavily.

The rain *is stopping* and the sun *is coming out*.

It often *rains* for a short time and then the sun *comes out*.

In the winter it sometimes *snows* all day but in the evening it *stops*.

So, if you are talking about facts which you know are generally true, you must use the (i) ...... Present Tense.

But if you are talking about particular actions or events (especially if you are actually looking at them or listening to them), you must use the (ii) ...... Present Tense.

17 (i) Simple

    (ii) Progressive

In the next programme, we shall look a little further at the differences between these two tenses.

Appendix II: Further comments on common-base rules for English and Chinese (See pp. 301–2)

Rule 2: Since the constituent Time never appears on the surface in our data no corresponding lexical items are given in the lexicon although the category has been subcategorized. (See comments on rules 9, 10 below.) It must be added that the omission of time lexical items from the lexicon is not due simply to practical considerations. There are theoretical difficulties involved caused by the requirement that only constituents which can be matched with single lexical items may be subcategorized. Hence the name 'lexical categories' to distinguish these (N, V, Adj, Art, etc.) from other non-terminal symbols. (See Chomsky 1965, p. 74.) But clearly our Time constituent is not a lexical category on this definition. Compare *He arrived last week* where there is a combination of lexical categories (realized by *last* and *week*) which constitutes the time adverbial. What seems to be needed here is a subcategorization of the phrase category Time (or even, as has been suggested, of the whole sentence). It should also be noted that lexical items indicating time (or time phrases for that matter) in the majority of cases do not inherently refer to past, present or future time; compare *He arrived on Monday* with *He arrives on Monday*. What controls the use of tense here is 'knowledge of the world' not the time adverbial. Given our requirements for contrastive analysis this knowledge of the world criterion should be represented as a set of three features (Past, Present, Future) attached to the time phrase (or possibly to the sentence).

Note that NP is a base category here. It has been argued that NP is a 'superficial' category (see Bach 1968). However, for our purposes we do not need to enter into this controversy.

Rule 3: This incorporates the four predicate types discussed on p. 297. Note that the preverb 'can' is generated in the base as a modal verb. There are two possible objections to this procedure. First, *can* when it expresses 'ability' is not a modal verb since it behaves differently from the 'real' modal verbs such as *must* and *may*:

She must be told = It is imperative that she (should) be told
He may go   = It is possible that he will go
He can swim   = *It is able that he swim.

The second objection is that modal verbs are secondary categories in the sense described on p. 300. They are dependent on other categories or configurations of categories in (semantic) deep structure. As an example note the ambiguity of *They must be married* ('Circumstances require that they marry' or 'I order them to be married'). Both objections are valid. However, since we are not discussing modal verbs or preverbs in this exercise we shall ignore the difficult problems associated with them and generate the category directly in the base. It is clear that, given our condition of semantic relevance something must represent *can* in the base.

Just to remind ourselves that the search for common categories is by no means an easy one, there are complications even within the non-modal subclass of the preverb *can* (that is, the one expressing 'ability'). Compare:

1 He can play the piano (He knows how to play the piano)
2 He can breathe again (*He knows how to breathe again)
3 He can pay the rent now (*He knows how to pay the rent now).

It seems that we must distinguish at least three types of non-modal *can*: (1) expressing 'acquired ability', (2) expressing 'natural ability', and (3) expressing what for want of a better term we may call 'circumstantial ability'.

Note that *tall* and *gao* are represented by the constituent Adj (= Adjective). It has been argued by some linguists that what have traditionally been called adjectives could be more adequately characterized as a subclass of verbs. This argument is particularly forceful for Chinese. However, without going into the details, we shall retain the traditional term. This is simply for convenience and should not be interpreted as a rejection of any alternative proposals.

Rule 5: We have already commented that articles are absent in the noun phrase, since 'definiteness' and 'indefiniteness' may be functions of the whole sentence (or parts of a sentence) rather than of the noun phrase. Note in this connection the different function of the definite article in the sentences *The cat sat on the mat* and *The cat is a furry animal* (or, indeed, *Cats are furry animals* or *A cat is a furry animal*). With regard to the indefinite article note the ambiguity of *She wants to marry a Norwegian* where the interpretation of the indefinite article as 'specific' or 'non-specific' depends on whether there exists a Norwegian whom the lady wishes to marry or whether it is her intention to marry any Norwegian. There are a great variety of ways in which this sort of information is expressed in Chinese, the point being that the semantic categories (of identification, specification, location, definition, etc.) are adequately expressed in Chinese without the category Article. Since the question of articles is not particularly relevant to the problem in hand we shall not pursue it further here.

The rewriting of NP as # S # represents the point where nominalization may take place in the base, this being a process which involves the recursive symbol S. The result will be, among other things, the English 'deep' string *He + want + he + buy + book and its Chinese equivalent *Ta + yao + ta + mai + shu (where in both cases the pronouns are co-referential). Eventually, by English-specific and Chinese-specific transformations, the contrastive grammar will generate the equivalent surface strings He wants to buy a book and Ta yao mai shu.

Rules 6, 7, 8: These rules express the fact that the lexical categories Adjective, Verb and Noun are 'converted' into complex symbols which are subsequently matched with the corresponding lexical items contained in the lexicon. There are no subcategorization rules as such in this grammar, that is, no rules of the type that Chomsky refers to as inherent feature rules, selectional rules and strict subcategorization rules (See Chomsky 1965, p. 90 ff.). The simplicity of the data allows us to omit these rules but they would of course have to be stated in a more comprehensive contrastive grammar of English and Chinese.

Rules 9, 10: Rule 9 expresses the fact (by metatheoretical implication) that the Time constituent is freely deletable on condition that it contains a feature [+Pro] (= Pro-form). This condition is necessary in order to guarantee recoverability of the deletion. This situation is analogous to the so-called 'agentless passive' in English. For example the sentence He was beaten presupposes linguistically the sentence He was beaten by somebody, where the word somebody is the non-referring pro-form of a Noun which has a feature [+Human]. The sentence in question does not presuppose linguistically the sentence He was beaten by Bill (by my father, etc.). In other words what is recoverable linguistically (with reference to context) from the agentless passive is the non-referring pro-form somebody and nothing else. Likewise, with regard to the Time constituent, what is recoverable from the sentence He bought a book is the pro-form 'at some time (in the past)' but not, say, yesterday or last year.

The formal status of rules 9 and 10 (and rules 11 and 12) as subcategorization rules is somewhat dubious but we merely follow Chomsky here who allows for rules like these (Compare Chomsky 1965, p. 107, his rule Article → [±Definite]).

Rules 11, 12: These rules subcategorize the Pronoun. They are rather primitive as stated here but all we need to describe the data are the features [+Sing] and [+3] to determine number and agreement in English.

The lexicon: The features attached to the orthographic forms of the lexical items are the ones needed for the present data. They define the conditions under which each individual item may be inserted into the pre-lexical strings generated by the grammar. For example, the feature [+————— #] for *gao/tall* expresses by implication the condition that this item must not be inserted in the environment [+————— Time]. This rules out the odd sentence *He was tall yesterday* and its Chinese equivalent. Unfortunately it also rules out the perfectly acceptable *He was tall and thin in those days*. Also, there are complications arising from Tense sequences such as *The man I saw yesterday was very tall* (but not *The man I saw was very tall yesterday*). Again, it must be emphasized that there is nothing final about these features. A conventional way of expressing this lack of finality is to use rows of dots. More often than not devices like this hide deep and controversial problems. Their presence in the lexicon should be interpreted with this in mind.

It should be noted that the place of the lexicon as part of the base component is not to be taken for granted. It is probable that a more comprehensive and adequate contrastive grammar which meets the identity condition on base components will have to allow for lexical insertion after certain transformations have applied, thus differing from grammars based on 'standard' transformational theory, according to which all the lexical items are inserted at a single point in the derivational history of a sentence, before any transformations have applied. This situation reflects the current debate among theoretical linguists, the two points of view being known as the 'lexicalist' versus the 'transformationalist' hypothesis on lexical insertion. For a discussion of this issue the reader is referred to Chomsky (1970). Since the question is not relevant here the lexicon is simply given as part of the base component.

Lastly, in a full contrastive grammar the categories in each base rule of the grammar will almost certainly have to form an unordered set (see Fillmore 1968 for a discussion).

Appendix III: Further comments on the grafting component of a contrastive grammar (See pp. 305–6)

The rules in Chapter 10 constitute only a small part of a contrastive grammar for English and Chinese and they will almost certainly have to be revised in the light of further data. It should be emphasized that the present rules are merely exemplificatory, and are not intended to be comprehensive.

Rule 1 creates a syntactic constituent Tense for English and expands it. In a more comprehensive grammar of English this rule is part of a complex of rules associated with the Auxiliary constituent which is usually formulated as follows:

Aux → Tense (Modal) (have + en) (be + ing)

Tense → $\begin{Bmatrix} \text{Preterite} \\ \text{Present} \end{Bmatrix}$

In other words, in a more comprehensive contrastive grammar an Auxiliary constituent would have to be created which directly dominates Tense and indirectly dominates Preterite and Present. This complex of rules would create fourteen possible branches any of which may be grafted on to the base tree on condition that one must be chosen, since all well-formed sentences in English contain at least one Auxiliary element (i.e., Tense).

Note that the extended Auxiliary expansion rule contains an optional Modal element. This leads to a difficulty, indeed a contradiction, in that the base grammar constructed for the data (see p. 302) already contains a Modal constituent. This means that the grammar could generate **He can can buy a book* after the grafting rule for the Auxiliary has applied. This difficulty can be remedied in one of two ways: (a) create an obligatory Modal deletion transformation which will remove one of the two modals (the one generated in the base) or (b) let Modal be a secondary category and create the corresponding primary categories in the base. The second of these solutions is obviously preferable, since the first one is not only ad hoc but also does not remove the theoretical contradiction in having the Modal constituent both as a primary and as a secondary category.

This problem concerning the Modal constituent is another example of the heuristic value of formalization in that it forces us to take a principled decision. Briefly, a distinction is made between 'epistemic' and 'non-epistemic' modals. Epistemic modals express the attitude of the speaker regarding the factuality, probability, etc. of the content of his utterance. According to this criterion the modal 'can' is non-epistemic when it expresses ability. It seems to be the case that there can only be one epistemic modal in a full clause and that certain non-epistemic modals may be 'assimilated' to epistemic modals on condition that there is not already an overt epistemic modal in the sentence. Hence 'He must be able to do it' (where 'must' is epistemic) but 'He can do it' (where 'can' is non-epistemic).[1] However, as already pointed out, it is not our task here to examine modals and consequently we shall have to adopt the first solution and allow it to pass without further comment. The unformulated rule 8 is meant to cover such cases.

Rule 2 is part of the Determiner complex in English. In a comprehensive grafting component the constituent Article would be stated as an immediate constituent of Determiner.

Rule 3 is one of the crucial grafting rules. It consists of an adjunction transformation plus a set of conditions governing the grafting of particular branches on to the base tree. The transformation itself, although basically of the adjunction type, is novel in that it adjoins a non-terminal constituent (in this case Tense) plus whatever constituents are dominated by it to an existing node (VP, in this case). Apart from this novelty the operations formalized by grafting transformations are identical to those expressed by the elementary transformation of adjunction. The new constituent is added to an existing constituent in such a way that both are dominated by the node which dominated the existing constituent before the operation took place. In this case the partial base tree (i) is transformed, for example, into (ii) or, if we allow for full Auxiliary expansion, into (iii):

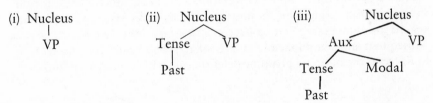

There is a problem, however, in that we might not wish to attach the Auxiliary node (Tense in our example) directly to the Nucleus but rather to an intervening node which Chomsky introduces and calls Predicate Phrase. He considers this node to be desirable for various reasons which basically concern the definition and domain of strict subcategorization

---

[1] I am grateful to John Lyons for drawing my attention to this.

(see Chomsky 1965, p. 106). Such an intervening node could be created in the grafting component (or indeed in the base component if the constituent were universal), but this is a relatively unimportant matter and we leave it open here.

Apart from the transformation itself a grafting operation is defined by a set of conditions as given in the second part of rule 3. Condition (a) which governs the grafting of a branch with Preterite as its lowest node, expresses the fact that this branch must be grafted on if the base tree contains Time [+Past]. This is indicated by the oblique stroke (normally used for context-sensitive rules) followed by the conditioning primary category. The row of stars serves as a reminder that there are undoubtedly several more primary categories which condition the use of the preterite in English but we are not particularly interested in these as far as the present problem is concerned.

Condition (b) specifies one requirement for using the present tense, namely the absence of a Time constituent in the base tree. As discussed earlier this is one way of specifying timeless sentences such as *He's tall*. The obligatory absence of a Time constituent is indicated in condition (b) by —Time. This convention is not part of transformational theory as such but corresponds to the notion of context-sensitivity. It may be interpreted as a 'tree-search' condition, i.e., 'This transformation applies if there is no Time constituent in the base tree'.

Rule 4 grafts an Article branch on to base Nouns so as to generate Noun Phrases like *a book*. As was noted earlier, the primary categories which condition the presence of the secondary category Article have not yet been fully clarified. This is indicated by the stars in conditions (a) and (b).

Rule 5 is unformulated since the matter of intervening nodes has been left open.

Rule 6 is Chomsky's affix permutation rule. For a more correct formulation (incorporating word boundary) see Chomsky (1957, p. 113). With regard to our example it converts *past+buy* into *buy+past*, and a subsequent morphophonemic rule conflates *buy+past* into *bought*.

Rule 7 is the optional pro-time deletion rule which changes (i) into (ii):

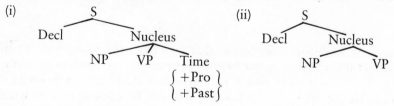

Rule 8 is unformulated for reasons given earlier (see comments on rule 1).

List of special symbols

Adj	Adjective
Adv-f	Frequency Adverbial
Adv-m	Manner Adverbial
Adv-p	Place Adverbial
Adv-t	Time Adverbial
Af	Affix
Art	Article
Aux	Auxiliary Phrase
Comp	Complement
Cop	Copula
CS	Complex Symbol
Decl	Declarative
Def	Definite
Det	Determiner
Indef	Indefinite
M	Modal
N	Noun
Neg	Negative
NP	Noun Phrase
PP	Predicate Phrase
Pred Nom	Predicate Nominal
Prep	Preposition
Pro	Pro-form
Pron	Pronoun
Prt	Particle
Q	Interrogative
S	Sentence
Sing	Singular
T	Tense
V	Verb
VP	Verb Phrase
VT	Transitive Verb
3	third person
$\neq$	is not equal to
$\equiv$	is equivalent to
$+ -$	concatenation signs
ø	zero
*	non-sentence
#	boundary marker
$\rightarrow$	rewrite as (phrase structure rules)
$\Rightarrow$	rewrite as (transformational rules)

Transcription conventions

Phonetic transcriptions are placed within square brackets [ ]. Phonemic transcriptions are placed within slant brackets / /. Phonetic symbols have the following values:

ɪ	*as in*	bit
e		bet
a		bat
o		pot
ʊ		put
ʌ		but
ə		*a*back
i		beat
ei		bait
ai		bite
oi		boy
iu		pew
au		cow
ou		hoe
u		two
iə		ear
eə		air
ɑ		car/calm
ɔ		court/caught
uə		tour
ɜ		bird
g		give
tʃ		church
dʒ		judge
ŋ		sing
θ		thin
ð		there
ʃ		sheep
ʒ		treasure
j		yes

Key-words are not required for the following consonant symbols since they have their customary English values:

p b t d k m n l r f v s z h w

References

Abercrombie, D. *Elements of General Phonetics.* Edinburgh: Edinburgh University Press and Chicago: Aldine, 1967.

Bach, E. Nouns and noun phrases. In E. Bach and R. T. Harms (eds.), *Universals in Linguistic Theory.* New York: Holt, Rinehart, Winston, 1968.

Bever, T. G. Session 1, The nature of writing systems: spelling-to-sound correspondences. In J. F. Kavanagh (ed.), *Communicating by language. The Reading Process.* Washington, D.C.: U.S. Dept. of Health, Education and Welfare, 1968.

Bloomfield, L. *Language.* New York: Holt, Rinehart, Winston, 1933, and London: Allen & Unwin, 1935.

Bloomfield, L. and Barnhart, C. L. *Let's Read.* Detroit: Wayne State University Press, 1961.

Carroll, John B. *The Study of Language.* Cambridge, Mass.: Harvard University Press, 1961.

Carroll, J. B. *Language and Thought.* Englewood Cliffs, N.J.: Prentice-Hall, 1964.

Catford, J. C. *A Linguistic Theory of Translation.* London: Oxford University Press, 1965.

Chafe, W. L. *Meaning and the Structure of Language.* Chicago: University of Chicago Press, 1970.

Chomsky, N. *Syntactic Structures.* The Hague: Mouton, 1957.

Chomsky, N. Current issues in linguistic theory. In J. A. Fodor and J. L. Katz (eds.), *The Structure of Language.* Englewood Cliffs, N.J.: Prentice Hall, 1964.

Chomsky, N. *Aspects of the Theory of Syntax.* Cambridge, Mass.: M.I.T. Press, 1965.

Chomsky, N. Remarks on nominalization. In R. A. Jacobs and P. S. Rosenbaum (eds.), *Readings in English Transformational Grammar.* Waltham, Mass.: Ginn & Co., 1970. Reprinted as a chapter in N. Chomsky, *Studies on Semantics in Generative Grammar.* The Hague: Mouton, 1972.

Chomsky, N. and Halle, M. *The Sound Pattern of English.* New York: Harper & Row, 1968.

CILT. Report No. 4. Centre for Information on Language Teaching, State House, 63 High Holborn, London, W.C.1., 1970.

Clegg, A. B. *The Excitement of Writing.* London: Chatto & Windus, 1964.

Commonwealth Office of Education, Sydney. *Situational English.* London: Longmans, 1967.

Corder, S. P. The significance of learners' errors. *IRAL,* 1967, **5**, No. 4, 161–70.

Crystal, D. Specification and English tenses. *Journal of Linguistics,* 1966, **2**, No. 1, 1–34.

Dakin, Julian. The teaching of reading. In H. Fraser and W. R. O'Donnell (eds.), *Applied Linguistics and the Teaching of English.* London: Longmans, 1969.

Dakin, Julian. *The Language Laboratory and Language Learning.* London: Longmans, 1973.

Davies, Alan (ed.). *Language Testing Symposium.* London: Oxford University Press, 1968.

Downing, J. *The i.t.a. Symposium.* London: National Foundation for Educational Research, 1967.

Ellis, R. W. B. Post-natal growth. In R. W. B. Ellis (ed.), *Child Health and Development.* Edinburgh: J. & A. Churchill, Ltd., 1966.

Fillmore, Charles J. The case for case. In E. Bach and R. T. Harms (eds.), *Universals in Linguistic Theory.* New York: Holt, Rinehart, Winston, 1968.

Finlayson, D. S. The reliability of marking essays. *Brit. J. Educ. Psychol.*, 1951, 21, 126–34.

Fraser, H. *Control and Create.* London: Longmans, 1967.

Gimson, A. C. *An Introduction to the Pronunciation of English.* London: Edward Arnold, 1962.

Gougenheim, G., Rivenc, P., Michéa, R. and Sauvageot, A. *L'élaboration du français fondamental (1er degré): étude sur l'établissement d'un vocabulaire et d'une grammaire du base.* Paris: Didier, 1964.

Halliday, M. A. K. *Intonation and Grammar in British English.* The Hague: Mouton, 1967.

Halliday, M. A. K., McIntosh, Angus and Strevens, Peter. *The Linguistic Sciences and Language Teaching.* London: Longmans, 1964.

Harris, Zellig S. *Methods in Structural Linguistics.* Chicago: University of Chicago Press, 1951. Reprinted as *Structural Linguistics*, 1961.

Hochberg, J. Session 2, Models for reading. In J. F. Kavanagh (ed.), *Communicating by Language: The Reading Process.* Washington: U.S. Dept. of Health, Education and Welfare, 1968.

Hope, K. *Elementary Statistics.* Oxford: Pergamon, 1967.

Hymes, D. On communicative competence. In J. J. Gumperz and D. Hymes (eds.), *Directions in Sociolinguistics.* New York: Holt, Rinehart, Winston, 1970.

Ingram, Elisabeth. Attainment and diagnostic testing. In A. Davies (ed.), *Language Testing Symposium.* London: Oxford University Press, 1968a.

Ingram, Elisabeth. Item analysis. In A. Davies (ed.), *Language Testing Symposium.* London: Oxford University Press, 1968b.

Jakobovits, L. A. Implications of recent psycholinguistic developments for the teaching of a second language. *Language Learning*, 1968, 11, Nos. 1 and 2, 89–109.

Jarvis, R. A. A study of conditional sentences in English with reference to the construction of a pedagogic grammar. Unpublished M.Litt. dissertation, Edinburgh University Library, 1971.

Jones, D. *The Pronunciation of English.* Cambridge: Cambridge University Press, 1956a (4th edition).

Jones, D. *Outline of English Phonetics.* Cambridge: Heffer, 1956b (8th edition).

Katz, J. J. and Postal, P. M. *An Integrated Theory of Linguistic Descriptions.* Cambridge, Mass.: M.I.T. Press, 1964.

Lado, R. and Fries, C. C. *Intensive Course in English.* Four volumes: *English Sentence Patterns, English Pattern Practices, English Pronunciation, English Vocabulary.* Ann Arbor: University of Michigan Press, 1943–.

Lado, R. and Fries, C. C. *English Pattern Practice.* Ann Arbor: University of Michigan Press, 1948.

Lado, R. *Linguistics Across Cultures.* Ann Arbor: University of Michigan Press, 1957.

Lado, R. *Language Testing.* London: Longmans, 1961.

Lakoff, G. On generative semantics, 1969. In D. D. Steinberg and L. A. Jakobovits (eds.), *Semantics: An Interdisciplinary Reader in Philosophy, Linguistics and Psychology.* Cambridge: Cambridge University Press, 1971.

Laver, J. The production of speech. In J. Lyons (ed.), *New Horizons in Linguistics.* Harmondsworth: Penguin, 1970.

Law, M. H. A special case. In *Onwards*, No. 1. York: Schools Council Modern Languages Project, 1970.

Lees, R. B. *The Grammar of English Nominalizations.* The Hague: Mouton, 1960.

Lyons, J. *Introduction to Theoretical Linguistics.* Cambridge: Cambridge University Press, 1968.

Lyons, J. Human Language. In R. A. Hinde (ed.), *Non-verbal Communication.* Cambridge: Cambridge University Press, 1972.

McIntosh, D. M. *Statistics for the Teacher.* Oxford: Pergamon, 1963.

Mackey, W. F. *Language Teaching Analysis.* London: Longmans, 1965.

McNally, J. and Murray, W. *Key Words to Literacy and the Teaching of Reading.* London: Schoolmaster Publishing Co., 1968.

Newmark, G. Grammatical theory and the teaching of English as a foreign language. *NAFSA Studies and Papers English Language Series*, 9. New York: National Assoc. for Foreign Student Affairs, 1964.

Nuffield Foundation Foreign Languages Teaching Materials Project. *En Avant Stage 2.* Leeds: E. J. Arnold & Son, 1968.

Ogden, C. K. Basic English Series, various titles. London: Kegan Paul, 1930–.

Palmer, H. E. *The Principles of Language Study.* London: Harrap, 1921. Reprinted in Language and Language Learning Series, London: Oxford University Press, 1964.

Pike, K. L. *Phonetics.* Ann Arbor: Michigan University Press, 1943.

Pilliner, A. E. G. Subjective and objective testing. In A. Davies (ed.), *Language Testing Symposium.* London: Oxford University Press, 1968.

Pimsleur, A. Language aptitude testing. In A. Davies (ed.), *Language Testing Symposium.* London: Oxford University Press, 1968.

Rivers, W. Grammar in foreign language teaching. *Modern Language Journal*, 1968, 52, No. 4, 206–11.

Roberts, P. *English Syntax.* New York: Harcourt Brace, 1964.

Rutherford, W. E. *Modern English.* New York: Harcourt Brace, 1968.

Saporta, S. Applied linguistics and generative grammar. In A. Valdman (ed.), *Trends in Language Teaching.* New York: McGraw-Hill, 1966.

Schools Council German Course. *Vorwärts Stage 4.* Leeds: E. J. Arnold & Son, 1973.

S.R.A. Reading Laboratory. Various levels. Chicago, Illinois: Science Research Associates, 1958 (Revised 1960).

Stott, D. H. *Roads to Literacy.* Glasgow: Holmes, 1964.

Sweet, H. *A Primer of Phonetics.* Oxford: The Clarendon Press, 1906 (3rd edition revised).

Temperley, Mary S. Transformations in 'English Sentence Patterns'. *Language Learning*, 1961, 11, Nos. 3 and 4, 125–33.

Valette, Rebecca. *Modern Language Testing: A Handbook.* New York: Harcourt Brace, 1968.

Venezky, R. L. English orthography: its graphical structure and its relation to sound. *Reading Research Quarterly*, 1967, 2, No. 3, 75–105.

Venezky, R. L. Session 1, The nature of writing systems: spelling-to-sound correspondences. In J. F. Kavanagh (ed.), *Communicating by Language, The Reading Process.* Washington, D.C.: U.S. Dept. of Health, Education and Welfare, 1968.

Vernon, P. E. *Secondary School Selection.* London: Methuen, 1957.

Ward, I. C. *The Phonetics of English.* Cambridge: Heffer, 1948 (4th edition).

Wardhaugh, R. *Reading: A Linguistic Perspective.* New York: Harcourt Brace, 1969.

West, M. Simplified and abridged, 1950. In W. R. Lee (ed.), *ELT Selections 1.* London: Oxford University Press, 1967.